Slovenia
From Yugoslavia to the European Union

Editors

Mojmir Mrak, Matija Rojec, and Carlos Silva-Jáuregui

THE WORLD BANK
Washington, D.C.

Cover photo: Dunja Wedam

Library of Congress Cataloging-in-Publication Data

Slovenia: from Yugoslavia to the European Union / edited by Mojmir Mrak, Matija Rojec, Carlos Silva-Jáuregui.
    p. cm.
Includes bibliographical references and index.
ISBN 0-8213-5718-2
    1. Slovenia—Economic policy. 2. Slovenia—Economic conditions. 3. European Union—Slovenia. I. Mrak, Mojmir. II. Rojec, Matija. III. Silva-Jáuregui, Carlos. IV. World Bank.

    HC406.S555 2004
    330.94973—dc22   2003066135

Contents

FIGURES

TABLES

Foreword

Slovenia's achievements over the past several years have been remarkable. Thirteen years after independence from the former Socialist Federative Republic (SFR) of Yugoslavia, the country is among the most advanced of the transition economies in Central and Eastern Europe and among the best prepared for membership in the European Union (EU), beginning in May 2004. The world has changed dramatically during these 13 years, and so has Slovenia. The process of transition to a market economy in Slovenia and the other countries in Central and Eastern Europe is unprecedented in scope. Slovenia's transition has been threefold: from socialism to a market economy, from a regional to a national economy, and from a part of SFR Yugoslavia to an independent state and member of the European Union. However, development is a long, difficult, and complex process, and Slovenia faces major economic challenges.

This book represents the work of a number of analysts reviewing the lessons from 13 years of transition in Slovenia. It reflects the knowledge and experiences of policymakers and academics in Slovenia and elsewhere, many of whom played a critical role in the country's transition. Several contributors to this book were at the center of decision-making in the process of gaining independence, during the transition, and during the process of accession to the European Union. Their policy choices changed the face and fate of Slovenia. Their reflections give us an insider's look at the options and alternatives that policymakers face.

The analysis is organized around three overarching themes. The first is Slovenia's road toward political and economic independence, and how Slovenia succeeded in separating from SFR Yugoslavia with far less pain than any of the other successor states. The second is Slovenia's socioeconomic transformation, and how Slovenia as an independent country chose its special transition path. The third is Slovenia's successful quest for membership in the European Union, and the country's path ahead.

With EU membership, Slovenia will face new challenges as well as new opportunities. Slovenia is ready to face those challenges. The effort and the sacrifices made in the past are starting to pay dividends. The priority for Slovenia's policymakers is to complete the remainder of the structural reform agenda and to accelerate growth. The future looks bright for Slovenia as it sets out to tackle this agenda.

The World Bank would like to express its appreciation to the contributors to this study and to those who assisted in its publication.

Shigeo Katsu
Vice President
Europe and Central Asia Region
The World Bank
March 2004

Preface and Acknowledgments

With 13 years of existence as an independent country, Slovenia is still a new state on the world map, yet the story of socioeconomic and political developments in Slovenia over those 13 years is a rich one and deserves a detailed account and analysis.

Publication of this book was undertaken for the following three reasons, among others:

- Slovenia has been undergoing a threefold transition. In addition to the transition from a socialist to a market economy, it has also faced the transition from a regional to a national economy, and the transition from being a part of the Socialist Federative Republic of Yugoslavia to being an independent state and a future member of the enlarged European Union.
- The process of Slovenia's transition and development is not well known to the world at large, and there is an obvious lack of literature on this subject. As a small state, Slovenia has been often neglected in cross-country analyses of transition economies.
- There are important lessons to learn from the transition process of Slovenia, particularly when many of the stories are told by critical figures in Slovenia's transition. In this book these practitioners in development share their experiences and reflections about the events that changed the face of the nation.

The main objective of the book is to analyze Slovenia's threefold transition in the context of a broader transition process in Central and Eastern Europe and to contribute toward filling the obvious gap in the literature on this subject. The book provides an overview of the most important developments faced by Slovenia during its transition—the achievements, the problems, and the challenges—and discusses the lessons that have been learned and the main challenges that Slovenia can expect to face in the years to come. Interdisciplinary in character, the book focuses on the socioeconomic and political aspects of the young

xi

country's transition and integrates them into the existing pool of knowledge about the transition process. This element gives the book a broader relevance in the context of transition literature.

Most of the authors who contributed to the book have been actively involved in the Slovenian transition process. Indeed, most of the leading creators of the Slovenian transition paradigm, as well as most of the leading figures who have been putting that paradigm into practice, contributed to the book. Their contribution gives the book an additional practical value for policymakers.

This book is the result of a collective effort of a number of people who have made invaluable contributions. First among them are the authors of the various chapters, not only for providing material of outstanding richness that increases the knowledge and debate about transtion economies, but also for finding the time and energy to present their theoretical knowledge and practical experiences on the Slovenian transition. We are lucky to have shared the creation of this book with the principal authors: France Arhar, Velimir Bole, Bistra Borak, Neven Borak, Bojko Bučar, Milan Cvikl, Jože P. Damijan, Polona Domadenik, Janez Drnovšek, Mitja Gaspari, Vladimir Gligorov, Aleksandra Gregorič, András Inotai, Božo Jašovič, Bartlomiej Kaminski, Tomaž Košak, Boštjan Kramberger, Jaime Garcia Lombardero, Boris Majcen, Jože Mencinger, Dušan Mramor, Rasto Ovin, Janez Potočnik, Janez Prašnikar, Dorota Pyszna-Nigge, Andrej Rant, Ivan Ribnikar, Marko Simoneti, Peter Stanovnik, Tine Stanovnik, Marjan Svetličič, Zlatko Šabič, Franjo Štiblar, Janez Šušteršič, Milan Vodopivec, Marko Voljč, and Wolfgang Wessels.

Publication of the book would not have been possible without the support of the three sponsors: the World Bank, the Bank of Slovenia, and the Government Office for European Affairs of the Republic of Slovenia, as well as of the Faculty of Economics of the University of Ljubljana, which has acted as the World Bank's counterpart in Slovenia in the preparation of the book. Although the book reflects the authors' views, and not necessarily those of the World Bank, its Board of Directors, or its member countries, its production was housed at the World Bank.

Special thanks go to Shigeo Katsu, Vice President of the Europe and Central Asia region of the World Bank, and to Roger Grawe, Country Director for Central Europe and the Baltics, for guidance and support of this project. Their genuine interest in Slovenia has made the publication of this book possible. Ksenija Maver from the Executive Director's office at the World Bank, Irena Sodin from the Ministry of Finance of the Republic of Slovenia, and Christine Castillo from the Central Europe and Baltics Country Unit have helped enormously in communications with the World Bank.

We would like to thank Martha Bonilla, who valiantly sought to manipulate our English into a more correct form; Slavica Mencin, who helped us in our extensive communication with the authors; Isabelle Chaal, for excellent support in the production of the manuscript; and Marianne El-Khoury, for her outstanding research and editorial support. We would like to thank those involved from the Office of the Publisher of the World Bank—Melissa Edeburn, Thaisa Tiglao, and Monika Lynde—for their superb assistance with the production of the book, print coordination, prepress, manufacturing, and e-book conversion. Our sincere thanks also go to Michael Treadway for his excellent editing of the book.

Mojmir Mrak, Matija Rojec, and Carlos Silva-Jáuregui
Ljubljana and Washington, D.C.
March 2004

Acronyms and Abbreviations

BRA	Bank Rehabilitation Agency
CAS	Country Assistance Strategy
CEE	Central and Eastern Europe
CEFTA	Central European Free Trade Agreement (or Area)
CEM	Country Economic Memorandum
CET	Common External Tariff
CFSP	Common Foreign and Security Policy
CGE	Computable general-equilibrium
COFOG	Classification of Functions of Government
CSCE	Conference on Security and Cooperation in Europe
DARS	Družba za avtoceste Republike Slovenije (Motorway Company of the Republic of Slovenia)
DM	Deutsche mark
EA	Europe Agreement
EBRD	European Bank for Reconstruction and Development
EC	European Community
ECE	Economic Commission for Europe
ECSC	European Coal and Steel Community
EEC	European Economic Community
EFSAL	Enterprise and Financial Sector Adjustment Loan
EFTA	European Free Trade Association (or Area)
EIPF	Ekonomski Inštitut Pravne fakultete (Economics Institute of the Faculty of Law)
EMU	Economic and Monetary Union
ERM-II	Exchange Rate Mechanism II
ESA95	European system of national and regional accounts 1995
ESDP	European Security and Defence Policy
EU	European Union
FAO	Food and Agriculture Organization
FDI	Foreign direct investment
FIE	Foreign investment enterprise

FRY	Former republic of Yugoslavia
FTA	Free trade agreement (or area)
FYM	Former Yugoslav market
FYR	Former Yugoslav Republic
GATS	General Agreement on Trade in Services
GATT	General Agreement on Tariffs and Trade
GDP	Gross domestic product
GEF	Global Environment Fund
GFS	Government Finance Statistics
IAEA	International Atomic Energy Agency
IBRD	International Bank for Reconstruction and Development
ICC	International Co-ordinating Committee
IDA	International Development Association
IFC	International Finance Corporation
IGC	Intergovernmental Conference
IHI	Institute for Health Insurance
ILO	International Labor Organization
IMAD	Institute of Macroeconomic Analysis and Development
IMF	International Monetary Fund
IPDI	Institute for Pension and Disability Insurance
ISA	Insurance Supervisory Authority
KAD	Kapitalska družba (pension fund)
LSE	Ljubljana Stock Exchange
M.A.S.T.E.R.	Managing Administrative Systems through Training, Education, and Research
MFERAC	Ministrstvo za finance enotno računovodstvo (Ministry of Finance Unified Accounting)
MFN	Most favored nation
MNCs	Multinational corporations
NATO	North Atlantic Treaty Organization
NBY	National Bank of Yugoslavia
NFA	New Financing Agreement
NKBM	Nova Kreditna Banka Maribor
NLB	Nova Ljubljanska Banka
NPAA	National Programme for the Adoption of the *Acquis*
NUTS	Nomenclature of Territorial Units for Statistics
OECD	Organisation for Economic Co-operation and Development
OSCE	Organization for Security and Cooperation in Europe
OTA	Ownership Transformation Act
OTC	Over the counter
PDIA	Pension and Disability Insurance Act
PHARE	Poland and Hungary: Aid for Economic Restructuring
PIFs	Privatization investment funds
QMV	Qualified majority vote

R&D	Research and development
SAS	Social Accounting Service
SBI	Price index of stocks listed on the Ljubljana stock exchange
SDK	Služba družbenega knjigovodstva (payment agency)
SFR	Socialist Federative Republic
SIERS	Strategy of International Economic Relations
SIGMA	Support for Improvement in Governance and Management in Central and European Countries
SIT	Slovenian tolar
SMA	Securities Market Agency
SMEs	Small and medium-size enterprises
SOD	Slovenska odškodninska družba (Restitution Fund)
SRD	Slovenska razvojna družba (Slovenian Development Corporation)
UN	United Nations
UNCTAD	United Nations Conference on Trade and Development
UNDP	United Nations Development Programme
UNESCO	United Nations Educational Scientific and Cultural Organization
UNICEF	United Nations Children's Fund
UNIDO	United Nations Industrial Development Organization
VAT	Value added tax
WTO	World Trade Organization

Overview: Slovenia's Threefold Transition

Mojmir Mrak, Matija Rojec, and Carlos Silva-Jáuregui

Historical accounts trace Slovenia's origins far back in time. Already in the sixth century A.D., the Slavic ancestors of today's Slovenians settled in what is now Slovenia. The country's legacy of statehood goes back to the seventh century, when an independent Slavic principality named Carantanum existed just to the north of today's Slovenia (Grafenauer 1979). Beginning in the eighth century, Slovenia formed part of the Frankish kingdom and later part of the Habsburg empire. After World War I, Slovenia joined Croatia and Serbia to form the Kingdom of Serbs, Croats, and Slovenes, a precursor to the Kingdom of Yugoslavia. At the end of World War II, Slovenia, along with five other republics, formed the Federative People's Republic of Yugoslavia, later renamed the Socialist Federative Republic of Yugoslavia (SFR Yugoslavia). Slovenia remained part of this federation until its declaration of independence in 1991.

Throughout its history, Slovenia kept its own language and culture as well as a homogeneous population. These factors have helped Slovenia maintain its own national identity and sociopolitical cohesion and, not least, encouraged Slovenians to vote overwhelmingly (with an 86 percent majority) for independence in the critical referendum held at the end of 1990. In the 13 years since that historic vote, Slovenia and its people have been involved in one of the most important projects in the history of the nation. That project is the subject of this book.

This overview chapter is composed of three sections. The first deals with the main features of Slovenia's transition. We discuss the main policies and reforms that lie behind the Slovenian transition and the main challenges that the country can expect to face in the years to come. The second section presents an overview of the World Bank's cooperation with Slovenia during this historic transition. The third section provides an overview of each of the chapters of the book and their findings.

THE CHALLENGES OF TRANSITION

During Slovenia's first 13 years as a modern independent state, the country has undergone a threefold transition. In addition to the transition from a socialist to a market economy, Slovenia has faced parallel transitions from a regional to a national economy, and from being a part of SFR Yugoslavia to becoming an independent state and an aspiring member of an enlarged European Union.

The fact that, before 1991, Slovenia was a part of SFR Yugoslavia has had two important impacts on the Slovenian concept of reform and on the reform process. In the decades before independence, Slovenia was part of a unique quasi-market socialist system, where transitional reforms began already at the end of the 1980s, and which ended with the collapse of the Yugoslav federation. As part of that larger federation, Slovenia was forced to follow the development patterns of the federation. During the 1980s a growing contradiction emerged between these patterns and the development aspirations of Slovenia, which was by far the most developed part of SFR Yugoslavia.

Slovenia's transition can be divided into two periods. The first was carried out in the context of creating the new independent state, and the second was driven by the process of accession to the European Union. Slovenia's reform process has been based on two sets of policies. The first relates to policies aimed at macroeconomic stabilization and internal and external liberalization. The second deals with structural and institutional reforms, including, among others, the building of institutions; the privatization of state-owned assets; and the reform of the enterprise sector, the financial sector, the public utilities, the pension and tax system, the social welfare system, and the public administration.

Slovenia's reform strategy has been conceptualized in several key documents.[1] From the point of view of the reform process and its policy impact, the most important has been the *Strategy of the Republic of Slovenia for the Accession to the European Union: Economic and Social Part* (Mrak, Potočnik, and Rojec 1998), adopted in January 1998. This policy document defines and outlines a consistent set of medium-term economic and social policy measures required to complete the economic transformation of the country into a market economy and to prepare it for accession to the European Union. The concept and contents of this strategy were fully endorsed by the European Union as well as by the major international financial institutions. In retrospect, one can observe that the reform program laid out in Slovenia's EU accession strategy was successfully implemented as part of the country's actual accession process.

Key Features of the Slovenian Transition

Three key features distinguish the transition process in Slovenia from that in other countries emerging from communism and central planning. First, Slovenia chose a gradualist approach to transition. Second, Slovenia's transition from a planned to a market economy was accompanied by a transition from a regional into a national economy. Third, Slovenia inherited from the former SFR Yugoslavia a unique enterprise ownership structure based on self-management, and a unique institutional setting. In contrast, most of the other transition economies embarked on their transition with an ownership structure dominated by the state (the exceptions being, of course, the other successor countries to the former SFR Yugoslavia). These facts make the

Slovenian transition quite unique and help account for the positive results achieved so far.

The gradualist approach. Slovenia opted for a gradualist approach in its transition from a planned to a market economy for several reasons, of which the following are some of the most important. One was the endogenous origin of Slovenia's transition, in which the old elites not only anticipated the transition but, by introducing important changes already in the pretransition period, also influenced their own future position in the society and economy in the aftermath of transition. Another reason was the country's relatively high level of development, which allowed a more cautious approach to the transition and which introduced into the cost-benefit analysis the consideration that it was important not to undermine some of the positive developments that had preceded the transition. A third reason was the generally cautious attitude of Slovenians toward economic reform, accompanied by a tradition of consensus building in the face of any major collective decision. Finally, the shock to the economy caused by the loss of the Yugoslav market, together with the unstable political situation in Slovenia itself during the early independence period, argued against a "big bang" approach to the transition.[2]

The gradualist approach was reflected in numerous areas of Slovenia's economic development throughout the 1990s, and in the privatization process in particular. Slovenia's privatization strategy established a relatively dispersed ownership structure in which internal, external, and quasi-governmental owners shared dominance. These ownership patterns have strongly influenced corporate governance processes in Slovenia in the wake of privatization. The gradualist approach has been key to the transformation of the financial sector as well. Although rehabilitation of the banking sector has been accomplished rather quickly, the privatization of the state-owned banks came very late on the economic policy agenda. For different reasons, the restructuring of the insurance sector is likewise lagging behind. Last but not least, Slovenia is still in the rather early stages of public utilities reform and in the reform of monetary and, more specifically, exchange rate policy. Slovenia also adopted macroeconomic policies aimed at smoothing the impact of the transition; for example, after the initial pure float, a managed floating exchange rate regime was chosen, with the central bank very much concerned to bring about a "controlled" appreciation of the new Slovenian currency, the tolar, so as to reduce pressures on the export sector.

The main argument in favor of a gradualist approach to transition, however, has been articulated as a counterargument against the big bang approach. Big bang reforms in other countries have typically been accompanied by large shocks to the economy, leading many times to temporary but severe losses of output and growing unemployment, and consequently to the threat of social instability and ultimately reversal of the reforms. A more gradualist approach gives economic agents more room to adapt, although it can also lead to a halt in the reform process. Gradualists believe that their approach is better because it allows some economic activity and some jobs to be reallocated between firms or industries rather than lost altogether.

Slovenia's economic record of the last decade clearly confirms the logic of its gradualist transition. The country has achieved one of the highest and least volatile growth rates among the current group of countries in line for EU membership. Moreover, after the initial stabilization, its stable and reasonably high growth rate was achieved without any major macroeconomic imbalances during the 1990s, and much the same can be said regarding social and political developments. All that said, however, gradualism seems to be a viable alternative only for relatively well-off economies and may not be an option for many other transition economies.

There can be no doubt that the overall economic, social, and political sustainability of the reform process has been a clear benefit of gradualism in Slovenia. However, as Jože Mencinger points out in Chapter 5 of this book, "the reality since independence has been an even more gradual transition than the most enthusiastic gradualists had suggested." Therefore it is not a surprise that Slovenia's gradualist and conservative approach has been accompanied by delays in the dynamics of the reform process. The same underlying reasons that led naturally to the choice of gradualism in Slovenia's transition are also responsible for its costs, which must be tackled if Slovenia wants to accelerate its development in the future. Strong political consensus and a tradition of economic and political reform were the main reasons why it was natural to choose a gradual approach in the early stage of transition. This approach was, however, not without its drawbacks, one of which was a stalemate among interest groups, leading to postponed decisions and less-than-optimal compromises, which delayed some crucial structural reforms. Recent developments have warned that the continuation of the gradualist approach might seriously hamper economic competitiveness and even backfire on a macroeconomic performance that has so far been remarkably stable.

Transition from a regional to a national economy. The second underlying pattern of Slovenia's transition is related to the fact that it is one of many countries where the transition from a socialist to a market economy has been accompanied by a transition from a regional economy (in Slovenia's case, part of SFR Yugoslavia) to a national economy.[3] When Slovenia became independent, its first tasks were not related exclusively to economic transition issues, but also included issues of key importance for creating a sovereign state. One of these tasks was the creation of the institutions of a sovereign state, which had not existed before independence, such as a central bank and a national currency, customs systems, and a worldwide diplomatic network under the direction of a ministry of foreign affairs. Another was the creation of economic conditions conducive to compensating for the loss of the larger part of the internal market of the former SFR Yugoslavia. A third was resolution of several open questions related to Slovenia's succession to the former SFR Yugoslavia; within this framework, the resolution of such issues as the apportionment of the former SFR Yugoslavia's external debt was a precondition for Slovenia's full integration into the international financial system. It was also an important hurdle to membership in such international organizations as the World Bank, the International Monetary Fund, and the United Nations.

All these activities directed to the building of a sovereign state have had a major influence on the transition process, especially in its early stages. Slovenia was obliged to establish some entirely new institutions and to drastically restructure others to the new environment created by independence. The sequencing of reforms has been influenced as well. For example, the creation of a national currency and a customs system were absolute priorities for the Slovenian authorities at the time of independence.

Legacy of the former SFR Yugoslavia. The third underlying pattern of Slovenia's transition is related to the legacy of the former SFR Yugoslavia's economic system. On the one hand, this legacy bequeathed some important benefits to Slovenia as it embarked on its transition. The country inherited a strong tradition of a quasi-market system with relatively independent enterprise management structures. Under the self-management socialist economic system of the former SFR Yugoslavia, Slovenian managers were to a large extent responsible for running their firms and, in contrast to managers in other planned economies, were directly exposed to some degree of competition.

On the other hand, the legacy of the former SFR Yugoslavia's economic system also had some strong negative effects. Two issues deserve special mention here. First, the tradition of self-management system influenced the approach that Slovenia took to privatization, in which a very important role was assigned to workers. A direct consequence of this type of privatization was a dispersed ownership structure of Slovenian enterprises, with a strong role for internal ownership, by managers, workers, and pensioners. This ownership structure has proved by and large to be an obstacle to efficient corporate governance and restructuring. Second, Slovenia also inherited huge internal and external imbalances from the former SFR Yugoslavia. At the moment when Slovenia introduced its own currency, inflation was running at over 30 percent a month (more than 2,200 percent on an annualized basis). At the same time, SFR Yugoslavia had an excessive external debt and no access to further international lending since 1982. The debt problem was further complicated by the fact that Slovenia was jointly and severally liable for a large amount of this debt.

Macroeconomic Policies and Structural Reforms

Thus, at independence, Slovenia inherited substantial economic imbalances, both internal (hyperinflation) and external (the large foreign debt), from the former SFR Yugoslavia. At the same time, Slovenia also lost markets in the former SFR Yugoslavia, had no foreign exchange reserves to back up its new currency, and had only begun to adopt an outward-looking, export-oriented development strategy, which required the liberalization of foreign transactions. For all of these reasons, macroeconomic stabilization and liberalization were an absolute necessity and top priority of Slovenia's early transition. As presented in Table 1, after the initial transitional recession, reflected in a decline in GDP per capita, Slovenia succeeded very quickly in regaining growth momentum and significantly cutting inflation. Already by 1993 economic growth had returned. In addition, throughout the transition period Slovenia sustained favorable positions in its fiscal and external accounts. One can therefore say that the country's macroeconomic policies aimed at stabilization and liberalization have been successful, thereby paving the way for structural and institutional reforms. These macroeconomic policies encompassed monetary policy, fiscal policy, incomes policy, and trade policy.

Monetary policy. A milestone in Slovenia's economic independence was the introduction of the new currency, the Slovenian tolar, in October 1991. At the time, the new Slovenian central bank, the Bank of Slovenia, was confronted with a wide range of institutional and macroeconomic difficulties: double-digit monthly inflation, a highly indexed economy, no international reserves, low confidence in the new currency, a huge legacy of nonperforming loans in two large commercial banks, and an absence of credibility in the newly established central bank itself and its policies. The central bank's primary concern was price stability. Accordingly, its main initial goal was to quickly bring inflation down from hyperinflationary levels. A monetary anchor was used to achieve this objective, but a floating foreign exchange rate regime was chosen. This regime implied that the bank would exercise control over the money supply but would intervene in the foreign exchange market only within the constraints set by the chosen monetary policy.

In the years that followed, Slovenia's monetary policy achieved a number of important goals. The central bank established itself as a credible institution, annual inflation was reduced to single-digit levels by mid-1995, the balance of payments position was strengthened, confidence in the new currency grew (as evidenced by strong growth and

TABLE 1   MAIN MACROECONOMIC INDICATORS OF SLOVENIA, 1991–2005

Indicator	1991	1992	1993	1994	1995	1996	1997	1998
GDP per capita								
In dollars at current exchange rates	6,331	6,275	6,366	7,205	9,431	9,481	9,163	9,878
In dollars at purchasing power parity	n.a.	n.a.	n.a.	n.a.	11,300	11,800	12,800	13,500
Growth rate of real GDP (percent)	-8.9	-5.5	2.8	5.3	4.1	3.5	4.6	3.8
Exports of goods and services (percent of GDP)	n.a.	63.1	58.5	58.9	55.3	55.6	57.4	56.6
Current account balance (percent of GDP)	n.a.	7.4	1.5	3.8	-0.4	0.2	0.3	-0.6
Unemployment rate[a] (percent)	n.a.	8.3	9.1	9.1	7.4	7.3	7.4	7.9
Gross fixed capital formation (percent of GDP)	n.a.	18.4	18.7	19.6	21.4	22.5	23.4	24.6
General government balance (percent of GDP)	2.6	0.2	0.3	-0.2	0.0	0.3	-1.2	-0.8
Inflation rate[b] (percent)	117.7	201.3	32.3	19.8	12.6	9.7	9.1	7.9

	1999	2000	2001	2002	2003[c]	2004[c]	2005[c]
GDP per capita							
In dollars at current exchange rates	10,109	9,531	9,803	11,004	13,534	14,299	15,154
In dollars at purchasing power parity	14,500	15,900	16,800	17,700	n.a.	n.a.	n.a.
Growth rate of real GDP (percent)	5.2	4.6	2.9	2.9	2.6	3.6	3.7
Exports of goods and services (percent of GDP)	52.4	56.5	57.9	57.9	56.9	57.2	57.3
Current account balance (percent of GDP)	–3.5	–2.8	0.2	1.4	0.3	0.5	0.2
Unemployment rate[a] (percent)	7.6	7.0	6.4	6.4	6.8	6.7	6.4
Gross fixed capital formation (percent of GDP)	27.4	25.7	24.0	22.6	23.0	23.5	23.9
General government balance (percent of GDP)	–0.6	–1.3	–1.3	–3.0	–1.5	–1.7	n.a.
Inflation rate[b] (percent a year)	6.1	8.9	8.4	7.5	5.8	4.9	4.0

n.a. = not available.
Note: The land area of Slovenia is 20,273 square kilometers; the population was 1,996,773 as of June 30, 2003.
a. As defined by the International Labour Organization.
b. Average for the year as measured by retail prices until 1998, and by the consumer price index after 1998.
c. Forecast.

Sources: Institute of Macroeconomic Analysis and Development (1996, 2003), Wiener Institut für Internationale Wirtschaftsvergleiche (1999), Eurostat (2003), Statistical Office of the Republic of Slovenia (2003).

an improved term structure of tolar bank deposits), domestic interest rates fell, foreign exchange reserves increased from practically zero to the equivalent of 7.1 months of total (goods and services) imports by the end of August 2003 (Bank of Slovenia *Monthly Bulletin,* September 2003), and the International Monetary Fund's Article VIII provisions on current account convertibility and stabilization of the banking sector were adopted.

Fiscal policy. A roughly balanced general government fiscal account and the creation of a fiscal environment capable of fostering economic growth were the main objectives of Slovenian fiscal policy. A strong fiscal stance was achieved through the reform of public finance institutions in 1991; these increased the effectiveness of tax collection and improved control over spending. Together these achievements formed one of the foundations of Slovenia's transition to a market economy and provided a key support for monetary policy in stabilizing the economy. However, balance in the general government accounts was achieved despite growing difficulties. Within the overall balance of public finances, significant problems continue to exist in the structure of expenditure and revenue. On the expenditure side, fiscal policy is limited by large and institutionalized social transfers and the relatively high fixed costs of state administration for a small country; on the revenue side, it is restricted by the close connection of revenue to wages: direct taxes and contributions for social security are important sources of revenue. In 1999 and 2000 Slovenia took two major, but still insufficient, steps toward the long-term viability of the fiscal balance. On the expenditure side, a pension reform was implemented, which to a certain extent relieved the single greatest pressure on public expenditure. On the revenue side, a new value added tax was introduced in mid-1999.

Incomes policy. Incomes policy could be potentially important for macroeconomic stabilization, employment, and export competitiveness in a small, open economy like Slovenia. Since independence, Slovenia has established an institutional mechanism in which collective agreements are the basic wage-setting apparatus, but individual agreements and legislation also play a role. Tripartite social agreements among the government, trade unions, and employers provide a uniform adjustment mechanism for wages. But these agreements have been insufficient to control wage growth. The wage indexation mechanism has been changed several times: starting from full monthly and quarterly adjustments of wages to price movements, steps have gradually been taken toward less frequent and partial adjustments, and from ex post to ex ante adjustments. Two decisive steps were the replacement, in 1997, of the quarterly wage indexation mechanism with a yearly adjustment, and the replacement, in 2001, of ex post with ex ante adjustment of base wages in line with increases in the consumer price index.

Wage developments in Slovenia did not adequately support the stabilization policy until 1996. Permanent increases in real wages per employee (recorded since 1992) contributed to a deterioration of export competitiveness. Despite a transition-induced drop in employment, the increase in real wages per employee exceeded the increase in labor productivity. Only in 1997, as a result of the new indexation mechanism, did real wage growth slow down. Control over wage growth in the public sector is yet to be achieved.

Trade policy. Because Slovenia is a small country, its only viable strategy for further economic development is an outward-looking, export-oriented approach and the adoption of policies to promote it. Since 1991, the share of foreign trade in GDP has increased significantly. Slovenia's most important partners are and will remain its European neighbors, primarily the EU member states. Slovenia undertook trade policy reforms aimed at reorienting its import substitution strategy to an export-oriented one already in the late 1980s, when nonprice protection was significantly reduced. Since independence, Slovenia has progressively introduced trade policy reforms (the reduction of customs duties and the elimination or reduction of nontariff barriers) in order to increase the openness of its economy, and it has established an institutional framework aimed at fostering the competitiveness of domestic producers. Today, Slovenia is on the threshold of membership in the European Union and is a member of the World Trade Organization.

Structural and institutional reforms. To develop a strong economy that is well prepared to absorb the shocks of transition, and to bring inflation down and maintain it at a low level, macroeconomic policies have to be accompanied by a wide range of structural and institutional reforms. In Slovenia these reforms are aimed, first, at creating the conditions conducive to increased investment, as required for sustainable economic growth and higher employment; second, at increasing the economy's international competitiveness by improving the efficiency of factor markets; and third, at designing policies and measures that will make the transition process socially and environmentally sustainable.

The process of structural and institutional reforms had begun already at the end of the 1980s but was intensified after independence with the process of privatization, bank rehabilitation, adjustments in social safety net measures, and other initiatives. In this context the Enterprise and Financial Sector Adjustment Loan (EFSAL) arranged between Slovenia and the World Bank in 1993 represented an important contribution in support of the transition (World Bank 1993). In view of the upcoming EU accession negotiations, a full-fledged program of structural reform was elaborated in the 1997 EU accession strategy document (Mrak, Potocnik, and Rojec 1998). The main components of these reforms and their sequencing are presented in Table 2.

TABLE 2 TIMETABLE OF MAJOR COMPONENTS OF MAIN REFORMS

Reform	1997	1998	1999	2000	2001
Tax system					
Approve VAT and excise tax legislation		▓			
Prepare to implement VAT and excise tax			▓		
Implement VAT and excise tax				▓	
Pension system					
Prepare White Paper on pension reform	▓	▓			
Discuss White Paper		▓			
Submit proposed legislation	▓	▓			
Adopt legislation		▓	▓		
Prepare reform			▓		
Start implementation of first phase of reform					▓
Continue implementation of successive phases					
Financial sector					
Open market to branch offices of foreign banks		▓			
Abolish interbank agreement on maximum deposit rates and tolar deposits on foreign credits			▓		
Privatize two largest state-owned banks[a]				▓	
Adopt legislation on bank privatization		▓			
Prepare for privatization and divestiture		▓			
Introduce new payment system					▓
Complete ownership transformation of insurance companies					▓
Rehabilitate and privatize insurance companies		▓	▓		
Open insurance market to foreign capital			▓	▓	▓
Broaden and deepen capital market	▓	▓	▓	▓	▓
Develop and improve legal and regulatory framework	▓	▓	▓	▓	▓
Harmonize with essential EU legislation	▓	▓	▓	▓	▓

Public utilities
Liberalize prices
Continue liberalization and competition, including privatization
Introduce regulation, including introduction of public procurement system

Price liberalization
Announce full program of price liberalization, with dates
Implement according to announced plan

Enterprise sector
Rehabilitate and privatize via Slovene Development Company
Replace distortive subsidies with transparent measures
Reduce subsidies to level compatible with Europe Agreement
Develop horizontal mechanism to stimulate competitiveness
Develop institutional and legal framework (takeovers, etc.)
Stimulate FDI and capital restructuring in privatized industries

a. Nova Ljubljanska Banka and Nova Kreditna Banka Maribor.
Source: Mrak, Potočnik, and Rojec 1998.

Slovenia has completed most of the needed structural reforms in full or in part, but its agenda in this area is not yet exhausted. Indeed, the intensification of the remaining structural reforms represents the main policy challenge facing the country in the near term. The elements of and progress achieved in the major areas of structural reform are briefly summarized below.

Institution building. The creation of appropriate institutions is probably the most important and the most complex issue in the transition from a socialist to a market economy. Institution building in Slovenia has been pursued in various dimensions: toward the creation of a national economy and state, in the transition from a socialist to a market economy, and, finally, toward accession to the European Union. Institution building is by its nature a gradual process, because institutions, however well designed, take time to mature. In the early postindependence period, Slovenia took a gradualist approach to institution building, but, in the course of the EU accession process, this approach was increasingly replaced by one aimed at more rapid change.

Enterprise sector reform. The restructuring of Slovenia's enterprise sector began back in the late 1980s. In the early phase, most of the attention in this area focused on three aspects of reform. The first was to establish an appropriate legal and institutional framework for enterprise creation and the promotion of entrepreneurial initiative. The second was the rehabilitation of the enterprise sector, toward which goal various programs of enterprise rehabilitation were launched. The third was privatization. For political reasons, quite some time passed between the passage of the Ownership Transformation Act in 1992 and the actual beginning of the privatization process. Slovenia's approach to privatization has been a mixture of free distribution of shares, internal buyouts at a discount, and commercial privatization. The emphasis on internal buyouts was the main implicit characteristic of the Slovenian privatization and served to maintain the status quo by avoiding larger layoffs, but at some cost to enterprise performance.

Financial sector reform. The dominant financial intermediaries in Slovenia are banks. During the early transition the banking sector went through an extensive, government-led rehabilitation, which was successfully completed by 1997. Since then the banking industry has undergone intensive consolidation and less intensive structural change in order to increase its efficiency. The largest bank in Slovenia, Nova Ljubljanska Banka, was partly privatized in 2002 but remains in majority state ownership. That same year the privatization of the second-largest state-owned bank was launched, but the attempt was not successful. In the insurance sector, consolidation and restructuring are lagging behind, largely because of unresolved ownership issues in the largest insurance company. In contrast to banking and insurance, the institutions of Slovenia's capital markets are new, free of any burdensome inheritances from the past. Capital market development was strongly influenced by the mass privatization process, but thus far it has not become an important channel for intermediating new savings. Market capitalization is low, and trading is concentrated in a rather limited number of large companies. Pension reform, with a greater emphasis on funded schemes, has been initiated, but its positive effects on long-term savings and the development of capital markets are to be expected only after several years.

Reform of public utilities and improvement of economic infrastructure. Soon after independence, Slovenia initiated reforms of its public commercial utility companies, but the pace of these reforms has been much slower than in other sectors of the economy and slower than is desirable for the developing market economy. The pace of reform was particularly slow in the first years of transition, and a slight acceleration was observed only in more recent years, in the context of Slovenia's negotiations toward EU membership. The relative inefficiency of the public utilities is an important structural reason for the persistence of inflation and hampers the competitiveness of the Slovenian economy.

Social security and pension system reform. Slovenia has succeeded in keeping its social security and human development systems (pensions, health care, education, and the social safety net) in good condition. Health care reform in 1992 introduced an additional, voluntary private health insurance pillar, which quickly became quasi-mandatory, as its coverage is nearly universal. Another comprehensive social security reform introduced during the transition was the pension reform launched in 2000. This reform modified the existing first pillar, which is in the form of a pay-as-you-go system, and introduced a second pillar in the form of a voluntary, fully funded scheme. Although these reforms have had a positive impact on fiscal stability, further steps in both areas are needed in order to maintain medium-term fiscal sustainability, especially when one takes into account the aging of the Slovenian population.

Challenges for the Future

Slovenia has made great advances along the path of transition and socioeconomic development. Although so far the transition can be judged relatively successful, and Slovenians' incomes are converging with those in the European Union, significant challenges remain. These are in part the result of delays in reform associated with the gradualist approach, but they are also linked to the normal development process and to Slovenia's maturing as a transition economy. These challenges need to be addressed in order to solidify the gains achieved thus far and to boost the benefits from EU membership.

In the macroeconomic domain, bringing down inflation is the most obvious challenge. Excessive inflation accompanied by a fixed exchange rate for the tolar within the Exchange Rate Mechanism-II (ERM-II) regime could cause major problems for economic stability in a highly export-oriented economy. But lowering inflation is not the only macroeconomic challenge. Slovenia also needs to maintain an overall macroeconomic policy framework that is consistent with and supportive of EU membership, including adoption of the *acquis communautaire* (the totality of the legal framework that has evolved over several decades of European integration) and other EU institutions. This macroeconomic framework is essential to securing economic stability for sustainable growth.

If, in the short term, reduction of inflation is the main challenge of macroeconomic policy, in the medium to long term the main challenges are likely to be in the areas of public finance and structural policies. Implementing the *acquis* will put pressure on the budget, even if the European Union pays some of the bill. Upon joining ERM-II, Slovenia will lose its monetary policy independence, which has been one of the main pillars of its economic policy and stability over the last 10 years. As a result, Slovenia's room to maneuver will be reduced. The loss of monetary policy independence will further enhance the relative importance of other macroeconomic policies, such as fiscal and incomes policies. These policies remain in the national competency but have to be coordinated with EU policies. If Slovenia's policies are not flexible enough, Slovenia's ability to manage shocks effectively will be severely limited and the risks of instability will be increased.

The challenges for structural reform are most noticeable in the restructuring and privatization of the corporate and financial sector, as well as of the public utilities. In the postprivatization process, the Slovenian enterprise sector faces certain problems, including ownership consolidation (with contradictions persisting between internal and external owners), the establishment of corporate governance (overcoming the lack of real long-term and strategic owners), and enterprise restructuring (which has been too slow because of corporate governance problems, insufficient incentive from macroeconomic and especially exchange rate policy, and persisting administrative barriers). In view of Slovenia's imminent membership in the European Union, these issues are becoming of crucial importance. Failure to address them would make it more difficult for the Slovenian enterprise sector to become a viable player in the internal EU market. In addition, to prepare the Slovenian financial sector to cope successfully with the competitive pressure of the single EU financial market, its competitiveness will have to be further strengthened and regulatory and supervisory measures efficiently implemented.

In reforming the public utilities sector, the strategic goal remains to provide reliable and cost-effective supply in the energy sector, transport, telecommunications, and local utility services. The ongoing reforms in the economic infrastructure include several sets of economic policy measures whose common denominator is to ensure that the development of this infrastructure is market oriented. The underlying principle of all reforms pursued in this field is to commercialize the services provided by this infrastructure. Efforts at reform should continue to aim at cost-effective production, the independence of economic agents in managerial activities, increased competition, efficient regulation, and continued investment.

More thorough reforms are also clearly visible in several areas. One of these is the pension system. Here a rather radical reform had originally been planned, but as numerous political compromises were made upon its implementation, further amendments, changes, and adjustments are going to be needed. Meanwhile comprehensive reform of the health care system needs to be implemented. Not enough has been done to reduce rigidities in fiscal expenditure, and very little has been done to develop public-private partnerships—investments are still made through traditional means, that is, budget resources and borrowing. All this, together with continuing labor market rigidities, keeps inflation relatively high and reduces Slovenia's export competitiveness. These problems need further attention in view of the quickly approaching date of EU accession.

Slovenia has made considerable progress in institutional development, but a number of deficiencies still exist. The problem of the so-called implementation gap—that is, the lag between the formal establishment of institutions and the ability of those institutions to act efficiently—is particularly relevant. Further improvements in institution building will proceed in parallel with changes in the role of the state.

There is little doubt that Slovenia is under pressure to intensify its structural reform processes so that it can enter the European Union and, later, ERM-II without major problems. To avoid potential threats and fully reap the benefits of EU integration, more effort is needed in many areas of structural reform so as to bring greater dynamism and growth potential to the economy. Public utilities reform has to be implemented with greater determination, and enterprise and financial sector policies must create the conditions for improved competitiveness of private business. Social policy has to be streamlined wherever it does not directly target the most vulnerable, and the institutional framework of economic activity has to be made simpler and more transparent. Implementation of these structural reforms will have to be accompanied by a more restrictive fiscal and wage policy, to ensure a soft landing for Slovenia in ERM-II, scheduled for the beginning of 2005, and the adoption of the euro in 2007. As in the past, there is no lack of awareness on Slovenia's part about what needs to be done. As Janez Šušteršič points out in Chapter 24, "what is needed now is the determination to act on those good intentions [to implement the agreed policy measures] in spite of pressure from special interests and in spite of the political risks associated with a less cautious approach to reform."

SLOVENIA AND THE WORLD BANK

In 1991 Slovenia emerged from the breakup of SFR Yugoslavia as the most economically advanced of the successor states. It became a member of the World Bank Group in February 1993, after issues related to the distribution of assets and liabilities at the Bank of the former SFR Yugoslavia among its five successor states were resolved.

In devising its approach to the transition economies, the World Bank's main challenge has been to accurately tailor the volume and composition of its assistance to each country's needs. The aim of the Bank's strategy was to complement countries' own efforts at domestic reform, enhancing their acceptance and sustainability. This was done by using the Bank's assistance to minimize the economic and social costs of reform. Striking a proper balance between the volume of financial assistance and the sequencing of reforms was important in order both to prevent an overaccumulation of debt and to facilitate a smooth and cost-effective implementation of reforms.[4]

Achieving restructuring and growth in the transition economies required addressing supply and demand constraints. On the supply side, the constraints were in the availability of resources—such as credit and infrastructure—needed to complement the growth of the private sector. On the demand side, constraints such as macroeconomic instability, a weak legal framework, or insufficient liberalization hindered the business environment and reduced investment incentives.

The World Bank Group also supported the transition economies with analytical and advisory activities. For some countries, like Slovenia, this form of assistance was as important as the financial support. These activities included policy advice, critical transfer of technical knowledge, economic and sector reports, seminars, training of government officials, and making the experience of international experts available to policymakers. The Bank's involvement in this historic transformation also helped the transition economies share their own local reform experiences with each other and with the rest of the world, bringing international recognition of their reform efforts and helping to boost their image abroad.

The World Bank's initial involvement in Slovenia after independence and before 1997 was relatively modest but nonetheless important. Project support included two environmental operations in an amount equivalent to $24 million in fiscal year 1996, to improve air quality and strengthen environmental management. Slovenia also received the equivalent of $32 million to continue the coastal water supply and irrigation project, the only active project inherited from SFR Yugoslavia, and the important Enterprise and Financial Sector Adjustment Loan (EFSAL, mentioned in the first section of this overview) provided support for the first phase of enterprise and financial sector reform in the amount of $80 million.

One of the two environmental projects was a technical support and investment project for the cost-effective phaseout of ozone-depleting substances, financed by a grant from the Global Environmental Facility. The project was completed in mid-1998. The second project involved a reduction in ambient atmospheric concentrations of particulate matter and sulfur dioxide along with the health damage associated with exposure to air pollution; the Ministry of Environment and Physical Planning also received assistance in developing standardized data sets and procedures to strengthen land use planning and environmental management. This project was completed in 2001.

The Slovene Coast Water Supply and Sewerage Project, prepared in 1987 and completed in 1998, was an important contribution to modernizing Slovenia's infrastructure. The project managed to eliminate previous water shortages, provide additional water supply capacity to meet industrial and domestic demand, reduce unaccounted-for water in the Rizana Water Works distribution network from 40 percent to 30 percent, and increase efficiency in the delivery of water supply and sewerage services.

From the policy point of view, by far the most important element of the World Bank's early support to Slovenia was the EFSAL, approved in fiscal year 1994. This was the Bank's first lending operation in the newly independent Slovenia and the first loan of its kind to a transition economy. The loan was designed to assist the country in its transition to a market economy by providing quick-disbursing balance of payments and budget support, facilitating enterprise privatization and restructuring, and accelerating the development of a strong and supportive financial sector. The last of these was accomplished through the rehabilitation of insolvent or seriously undercapitalized banks, including the severance of ownership links between enterprises and these banks; the exchange of the frozen claims of all Slovenian banks against the National Bank of Yugoslavia for bonds issued by the Republic of Slovenia; the enhancement of the legal and regulatory framework for banking and the strengthening of bank supervision; and bank privatization.

Starting in fiscal year 1997, the World Bank strengthened its cooperation with Slovenia following growing requests for support by the Slovenian government. The blueprint of this assistance for the following three years was formulated in the first Country Assistance Strategy (CAS) for Slovenia. The CAS was designed to support Slovenia's transition reforms and institution building, as well as its quest to become a member of the European Union. The CAS also set the stage for Slovenia's eventual graduation from World Bank borrowing.

The CAS focused primarily on analytical and advisory activities, with some small targeted lending. Two lending operations, the Real Estate Registration Modernization (in the amount of $15 million) and the Health Sector Reform Project ($9.5 million) were approved in fiscal years 1999 and 2000, respectively.

The greater part of World Bank assistance to Slovenia during the CAS period (fiscal years 1998–2000) came in the form of analytical and advisory services. This type of assistance served Slovenia well and was appropriate for its relatively advanced level of development. The work program of these services included analytical papers, reviews, technical notes, workshops, and seminars. Its success was reflected in the promotion of important reforms in a number of areas, including banking and capital markets, the pension system, health sector finance and management, property rights and housing finance, and the launch of the privatization of some state-owned assets, including the two state-owned banks. In addition, institutional capacity was deepened in the area of debt management, and frameworks were developed to better promote foreign direct investment, expand the role of the private sector in infrastructure investment, and more effectively enforce and monitor the environmental regulatory regime.

In addition, the CAS allowed the preparation of a series of freestanding sector reviews that provided an assessment of remaining structural weaknesses and discussed policy options to address the challenges faced by Slovenia in its pursuit of EU membership. These reviews covered agriculture, trade, and labor markets and included a comprehensive Country Economic Memorandum (CEM) focused on EU accession. The CEM, delivered to the government in March 1999 and broadly disseminated within Slovenia and the European Union, was the first prepared for Slovenia and served to highlight the country's reform progress and remaining challenges and to reinforce the ideas behind the EU accession strategy document referred to above (Mrak, Potočnik, and Rojec 1998). The CEM was also important in showcasing Slovenia before the international community.

Slovenia will be the first of the transition countries from Central and Eastern Europe to graduate from World Bank borrowing. The country is slowly changing its status from that of a recipient of resources from the World Bank to that of a donor. The Bank's assistance program to Slovenia has been declining as the country moves closer to EU membership. A small number of additional analytical and advisory services are planned as final elements of the Bank's active support to Slovenia. At the same time, Slovenia is taking over the responsibilities associated with donor status. The country is participating normally in the thirteenth replenishment of International Development Association funding (IDA-13). It will also make contributions for the IDA-9 to IDA-12 replenishments so that its share in the capital of this institution will remain unchanged. In addition, Slovenia has been a member of the Global Environment Fund (GEF) since its creation in 1994. The country participated in the second (1998–2002) replenishment of the GEF Trust Fund, with a contribution of SDR 1 million, and it plans to participate in its third replenishment (2003–06) with an equal amount.

The World Bank and Slovenia have walked the transition path together as good partners. Both Slovenia and the Bank have learned from each other and have benefited from this partnership. The journey has so far been successful, and a major milestone will be reached when Slovenia becomes a full-fledged member of the European Union in May 2004. The experience of the relationship between the World Bank and Slovenia during the past 13 years has produced many lessons that will be useful to other transition economies. As Slovenia continues to move forward, at its own pace in the Slovenian way, it will face new challenges, but already the short history since independence allows one to foresee that it will address them successfully.

A CHAPTER-BY-CHAPTER SYNOPSIS

This book is composed of 24 chapters grouped into three main parts. These three parts are, by and large, arranged chronologically. The first, "The Road Toward Political and Economic Independence," discusses the political, economic, and social environment in SFR Yugoslavia that created the conditions for Slovenia's independence, and it presents the main building blocks of Slovenia's economic and political independence. The second part of the book, "Socioeconomic Transformation—The Slovenian Way," presents and analyzes the main features of Slovenia's transition to a national market economy. Those aspects of the socioeconomic transition in Slovenia whose design and implementation were at variance with the conventional recipes followed by most transition countries are given particular attention. The third part, "The Quest for EU Membership," deals with the process of Slovenia's EU accession and with the country's prospects as a member of an enlarged European Union.[5]

Part I: The Road Toward Political and Economic Independence (Chapters 1–7)

Political factors contributed decisively to the dissolution of SFR Yugoslavia. In the late 1980s, two political visions competed on how to reform the federation. On the one hand was the vision of a democratic and decentralized Yugoslavia, advocated primarily by Slovenia and Croatia. The opposing vision, whose major proponent was Serbia, was far more authoritarian and centralized; it was also clearly nationalistic and ethnocentric. In *Chapter 1* of this book, *Janez Drnovšek* claims that the dissolution of SFR Yugoslavia clearly shows that greater centralization is not the right recipe for reforming an already rather decentralized multinational federal state when huge differences separate the constituent parts. On the contrary, the creation of conditions that would allow the democratic concepts of tolerance and cooperation to prevail, rather than nationalistic concepts founded on exclusion, was the only way for the successor countries of SFR Yugoslavia to go forward on the road to stability and prosperity. The European Union can and should be a major actor in these processes, and Slovenia as an imminent member of the European Union can also play a useful part.

In the aftermath of the breakup of SFR Yugoslavia, at least two economic explanations of that disintegration have been advanced. The first holds that disintegration was a consequence of the great economic diversity that existed in the country. The second argues that the dissolution occurred because of differences among the republics in the gains they expected from transition and integration into the world economy and especially into the European Union. According to *Vladimir Gligorov*, in *Chapter 2*, from an economic point of view the key element in the disintegration of SFR Yugoslavia was the concept of social ownership and the difficulties it introduced in developing a consistent macroeconomic governance setup. The regime of self-management lacked a clear understanding of the role of macroeconomic institutions and policy. The disarray in public governance, the inability to deal with problems, and the lack of adequate instruments of economic policy management, together with large macroeconomic imbalances, contributed to the disintegration, although it was mainly driven by political interests. Still, the author believes, from an economic point of view this was not a necessary development. Although the system of social self-management was neither representative nor efficient, it could have been reformed. In a way, the Slovenian transition itself makes that point clear.

The political and economic differences among the Yugoslav republics might not have been sufficient to lead to the dissolution of SFR Yugoslavia had they not occurred during a historic "window of opportunity" for republics to claim independence and seek integration into the international community. In *Chapter 3* of the book, *Bojko Bučar* identifies two sets of developments, internal and international, whose synchronization paved the way to Slovenia's independence and international recognition. The internal developments were characterized by the political and economic reasons for the dissolution of SFR Yugoslavia, enumerated above, whereas the international developments can be summarized by the fall of the Berlin Wall and all that followed. The specific internal developments in Yugoslavia, combined with the tectonic changes in the international community, made possible the independence of Slovenia as a sovereign state. The key word here is "synchronization." Slovenia probably achieved its statehood in a narrow window of time when the conjuncture of events was favorable for such an event. At any other time, things might have gone in another direction. Still, as Bučar says, one should not neglect the determination of a people and its political representatives to establish a sovereign and independent state. At the end of the day, without that determination, not much would have happened.

In the process of gaining independence, Slovenia first had to create the institutional setting for a new independent state, undertake the necessary system changes and policy initiatives that precede independence, establish monetary sovereignty, and resolve the issue of the succession of SFR Yugoslavia's external debts and establish financial independence. At the outbreak of the Yugoslav political crisis in the second half of the 1980s, SFR Yugoslavia already functioned as an asymmetric federation. The constituent republics effectively took over federal responsibilities, thus narrowing the role of the federation and transferring several sovereign rights to themselves. Although Slovenia possessed many of the competencies of a state at the time of independence, many institutional gaps remained. This to a great extent defined the priorities of institution building in the new state. As described by *Neven Borak* and *Bistra Borak* in *Chapter 4,* these efforts concentrated on the building of a constitutional system, a fiscal system, and a monetary system, as well as institutions for conducting foreign policy and ensuring national security. Slovenia's new constitution established a system of parliamentary democracy based on a social market economy, combining a parliamentary system with a weak presidency. The creation of a fiscal system established state control over the public finances while building the institutions necessary to run an independent state. Creation of the monetary system included the establishment of an independent and accountable central bank and the introduction of the new Slovenian currency.

In *Chapter 5* of the book, *Jože Mencinger* analyzes Slovenia's approach to transition and the policy activities undertaken in the period before and shortly after independence. The economic policy of the Slovenian government that came to power after general elections in May 1990 aimed at achieving three major goals: first, the survival of the economy in the period of stabilization and transformation; second, the construction of a market-oriented economic system; and third, the gradual takeover of economic policy tools from the federal government. Pragmatism and gradualism were the pillars of this strategy, aimed at making the costs of transition socially bearable, facilitating rapid adaptation to highly uncertain political decisions, and generating proper responses to the economic policies of the federal government. Systemic changes were made cautiously as well. Two types of statutes were introduced. On the one hand were those aimed at facilitating the functioning of a normal market economy (such as a new tax system and budget), and on the other were those needed for the transition to independence (such as the statutes regulating monetary policy and the financial sector).

Gradualism was thus the dominant pattern of the Slovenian transition both before and after independence. However, as Mencinger observes, the reality since independence has been an even more gradual transition, in terms of both economic policy and actual changes in the economic system, than the most enthusiastic gradualists had proposed. Gradualism was in a sense a natural heritage of the previous systemic changes within SFR Yugoslavia, entrenched in initial economic conditions and consistent with political developments. The transition process in Slovenia can be disentangled neither from the legacy of the Yugoslav type of socialism nor from the process of the disintegration of SFR Yugoslavia. The latter, and the task of creating a new state, slowed and softened the transition measures undertaken as well. The gradualism of Slovenia's transition, as reflected in the dilemmas and controversies the country faced in the early postindependence transition, is most explicitly reflected in two issues, privatization and macroeconomic stabilization, and within the latter, in the choice of exchange rate system in particular.

From the economic point of view, asserting monetary sovereignty was probably the single most important and demonstrative act of Slovenian independence. The October 1991 introduction of the new Slovenian currency, the tolar, by the Bank of Slovenia, acting as the fully independent central bank of the new sovereign state, was only the final step in a process that had started long before. In SFR

Yugoslavia, monetary policy had been the responsibility of the National Bank of Yugoslavia, but its implementation was left, to a large extent, to the central banks of the individual republics. Monetary policy in the Yugoslav federation was not conceived as independent from the specific financing needs of enterprises, especially in agriculture and the export sector. In this administratively governed system, banks were used primarily as channels for serving the needs of enterprises. The latter were at the same time the main beneficiaries of the foreign credits whose buildup resulted in a huge external debt. According to *Andrej Rant* in *Chapter 6,* the National Bank of Serbia's illegal raid on the Yugoslav monetary system in 1990 was not a simple breach of the existing federal rules. It was rather an attempt to set new rules whereby the federal monetary function was taken over by a single republic in the federation. The exclusion of Slovenia and Croatia from the monetary system in June 1991 was another step in the same direction. As a consequence of these developments, Slovenia had no alternative but to speed its preparations for monetary autonomy, which ended with the introduction of the tolar and the assumption of responsibility for Slovenian monetary policy by the Bank of Slovenia.

Less than one year after its June 1991 declaration of independence, Slovenia had become a full-fledged member of the international political community. Political recognition was a precondition for intensifying the country's efforts toward another strategic objective, namely, constituting its independent financial position and delinking it from the country risk of what used to be SFR Yugoslavia. Achieving this objective was essential if Slovenia was to normalize its relations with international capital markets and, as a result, to create the conditions for normal access of Slovenian entities to these markets. As presented by *Mojmir Mrak* and *France Arhar* in *Chapter 7,* two main areas of activity have been crucial in reaching this strategic objective. The first was the admission of Slovenia to membership in international financial institutions, especially the International Monetary Fund, the World Bank Group, and the European Bank for Reconstruction and Development. Successful completion of the procedures for membership not only opened the way toward renewed access of Slovenia to the financial resources of these institutions, but also established the key principles for apportioning the external debt that SFR Yugoslavia owed to other groups of foreign creditors. Having first established the principle that Slovenia was one of five equal successors to SFR Yugoslavia, Slovenia had completely regularized its relationship with foreign creditors by mid-1996. The "Slovenian model" of debt apportionment was reconfirmed de facto by the Agreement on Succession Issues signed in May 2001 by representatives of all five successor states.

Part II: Socioeconomic Transformation—The Slovenian Way (Chapters 8–20)

Slovenia enjoyed some of the most favorable initial conditions of all the transition economies, including a good geographical location, skilled human capital, and significant trade links with the West. However, upon independence, Slovenia lost important markets in the rest of the former SFR Yugoslavia, and the transformation of its economic structures during the early transition period was not painless. Slovenia suffered a severe economic shock from the combination of these two events. The country also inherited from SFR Yugoslavia a high degree of macroeconomic instability, reflected in a skyrocketing inflation rate and a large external debt burden. All these factors together resulted in a considerable fall in the country's GDP.

Slovenia responded with a strong adjustment program aimed at retaking control of its economy. The implementation of a macroeconomic stabilization program, characterized by trade liberalization and the synchronization of monetary and fiscal policy, was among the most important economic tasks of the newly established state. In *Chapter 8* of the book, *Carlos Silva-Jáuregui* concludes that the overall impact of this adjustment program was remarkable, and he observes that the beginning of the economic turnaround, after the initial adjustment shock, was visible already by early 1993. Already by 1996, output had risen to levels above those prevailing before the transition. Today Slovenia has a functioning market economy, one that will be capable of facing competitive pressures within the European Union. The country has made good progress in adopting and implementing the *acquis communautaire*, as well as in developing the necessary institutions. Slovenia has the highest income per capita among the current group of EU accession countries, and the past decade has witnessed a considerable convergence of its income per capita toward the EU average.

Trade liberalization, together with monetary policy (including the management of capital flows) and fiscal policy, has been one of the pillars of Slovenian macroeconomic stabilization and liberalization. *Boris Majcen* and *Bartlomiej Kaminski* argue, in the first part of *Chapter 9*, that the greater part of Slovenia's foreign trade liberalization happened while Slovenia was still part of SFR Yugoslavia and in the first years of independence. Trade liberalization within SFR Yugoslavia started with a radical removal of nontariff barriers in the late 1980s. Independent Slovenia continued this process by eliminating the remaining nontariff barriers and adopting a new tariff schedule, which ultimately abolished all other import charges except tariffs, in order to adapt it to its own structure of production. This unilateral trade liberalization further evolved into a multilateral phase with Slovenia's accession to the General Agreement on Tariffs and Trade and the World Trade Organization. The second phase of Slovenia's trade liberalization has been bilateral, driven by the process of EU accession, through a number of free trade agreements and the Europe Agreement. The combined result of all these processes is that the existing level of foreign trade liberalization in Slovenia is lower than expected at the time of independence, and lower than it would have been in the case of multilateral reduction of most-favored-nation tariff rates. EU membership and the consequent adoption of the Common External Tariff will align the level of Slovenia's trade liberalization with that of the European Union.

In October 1991, when Slovenia introduced its new currency, the tolar, the economy was facing galloping inflation. Even as it confronted a tremendous need to build up appropriate foreign exchange reserves, which then amounted to only four days of imports, the Bank of Slovenia was obliged to reduce the inflation rate. As the banking system was very liquid at that time, the central bank shrank base money toward its estimate of the amount demanded by the economy. In the early postindependence period, the central bank conducted monetary policy in accordance with an exogenous money supply and a floating exchange rate. In *Chapter 10* of the book, *Ivan Ribnikar* and *Tomaž Košak* argue that this approach to monetary policy was successful in that it contributed to a rapid fall in inflation by mid-1992. At that time the Bank of Slovenia already faced increasing capital inflows, which intensified in the following years, partly because of high domestic interest rates and partly because of the reduced foreign exchange risk premium for borrowing abroad. To sterilize these inflows, the central bank issued bills denominated in foreign currency as well as so-called twin bills (denominated partly in foreign currency and partly in tolars). Until recently, the transmission of monetary policy changes through the interest rate channel had proved to be weak in Slovenia. Its effectiveness was diminished by the widespread use of indexation mechanisms in financial contracts, a direct consequence of the high inflation experienced while part of SFR Yugoslavia. In line with the planned convergence to conditions in the European Union, in November 2001 the Bank of Slovenia framed its new monetary policy for the period before entering European Monetary Union. According to Ribnikar and Košak, this policy rests on two pillars: the first takes into account the quantity of money in circulation, whereas the second takes into consideration various indicators that provide supplementary information about the economic situation in general.

Chapter 11, by *Velimir Bole*, also discusses monetary policy in Slovenia. The focus here is on a specific topic of extreme importance for Slovenia's macroeconomic policy, which the previous chapter has already touched on, namely, foreign exchange policy and the management of foreign capital flows. Slovenia's exchange rate policy was at first based on free floating of the tolar. According to Bole, immediately after independence, a pure float and exogenous money were the only real option in a context of galloping inflation, almost negligible foreign exchange reserves, and total lack of access to foreign credit. In such circumstances, Slovenia had to proceed on two tracks simultaneously: building foreign exchange liquidity and reducing inflation. Once basic control over the economy was restored and foreign exchange liquidity strengthened, policymakers were able to tackle the harmful effects of increasing net foreign financial inflows and microeconomic distortions on the product and labor markets. Therefore, after 1992, policymakers started to manage the floating exchange rate and to target the money supply. During most of the 1990s, the relative prices of nontradables and foreign financial flows were the most important constraints on the design of the exchange rate regime and on the choice of monetary policy measures. Until 1999, the economy had been stabilized using monetary targeting; after capital controls were lifted, monetary policy switched from targeting money to targeting the real interest rate. Although the implementation of managed floating has changed several times, depending on the ability to control the harmful effects of foreign financial flows, exchange rate interventions were used in a coherent fashion to support the effectiveness of monetary control.

In their analysis, in *Chapter 12*, of fiscal policy and public finance reform in Slovenia, *Milan Cvikl* and *Mitja Gaspari* ascertain that, in the first phase of the transition, a surplus in Slovenia's fiscal accounts supported a restrictive monetary policy (discussed in the previous chapters) in achieving macroeconomic stabilization. This surplus was achieved through actions both on the revenue and on the expenditure side, by centralizing control of the public finances and introducing hard budget constraints. In the second phase, fiscal policy has aimed at supporting enterprise and bank restructuring by creating room on the expenditure side for the costs associated with this restructuring and by implementing pension reform. In this context, fiscal policy assisted the liberalization of the enterprise sector, fostered the growth of the private sector, and contributed to successful rehabilitation and reform of the financial sector. In 1999 Slovenia passed modern budget legislation and reformed the tax system with the introduction of a value added tax and excise taxes. Although the second half of the 1990s saw major improvements in public expenditure management, the goal of a balanced general government budget over the business cycle has not been met. According to Cvikl and Gaspari, several further tasks must be undertaken in the areas of fiscal policy and reform and of public expenditure management in the years to come. First, the commitment by the authorities to implement Exchange Rate Mechanism II will require that a restrictive fiscal stance remain a top priority.

Second, further progress is needed in the design and implementation of methods and procedures for full medium-term economic forecasting and budgetary planning. Third, performance-oriented budgeting must be designed and implemented as an ultimate instrument that will increase the efficiency of government services and change the role of the state. This will include reforms in a range of government services including education, health, social assistance, the judicial system, defense, security, and market regulation.

Building a consistent set of institutions is one of the basic pillars of each country's transition strategy. However, institution building is not very popular among politicians and policymakers, because it involves high political risk and is very difficult to implement. In *Chapter 13* of the book, *Rasto Ovin* and *Boštjan Kramberger* note that, during the early transition in Slovenia, a lack of political will for institutional change led to the adoption of a gradualist approach to institution building. However, in the course of the EU accession process, this approach has been increasingly replaced by a more aggressive one, as Slovenia strives to meet the requirements of the *acquis communautaire*. Although Slovenia has made great strides toward creating the institutional setting for a modern market economy, backlogs remain. Problems in the financial sector, the public utilities, the judiciary, and elsewhere all have their roots in deficient institutions. The problem of the so-called implementation gap—that between the normative institutional setting where institutions mostly exist, and their inability to act effectively—is particularly important. The authors claim that improvement of the institutional setting in Slovenia will have to go hand in hand with changes in the role of the state.

Slovenia's approach to enterprise privatization and the process of postprivatization restructuring is typical of the country's gradualist approach to the transition. *Marko Simoneti, Matija Rojec,* and *Aleksandra Gregorič* claim, in *Chapter 14*, that this approach was mostly driven by the aim to reach a consensus among the main stakeholders and to distribute the burden of transition among governmental, semi-governmental, and private entities. This approach proved appropriate for several hundred relatively small and labor-intensive companies and for about 100 well-performing, large, capital-intensive companies. However, the privatization program as designed was inappropriate for those relatively large and capital-intensive companies requiring substantial restructuring and, hence, extensive outside strategic financing. Except in those unprofitable companies that were subject to a governmental restructuring program, conflict between company insiders and outsiders slowed restructuring in these firms. Two problems resulting from Slovenia's chosen approach to privatization seem especially relevant. The first is the problem of "employeeism," where worker-owners wield enough power to influence company decisions toward excessive wages and employment. The second problem is that of insider control, which frequently prevents dispersed outsiders from efficiently transforming ownership into effective control, despite holding a majority of voting shares. Yet another consequence of Slovenia's approach has been a low level of foreign direct investment (FDI). Existing analyses and empirical data leave little doubt that FDI has made a positive and relevant contribution to the restructuring of Slovenia's enterprise sector, but also that it has played only a modest role in privatization overall and in the postprivatization consolidation of ownership.

According to the authors, the consolidation of control and corporate governance—the necessary precondition for a thoroughgoing restructuring—is still in its infancy in many privatized companies. Although, in the 1994–98 period, private companies that were not part of the privatization process expanded their activities through offensive restructuring (new investment and increased employment) and hence increased their advantages in terms of productivity and financial performance, privatized firms in general were not expanding but rather improving their productivity very slowly, mostly through defensive restructuring. Nonprivatized firms meanwhile remain in the red, although they have managed to cut their operating losses and increase their labor productivity, mostly through defensive restructuring and downsizing, reduced employment, and disinvestment. Given that firms with well-defined domestic and foreign ownership seem to perform better in the same institutional environment, the following steps should be taken to further improve the performance of the Slovenian enterprise sector: complete privatization of poorly performing nonprivatized companies, accelerated ownership consolidation and improvements in corporate governance in privatized companies, elimination of barriers to FDI, and, finally, measures to promote the establishment and growth of new companies.

Chapter 15 provides a somewhat different perspective on the process of enterprise restructuring in Slovenia. *Polona Domadenik* and *Janez Prašnikar* claim that the restructuring of existing firms was a primary impetus to economic growth in Slovenia in recent decades. The preprivatization restructuring of firms was largely influenced by the old self-management system, signaling a steep tradeoff between investment and wages. More precisely, in the early transition period, before these firms were privatized, the reduction of government influence over them, in the absence of market competition, resulted in rent sharing by workers and increases in wages at the expense of investment. In the wake of privatization, empirical evidence suggests that privatized Slovenian firms have undertaken limited and slow defensive restructuring but have been relatively successful at strategic restructuring compared with their counterparts in other transition economies. The immediate defensive adjustment in employment has been sizable, but too slow and incomplete. Defensive restructuring was slower in firms where employees had more influence, indicating the presence of rigid labor market regulations. As far as strategic restructuring in Slovenia is concerned, Domadenik and Prašnikar argue, in contrast to the authors of the previous chapter, that the form of ownership structure has had no significant impact on investment activities or labor adjustment in the enterprise sector. The difference between the two chapters on this score may be smaller than it seems, however, because Chapter 15 is focused on the more recent period, when a smaller impact of the ownership structure would have been expected.

Two factors have been of key importance in the strategic restructuring of Slovenian firms. The first is an inadequate institutional structure, reflected in underdeveloped capital markets resulting in underprovision of loans, a labor market with centrally set minimum wages and restrictive employment legislation, slow labor adjustment, and increasing discrepancies between the tradables and nontradables sectors. Second, a group of leading, internationally distinguished Slovenian firms have accumulated resources internally and are no longer limited by external constraints in obtaining the funds they need for their investment activity. These firms, which have shouldered the largest share of the burden of Slovenia's transition, differ among themselves in their ownership structure. Many in fact took advantage of internal buyouts, but their workers behave more like shareholders than like other types of stakeholders. The authors suggest that the state should accelerate its withdrawal from the productive sector and abandon its paternalistic role, manifested in the slow pace of institutional change in capital and labor markets. Further microeconomic reforms not only will induce faster economic growth but will also prove important in the approach to EU membership.

The distinguishing features of Slovenian banking, including the early introduction (in the late 1950s) of a two-tier banking system, ownership of banks by enterprises, and openness to the world, put Slovenia's banks in a unique starting position at the beginning of the 1990s and led to specific solutions in the area of bank restructuring. The cornerstone of banking sector restructuring in Slovenia was the rehabilitation of the two largest "old banks" starting in 1993. These two banks accounted for more than half of the entire banking sector at the time. Their rehabilitation, which was successfully completed in 1997, entailed a mixed centralized-decentralized approach, in which a large portion of the banks' bad debts was swapped for DM 1.9 billion in government bonds, the equivalent of approximately 6 percent of GDP in 1997. The privatization of state-owned banks in Slovenia has been pursued very gradually, in line, as explained by *Franjo Štiblar* and *Marko Voljč* in

Chapter 16, with the strategy of the less developed EU countries. With only about one-third of the banking sector under foreign control, Slovenia is the only transition economy where banking is not yet majority foreign-owned. As far as performance is concerned, the authors claim that there has been a slow and continuous growth and deepening, and that the efficiency with which the sector generates income has been increasing. The authors predict that although membership in the European Union will have an impact on the Slovenian banking sector, major shocks are not expected, because adjustment to the competitive environment has already been under way for some time.

Whereas banks were already well established in Slovenia in the preaccession period, the capital market has only emerged recently as an entirely new segment of the country's financial sector. According to *Dušan Mramor* and *Božo Jašovič* in *Chapter 17,* the main dilemma for capital market development in Slovenia is linked to the privatization process and its consequences. Two competing concepts have emerged. The first envisions the capital market as an unfettered tool for the rapid redistribution of corporate ownership in the wake of privatization, likely resulting in its concentration, which should lead to more efficient industry under the watchful eyes of shareholders. The second, on the other hand, argues that the capital market should be closely managed in order to preserve economic and social stability, with prices kept at levels consistent with an active market for primary issues and an acceptable ultimate distribution of ownership.

In the past decade Slovenia has made considerable progress in the development of its capital market, especially if one considers the status of the legal environment, its enforcement, and other elements of well-organized capital markets. Although the privatization process dominated capital market development in the recent past, it will gradually become less important in the future, and meanwhile the importance of pension funds and the insurance industry is expected to increase. The additional demand for securities induced by the introduction of funded pension schemes and the growth of the still-underdeveloped insurance industry will undoubtedly promote the development of the securities market. Nevertheless, it is very likely that the opportunity for the capital market to play a central role in the Slovenian financial system has been lost. Further development of the capital market will probably mean targeting a complementary role, emphasizing its competitive advantages in such fields as the management of pension and life insurance savings. If this happens, the Slovenian capital market will most likely come to resemble those in Germany, Austria, and Switzerland.

In line with its general approach to transition reforms, Slovenia undertook labor market reforms rather cautiously. The country has retained fairly strict employment protection legislation, particularly for regular employment, and maintained a costly unemployment benefit system, which, even after the sharp reduction in entitlements in 1998, remains the most generous among transition economies. In addition, Slovenia has imposed a heavy tax burden on labor and has kept minimum wages relatively high. To stimulate reemployment, it has also spent considerable resources on active labor market policies. In *Chapter 18* of the book, *Milan Vodopivec* argues that, regardless of whether these policies helped or hindered labor market adjustment, the empirical evidence suggests that by 2000–01 the Slovenian labor market had completed its transition.

The systemic shock of the early 1990s dramatically increased worker and job flows, with worker separations and job destruction leading the way. As a consequence, unemployment increased sharply but then slowly declined. Similarly, after an intense but short-lived reduction in the early 1990s, both employment and wages started to increase, with the turnaround occurring in 1993–95. In 2001 total employment and the total labor force exceeded their 1991 levels, and unemployment stabilized at a level that was low in international comparisons. All these developments clearly show a strengthened role for market forces. According to Vodopivec, increased worker and job flows in the early transition suggest that one of the key tasks of transition—the reallocation of labor—proceeded vigorously. The process was fostered by an increased flexibility of the wage determination system, and documented increases in the returns to education show that market forces were strongly at work in this area, too. Also on the plus side, the gender wage gap has not widened and has stabilized at a level that is low by international standards. On the minus side, however, is the distortion of the wage structure due to automatic increases in the basic wage with seniority, as called for under collective agreements.

The social protection system played an extremely important role in Slovenia's transition. *Tine Stanovnik*, in *Chapter 19,* describes the system as a rock of stability in a tempestuous period of rapid economic, political, and social change. This is not to say that the system was rigid and inflexible. It did evolve, but in a gradual and orderly fashion. The system has also remained generous, particularly in comparison with those of other countries in the region. This strong performance was made possible by the well-developed administrative capacity of Slovenia's autonomous social security institutions, and by the fact that Slovenia has preserved a centralized system of tax and contribution collection, which prevented an erosion of compliance. As a percentage of GDP, the costs of social expenditure in Slovenia are very close to the current EU average. Slovenia has so far been successful in balancing, in Stanovnik's words, "providing acceptable benefits from the combined . . . social protection system while keeping the costs acceptable to the general population." Nevertheless, the level of expenditure on social protection remains a cause of constant concern, because the resulting high labor costs reduce the competitiveness of the Slovenian economy. Although reforms of the various parts of the social protection system have pursued multiple goals, financial sustainability was certainly at the forefront. Reforms of the pension and health care systems, for example, were triggered by the need for cost containment and the desire to ensure their financial viability at least in the medium term. These reforms reduced benefits within the public system and assigned a greater role to private provision. This strategy proved quite successful in the health care reform of 1992 and in the 1999 pension reform.

Chapter 20, the last chapter in this part of the book, addresses an issue of the transition that is specific to Slovenia among the current EU accession countries, namely, the problems Slovenian enterprises face in reentering the markets of the former common state. The loss of these markets both before and, especially, after independence was one of the major causes of the loss in output of the Slovenian economy in the early 1990s. In the last few years, however, Slovenian enterprises have increased their trade and investment in the markets of the former SFR Yugoslavia. According to *Jože P. Damijan,* these increased flows might point toward a reintegration of these markets and the creation of new (or the restoration of former) patterns of trade and production specialization characterized by a supply-chain organization.

The attractiveness and increased importance of the countries of the former SFR Yugoslavia as export markets for Slovenian firms has a clear sectoral pattern: those Slovenian industries that are less competitive in EU markets tend to specialize in exports to these markets. Yet Damijan warns that, however attractive these markets may appear to Slovenian firms today, without a change in their market access strategy their market shares in the region may become endangered in the near future. One reason is that all of the countries of the former SFR Yugoslavia are running large balance of payments deficits, which may not be sustainable. Another is that after Slovenia joins the European Union in 2004, it will have to abandon the free trade agreements currently in effect with these countries. This will seriously weaken the market access advantage that Slovenian firms now enjoy over their EU competitors. To avoid possible unfavorable trends in the future, Slovenian firms, especially those in less competitive sectors, should place more emphasis on the possible relocation of some of their manufacturing activity to the other former Yugoslav republics, through FDI, rather than rely on export specialization as at present.

Part III: The Quest for EU Membership (Chapters 21–24)

Membership in the European Union was judged to be the most suitable strategic option for Slovenia for various reasons, including the promise of greater external security, legal harmonization, and stability; the prospect of involvement in European decision-making processes; and the allure of access to a single European market of 450 million consumers, with free movement of goods, services, capital, and labor across borders. EU membership also offers Slovenia the opportunity to become an active partner in European and global development, and at the same time to use EU membership as an umbrella of protection against the negative impacts of globalization on a small country. Yet despite a high degree of consensus among all the main political actors and the population at large, Slovenia's process of EU accession was accompanied with greater realism and a different set of concerns than in some other candidate countries. This can be attributed to Slovenia's higher level of development and to the fact that Slovenia became an independent nation-state only a few years ago. According to *András Inotai* and *Peter Stanovnik*, in *Chapter 21,* the view generally held among the political elite in Slovenia, as well as by the vast majority in the society, is that EU accession is a positive-sum game. This shared assessment is reflected in the highly successful referendum on accession in early 2003, in which 86 percent voted in favor. However, there is also widespread awareness that the benefits and costs of EU membership will be unevenly distributed across sectors and regions. Other concerns include a possible rise in prices and unemployment, the likely bankruptcy of some small and medium-size companies, the danger of a budgetary crunch, and the inevitable loss of some degree of sovereignty.

Slovenia's road to EU accession, the topic of *Chapter 22,* started at the Luxembourg European Council meeting in 1997. The objective of Slovenia's negotiations toward accession, which started in April 1998 and were completed in December 2002, was basically to reach agreement on how and by when Slovenia could align its legislation with the *acquis communautaire*, and whether it had set up the administrative structures and bodies necessary for effective implementation of those common rules. *Janez Potočnik* and *Jaime Garcia Lombardero* observe that, for Slovenia, the most difficult part of the negotiations was that concerning the financial package. The package eventually agreed upon is balanced for Slovenia in the short run and includes elements that should have important positive effects on the country's long-term orientation, thus contributing to stability of the public finances. Slovenia's accession process and negotiations undoubtedly created a favorable basis for its successful integration in the European Union and enhanced the prospects of real convergence. It now is up to Slovenia itself to determine how it will use the opportunity at hand.

Looking back on Slovenia's road to membership in the European Union, Potočnik and Lombardero list a number of issues that arose in that process that might be of relevance for other countries seeking to follow the same path. In Slovenia, EU integration has always been seen as a means of strengthening the transition process, and not as an objective in itself. It was recognized quite early that transition and accession are two mutually reinforcing processes, and that EU integration is the most natural and the best way to accelerate and deepen the transition process. It is no surprise that the accession process has, on a number of occasions, helped the Slovenian government push forward some necessary transition reforms that would otherwise have faced serious opposition at home. Indeed, one can say that the negotiations started at home rather than in Brussels, because they required a lot of adjustments for which, first of all, domestic consensus had to be found.

Chapter 23 deals with the position of smaller states, like Slovenia, within the European Union. *Zlatko Šabič, Marjan Svetličič, Dorota Pyszna-Nigge, and Wolfgang Wessels* argue emphatically that size does matter in the European Union. Although all recognized states are accorded formal equality in the international community and within the European Union, actual equality is another matter. The final product of the Convention on the Future of Europe, the Draft of the Constitutional Treaty announced in the summer of 2003, leans toward certain limitations on the role of smaller states. This is not to say, however, that the European Union that Slovenia is now joining will be very different from the one to which it first sought accession. The core advantages of EU membership remain, and they remain considerable for smaller countries. Apart from the advantages of being a part of a large internal market, membership brings an opportunity to participate actively in EU policymaking and in setting the European agenda, and to be part of, and form, coalitions with other member countries that will advance Slovenia's priorities. Membership also offers an opportunity to participate within an important group in international fora and organizations, and a chance to influence discussion and decisionmaking at an international level, and so to upgrade the country's international status and position.

Although size does matter, the future of countries such as Slovenia in the European Union is not determined by their small size. Probably the most important challenge for smaller states is how to seize most effectively the new opportunities stemming from EU membership, given their objectively limited human and material resources. According to the authors, Slovenians should be aware that a truly unified bloc of small states is close to a political fiction—something that rarely, if ever, comes to pass. Smaller states can be expected to behave rationally, follow their own interests, and choose their allies accordingly. Therefore, retaining flexibility in seeking cooperation and support, as determined by what the country really wants to accomplish in a given field, should be the main guideline for Slovenia in pursuing its own goals as a member of the European Union.

Chapter 24 appropriately concludes the book by analyzing the underlying pattern and determinants of Slovenia's transition process, presenting its main positive and negative aspects, and, finally, providing a perspective on future reforms and other steps that Slovenia should undertake in order to become a successful member of the European Union and a viable actor in the EU internal market. According to *Janez Šušteršič*, Slovenia is a prime example of the gradualist approach to transition. One of the main arguments in favor of gradualism is that it entails fewer and smaller shocks and, consequently, smaller losses of output and jobs, less social unrest, and therefore less of a danger that reforms will be reversed. The record of Slovenia's transition confirms this judgment. Šušteršič points to two specific factors that favored gradualism in Slovenia. The first is the endogenous nature of the transition in Slovenia, and the second is the favorable initial economic conditions that Slovenia enjoyed. However, a cautious reform is not without its costs. If Slovenia is to avoid potential threats and to fully reap the benefits of EU membership, more effort is needed in many reform areas, to bring greater dynamism and growth potential to the economy. Šušteršič proposes that structural reforms, particularly in the public utilities, be carried out with greater determination, and that industrial policy concentrate on fostering the restructuring and enhancing the competitiveness of the private business sector. A more restrictive fiscal and wage policy, as well as a less accommodative monetary policy, is needed to bring inflation down to sustainable levels. Social policy has to be streamlined wherever it does not directly target the most vulnerable in the population; the cost efficiency of the public sector has to be improved; and the institutional framework of economic activity has to be made simpler and more transparent. There is no lack of awareness that all this needs to be done, and official government documents are full of declarations on this score. What is most needed now is the determination to implement those declarations, despite the pressures of special interests and the political risks associated with a less cautious approach to reform.

REFERENCES

Dervis, K., M. Selowsky, and C. Wallich. 1994. "The Evolving Role of the World Bank: Transition in Central and Eastern Europe and the Former Soviet Union." World Bank, Washington, D.C..

Eurostat. 2003. *Statistics in Focus, Economy and Finance.* Theme 2-46. Luxembourg.

Grafenauer, B. 1979. "Samova 'država' in država karantanskih Slovencev." In *Zgodovina Slovencev*. Ljubljana: Cankarjeva založba.

Institute of Macroeconomic Analysis and Development. 1996. *Autumn Report 1996*. Ljubljana.

_____. 2003. *Autumn Report 2003*. Ljubljana.

Mrak, M., J. Potočnik, and M. Rojec, eds. 1998. *Strategy of the Republic of Slovenia for the Accession to the European Union: Economic and Social Part*. Ljubljana: Institute of Macroeconomic Analysis and Development.

Potočnik, J., M. Senjur, and F. Štiblar, eds. 1995. *The Strategy for Economic Development of Slovenia: Approaching Europe—Growth, Competitiveness and Integration*. Ljubljana: Institute of Macroeconomic Analysis and Development.

Statistical Office of the Republic of Slovenia. 2003. *Republic of Slovenia Statistical Yearbook 2003*. Ljubljana.

Šušteršič, J., M. Rojec, and M. Mrak, eds. 2001. *Strategy for the Economic Development of Slovenia 2001–2006—Slovenia in the New Decade: Sustainability, Competitiveness, Membership in the EU*. Ljubljana: Institute of Macroeconomic Analysis and Development.

Wiener Institut für Internationale Wirtschaftsvergleiche. 1999. *Countries in Transition 1999: WIIW Handbook of Statistics*. Vienna.

World Bank. 1993. *Slovenia: Enterprise and Financial Sector Adjustment Loan*. Washington, D.C.

NOTES

1. The three most important of these are *Strategy for Economic Development of Slovenia: Approaching Europe—Growth, Competitiveness and Integration* (Potočnik, Senjur, and Štiblar 1995), *Strategy of the Republic of Slovenia for the Accession to the European Union: Economic and Social Part* (Mrak, Potočnik, and Rojec 1998), and *Strategy for the Economic Development of Slovenia 2001–2006—Slovenia in the New Decade: Sustainability, Competitiveness, Membership in the EU* (Šušteršič, Rojec, and Mrak 2001).

2. Interestingly, in some other transition economies, such as the Baltic states, this very argument was used to argue for exactly the opposite transition strategy (the big bang approach).

3. Other countries that experienced similar transitions in this respect include the successor states of the former Soviet Union, the Czech Republic, and Slovakia.

4. See Dervis, Selowsky, and Wallich (1994).

5. This overview is strictly based on the texts of the chapters themselves and therefore reflects the views as expressed by the chapter authors, as interpreted by the editors.

Part I: The Road toward Political and Economic Independence

Chapter 1
The Political Reasons for the Dissolution of SFR Yugoslavia

Janez Drnovšek

It has now been 13 years since the disintegration of SFR Yugoslavia, during which time sharp differences and even armed conflict have divided the countries that have emerged on its territory. Today, however, the integration of these countries into the European Union is appearing more and more as a common goal. With the exception of Slovenia, which has already all but completed the often-demanding path to membership in the European Union, the countries of the former SFR Yugoslavia are only taking their first steps in that direction. Yet the conviction is rapidly gaining ground that integration into the European Union offers the best guarantee not only for the permanent attainment of stability and prosperity, but also for overcoming the conflicting interests that still prevail among the various ethnic groups and entities in the territory of the former SFR Yugoslavia. It is hoped that EU membership—and the preparations for membership—will help to solve these differences.

Slovenia's imminent entry into the European Union, as the first former Yugoslav state to have met all the criteria for membership, provides a fitting occasion to look back on the historic events that defined the disintegration of the common state. One question raised— a serious one, given the tragic events following SFR Yugoslavia's disintegration—is whether the ensuing chaos and bloodshed could have been prevented. In answering this question, the political reasons for the disintegration of the federal state are of primary importance. In this chapter I shall therefore analyze in more detail the events and developments of the years preceding the disintegration, paying particular attention to the contrasting political visions whose mutual opposition sealed the fate of SFR Yugoslavia.

TWO OPPOSING POLITICAL VISIONS

At the end of the 1980s, two visions of SFR Yugoslavia's political future existed in a kind of uneasy juxtaposition within the country, becoming more and more irreconcilable as time went on. On the one hand was the democratic vision advocated by the Slovenians and some others. Besides seeking all the fundamental institutions of democracy—free and fair elections, the rule of law, and all the rites and rituals of a multiparty system, which by 1990 were not just distant possibilities in Slovenia but were suddenly something real and tangible—this democratic vision of how to run the affairs of the state placed a high primacy on negotiation, compromise, and a peaceful settling of differences.

The opposing concept was far more authoritarian; it was also clearly nationalistic and ethnocentric. In this countermethodology of how to run a state, force was not necessarily seen as a last resort; cen-

4

tralized control was viewed as a prerequisite, and concepts such as negotiation and compromise were perceived as synonymous with weakness, not strength. This second model of state management was characteristic of the Serbian regime. By 1990 it was clear that the regime of Slobodan Milošević had convinced itself (and, just as important, the Serbian people) that it had been denied its proper status and its rightful weight within the arrangements of SFR Yugoslavia. This idea was directly responsible for setting into motion the historic events that made their devastating and very bloody march across the rest of the decade.

SFR Yugoslavia began to fragment with the Kosovo crises of 1989 and 1990. Kosovo, an autonomous province within Serbia's borders, was the first target of Milošević's nationalistic vision of a Greater Serbia. The fate of that province therefore represented a kind of litmus test for whether a multiethnic SFR Yugoslavia could be democratically transformed. Many countervailing forces were still at play then, and many attempts were made in those years to keep the country together and to reorganize it on democratic principles. But when the forces of authoritarianism and nationalism prevailed in Kosovo at the beginning of the 1990s, it became clear to many of those favoring democratic change that they would be unable to achieve their goals within SFR Yugoslavia. The 1989–90 Kosovo crisis, then, was when the dissolution of the country became inevitable—just as the 1999 Kosovo crisis was the definitive moment when Serbian policies were revealed as an unambiguous failure.

As the head of Yugoslavia's collective presidency for a one-year period during this earlier Kosovo struggle, I took steps to oppose Milošević's agenda by advocating the ideas of dialogue, tolerance, European integration, economic efficiency, and prosperity. Such an approach may have been perceived as naïve at the time. The authoritarian approach of the opposing side may have seemed more powerful, more realistic, and, not least, more likely to prevail.

EARLY STAGES OF DISSOLUTION

Josip Broz Tito, Yugoslavia's leader throughout the early postwar era, had created an intricate structure of political weights and balances to try to satisfy the different constituent parts of that multinational country. SFR Yugoslavia was formally a decentralized federation, with significant autonomy granted, at least on paper, to its six republics (Bosnia and Herzegovina, Croatia, Macedonia, Montenegro, Slovenia, and Serbia) and to the two autonomous provinces that existed within the framework of Serbia. These were Vojvodina, with its sizable Hungarian population, and Kosovo, with a majority Albanian population.

While Tito remained firmly in power, the actual sovereignty of the federal republics and autonomous regions was limited in practice. But after Tito's death in 1980, power gradually started to devolve from the center, and the Communist Party itself became more and more decentralized. Toward the end of that decade, with the winds of change blowing unmistakably through Eastern Europe, some republics—notably Slovenia and Croatia—intensified this ongoing process of political change. Differences between the republics increased, largely because of these different speeds of democratization. It could be said that Slovenia was leading the process and that Serbia, under Milošević's rule, was heading in a very different direction.

Slobodan Milošević first became the leader of the Serbian Communist Party in 1987. As is by now well known, his political breakthrough took place in Kosovo, and that breakthrough was due specifically to his nationalistic, hard-line approach. Having seen the political potential of harnessing populist anger, Milošević self-consciously profiled himself as the defender of the Serbs in Kosovo against the "Albanian danger" and claimed that the Serbs deserved more power than they had been allotted under Tito's Yugoslavia. Put simply, Milošević wanted to change the political and ethnic balance in the country.

Well before war broke out, however, Milošević took his first steps in that direction, managing to install Serbian-controlled puppet regimes in the Republic of Montenegro as well as in the two autonomous provinces. He did this by organizing large mass-media campaigns and by threatening large public demonstrations (the so-called yogurt revolutions of 1988). Understandably, the Albanian majority in Kosovo protested in massive numbers when the Serbian regime eliminated their autonomous status. The police responded, and many were killed in the demonstrations. As a consequence, the federal presidency introduced martial law in Kosovo. By the beginning of 1989, the whole Yugoslav picture had become more and more gloomy and frightening.

This was when I personally came into the picture. Partly in response to the extreme events in the southern part of the common state, the Slovenian political leadership was already experimenting with democracy. In a sense, the authoritarianism in the south had reinvigorated its opposite elsewhere—a phenomenon not uncommon in history. For the first time in the history of SFR Yugoslavia, free elections were held for the position of Slovenia's representative on the Yugoslav collective presidency.[1] Much to the surprise of the political establishment, an independent candidate—myself—defeated the representative of the Communist Party and was elected to this body.

In keeping with the democratic means by which I was elected, what I brought to the Yugoslav presidency were the general feelings and aspirations of the Slovenian people, including a desire for greater economic efficiency, increased democratization, and integration into Europe. But I also brought fears. Seeing the increasingly hard-line nature of the Belgrade regime, Slovenians were afraid that something terrible would happen in the country. There were fears of further yogurt revolutions, of civil war, of military takeover, of economic chaos.

It should be said, however, that despite these fears the Slovenian demand for independence was not explicit at first. Too many risks were involved. At the time, the Slovenian people would have simply preferred an improvement in their living conditions and their security. Only gradually, as events proceeded along their inexorable course in Serbia, did people become alarmed and realize that compromise was less and less likely—and finally impossible. It became increasingly clear that the only way out for Slovenia was into independence. Directly to the west of us, a peaceful, prosperous, and democratic Europe was integrating. Slovenia gradually developed the idea of joining this process—I myself experienced a similar evolutionary conversion. Meanwhile I tried to do my job as the Yugoslav president as best I could. I tried to reconcile Serbs and Albanians, and I tried to organize a constructive dialogue between Milošević and the opposition Albanian leaders.

CONFRONTATION OVER KOSOVO

In my year as head of the collective presidency of SFR Yugoslavia—from May 15, 1989, to May 15, 1990—I tried patiently, step by step, to diminish the escalating tensions. Gradually I succeeded in freeing the Albanian political prisoners—of which there were several hundred—and in ending the Serbian-sponsored martial law in Kosovo, which was limiting communications and the free movement of people as well as imposing strict police control. However, my efforts to bring the Albanians and the Serbs to the negotiating table were fruitless. The Serbs relied only on force, refusing dialogue. Both in formal meetings of the presidency and in informal talks, I tried to bring the two sides together. Milošević could be a charming person to talk with about many issues, but when discussing Kosovo he hardened, and compromise was impossible.

When I managed to get a majority in the federal presidency and to free Kosovo's political prisoners—including the Kosovo Albanian freedom fighter Adem Demaci, who had spent 28 years in prison—Milošević was furious. And because of my efforts to establish a dialogue leading to a solution of the Kosovo problem, I was often accused in Serbia's controlled media of being a traitor to federal Yugoslavia and to Serbia. But in fact this was the last real effort to help the country avoid disaster. I once said to Milošević, "Your policy is like riding a tiger. While you ride it you probably feel very powerful. But sooner or later you'll have to come down, and the tiger will eat you." Alas, I did not succeed in changing his politics or his behavior. And the course of history proved my words right. In the end, in April 2001, Milošević was handed over to the International Criminal Tribunal for the Former Yugoslavia under charges of genocide, crimes against humanity, and grave breaches of Geneva conventions.

During my entire term as head of the Yugoslav presidency, I advocated tolerance, compromise, and discussion and tried to win over the Serbs. I attempted to inject a tone of reasonableness, and I tried not to be only a Slovenian in the presidency but to improve the climate for everyone. I introduced the idea of joining the Council of Europe and later the European Community; I expressed this intention not only within the presidency of Yugoslavia but also to European leaders. When I met with the latter, I explained to them that a race was under way in my country between a rampant nationalism and a more rational, tolerant, and democratic vision.

Unfortunately, as history has recorded, the process of destruction finally outran the process of democratic consolidation. Sometimes I wonder if the democratic option really had a chance at all. It would have demanded tolerant and responsible politicians in all the Yugoslav republics—but particularly in Serbia and Croatia. (People in Bosnia and Herzegovina feared the nationalistic pressures emanating from both Serbia and Croatia and felt premonitions of a disaster.) Still, it must be said that, during my one-year term as president, I had much public support. Many felt that this would be the right way to go. For a short time, it even looked as though I might succeed. But this was only an illusion—the calm before the storm.

That storm hit not long after I stepped down as president. When my term came to an end, the Serbian member of SFR Yugoslavia's rotating presidency replaced me. He immediately introduced very different rhetoric, followed closely by action: repression against the Albanian separatists must be instituted, he said, and the interests of the Serbs, wherever they live, must be protected. I had barely left office when the Serbian regime dissolved the Kosovo parliament and police repression was revived. In a secret meeting of their assembly, the Albanians of Kosovo responded by declaring their own republic.

From then on, no further attempts were made to find a peaceful and democratic solution in Kosovo. The Kosovo Albanians organized parallel informal institutions, including schools. For almost this entire decade, the Kosovo Albanian community, to their great credit, followed Ibrahim Rugova's policy of passive resistance. They awaited the outcome of FSR Yugoslavia's self-destruction; more than anything else, they hoped for the fall of the Milošević regime. But Milošević survived. His military and police forces remained practically untouched throughout the Yugoslav wars. And in the end, the Kosovo Albanians saw no alternative but armed resistance.

SLOVENIA'S PATH TOWARD INDEPENDENCE

In April 1990—just before the end of my term as Yugoslav president—free parliamentary elections were held for the first time in Slovenia and Croatia. New political groupings won that were clearly on the path of democratization. They focused on issues of national identity and sovereignty—still within the framework of a federative or confederative Yugoslavia. But Serbia's uncompromising pressure to change the structure of power in SFR Yugoslavia gave a real push to Slovenian and Croatian demands for independence. There were clearly precious few options left within SFR Yugoslavia. After Serbia terminated the autonomy of Kosovo, Vojvodina, and Montenegro, the picture had become very threatening to the other republics. Suddenly Serbia, previously one vote out of eight, spoke with four votes in the federal presidency. This was particularly important because the federal presidency held formal command of the Yugoslav army.

At the end of 1990 and during the first months of 1991, Milošević tried to obtain a majority vote in the presidency and to get the army to move toward Croatia and Slovenia—all under the pretext of defending Yugoslav sovereignty. At the time there was much speculation that the army would intervene directly in the political scene. However, the generals did not want to act without the formal approval of the presidency, and the presidency blocked such attempts several times.

One thing not commonly recalled when considering this period is that, in 1990, Slovenia and Croatia were still willing to negotiate a new, looser confederation. But they were confronted with the Serbian idea of a centralized federation. Since such a federation would have meant that Milošević would rule Yugoslavia, he had very good reasons for blocking the Slovenian and Croatian proposals. In the ensuing deadlock, the momentum of the Slovenian and Croatian independence movements grew in the second half of that year (compounded by the popular reaction to the brutalities unfolding in Kosovo). I cannot say that it would not have developed anyway, especially in Croatia. But as a consequence of these events, this move toward independence could be seen as inexorable and directly attributable to Serbian pressure.

In December 1990 Slovenia and Croatia took the fateful step of announcing their intention to become independent. However, they concurrently proposed a six-month period to negotiate relations among the republics peacefully and to establish the new political situation. In light of all these facts, I certainly cannot agree that Slovenia and Croatia forced their independence and that they are somehow the culprits in SFR Yugoslavia's breakup (a view still espoused by some). By now it should be more than clear: the Yugoslav split began in Kosovo in 1989 and 1990.

Given the path chosen by the Belgrade leadership at the time, what the rest of the world still saw as a unitary state went through some very tense times in the first half of 1991. An explosion seemed possible at any moment. In a referendum at the end of December 1990, a large majority of Slovenians decided on independence. Within the federal presidency and with the presidents of the republics, we negotiated the nonexistent political future of SFR Yugoslavia. In keeping with the democratically verified wishes of my country—which were also my own convictions—my own goal now was to achieve at least a peaceful dissolution of the country.

Slovenia is ethnically homogenous and could establish its independence without too many problems. Croatia was more difficult: a large Serbian minority lived there. And Bosnia and Herzegovina was the most complicated situation of all: Serbs, Croats, and Muslims were all mixed together. Although serious attempts were made, a solution was almost impossible to find. One proposal would have allowed Slovenia to become independent while, to satisfy its Serb minority, Croatia maintained some loose link with the rest of the federation. Sometimes we seemed to be very close to a solution, but when I look back today, I can see that the Serbian regime was already working on a military solution. They were simply waiting for Slovenia and Croatia to proclaim independence.

FROM ARMED INTERVENTION TO INTERNATIONAL RECOGNITION

On May 15, 1991, the day the Serbian term as head of the federal presidency expired—and one year after I left office—Belgrade blocked the succession by refusing to accept the Croatian member as president. The result was that the Yugoslav presidency ceased to function as the supreme commander of the army. When Slovenia and Croatia declared independence on June 25, 1991, the Yugoslav army intervened in Slovenia. It was a catastrophic decision—not for Slovenia, which was able to defend itself and achieve independence, but for the rest of Yugoslavia, which remained in chaos and war for the rest of the decade. The military advance on Slovenia was the first crucial step from negotiations to politics conducted, as the saying has it, "by other means"—that is, outright war. At the time of the decision to intervene in Slovenia, the Yugoslav army was still a federal body. But it soon became clear that the Croats, Macedonians, Bosnians, and Albanians caught in uniform did not want to fight the Slovenians. They knew that tomorrow the same thing could happen to their own people.

Slovenia had made its decision and stood firm, and during the 10-day war the old multiethnic Yugoslav army disintegrated, soon to be replaced by what was effectively a Serbian army. After a cease-fire came negotiations: the so-called Brioni agreement was reached between the federation and Slovenia, with the European Union as mediator. This was the first successful European attempt in managing the Yugoslav crisis, and for almost a decade the last one—until the successful EU mediation in the Macedonian armed conflict in 2001.

The agreement reached at Brioni was not very clear, however. Rather, it was written with a kind of constructive ambiguity. Slovenia and Croatia had to accept a three-month moratorium on their sovereignty, and I was supposed to return to the federal presidency for three months. It was not clear what would happen after that.

What did happen was that developments came thick and fast. In the first session of the Yugoslav presidency, we agreed that the Yugoslav army would retreat completely from Slovenia. As a result, my country was able to establish complete control over its territory. At first, the international community was reluctant to recognize the new state, but at the end of 1991 and the beginning of 1992, the first international diplomatic recognition came. Slovenia had become independent; it had actually managed to escape the growing Yugoslav disaster.

ARMED CONFLICT ELSEWHERE IN SFR YUGOSLAVIA IN THE 1990s

The war soon spread to Croatia and then to Bosnia and Herzegovina before events came full circle back to Kosovo. The modus operandi of the Serbian regime was to opt for force whenever it appeared that more could be achieved that way than with negotiations. The Serbians' intent was unambiguous, even if skillfully hidden behind rhetorical smokescreens: to establish control over the whole Yugoslav federation if possible; if it was not, to let Slovenia and part of Croatia go and to establish control of Serbia's ethnic borders. Either way, they would have realized the idea of a Greater Serbia.

The lesson Slovenia learned from its experience with the Serbian regime in 1991—that it would readily resort to force, if force was to its advantage—was repeated later in the wars in Croatia and in Bosnia. Unfortunately, the international community was slow to realize that it was not dealing with a tolerant and democratic regime in Belgrade, and until then it was only too willing to take what its representatives said at face value.

Hundreds of thousands were killed during the wars in Croatia and in Bosnia and Herzegovina. Millions more became refugees. I consistently advocated an early international military intervention in order to stop the atrocities. Unfortunately, events unfolded differently. The international community tried to mediate in other ways, without much to show for it. Neither UN resolutions, nor EU observers, nor a UN "peacekeeping" force could stop the fighting. Only in 1995, when the United States decided to bomb Serbian positions in Bosnia, did the conflict wind down. Together with increasing Croatian military pressure, this brought an end to the war. The Dayton agreements that followed finally established a measure of peace and relative order in an exhausted Bosnia and Herzegovina.

Clearly, international military intervention in 1992 could have prevented many atrocities. It would also have made it easier to protect the multiethnic structure of that republic. Now, after years of killing, it is much more difficult to rebuild the necessary confidence and to normalize life in the multiethnic state. Without a strong and long-lasting international presence, it will be impossible. Even with it, it will be very, very difficult, requiring much patience and resources.

This last point is crucial. The fact that the international community had left Kosovo under Serbian martial law made Ibrahim Rugova's policy of nonviolent resistance to Serbian domination less and less tenable. When, in 1998, the Kosovo Albanians started a more organized armed resistance—under what became known as the Kosovo Liberation Army—Milošević responded with police and paramilitary terror. In what had by now become a wearisome routine, the international community attempted to reason with Belgrade, and new interim agreements were reached.

But the violence continued, and in February 1999 the so-called contact group (consisting of France, Germany, Italy, Russia, the United Kingdom, and the United States) organized the Rambouillet conference. Serbs and Kosovo Albanians were asked to meet and discuss a peace plan that had been prepared in advance.

The Rambouillet plan, which presented a transitional solution to resolving the Kosovo problem, would have provided autonomy for Kosovo but kept it formally within the framework of Serbia and Yugoslavia. A substantial international force would have ensured peace. The Kosovo Albanians did not get a sovereign state, and this was understandable. There was already an Albania, and there was a large Albanian minority in Macedonia. Would they all join and form a Greater Albania, or a Greater Kosovo? Why would either be any better than a Greater Serbia?

These "negotiations" proceeded a bit differently from the textbook definition. In what has been described as a take-it-or-leave-it approach, both sides quickly discovered that they were not supposed to change the plan or really negotiate. If the Serbs did not accept the Rambouillet proposal, they were informed, NATO would bomb Serbia. If the Kosovo Albanians refused, they would lose the support of the international community. It was not easy to convince the Albanians to accept the terms of the Rambouillet agreement, but after a two-week break, they came around. The Serbs, however, refused outright, and it took that year's large-scale NATO bombing of the Federal Republic of Yugoslavia to convince them. Two years after the NATO military campaign, Milošević was arrested and handed over to the Hague tribunal, opening the way for new democratic development in Serbia.

CONCLUSIONS

Looking at the situation in the territory of the former SFR Yugoslavia today, one can establish one thing above all, namely, that the continued involvement and commitment of the international community remain crucial for the success and permanent consolidation of the region. The greatest challenge is to answer the question of what would be better than the present status quo.

This goes for federal Bosnia and Herzegovina, as mapped out through the Dayton Accord, in which the most essential issues regarding ethnic relationships have not yet been resolved. Cooperation between entities in that country is being established slowly, and political life follows ethnic divides too closely. The same goes also for Kosovo, whose temporary status as an international protectorate cannot continue indefinitely; some form of permanent solution will be required. The situation of the State Community of Serbia and Montenegro, an unprecedented form of cohabitation of two separate political, economic, and administrative entities, is also very complex. The integration of these entities during the period set by the international community for their cohabitation may well give way to the selection of independent paths at the beginning of 2006. The same also goes for FYR Macedonia, which in 2001 avoided slipping into a civil war by a hairsbreadth, largely because of the international community's decisive role. Tensions between the ethnic Macedonian majority and the ethnic Albanian minority are still very much alive. It is essential for the successful implementation of the 2001 Ohrid agreement—which addresses the requirements set by the ethnic Albanian minority for improving their political and cultural status—that the process have the support of the international community.

The transnational (cross-border) identities of the region's inhabitants, and the unanswered questions regarding the functioning of local political entities and ethnic relationships, continue to hold the potential to destabilize the region. I believe that, after a decade of repeated conflicts and of attempts to halt or at least contain them, the importance of the region's stability for its own security and that of Europe as a whole hardly needs further elaboration.

The lessons to be learned from SFR Yugoslavia's disintegration are of vital importance for the development of democracy and the provision of security and stability in the region. It is necessary to establish conditions that will not allow the persistence of nationalistic thinking founded on exclusion, but will ensure instead the spread of democratic ideals of tolerance and cooperation.

Such conditions in the region can be ensured only by the real prospect of integration into the European Union. That prospect and the very process of adopting rules and democratic standards, and of establishing and consolidating the existing market economy—all of which must include the relevant economic supports—can contribute significantly to securing the long-term stability and success of the region. Slovenia as an imminent member of the European Union can play an important role in these processes. On the one hand, other countries in the region can relate to Slovenia, which for them is a kind of role model. On the other hand, Slovenia, thanks to the comparability of the systems from which these countries have emerged, is in a position to help, particularly with its advice, as these countries adopt the regulatory and institutional systems of the European Union.

NOTES

1. Under the then-existing political system, the representatives of the constituent republics and the autonomous regions were members of Yugoslavia's collective leadership, each in turn becoming the president of the country for a one-year term.

Chapter 2
Socialism and the Disintegration of SFR Yugoslavia

Vladimir Gligorov

The collapse of the Yugoslav type of socialism has been connected with the disintegration of that country, but the connection is not altogether straightforward. This chapter addresses this question by first describing the institutional setup of self-management socialism based on the concept of social ownership. This is followed by a description of the political economy of that system. Next, developments in the decade preceding SFR's disintegration are reviewed. Finally, the causal link between the collapse of socialism and the disintegration of the country is reassessed, with the help of hindsight. In that context the issue of continuity and discontinuity is considered, with special emphasis on the transition in Slovenia.

Describing the Yugoslav model of socialism is not a straightforward task either, in part because its initial motivation was political, and in part because the system developed over time, influenced by both internal and external factors. Internally, there was an interplay of political and ideological motives. Externally, there was the actual economic performance of the system as well as international influences. Therefore the logical consistency of the system and its development are not all that easy to ascertain. In addition, the difference between the institutional setup and its actual implementation has to be taken into account. Thus perhaps the best way to describe the system is by first setting out what one may call the set of ideal types, in the sense of Max Weber, of the main conceptual grid of the system. Then its internal development can be analyzed, and finally its adaptability to internal and external shocks can be looked at.

One last introductory comment is also necessary. The ideal model of social ownership and self-management that I will describe is different from the model of self-management socialism that has been developed in the economic and sociological literature. Although the links cannot be disregarded completely, the initial motivation and the dynamics of the development of institutions of the Yugoslav type of socialism cannot be simply reduced to a theoretical and ideological discussion about the consistency and efficiency of the so-called model of market socialism. That discussion is not irrelevant, but consistency and efficiency were not the determining factors in the institutional development of socialist Yugoslavia.

FROM SELF-MANAGEMENT TO SOCIAL OWNERSHIP

In Marxist socialism, ownership is fundamental. Private ownership both misallocates resources and supports the unequal distribution of incomes. Therefore state ownership is preferable. The Yugoslav communists, however, recognized early on that state ownership of resources and their allocation through central planning are inefficient. This issue arose because of the severe crisis that the country experienced after the break with the Soviet Union in 1948. The governing Communist Party also needed to secure domestic political support and legitimacy. Thus it decided to devolve managerial responsibilities from the central planners to the firms. Also, it gradually came to the conclusion that it needed to diminish the excessive centralization of state functions and devolve some of those functions to the member states of the federation. Leaving the latter issue aside for the moment, it is clear that the idea of self-management—originally workers' self-management—preceded the idea of the need to reform the ownership of resources.

The need to tackle the issue of ownership was realized gradually, but it became almost urgent in the early 1960s. Again an external shock precipitated the internal change. SFR Yugoslavia needed to borrow money from abroad, because aid and grants were diminishing. Thus a far-reaching reform was initiated, which abolished the system of central planning and introduced commercial banking and elements of macroeconomic management. Central planning was replaced with the market, state investment funds were essentially abolished, and monetary and fiscal policies were made responsible for stability and growth.

In that context the issue of material responsibility of firms and banks for their self-managerial decisions had to be addressed. Because the return to private ownership was ruled out in the late 1960s, essentially after mass student demonstrations in 1968, the remaining alternative was to elevate the idea of social ownership to the position of the key systemic concept. Thus most of the institutional creativity, if that is the proper word, was concentrated on answering the question, What *is* social property or social ownership?

No satisfactory answer was ever found. The initial ideas of collective management were transformed into the concept of a firm that makes all its decisions autonomously but has no clear objective function and no obvious locus of responsibility. Thus social ownership came eventually to be defined as nonownership. As a consequence, the Yugoslav type of socialism was one of self-management of assets that were not owned by anyone. Indeed, in the legal system that developed in the 1970s, state ownership was also abolished, so that the only ownership that existed at all was private ownership, but that was severely restricted where it was not outlawed outright.

These two concepts—social ownership and self-management— define the Yugoslav system of market socialism, at least at the microeconomic level. A voluminous debate developed on whether such a system can allocate resources efficiently, in the usual sense of "efficiency." Two effects were discussed more than others: the Ward effect and the Furubotn-Pejovich effect. It is convenient to use these concepts in discussing these issues, as the first treats the efficiency properties of self-management, whereas the second deals with the problems of efficient allocation associated with social ownership.

The basic point that the Ward effect is supposed to highlight is that a self-managed firm does not allocate labor efficiently. A simple way to see this is to assume that the self-managed firm maximizes the average wage, and one way to do that is to minimize the number of employees. Thus a firm that maximizes profits will produce more and employ more people than a self-managed firm. This assertion has been disputed both theoretically and empirically, but it does highlight the crucial fact about the self-managed firm, which is that it is not immediately evident what the objective function of such a firm is.

The objective cannot be to maximize the value of the firm, because a self-managed firm cannot be traded. Thus there is an issue with the investment function of such a firm. This is the basis of the Furubotn-Pejovich effect. Assuming that an individual has a choice to invest in a socially owned firm or in a private firm, in a market economy he or she will prefer the latter. In other words, voluntary investment in the socially owned firm will be insufficient. If no private investment is available, consumption will be preferred to investment. In any case, investment will be lacking in an economy based on social ownership. This assertion, too, has been disputed in a number of ways, but the effect does point to the obvious lack of clear responsibility for the assets of the socially owned firm.

The system developed in the 1970s did attempt to deal with these problems, but the normative structure that was designed could not be consistently implemented. Also, the economy remained highly regulated, so that the institutional setup only indirectly governed the functioning of the economy.

FROM SOCIAL OWNERSHIP TO SELF-GOVERNMENT

As already mentioned, the break with Soviet-type socialism also implied the further federalization of the state. Without going into the political reasons for the increase in the autonomy of the federal states, it is not difficult to see what the economic reasons were. The increased autonomy of firms (and of banks, although that is a somewhat separate issue) and their marketization—that is, commercialization together with the legalization of social ownership—opened up the issue of public governance. Once central planning was abolished, the need remained to allocate responsibility for microeconomic management of the economy. Leaving macroeconomic management aside for the moment, the state still needed to get involved in quite a number of decisions, from the appointment of managers down to the smallest investment decisions. It was accepted that a decentralized system of public governance would be better than the existing centralized one. Thus the Yugoslav system of public governance became increasingly decentralized, not only at the level of the member states but also at the level of counties and municipalities. This whole system was called "social self-management," and indeed it called for the increasing importance of self-government at the local level and at the level of the federal states.

This decentralization had two significant consequences, which determined the development of the Yugoslav system of socialism. On the one hand, the role of the centralizing power remained with the Party and the military. Other federal institutions became increasingly irrelevant. The issues of macroeconomic management will be discussed later; here it is sufficient to note that federal political institutions—such as the parliament, the supreme court, and all political organizations—gradually lost their power and influence. Indeed, after the adoption of the constitution of 1974, there were no directly elected representatives either to the federal parliament or to any of the bodies and institutions at the federal level. That, of course, made it impossible for the ruling party and the military to seek any kind of institutionalized legitimacy.[1]

On the other hand, most of the power that mattered was transferred to the level of the member states. Thus, after the late 1960s, the really important political developments were those in the republics and not in the federation. This devolution of power was legalized in the constitution of 1974, although the ruling party and the military retained the residual power at the federal level. Thus an inconsistent distribution of power developed. The main decisions were made at the level of the member states, but some important powers—the ruling party, the army, the central bank—were run as if in a centralized state.[2] Clearly, something had to give. The first institution to disintegrate was the ruling party, followed by the army, and then the country. In the end, both the experiment in market socialism and the experiment in institutionalizing a socialist federation collapsed.[3]

MARKET SOCIALISM: MICROECONOMIC AND MACROECONOMIC POLICY

The institutional setup that worked out in the 1970s was put to a severe test at the beginning of the 1980s, when the country proved unable to service its foreign debt. Throughout the 1980s the economy was under serious pressure; indeed, at the time it was accepted that it was in a state of a persistent crisis, a crisis of public governance. Putting aside purely political issues, this crisis of public governance had two aspects. One was the problem of building a consistent economic policy structure for a self-managed economy; the other was the design of a proper stabilization policy in the context of social ownership and significant federalization.

The regime of self-management lacked a clear understanding of the role of macroeconomic institutions and policy. During the institutional reform of the 1960s, liberalization, commercialization, and even (limited) privatization were to be supplemented by a convertible currency and a balanced budget. All of these goals were essentially abandoned in the system that was put in place in the 1970s. Although some of the microeconomic elements were retained, the macroeconomic structure that was built into the system lacked any understanding of the needs of macroeconomic policy.

This is not necessarily because no consistent macroeconomic policy can be designed for a market socialist economy. Indeed, building on the lessons from the failed reform of the 1960s, Aleksander Bajt, the leading Slovenian economist of that era, proposed an economic policy framework that he thought could be consistent with an economic regime based on social ownership.[4] This proposal can be understood as the final model of a Yugoslav type of market socialism. The key elements were as follows.

First, there was to be thorough marketization and commercialization of socially owned and self-managed enterprises. They were not supposed to be subsidized: the only help they could hope to get from the government was restrictions on the expansion of private ownership. Absent such restrictions, Bajt thought, because private firms are more efficient than socially owned firms, the latter would not survive in a freely competitive market for ownership rights.

Second, markets would be completely liberalized; that is, domestic and foreign trade would be completely free, and markets alone would set prices. No monopolies and no administrative prices were to be allowed or would be introduced.

Third, markets would also be responsible for the allocation of labor. It was not altogether clear how new firms would come into existence and what would happen to those that should go out of business. In any case, there was supposed to exist a free market for managers, which would allocate managerial ability efficiently.

Fourth, macroeconomic policy should be based on a balanced government budget and a balanced current account. Indeed, the budgets of the republics were required to be balanced in socialist Yugoslavia. Whether they were in fact balanced is another matter. Certainly, in the less developed regions, budgets were in a mess, partly because they relied on aid and subsidies from the federal budget. In the more developed states, budgets probably were balanced, because taxes were the only source of revenue.

Balancing of the current account is a different matter altogether. Clearly, it required that the local currency be convertible in current account transactions. The exchange rate would have to float in order to balance exports and imports. Inward foreign investment, however, would be restricted, partly for current account purposes and partly in order to protect social ownership, or rather to ensure its survival. The control of inflation would be left to monetary policy, that is, to the interest rate that would be determined in the money market. Banks would, of course, be in social ownership but would operate on commercial principles.

The issue of current account balance is an important one because, if implemented, it would bring very significant changes in the Yugoslav economy. The reason is that, after the mid-1960s, the economy developed under the influence of the large outward migration of those years. Close to 1 million people left SFR Yugoslavia to work in a number of Western European countries. The outflow diminished significantly later on, but it never really stopped. As a consequence, shortly thereafter the country began to receive large inflows of remittances and private transfers. Together with the large amount of borrowing undertaken in the second half of the 1970s, they led to a persistent trade deficit. Although there was a surplus in services trade—indeed an increasingly large one, due to the growth of tourism—exports of goods never really caught up with these developments. The crisis of the early 1980s meant that investment, which in a socialist economy means public investment, had to fall to make room for those budget programs that targeted social welfare. Thus, balancing the current account would have meant a radical change in economic policy and in the structure of the Yugoslav macroeconomy. Indeed, of all the states that came out of SFR Yugoslavia, only Slovenia has succeeded in balancing its current account. All the other former Yugoslav republics are struggling with stagnating exports and large current account deficits, leading to persistent increases in their foreign debt.

Thus the economics of social ownership and self-management was ideally to be based on free trade, competition among socially owned firms, a developed market for managerial skills, and an open economy with a balanced budget and current account. It would be an exaggeration to say that this version of the economics of socialism provided the theoretical solutions of the Ward effect and the Furubotn-Pejovich effect discussed above. Indeed, this version was also not a realistic proposal for dealing with the political and economic crisis in which SFR Yugoslavia found itself during the 1980s, to which I now turn.

POLITICAL ECONOMY OF THE 1980s CRISIS

At the beginning of the 1980s, SFR Yugoslavia became unable to service its foreign debt. The debt itself was not very large as a share of

GDP or of trade in goods and services. Total foreign debt was not more than $20 billion. Yugoslav GDP, measured at the then-current exchange rate, was certainly not below $3,000 per capita, or at least $60 billion in total. Exports of goods and services were probably not much below $20 billion. However, the current account deficit was large, reflecting an unrealistic exchange rate. Thus, once world interest rates shot up at the beginning of the 1980s, the cost of debt service increased significantly, and the dinar collapsed.

The crisis itself was neither exceptional nor of a type specific to a socialist economy. Indeed, it mirrored the crises that a number of countries were going through in both the capitalist and the socialist world. What it revealed, however, was the weakness of the institutions of public governance—even more strikingly because SFR Yugoslavia enjoyed a good relationship with the international financial institutions and was able to rely on their support throughout the 1980s. Internally, however, the country proved incapable of coming to grips with the macroeconomic problems it faced, and the crisis dragged on for a whole decade, leading eventually to the collapse of the country.

From the macroeconomic point of view, the key cause of the crisis was inadequate monetary policy—not only the essentially fixed exchange rate that prevailed in the period before the crisis erupted (that is, in the 1970s) but, even more fundamentally, the inability to control inflationary pressures. The pressures originated in the nature of social ownership. As revealed by the Ward and Furubotn-Pejovich effects, there were constant pressures to increase wages, and investment was undersupplied. To finance investment, therefore, inflation was kept high enough to drive real interest rates into negative territory. External borrowing was, in the end, where the supply of money (that is, of savings) came from. With fixed exchange rates, that meant a constant real appreciation of the dinar and an increase in the current account deficit. Once borrowing abroad stopped, the system had to collapse.

Against this background the whole debate and political frictions of the 1980s can be seen rather clearly. Once the supply of credit from abroad dried up, investment dropped sharply and the economy went into a prolonged stagnation. Indeed, at the end of the 1980s, output had hardly grown at all: in 1989 the GDP of SFR Yugoslavia was essentially where it had been in 1979. Unemployment increased significantly, however, and inflation was increasing year after year, to reach about 100 percent in 1988. In addition, the country now faced constant problems in servicing its foreign debt. More important, none of the problems had been solved, and no institutional changes had been introduced. This total impotence of public governance eroded the legitimacy of the system, which could not have been insignificant at the outset, given that it was capable of surviving a decade of public incapability and mismanagement of just about everything that the government attempted to do.

The crisis highlighted two issues that were directly connected with the system of social ownership and self-management. Both were essentially problems of responsibility: responsibility for the country's assets and responsibility for macroeconomic stability, which basically meant responsibility for fiscal and monetary policy. The solution for the first problem was to be found in privatization, and that for the other in reliance on democratic legitimacy. Both solutions implied significant redistribution of wealth and power. It took 10 years of political stalemate for it to become clear that the system as it was could not deliver the necessary reforms that would solve these two problems of responsibility and legitimacy. Thus, in the end, the responsibility for reforms had to be located where power was already mostly located, namely, in the member states.

THE LAST STAND

The country did not go down before making a last attempt to reform and transform itself. In 1989 a far-reaching reform was initiated, aimed at addressing the main deficiencies of the socialist system as it had developed in SFR Yugoslavia. Here a brief comparison with parallel developments in Poland may be useful, as the reforms were very similar and were introduced at the same time, but they succeeded in Poland and failed in SFR Yugoslavia. Why? The basic reason is indeed very important, because it also explains, to a very large extent, the later success observed in Slovenia and the disappointing developments in other successor states of SFR Yugoslavia.

The pattern of transition that was implemented in the more successful states in Central and Eastern Europe has been summarized in the following strategy: *First democracy, then reform*.[5] This is exactly what distinguishes the reforms introduced in Poland from those in SFR Yugoslavia. Whereas in Poland it was the new, democratically elected government that took responsibility for the reforms and for the transformation in general, in SFR Yugoslavia the reforms were initiated without the appropriate political changes. Indeed, the ruling Communist Party disintegrated practically at the very moment that the reform process started. No substitute was looked for, and thus none was found. Therefore the federal government took responsibility for the reform without securing the necessary political legitimacy. Policymakers in the reform government believed that the success of the economic reforms would carry over to the introduction of the necessary political changes. That turned out to be a mistake.

There were two main reasons why this was a mistake. One was that the government misjudged how far its credibility had sunk after a decade of mismanagement and sheer impotence. Thus, although the program was indeed popular, as were the leading reformers, the federal institutions they led were not. Indeed, as already mentioned, they went into a process of rapid disintegration at the very time that the main reforms had to be developed and implemented.

The other reason was the reformers' gross misjudgment in thinking that the enormous redistribution of power and wealth implied by the transition could be realized without very strong institutional support. It turned out almost from the start that most of the institutions needed for macroeconomic management were essentially incapable of carrying out the tasks of reform. The problem was not only that the personnel were inadequate, but also that their loyalties were local, as that was the way the system was set up constitutionally. Thus, without support in the member states, reform was doomed. And, indeed, the reformers failed to secure the support of the two key states of the Yugoslav federation: Croatia and Serbia. Thus the whole attempt was a nonstarter.

The more specific mistake was in the sequencing of reforms. Clearly, stabilization was the first task, because prices were rising at hyperinflationary levels at the end of 1989. The government fixed the exchange rate to the German mark, the preferred currency in SFR Yugoslavia since the mid-1960s. Inflation fell quickly and foreign exchange reserves increased dramatically. The situation improved to such an extent, and so rapidly, that the government was able to start repaying its foreign debts ahead of time. Also, the introduction of laws freeing private entrepreneurship led to a significant inflow of investment. Indeed, foreign financial support was substantial, although it is now clear that money was not the essential problem.

Fiscal policy proved to be the main problem. Because of the significant fiscal decentralization, the federal budget was not the key problem, although clearly military spending was high and could have been reduced. But the main expenses—social security, education, public services, subsidies—were paid out of the budgets of the member states. The macroeconomic strategy adopted was to use the fixed exchange rate and complementary monetary policy to force the republics to adjust their fiscal policies. This did not work, because the federal government and the central bank did not anticipate that the republics could use the country's financial institutions to raid the federation's foreign currency reserves. SFR Yugoslavia had a parallel payments system outside of the banks (the Social Accounting Service; see chapter 6). This system could channel money wherever it was wanted. Thus in early 1991 the Serbian government diverted about $2 billion through this system, even though the banking system had collapsed some time before that because of the run on the banks in the early autumn of 1990. In the end, the stability of the currency had to be sacrificed, and the reform failed.

In hindsight it is clear that the reasons for the failure of reform in Yugoslavia are to be found in the system of social ownership and the attendant fiscal and monetary institutions. Self-management was less of a problem, as it was somewhat constrained by the role of the market and by the increasing competition, especially in those industries where there was also foreign competition. Although the large trade deficit was a problem, foreign competition through imports did lead to an increase in the productivity and efficiency of the exporting industries. Macroeconomic policy was mostly not helpful, however, and the constant shocks emanating from that quarter proved too much for a system that already had significant problems of its own.

WAYS OUT

Although the system of social self-management collapsed with the disintegration of the country, this did not necessarily mean that it could not be reformed and transformed into a system appropriate to a market economy. Once commercialized—that is, put under hard budget constraints—the self-managed firms could function with some efficiency, although they could not be expected to survive without some support from the government. Also, macroeconomic stability could be maintained as long as there was appropriate control over fiscal policy. The banking sector could prove to be a problem as long as the banks were under social ownership, because that meant that borrowers and lenders were the same agents, at least when it came to the business sector.

One possible transition strategy was to reintroduce state socialism. This was the preferred strategy in Serbia, although it was never really implemented—the reason being the collapse of the Soviet type of socialism everywhere, and especially in Russia. Thus the government decided to muddle through, as it was left with no other strategy and was in any case preoccupied with war throughout the 1990s. This led to one of the worst performances among all the transition economies, however assessed.

The other possibility was to nationalize, which was the preferred strategy in Croatia. This strategy was to some extent implemented because the government of Croatia decided, after independence, to nationalize its socially owned enterprises and then sell them to private owners, mostly handpicked by the government itself. This led to a substantial misallocation of resources that has cost Croatia dearly.

Slovenia adopted an alternative approach. Much of what Aleksander Bajt had suggested was implemented in the Slovenian transition. Macroeconomic balances were preserved through appropriate exchange rate and monetary policy. Social ownership was abandoned in the area of banking and public services, and the latter were nationalized. Socially owned and self-managed firms were privatized, but in a way that preserved the continuity of ownership and the survival of existing firms. An interesting approach to social ownership was taken. As noted at the outset, the legal definition of social ownership was such that it was in fact a nonownership, which perhaps can be understood to mean that a socially owned firm is not tradable. However, their employees and managers saw these self-managed firms as belonging to them. Thus, de facto if not de jure, socially owned firms were seen as basically worker owned. Accordingly, the most natural, if not necessarily the most efficient, way to privatize these firms seemed to be to sell them to the employees, or distribute their shares to employees, and then let the capital markets determine the eventual ownership structure. Although significant inefficiencies persisted in these firms after they were privatized, few went bankrupt, and the restructuring did not lead to a very sharp increase in unemployment.

The Slovenian case also shows that the institutional setup was not so poor after all. Fiscal institutions proved especially strong, capable of preserving the rather large revenue stream from taxes. Again, Slovenia chose to reform the tax system only very gradually, and the same gradualism was applied to the payments system, which indeed played a crucial role in keeping tax revenue coming in. And because public revenue did not collapse, public services did not collapse either. As a consequence, Slovenia went through a mild and short transitional recession and has enjoyed sustained growth ever since.

Clearly, then, the system of social ownership and self-management was capable of being reformed. The key issues of responsibility for assets and for public finances were tackled, and macroeconomic imbalances were not allowed to develop.

A DIGRESSION: AN ECONOMIC THEORY OF DISINTEGRATION

In the aftermath of the breakup of SFR Yugoslavia, at least two economic explanations of that disintegration have been advanced. The first argues that it was a consequence of the country's great economic diversity. More generally, this argument holds that there is a level of diversity beyond which political integration does not make sense. In the case of SFR Yugoslavia, it was often pointed out that the most developed region, Slovenia, had perhaps six or seven times the GDP per capita, depending on the year in question, of the least developed region, Kosovo.

TABLE 2.1 GROSS SOCIAL PRODUCT PER CAPITA IN SFR
        YUGOSLAVIA
(Slovenia = 100, unless otherwise indicated)

Republic or province	1952	1965	1974	1980	1989	1997[a]	1999[b]
Slovenia	100.0	100.0	100.0	100.0	100.0	100.0	10,078
Croatia	66.7	65.8	62.5	64.1	64.1	48.0	6,464
Vojvodina	49.1	60.9	58.0	57.1	59.6	24.3	6,006
Serbia proper	56.7	52.2	48.0	49.5	52.0	18.9	5,243
Serbia incl. Vojvodina and Kosovo	51.5	50.0	45.0	45.5	46.0	17.1	4,632
Montenegro	48.5	41.3	34.0	39.9	36.9	16.1	3,716
Bosnia and Herzegovina	52.6	39.1	33.0	33.3	34.3	10.2	3,461
(FYR) Macedonia	39.2	36.4	34.0	33.8	33.3	20.3	3,359
Kosovo	25.7	19.6	16.0	14.1	12.6	5.1	1,272

a. Data refer to gross material product per capita for Serbia, Montenegro, Vojvodina, and Kosovo and to GDP per capita for other countries.
b. Data are actual GDP per capita (in dollars at the then-current exchange rate) for Slovenia, and the hypothetically attainable level of GDP per capita (in dollars at exchange rate) for the others, under the assumption that regional discrepancies (as measured in GDP per capita) are the same as in 1989.
Source: OECD data.

Table 2.1 gives an indication of the regional differences in gross social product per capita (similar to the gross material product concept used in other socialist countries) across the republics and provinces in former Yugoslavia over a long period. The table also shows GDP (or gross material product) per capita among the newly established states and the provinces of Vojvodina and Kosovo in the late 1990s. As can be seen, the differences were rather stable throughout most of SFR Yugoslavia's history, with the exception of Kosovo, where output fell sharply.[6] The different states' fortunes diverged markedly, however, after the breakup.

Assuming significant transfers from the richer to the poorer regions in SFR Yugoslavia, the richer ones would have an obvious incentive to become independent. Even if it turned out, as indeed it did, that some of the poorer regions were also interested in independence, a modified explanation based on diversity could be applied. The common level of taxation may have been higher or lower than the poorer regions needed, and the transfers may not have been enough to make up the difference. In that case the poorer regions would have had an incentive to seek independence even though they would have to forgo the transfers from the richer regions. Indeed, an argument could be made that disintegration was better for everyone—that is, Pareto-improving—if tax rates and transfers differed too much from what they would be if the regions were independent states. Thus it could, in fact, be the case that disintegration would emerge as a

TABLE 2.2 EXPORTS OF GOODS IN SFR YUGOSLAVIA
(percent of GDP)

Republic or province	1970	1976	1983	1987
Slovenia	17.7	17.1	41.9	22.2
Croatia	15.6	14.9	25.5	14.3
Vojvodina	10.9	11.1	22.7	13.1
Serbia proper	17.4	14.9	31.4	20.3
Serbia incl. Vojvodina and Kosovo	15.0	13.9	28.2	17.6
Montenegro	8.6	17.5	24.6	17.5
Bosnia and Herzegovina	12.9	15.9	32.3	19.8
Macedonia	13.7	15.0	26.6	17.8
Kosovo	7.7	17.5	22.6	11.4
SFR Yugoslavia	15.1	15.1	30.0	17.9

Source: OECD data.

Pareto-improving option if the level of diversity were high enough (see Bolton and Roland 1997).

This theory takes the state to be simply a fiscal agent. This makes sense if the state is a small, open economy, in which case markets determine almost everything else. Thus perhaps the only thing left to a state as an agent of economic policy is fiscal policy (in the broader sense, adding the fiscal effects of regulation to taxes and their rates). Then different preferences about the level of public spending and the distribution of the fiscal burden would provide incentives to consider the trade-off between fiscal independence and integration. The theoretical question then becomes whether there is much room for fiscal divergence for a small, open economy. The answer is likely to be that there is not. Indeed, as a rule, less developed countries would tend to have smaller public sectors than more developed ones, partly for reasons of competitiveness and partly because of differences in demography. In any case one cannot simply assume that independent small, open economies would be able to set their tax rates independently of the rest of the world.

The crucial assumption here is that the country in question is a small, open economy. In fact, SFR Yugoslavia was not such a country: it was small but not very open (Table 2.2). Clearly, liberalization was one of the goals of the transition process on which the country was embarking at the moment of its dissolution. Thus the Pareto-improving fiscal arrangements that dissolution would arguably bring would have to be seen as expected future benefits.

This is where the second explanation comes in. Many have argued that the dissolution of SFR Yugoslavia occurred because of differences among republics in the expected gains from transition and integration into the world economy, and especially into the European Union. For instance, it is conceivable that the more developed regions expected to benefit more from external markets than the less developed regions. In other words, it might be the case that the richer and poorer regions did not form an optimal customs union. A less developed region might need a higher level of protection than a more developed one. In that case the more developed region would have an incentive to secede, because its gain from access to the larger outside market suffices to compensate for the loss of the internal market.

But can one assume that the less developed a country is, the more protection it needs? Although it is true that, in SFR Yugoslavia, protectionist interests were rather strong in the less developed regions, they were strong in some of the more developed regions as well. In any case those interests cannot be easily rationalized with the help of economic theory, which advises openness rather than reliance on protection and self-sufficiency. Of course, political incentives may differ from economic incentives, and indeed that was the case in SFR Yugoslavia.

Thus, economic explanations of SFR Yugoslavia's political disintegration rely on the idea that either

- disintegration is a Pareto-improving move, because all regions of a country stand to benefit when they become independent states (although the distribution of benefits may not be equal), or
- the preservation of the common country is a Pareto-optimal situation in which disintegration benefits some, usually richer, regions but disfavors the other, mostly poor regions; that is, preservation is Pareto-optimal but not an equilibrium state of affairs.

These two explanations can be included in a variety of more general theoretical models in order to determine the influence of a number of other political and economic developments on the stability of a country. Clearly, if a country has a closed economy, it may become destabilized when it liberalizes its foreign economic relations. Thus, as some have argued,[7] globalization of free trade may lead to an increase in the number of countries, because access to the world market makes any advantage of closed local markets disappear, in which case the size of a state ceases to matter.

Democratization has a similar effect. By taking into account the political preferences of the citizens, it reveals the differences in desirable tax rates. This assertion is sensitive to gerrymandering, however. Therefore it is often assumed that diversity increases with size. For instance, any state within the United States, or any member state of the European Union, should be more homogeneous than their union is. If that is the case, at some point the diversity will be much more than a common state can accommodate. Incentives to disintegrate will emerge, which cannot be suppressed if decisions are made democratically.

There are other economic accounts of the breakup of states, but in one way or another they collapse into these two. As long as the world is not globalized, larger states have advantages over smaller ones. Once there is free trade, however, the size of a state becomes irrelevant except in terms of the level of redistribution that different agglomerations of individuals are ready to accept. Then there are two possibilities: either disintegration is Pareto-improving or it is not. In the latter case, there may exist a conflict of interests—a lack of equilibrium—which can be resolved in a number of ways, one of them being integration into a wider economic and political area or union.

These explanations do account for a number of features of the Yugoslav disintegration but do not identify the key cause. As argued in this chapter, the key contributing element to the disintegration of SFR Yugoslavia, at least from an economic point of view, was the concept of social ownership and the difficulty that it introduced in developing a consistent setup for macroeconomic governance. And even these factors are subordinated to the political ones, which are not discussed here in any detail.

CONCLUSION

The economic setup of SFR Yugoslavia and the macroeconomic policies it pursued contributed to the country's disintegration. From an economic point of view, this was not a necessary development, although the leading political economy theory on the integration and disintegration of states might claim otherwise. Although the system of social self-management was neither representative nor efficient, it could have been reformed. In a way the Slovenian transition makes that point clear. Nevertheless, the public governance mess, the political system's inability to deal with problems, and the lack of adequate instruments of economic policy management, together with large macroeconomic imbalances, did contribute to the disintegration of the country, even though that disintegration was mainly driven by political interests, leading to a decade of violent conflict.

REFERENCES

Alesina, A., I. Angeloni, and F. Etro. 2003. "International Unions." Harvard University, Cambridge, Mass. Processed.

Alesina, A., and E. Spolaore. 1997. "On the Number and Size of Nations." *Quarterly Journal of Economics* 112(4): 1027–56.

Alesina, A., E. Spolaore, and R. Wacziarg. 2003. "Trade, Growth and the Size of Nations." *HIER Discussion Paper* 1995. Harvard Institute of Economic Research, Cambridge, Mass.

Bolton, P., and G. Roland. 1997. "The Breakup of Nations: A Political Economy Analysis." *Quarterly Journal of Economics* 112(4): 1057–90.

Gligorov, V. 1994. *Why Do Countries Break Up? The Case of Yugoslavia.* Uppsala, Sweden: Acta Universitatis Upsaliensis.

_____. 1998. "Yugoslav Economics Facing Reform and Dissolution." In Hans-Jürgen Wagener, ed., *Economic Thought in Communist and Post-Communist Europe.* London: Routledge.

_____. 2001. "Economic Future of Kosovo." European Centre for Minority Issues, Flensburg, Germany. Processed

_____. 2003. "Economics of Integration and Disintegration." In Alina Mungiu–Pippidi and Ivan Krastev (eds.), *Postcommunist Nationalism: Lessons Learned.* Budapest: Central European University Press.

Roland, G. 2000. *Economics of Transition.* Cambridge, Mass.: MIT Press.

NOTES

1. The issue of legitimacy in socialist Yugoslavia is a much more complicated one and beyond the scope of this chapter.

2. Of course, both the states and the federation were run in an autocratic manner, as political pluralism and private entrepreneurship would have been in contradiction with the socialist character of the political and economic system.

3. I discuss the disintegration of SFR Yugoslavia in greater detail in Gligorov (1994).

4. I discuss this subject in more detail in Gligorov (1998).

5. For more on this subject, see Roland (2000).

6. There the divergence was mostly due to the rapid growth of population rather than to slower economic growth. For more on that subject see Gligorov (2001).

7. See Alesina and Spolaore (1997); for more recent statements, see Alesina, Spolaore, and Wacziarg (2003) and Alesina, Angeloni, and Etro (2003). For further comments see Gligorov (2003).

Chapter 3
Independence and Integration into the International Community: A Window of Opportunity

Bojko Bučar

Slovenia has gained independence and international recognition within a sophisticated and complex historical situation, both in the world at large and, specifically, with respect to internal political developments in SFR Yugoslavia. For Slovenia to become a sovereign state, both these windows of opportunity—internal developments and international relations—had to be synchronized. And, as so often happens, internal developments influenced international relations and vice versa. To attempt to understand the one without the other is often futile.

After the fall of the Berlin Wall in 1989, it became clear that regime changes in other central and eastern European (CEE) countries would soon follow. Even so, the transformation of communist regimes throughout the region into governments of genuine democracy came at a pace that the rest of the world had not expected in its wildest dreams. Observers had to wait for some 10 years to see the peaceful transformation come about in Poland, but it took only about 10 months in Hungary, 10 weeks in eastern Germany, and 10 days in Czechoslovakia.[1] Small wonder, then, that the Western democracies, which had long hoped for these changes, were somewhat taken by surprise and had no policies of their own for such a scenario. Only in the former Soviet Union and in parts of the former SFR Yugoslavia does the transformation seem to have lingered.

This chapter seeks to analyze selected internal political developments and the international context that led to the disintegration of SFR Yugoslavia and the independence of Slovenia. The first section deals predominantly with internal developments up until the declaration of independence, and the next section predominantly with the international context and developments since then. The chapter ends with a short conclusion.

INTERNAL DEVELOPMENTS IN SFR YUGOSLAVIA IN THE PERIOD UP TO SLOVENIA'S DECLARATION OF INDEPENDENCE

To some outside observers in the late 1980s, the processes leading toward genuine democracy might have seemed to have progressed more slowly in SFR Yugoslavia than in the rest of CEE. This may have been superficially true, yet it certainly has not been true in substance. In striving to become a democratic nation, the country did surely encounter enormous difficulties. Generally speaking, precisely because Yugoslavia in the post–World War II period had a more liberal system than the rest of CEE, change did seem slower in coming and less profound. As in the Soviet Union, whose hegemonic international tendencies after World War II led to the development of liberalism in SFR Yugoslavia after the initial break with Stalin in 1948, this phenomenon is usually attributed to two facts: greater legiti-macy of the communist regime,[2] and the multinationality of the state. This made decisions somewhat more difficult to reach, but says noth-ing about the depth of the changes undertaken. Similarly, the more liberal system of SFR Yugoslavia after 1948, compared with the rest of CEE, made certain changes less visible and dramatic at first, but this says little about the quality of the processes.

SFR Yugoslavia has always been a land of diversity. After World War II it was conventional to describe it as one federal state with six republics (federal units constitutionally defined as states),[3] five nations, four religions, three languages, and two alphabets, under the single leadership of "the last Hapsburg," Marshal Josip Broz Tito. The idea of self-management socialism (sometimes understood as self-management in the economy and self-government in politics), with its unique notions of equality and democracy, tried to cover over social, national, and other differences by instead emphasizing Marxist-style class antagonism. In essence, however, the state was torn between the north and the south, the north being richer and belonging to the mid-dle European cultural and historical area, the south poorer and belonging to the southeastern European cultural heritage.[4] In a way, this internal north-south relationship was similar to the classic North-South relationship well known in international relations (Borak 2002).

As an important leader of the global nonaligned movement, SFR Yugoslavia was basically a developing country, and like many such countries, it was hit hard by the world debt crises of the mid-1980s. The economy (and the state) eventually found itself choking in debt, and the deteriorating economic situation toppled into the political vacuum created by Tito's legacy.[5] In the attempt to solve these prob-lems, two tendencies emerged. The centralist option was advocated by the federal government (and in the beginning by some of the less developed republics); the decentralist solution was advocated initially by the richer republics, but was soon to be championed by virtually all, if for quite different political and economic reasons. The central-ist tendencies stayed more or less with the federal institutions.

To understand these processes and how they came about, one must look at the second half of the 1980s, when the "cohabitation" of the nations of SFR Yugoslavia seemed no longer possible, primarily for economic reasons. There was still a single Communist Party in power, but in an attempt to preserve legitimacy and stay in power, the state party had started dissolving itself into six national parties, which clothed themselves in national garb, defending not class but national or class-national interests. The classic North-South debate of who was exploiting whom started between the republics. This resulted in the first serious breakthrough toward freedom of the press, which could not have been contained to economic issues of exploitation only. Growing press freedom slowly enabled political demands to be expressed publicly, not only within the republics but also within the federation itself. The central authorities started losing the support of the republics because of the internal political struggle for power as well; in addition, international events were favorable. The nonaligned movement had lost its political prestige since the end of the 1970s, and changes in East-West relations were under way. Central and eastern Europe experienced the first political changes, and the internal opposition, especially in the north of SFR Yugoslavia, started looking toward the values of Western Europe. The political and economic crises in SFR Yugoslavia resulted in a political decision to change the federal constitution of 1974, which in itself was nothing new—major constitutional changes had already been made in 1946, 1953, 1963, 1967, 1968, and 1971.

The main reason for the decision to change the constitution was to initiate reforms toward a market economy. However, it was generally recognized that simultaneous political reforms would be necessary as well, if the attempt dared hope for greater success than previous "socialist reforms." The two political tendencies toward more or less centralization resulted in compromise, in the form of the constitutional amendments of 1989.[6] Yet because of the change in the federal constitution, the constitutions of all the republics had to be changed as well. Since political changes were already under way, the Slovenian constitution had been changed in a way that enabled—roughly speaking—direct elections by secret ballot and a multiparty system. Now this constitutional change was challenged before the federal constitutional court, which decided that it violated the federal constitution. Nothing could be done, however, because the legal system did not provide for effective enforcement of the court's decisions.

As an institution, the court was in any case rather an anomaly in the socialist world. As a socialist, communist society, SFR Yugoslavia was founded on the ideological notion that the only possible social conflict—that between classes—was to be resolved in a political way. Other than that, SFR Yugoslavia was considered a conflict-free society, and therefore adequate mechanisms of conflict resolution were lacking. Most changes were brought about through political means, in disregard of the legal system of the state. The rule of law simply did not exist, and this had far-reaching consequences for the whole process, once the federal League of Communists had lost its unity.

Slovenians claimed that they as a nation were sovereign, even according to the constitution of 1974, and therefore they would not be prepared to submit changes to their constitution to approval by a higher authority, that is, to make such changes only within the limits of the federal constitution. Starting from the notion of the sovereignty of nations, the federal constitution could only be based on the previous change of the constitutions of the republics, since only they could define and determine their common interest to be exercised within the federation.[7] But even more serious than this constitutional or legal crisis was the political one. The federal Communist Party no longer existed,[8] and, in contrast to the south, a multiparty system emerged in the north. The two systems became incompatible. A cumulative effect was reached with the economic reforms of the federal government, which became a challenge for the economy and worsened the situation of ordinary people. On top of that came the human rights issue in the south.

The latter issue has many dimensions, but here I shall deal with only one of them: the right of peoples to self-determination. According to the 1974 constitution, one of the republics, Serbia, had two autonomous provinces within its territory, both of which were represented in the federation directly.[9] But in early 1990, for political reasons, Serbia abolished the autonomy of both provinces, claiming that it was an internal matter of a sovereign nation.[10] Yet the federal constitution was left unchanged, so that the two provinces kept their representation at the federal level. Representatives of all sovereign nations and nationalities within Yugoslavia (republics and both autonomous provinces) used to vote or form political coalitions at the federal level primarily according to their economic interests.[11] There was little concern that the less developed units (Montenegro, Macedonia, Bosnia, or Kosovo) would side with a political proposal by the more developed units (Serbia proper, Croatia, Slovenia, or Vojvodina), especially if it enshrined centralization and possibly domination by one of them. Yet once both autonomous provinces had been abolished by the political will of the republic of which they had been a constituent part, the question arose, which constituency would they henceforward support at the federal level, especially bearing in mind the unanswered question of who might recall, replace, or reappoint them? The fear that Serbia would thus have three votes in the federation proved to be wrong in practice, primarily because of the traditional patterns of loyalty based on differing levels of development, and consequently diverse economic interests, of Serbia and the two provinces. Nevertheless, Slovenia regarded this as a unilateral change in the federal constitution and therefore felt justified in declaring its sovereignty, which it did in June 1990 (Bučar 1990). This political declaration was also a demand for a modified concept of democracy. Although only a political statement, the declaration demanded in juridical terms that the laws of the republics prevail over federal laws, and it rejected cooperation in federal structures where decisions could be reached by majority vote instead of consensus. This challenge to the "one man, one vote" rule in a multinational federation proved far-reaching, affecting all later discussions of the concept of a new common state. The political declaration of June 1990 found its legal expression in the Slovenian constitutional amendments and two constitutional laws of September 27, 1990.

Meanwhile, in the second half of 1990, elections were held in all republics, although with quite different results. An analysis of how the different parties or coalitions came to power in the various republics, and the consequences thereof, would be far beyond the scope of this chapter. But the fact was that a change in the structure of the state could only have been negotiated among the republics, and the political elites in the different republics simply could not agree on federal elections. In addition, in the last days of 1990, Slovenia held a referendum on independence, and Croatia adopted its new constitution.[12] In light of previous developments, these steps amounted to a clear manifestation of the will of both republics to become independent states and to be recognized as such by the international community.

This development might be seen also as part of the evolution of political ideas about the future of the common state. As long as it had a one-party system, the federation seemed to guarantee the equality of the constituent republics. Economic and political developments in the 1980s opened, among other things, a political debate precisely on this issue of equality, and some (especially in Slovenia) felt that the form of the state should be changed to a kind of asymmetric federation, leaving the centralist option open for some republics, and the decentralist option for others. Centralist tendencies in 1989 were still present in some of the southern federal units, notably Serbia, where the argument went another way. The Serbians claimed that the existing federation was not a federation at all, and that therefore it should be turned into a modern federation on the principle of "one man, one vote" and majority decisionmaking. The requirement of consensus within federal structures, they claimed, meant that the federal state had been in reality a confederation.[13] Once the term "confederation" had been launched in the political arena, Slovenia and Croatia claimed that was what they wanted, whereas the southern republics demanded a modern federation. (The northern republics' claim that they wanted a confederation but not secession seemed a contradiction in terms. What the two sides seem actually to have meant was a "loose federation" and a "unitary state," respectively.) The federal presidency developed a plan for a referendum with four options: a confederation, a federation, a confederation for some and federation for others, and dissolution of the state. This plan was rejected, however, because of political mistrust and the belief that the republics alone had the right to determine how they would decide.

In the second half of 1990, however, after elections had been held in most of the republics, the right to self-determination and even secession became a legitimate principle.[14] In October 1990 Croatia, and in a less elaborate form Slovenia as well, introduced a plan for a confederation that in essence was a copy of arrangements in what was then the European Community.[15] By then, all of the republics recognized these issues as legitimate, but serious technical (in essence, political) questions were raised on the issue of borders and other rights and duties arising from secession. Suddenly, the republics that had seemed the most eager to secede started to have second thoughts, since in legal and substantive terms there is a difference between secession from a state, whereby the old state keeps its existence, and the dissolution of a state, whereby the old state ceases to exist. In a nutshell, secession leaves most of the seceding state's rights and assets with the old state and imposes mainly duties and liabilities on the seceding state. In contrast, when a state is dissolving the rights and duties are equally divided among the successor states (Trifković 1999, 188–91). Therefore the issue became not how to break away from the federal state but how to break it up. This started a new round of negotiations, since, in practice, the difference could have had considerable economic impact.

The federal government and the army, encouraged by the international community, remained opposed to any form of dissolution or secession. Because of its eagerness to proceed with economic reform, the federal government had international credibility. It did not have to worry too much about social issues, since this was within the competence of the republics, and, because of the lack of unity among them, it did not have to fear for its own position. In order to proceed with economic reform, including monetary reform, the federal government demanded more central power. But for the same reason, which made it a stable government, it could not get more power, since there was no unity for any kind of agreement among the republics. Meanwhile the army had strong and vital interests of its own for wanting to keep the federal state going (Radaković 2003).

The causes of the disintegration of SFR Yugoslavia were numerous (Bučar 1991a). Yet from the point of view of international relations and foreign policy, the European orientation of some of the republics seems to have been decisive. The widening economic gap between SFR Yugoslavia and the countries of Western Europe was considered to be due in part to the unwillingness of some republics to undertake not only economic reform but also the necessary political changes. The goal of establishing genuine democracy, the rule of law, and respect for human rights seemed to be drifting into the distant future.

The debate among the republics was to a considerable degree based on constitutional issues. According to the basic principles of the 1974 constitution, the bearers of sovereignty were "the working people and the nations and nationalities,"[16] who were entitled to "exercise their sovereign rights" in the republics and in the federal state only "when in their common interest it is so specified" by the constitution. Furthermore, it was written that "the nations of Yugoslavia, proceeding from the right of every nation to self-determination, including the right to secession" have united in a federal state. The concept of the right of peoples to self-determination became a hot issue (Kristan 1992).

The focus on the right of the Yugoslav peoples to self-determination seemed to come at a perfect time from the standpoint of the international community as well. The Berlin Wall had just fallen, and in the document of the Conference on Security and Cooperation in Europe (CSCE) of 1990,[17] titled "Charter of Paris for a New Europe," the international community had, among other things, recognized the right of the German nation to self-determination—in other words the right to unify. This was certainly an important milestone in the implementation of the right of self-determination.

For Slovenia the notion of the right of peoples to self-determination within the constitutional system of SFR Yugoslavia, as well as in the international community, was of utmost importance (Bučar 1997). In domestic politics Slovenia started to argue that if the federal state of SFR Yugoslavia had been established on the free will of all the nations, the departure of one or more nations from the state would not constitute secession, but rather the dissolution of the state. The difference in legal and material terms, in national as well as in international politics, is of course significant. In international politics and law the existence of the right to self-determination presumably imposes a duty on states to respect this right, which not only would facilitate recognition of a newborn state but would also require assistance to peoples claiming this right. Slovenia tried to convince foreign governments and international public opinion of its right, and it refused to recognize that, throughout history, the right of peoples to self-determination had been mostly achieved through war and bloodshed, precisely because that right conflicted with the equal right of states to maintain their territorial integrity. Slovenia also failed to acknowledge other limitations of the right to self-determination, which were, mainly for security reasons, always present as political considerations in the international community.[18]

At the beginning of 1991, all six republics seem to have agreed that a new form of the state was inevitable. But the federal government and the army still opposed this, not only because of their constitutional obligations, but also because of their own vital economic and political interests. The federal government enjoyed a good reputation in the international community, partly because of the well-known history of SFR Yugoslavia's leadership in the nonaligned movement, and partly because of the seemingly successful economic reforms it had introduced. Yet for practically the same reason, the federal government enjoyed little support internally. This was partly because the economic reforms had caused adverse social effects, which the republics, and not the federal government, were responsible for alleviating, and partly because of political and nationalistic antagonisms between republics. Departing from the concept of the sovereignty of nations, the republics started to negotiate on the future of the state without the presence of the army and the federal government.[19] A decision was reached to put the matter to the will of the people, by way of a referendum in each of the republics in 1991, except in Slovenia where a referendum had already been held. The escalation of the conflict in Croatia made the implementation of this decision impossible (Bučar 1993), and the negotiations broke off.[20]

To achieve independence, Slovenia had only three options. The first was to reach an agreement among all the parties to the dispute. The international community favored this. The second was to reach independence by way of a unilateral decision—and hope that the outcome did not follow the unsuccessful example of Lithuania. The third option was to start a secessionist armed conflict. The first option could not be achieved for at least two reasons. First, the federal government and the army were interested parties but were not part of the negotiations among the republics. Second, negotiations among the republics failed, and subsequently the federal government was not interested in negotiations with only one of them. The third option seemed possible but not probable and was regarded as unlikely, especially in view of contemporary developments elsewhere in Europe. The second option, then, was the only viable solution, and Slovenian authorities had to proceed with it, since they were bound by the special law on the plebiscite to declare independence within six months. The Slovenian legislature decided, against some better advice from within and outside the country, to declare independence on June 25, 1991, and it immediately sought international recognition (Ministry of Foreign Affairs 1992).[21]

AFTER THE DECLARATION OF INDEPENDENCE: THE INTERNATIONAL CONTEXT

The international community was well aware of the growing crisis in Yugoslavia, having been informed by their countries' own diplomatic agents,[22] special envoys, media reports, the Yugoslav federal government, and the governments of the republics. The message that foreign governments, especially those of the other European states and the United States, were sending was clear enough. They were not ready to recognize a secessionist state, and still less the dissolution of a state, unless there was a consensus within the existing state on secession or dissolution. The reasons were numerous. The first was economic: who would pay the old state's debts once it ceased to exist?[23] There was also the concern that disintegration would result in a considerable shrinkage of the internal national market.[24] Security reasons were perhaps even more important. A disintegration of the state could end in armed conflict that might prove hard to contain. SFR Yugoslavia's disintegration also would have set a bad example for the Soviet Union, still in existence at that time. With its numerous constituent nations, many of which aspired to national self-determination, and with its vast nuclear arsenal, the Soviet Union could not be allowed to disintegrate in an uncontrolled manner. To these considerations could be added a general discomfort in view of the possible future international influence of a reunited Germany. There was also some worry about the influence that the Yugoslav case might have on other states with substantial ethnic or other minorities, including some Western democracies. In addition, the integration processes then proceeding, especially elsewhere in Europe, made all processes working in the opposite direction appear, at least at first glance, anachronistic and obsolete. Finally, international legal principles had to be respected, and primarily the obligation to respect the territorial integrity of states and the principle of nonintervention in their internal affairs.

Since no consensus could be reached within the state of SFR Yugoslavia, the international community decided to support the federal government. By the end of May 1991 at the latest, it terminated all contacts with the republics, and once again the federal government became the sole representative of SFR Yugoslavia in international affairs. Since Slovenia had by then declared independence, the federal government of SFR Yugoslavia reacted much as did the central government of the Soviet Union to Lithuania's similar declaration. On the day of Slovenia's declaration, the federal legislature declared the act illegal and called upon the federal government to protect the borders of the federal state. The next day the federal army and some detachments of the federal police tried to close the borders by force, federal authorities closed the air space by decree, and the federal national bank took all necessary measures to discipline the disloyal republics in monetary matters, limiting access to foreign exchange, interrupting all credit transactions, and so on. Unlike Lithuania, however, Slovenia had its own territorial army and police force. The 10-day war of June 1991 began.[25]

The criteria for statehood generally recognized in international law include a defined territory and population under the control of a government.[26] Although in theory the definitions of "territory" and "population" might create problems, this was not the case in either Slovenia or Lithuania. The problem was rather in the criterion "under the control of a government" (or "effective authorities"). In essence the question was one of sovereignty, which in international relations means the absence of any higher authority.[27] Sovereignty enables the state to exercise the power to make treaties, the right to representation, and the right to wage war. In cases of secession, who the "effective authorities" are becomes a crucial issue, and, as the cases of Slovenia and Lithuania show, it was exactly on this criterion that the central authorities tried to halt the aspirations of peoples for a new state and the recognition of these states by foreign governments. Yet by that time it seemed that the focus had shifted from "the control of government" to "how control is exercised." [28] It was becoming an issue of human rights invading the stronghold of the principle of noninterference in internal affairs.

The armed conflict of June 1991 shocked the international community. It was happening in the midst of a Europe that had long been mostly at peace, and the outcome was hard to predict (Bučar 1991b). The European Community, which at that time did not have its Common Foreign and Security Policy (CFSP) even on paper, offered its good offices in the conflict. It threatened economic and political sanctions (that is, unfriendly but legal actions) if the conflict were not solved by peaceful means. SFR Yugoslavia accepted the offer, and in practice the European "Troïka" turned its services toward mediation.[29] Their basic aim was to stop all hostilities and encourage all parties to conduct peaceful negotiations in good faith toward a peaceful settlement. If the parties agreed, the European Community would continue cooperation with all concerned; otherwise it would break off all relations. In addition, the federal government was put under pressure: it was made to understand that if it continued with the armed intervention, the European Community would recognize Slovenia and Croatia as independent states. On the other hand, the republics had to return their representatives to the federal bodies from which they had previously withdrawn.

The European Community's mediation resulted in the signing of the Brioni declaration of July 7, 1991, in which all parties basically agreed to a three-month cooling-off period in which no unilateral actions that might worsen the situation should be taken, and in which they would try in good faith to reach a peaceful solution for the future of the state. This meant Slovenia had to suspend its declaration of independence for at least three months. But in this way the conflict in SFR Yugoslavia again became internationalized—it ceased to be an internal affair—and Slovenia was acknowledged as a party to the dispute. The solution suggested by the European Community clearly demonstrated a will to preserve the territorial integrity of the state; it caused the termination of hostilities, yet it did not push for a specific political solution of the crisis.[30] This was left to the parties to the conflict.

But the three months brought no progress. The parties failed to reach any significant compromise or agreement on the issue of borders (the self-determination of peoples versus the self-determination of republics) or on the question of who should be recognized as the successor to the old state (secession from versus dissolution of the old state). Federal bodies were not able to resume their work, because the republics were unwilling to participate in good faith. The federal army agreed to withdraw from Slovenia, only to get engaged in another armed conflict in Croatia, which in turn could already be seen as a prelude to the war in Bosnia. The Hague Conference on Yugoslavia, presided over by the European Community,[31] was unable to change the course of developments on the ground, where it became obvious that the old state no longer existed, and some political forces thought that maps of new states could be drawn at random. At the same time, significant developments were occurring elsewhere in the international community. It became clear that the Soviet Union was falling apart, that new states were emerging, and that the era of *perestroika* and *glasnost* had come to an end.[32]

The armed conflict in Croatia resulted in Slovenia and Croatia becoming de facto independent states, although they still lacked international legal recognition. But it was precisely the armed conflict that caused foreign governments and international organizations to tolerate the existence of these de facto states and allowed for economic and other cooperation, which in cases of nonrecognized states would normally not be possible. In economic matters, for example, the beneficial toleration of the situation by the European Community and by the General Agreement on Tariffs and Trade (GATT) was especially important. In any case Slovenia finally fulfilled the criterion of possessing "effective authorities." But as part of the requirements under international law for an entity to be recognized as a state, the recognizing state is required to make a determination, reasonably based on fact, that the entity claiming statehood shows reasonable indications that the international legal requirements will continue to be satisfied. In the case of secession or dissolution of a state, this occurs when the old government renounces its pretensions or when it is obviously no longer in a position to reconquer the entity claiming statehood. Otherwise recognition might be considered premature and in violation of international law.[33] Also, the economic, political, and security reasons that a few months earlier had argued in favor of the integrity of the state as a whole suddenly either became irrelevant or even argued in favor of the opposite position.

Because of its cooperative policy at The Hague Conference on Yugoslavia, which had started on September 5, 1991, Slovenia was enabled to proceed toward independence on October 7, 1991, after the three-month period stipulated by the Brioni declaration had passed. The situation in the rest of SFR Yugoslavia was worsening rapidly, and on November 29, 1991, a special Arbitration Commission of the Peace Conference on Yugoslavia found that SFR Yugoslavia was in fact disintegrating.[34]

Meanwhile, on the ground, the Yugoslav army engaged in a fierce battle for the Croatian town of Vukovar, which, like Stalingrad in World War II, became a symbol of resistance against foreign domination (and centralization). The drawn-out street battles, mainly between a well-organized armed force on one side and more or less fierce civilian resistance on the other, sobered the European states. Germany, in particular, a strong player in international economic relations yet up until then rather coy in its foreign policy actions, pushed for a change in what then was still the common stance of the European Community. The reason was plain enough: if the insistence of the international community on the territorial integrity of Yugoslavia was going to result in civilian massacres in Vukovar and in artillery attacks on the historic town of Dubrovnik (under the special protection of UNESCO), then maybe an end to the fighting could be reached by recognizing SFR Yugoslavia's republics as states.[35] Furthermore, international conditions were also favorable. The Soviet Union was in the process of disintegration, and it was dissolved peacefully on December 20, 1991. It was the German position that influenced a change in the attitude of the member states of the European Community, and consequently of the international community. Germany, in keeping with its own foreign policy strategy and in accord with international expectations, had always been keen on restraining the exercise of its sovereign powers in favor of European integration. What it called for now was a new approach toward integration. The United Kingdom and France, which had always had active foreign policies of their own, were somewhat reluctant to follow.[36] However, the diplomatic formula for how it should be done was probably invented by Italy.[37] And, in the end, it was a common decision of all the European Community member states and not, as often claimed, of Germany alone.

In short, faced with a situation that it could not tolerate any longer, the European Community on December 16, 1991, adopted a declaration on "Guidelines on the Recognition of New States in Eastern Europe and in the Soviet Union" (European Community 1991a), as well as a "Declaration on Yugoslavia" (European Community 1991b), whereby it decided to recognize, subject to certain conditions, the former Yugoslav republics as sovereign states, effective January 15, 1992. On the basis of this decision, Slovenia was recognized as a sovereign state by Iceland, Sweden, and Germany on December 19, 1991, by Belarus on December 27, 1991, by the Holy See on January 13, 1992, and by San Marino on January 14, 1992. The rest followed on January 15, 1992, and thereafter.[38] For various reasons of domestic and international politics, the U.S. administration recognized Slovenia only on April 7, 1992 (Petrič 1994), although it did so in accord with the decision of the European Community (United States and European Community 1992).

Whether the republics met the European Community's special requirements for recognition was judged by the Badinter Commission, which also had to respect international law. This body declared that two federal units (Slovenia and FYR Macedonia) had satisfied the requirements and that one federal unit (Croatia) had done so partially; the fourth (Bosnia and Herzegovina) had at that time not been fully established (Badinter 1992).[39] Regardless of this legal opinion, requested by the European Community itself, Slovenia and Croatia were recognized immediately (EC Presidency 1991), Bosnia shortly thereafter, and FYR Macedonia much later. This timing certainly supports the hypothesis that political interests and decisions determine the recognition of a state.

After Slovenia had been recognized by the European Community member states, it was only a matter of time until it was admitted into international organizations. Not surprisingly, Slovenia first became a member of the CSCE on March 24, 1992, since this organization had been involved in the Yugoslav crisis virtually from the beginning.[40] On May 22, 1992, only 11 months after declaring independence and 4 months after its recognition by the European Community, Slovenia became a member of the United Nations. Soon thereafter it became a member of various specialized UN agencies and other international organizations (Journal of International Relations 1994b). Somewhat more complicated was Slovenia's accession to the international financial organizations (Mrak 1994), and indeed the question of succession drags on even today.[41] First, Slovenia joined the European Bank for Reconstruction and Development on December 23, 1992. Following certain decisions by the United Nations,[42] Slovenia became a member of the International Monetary Fund on January 15, 1993, and of the World Bank (the International Bank for Reconstruction and Development and the International Development Association) and the International Finance Corporation on February 25, 1993. In joining these organizations it was important that Slovenia be considered one of the successor states of SFR Yugoslavia. Somewhat more time consuming for Slovenia were its efforts to become a contracting party to the GATT (and later its successor the World Trade Organization). Immediately after recognition, Slovenia had applied for GATT membership, yet given the precedent its admission might set for other potential members (for example, Ukraine, Russia, and China), negotiations dragged on until October 30, 1994. In this way Slovenia accomplished most of the goals of its foreign relations strategy, which had been designed before independence,[43] except for membership in the Organization for Economic Cooperation and Development.

CONCLUSIONS

As this chapter has shown, specific internal developments in SFR Yugoslavia and the tectonic changes in the international community that influenced international relations during the same period made possible the independence of Slovenia as a sovereign state. Slovenia probably achieved its statehood during a narrow window of time when conditions were favorable for such an event. At any other time, things might have gone quite differently. Yet the determination of a people and its political representatives to establish a sovereign and independent state should not be underestimated, and considering Slovenia's referendum on independence, it is taken for granted in the analyses above. It is certainly on the one hand a crucial factor in favorable internal and external circumstances, possibly also without the latter. Favorable internal circumstances have to encompass a determined people as an actor, who might not be able at the same time to influence favorable external circumstances and may even be indifferent to them. On the other hand, as the history of international relations teaches, internal and external circumstances, especially the latter, can either prevent or facilitate international recognition, regardless of the will of the people and its political elites. In the case of Slovenia, they have certainly facilitated if not contributed to its independence.

REFERENCES

Badinter, R. 1992. "Report of the Arbitration Committee—15 January 1992." AVIS 4, 5, 6 and 7. *Review of International Affairs* 43(1001): 15–21.

Borak, N. 2002. *Ekonomski vidiki delovanja in razpada Jugoslavije.* Ljubljana: Znanstveno in publicistično središče.

Bučar, B. 1990. "Declaration on the Sovereignty of Slovenia." *Regional Contact* 1: 19–22.

————. 1991a. "Political Developments in Yugoslavia." In W. Mantl, ed., *Die neue Architektur Europas: Reflexion en in einer bedrohten Welt.* Vienna: Böhlau Verlag.

————. 1991b. "Nekatere mednarodne dileme in pogledi na samostojnost Slovenije." *Teorija in Praksa* 28(8–9): 1008–14.

————. 1993. "Der Bürgerkrieg in Jugoslawien." In K.-D. Grothusen, ed., *Ostmittel-und Südosteuropa im Umbruch.* Munich: Südosteuropa Gesellschaft.

_____. 1997. "The International Recognition of Slovenia." In D. Fink-Hafner and J. R. Robbins, eds., *Making a New Nation: The Formation of Slovenia.* Aldershot, United Kingdom: Dartmouth Publishing.

European Community. 1991a. "Guidelines on the Recognition of New States in Eastern Europe and the Soviet Union (17 December 1991)." *Review of International Affairs* 42(998–1000): 27–28.

_____. 1991b. "Declaration on Yugoslavia (17 December 1991)." *Review of International Affairs* 42(998–1000): 28.

EC Presidency. 1991. "Statement of the EC Presidency on the Recognition of Yugoslav Republics (15 January 1992)." *Review of International Affairs* 42(1001): 13.

Hannum, H., and R. B. Lillich. 1980. "The Concept of Autonomy in International Law." *American Journal of International Law* 74: 858–89.

Journal of International Relations. 1994a. "Chronologic List of States, which Have Recognised the Independence and the Sovereignty of the Republic of Slovenia (until 22 October 1993)." *Journal of International Relations* 1(1): 82–84.

_____. 1994b. "Membership of the Republic of Slovenia in International Governmental Organizations—Chronological Order (from 24.3.1992 until 24.5.1993)." *Journal of International Relations* 1(1): 85–87.

Kristan, I. 1992. "Das Recht auf Selbstbestimmung." In K.-D. Grothusen, ed., *Staatliche Einheit und Teilung—Deutschland und Jugoslawien.* Munich: Südosteuropa-Gesellschaft.

Lucarelli, S. 2000. *Europe and the Breakup of Yugoslavia—A Political Failure in Search of a Scholarly Explanation.* The Hague: Kluwer Law International.

Ministry of Foreign Affairs. 1992. *Poročilo Ministrstva za zunanje zadeve za leto 991* (Report of the Ministry of Foreign Affairs for 1991). Ljubljana (January 5).

Mössner, J. M. 1977. *Einführung in das Völkerrecht.* Munich: Verlag C.H. Beck.

Mrak, M. 1994. "Slovenia—Creating Its Own Identity in the International Financial Community." *Journal of International Relations* 1(1): 23–34.

Petrič, E. 1981. "Regionalism in Yugoslavia—Some Constitutional Aspects." In *Regionalism in Europa,* Vol. I. Munich: Internationales Institut für Nationalitätenrecht und Regionalismus.

_____. 1994. "Dolgoročni vidiki ameriške zunanje politike." *Teorija in Praksa* 31(1–2): 79–87.

Radaković, I. T. 2003. "Besmislena YU-ratovanja 1990–1995. Drugo dopunjeno izdanje." Belgrade: Društvo za istinu o antifašističkoj narodnooslobodilačkoj borbi u Jugoslaviji 1941–1945.

Trifković, M. 1999. "Fundamental Controversies in Succession to the Former SFR Yugoslavia." In M. Mrak, ed., *Succession of States.* The Hague: Martinus Nijhoff.

United States and European Community. 1992. "US/EC Declaration on the Recognition of the Yugoslav Republics (Bruxelles, 10 March 1992)." *Review of International Affairs* 43(1003): 17.

NOTES

1. It seemed to happen even more quickly in Bulgaria and Romania (and years later even in Albania), yet there the transformation did not come about peacefully.

2. After World War II, unlike the rest of CEE, SFR Yugoslavia was not "liberated" (that is, occupied), by the Red Army, and consequently its leadership had not been installed by the Soviet Union.

3. The federal units, most of which later became sovereign states, were Bosnia, Croatia, Macedonia, Montenegro, Serbia, and Slovenia. Each had its own state structures: a government (executive) with its administration, a legislature, a judicial system, a central bank, and so forth. Even the communist party was organized on the territorial principle, as a league of communist parties composed of (roughly speaking) the communist parties of the federal units.

4. The dividing line between the Western and Eastern Roman Empire, which later became the dividing line between the Catholic and the Orthodox Church, the Latin and the Cyrillic alphabet, and still later the border between the Ottoman and the Hapsburg Empire, ran right across what became SFR Yugoslavia.

5. In the media the debt crisis has been cited as the main source of all SFR Yugoslavia's economic difficulties. It seems, however, that the debt itself would not have been alarming had it not been for the unfavorable ratio and structure of imports and exports. This caused constant balance of payments difficulties and a shortage of hard currency, and in turn a shortage of intermediate materials and of consumer goods. In the end this made it even harder to service the debt.

6. The compromise allowed for economic reforms, and the northern republics managed to retain the legal and political arrangement of consensus among republics for the making of vital decisions. Unlike under the previous arrangement, however, federal law now prevailed over the laws of the republics. This was the last compromise that would be reached: shortly thereafter the federal Communist Party (the League of Communists), where major decisions had always been made, fell apart.

7. According to the Yugoslav Constitution of 1974, the political holders of sovereignty were all working people and citizens, nations, and nationalities. They exercised their sovereign rights in the republics (constitutionally defined as states) and—only if in the common interest—within the federal state (Petrič 1981). The history of constitutional changes in the postwar period does not necessarily justify this notion, since it has always been changes in the federal constitution that determined changes in the constitutions of the republics. However, such changes were always made with the consent of the representatives of all the republics.

8. On January 23, 1990, the Slovenian delegation left the Fourteenth Congress of the League of Communists of Yugoslavia. This event signified the end of unity among the alliance of national communist parties.

9. "Autonomy" is one of the most nebulous of concepts, as the late John Chipman Gray claimed (Hannum and Lillich 1980). In SFR Yugoslavia the autonomous provinces had the same substantial rights and duties as republics. They even had the same state structure. Nevertheless, constitutionally, they were not considered federal units but only "elements of federalism." In hindsight it seems that the only substantial difference was that people in the republics would have the right to self-determination, including secession, whereas people in the autonomous provinces internally lacked this right.

10. In theory, the issue was a classic conflict between the right of a state to territorial integrity and the right of its peoples to self-determination, including secession. In this case, the Albanian majority in one of the autonomous provinces (Kosovo) demanded the status of a federal unit, that is, a republic.

11. Within SFR Yugoslavia, Slovenia and Croatia were considered developed, as was also, at least formally, Serbia proper (that is, Serbia minus the two autonomous provinces). Whether Serbia proper was developed was somewhat questionable. Again at least formally, Bosnia was considered less developed, as were, less ambiguously, Montenegro and Macedonia. One of the autonomous provinces was considered developed (Vojvodina), and the other (Kosovo) less developed (the classification in both these cases corresponding to the actual situation).

12. In Slovenia a special law had been passed, and on December 23, 1990, an overwhelming majority of the voters opted for an independent state (of the 93.5 percent turnout, 88.5 percent of the votes were in favor of independence). The same law empowered the Slovenian legislature to enforce this decision in six months' time. Croatia, on the other hand, decided that its political parties were sufficiently legitimate representatives of the will of the people, and on that basis the Croatian parliament, on December 22, 1990, adopted a new constitution.

13. According to the constitution of 1974, the federal legislature was composed of a federal chamber and a chamber of republics and provinces. In the latter, for vital decisions concerning nations, consensus was required. Also, for example in the federal presidency, decisions could be reached legally by majority vote, yet in practice consensus was always sought.

14. The right to self-determination was also written in the 1974 constitution, but the somewhat ambiguous wording made room for the argument that this right had been exercised once and for all in the past by the formation of the state of Yugoslavia in 1945.

15. The Treaty on European Union had been signed in February 1992 and came into force in November 1993. Until then the legal name was "European Communities," but following common usage (and the recommendation of the European Parliament), I use here the term "European Community."

16. The term "nations" designates SFR Yugoslavia as a multinational state; the term "nationalities" meant minorities.

17. The CSCE is the organization known since January 1, 1995, as the Organization for Security and Cooperation in Europe (OSCE).

18. For example, in the State Treaty of 1955, Austria was denied the right to integrate with Germany; Cyprus in 1960 was denied the right to unite with Greece; and the Federal Republic of Germany had to exert considerable diplomatic effort to be allowed to unite with the German Democratic Republic.

19. Negotiations started on March 28, 1991, and lasted for five weeks. No agreement on a new form of the state could be reached. Slovenia and Croatia favored a confederation, Serbia and Montenegro a federation. Bosnia pushed for a compromise, a federation of sovereign states. Macedonia would opt for a federation only if all the republics would stay together; otherwise it preferred a confederation.

20. Croatia was the first of the republics to be unable to organize a referendum on the whole of its territory. In certain parts of the republic there was strong, even armed resistance on the part of the (predominantly Serb) population, supported by units of the federal army. Serbia supported the idea of determining the will of the people by way of a referendum but would not have it confined within borders of the republics. It claimed that the right of peoples to self-determination was not identical with the right of republics to self-determination.

21. Croatia was the only state that recognized Slovenia immediately on June 26, 1991. It had declared independence a day before Slovenia, but at the time, it was rather declaratory. Slovenia's actions were much more constitutive. It had not been forwarding customs duties into the federal budget for some time and had taken other measures to secure sovereign authority.

22. It seems that countries have been poorly informed by their own diplomatic agents, probably because members of the diplomatic corps rarely left the capital and neglected regional news and newspapers, especially in languages other than Serbo-Croat.

23. Data on SFR Yugoslavia's external debt vary somewhat. Estimates are that external debt in convertible and in nonconvertible currencies totaled about $18.2 billion (Mrak 1994: 31). International law in cases of succession is somewhat vague, and the differences between the wealthier north of the country and the poorer south posed additional complications.

24. The Yugoslav market consisted of about 21 million people, and its disintegration into several smaller markets was in the interest neither of importers to the country nor of investors.

25. According to some media reports, the White House might have known of the planned armed intervention by federal authorities but did not foresee the armed resistance.

26. Point 1b of the Report of the Arbitration Committee of the Conference on Yugoslavia of December 10, 1991, states "that the State is commonly defined as a community which consists of a territory and a population subject to an organized political authority; that such a state is characterized by sovereignty."

27. All other facts—for example, monetary independence and the presence of foreign troops—seem to bear less importance.

28. Point 1c of the Report of the Arbitration Committee of the Conference on Yugoslavia reads: "for the purpose of applying these criteria [for the recognition of states] the form of internal political organization and the constitutional provisions are mere facts, although it is necessary to take them into consideration in order to determine the Government's sway over the population and the territory."

29. Since the beginning of the 1970s (the Middle East mission), the "Troïka" has been an ad hoc foreign policy mechanism of the European Community, which in 1981 became formalized within European Political Cooperation (EPC). In 1992 it developed into a "permanent formation," and today it is part of the CFSP. Its composition and functions have varied considerably over time. In 1991 the Troïka consisted of the foreign ministers of the country that currently held the Presidency of the European Council, the country that preceded it, and the country that was to follow. Since the Presidency rotated among countries every six months by alphabetical order, so did the composition of the Troïka. At the time in question, it consisted of the foreign ministers of Italy, Luxembourg, and the Netherlands; after July 1, 1991, it consisted of the foreign ministers of Luxembourg, the Netherlands, and Portugal (Lucarelli 2000, 19).

30. Austria, for example, which seemed somewhat biased in favor of the secessionist republics, had been warned by the SFR Yugoslav authorities and other governments of European states to stay neutral. Its stand also became a domestic issue, since Austria has for a long time been a permanently neutral state, and in time the legal concept had become part of Austria's identity.

31. To manage the conflict more effectively, the European Community in August 1991 convened a "Peace Conference on Yugoslavia" at The Hague, which lasted for a year. After a year, when the situation on the ground had deteriorated and Russia and the United States had become involved, the conference came under the joint presidency of the United Nations and the European Community and was transferred to London. It became known as the International Conference on Former Yugoslavia.

32. In August 1991 the unsuccessful coup attempt in the Soviet Union led to the recognition of the Baltic states (Estonia, Latvia, and Lithuania) and ended the Gorbachev era.

33. Recognition in such circumstances would constitute interference in the internal affairs of a state and could be considered a violation of its territorial integrity. However, there were cases, especially in the colonial situation, where states recognized entities that did not entirely meet the required criteria. Recognition in these cases was a political sign of support for the new state, and states used political, not legal, arguments to justify such actions (Mössner 1977: 64–65). This seems to have been the case in Slovenia's recognition by Lithuania on July 30, 1991, of Georgia on August 14, 1991, of Latvia on August 29, 1991, of Estonia on September 25, 1991, and of Ukraine on December 12, 1991.

34. Opinion No. 1. Also relevant are opinions 2–3 (1991), 8–10 (1992), and 11–15 (1993). The Arbitration Commission was composed of five judges from European Community member states and presided over by the French judge Robert Badinter (hence it is often called the Badinter Commission). Its functions were, among others, to give advice on any legal question submitted to it by the chairperson of the conference. The commission continued its work for the London conference as well and changed its name accordingly, to the Arbitration Commission of the International Conference on Former Yugoslavia.

35. The escalating military conflicts in the old state clearly expose the fallacy that the international recognition of republics as independent states instigated the wars in Yugoslavia.

36. The German stance might have influenced the European Community member states to assent to the idea of a CFSP in the then-evolving Maastricht Treaty establishing the European Union.

37. Italy, which after World War II had, among other things, lost some territory to SFR Yugoslavia, always considered the latter a powerful neighbor. For its own security concerns, it was somewhat cautious toward developments in its neighborhood. On the other hand, Italy was favorably disposed toward the dissolution of the neighboring state at the appropriate time.

38. By the end of 1992 about 100 states had recognized Slovenia, and diplomatic relations have been established with most of them (Journal of International Relations 1994a).

39. Two federal units (Serbia and Montenegro) never applied for recognition, since they never recognized the dissolution of the state and claimed to continue its existence.

40. Annex II of the Joint Brioni Declaration (July 7, 1991) already provided for a CSCE monitoring mission.

41. The agreement on succession was signed by all the former Yugoslav republics in Vienna in June 2001, but as of the end of 2003 it still had not been ratified by one of them (Croatia).

42. In a manner similar to the decision of the Arbitration Committee of the Conference on Yugoslavia, the United Nations Security Council in Resolutions 777 (1992) and 821 (1993) decided among other things that FR Yugoslavia (Serbia and Montenegro) had to apply for membership to the United Nations as a successor state. This has been repeated in General Assembly Resolutions 47/1 and 47/229.

43. "Temelji strategije zunanje politike Republike Slovenije [Foundations of the Foreign Policy Strategy of the Republic of Slovenia]." *Poročevalec Skupščine RS in Skupščine SFR Jugoslavije* [Reporter of the Assembly of the Republic of Slovenia and the Assembly of SFR Yugoslavia] No. 11, March 26, 1991, pp. 11–15.

Chapter 4
Institutional Setting for the New Independent State

Neven Borak and Bistra Borak

Slovenia was an integral part of post–World War II Yugoslavia's constitutional and legal system. As a federal unit (a republic within the federation), it shared the common, relatively independent status of the other republics, as implemented by the first federal constitution in 1947 and constantly deepened in successive constitutional reforms aiming at further decentralization. Finally, in 1974 a new constitution granted the six republics and two autonomous provinces elements of confederate status while reserving for the federal government authority over defense, foreign affairs, and monetary matters.

At the outbreak of the Yugoslav political crisis in the second half of the 1980s, SFR Yugoslavia was already functioning as an asymmetric federation. Republics effectively took over federal responsibilities, thus narrowing the role of the federation and transferring several sovereign rights to the republics. Therefore it could be said that, at the outbreak of war on the territory of SFR Yugoslavia in 1991, the republics were de facto sovereign states, although they were not yet internationally recognized. Although SFR Yugoslavia was still in existence, the federal authorities had been effectively "captured" by the Republic of Serbia. They served as a shield covering Serbia's way to sovereignty and backing its plans to become the only legitimate successor state of SFR Yugoslavia.

This chapter presents a very broad outline of the overall institutional setting established in Slovenia after independence. The chapter consists of three parts. The first presents the key features of the Slovenian constitution. In the second the main outlines of the three branches of the state's institutional setting—legislative, executive, and judicial—are discussed. The third part provides an overview of selected policies of key importance for governing an independent Slovenia. Attention is given to those aspects of the institutional setting that are specific to an independent state. Already before independence, Slovenia had many of the competencies of a sovereign state. However, at the time of independence, there were several vitally important "independent state-specific" institutional gaps, the most obvious being the lack of a constitution, an independent monetary system, a foreign policy, a national security apparatus, and control of fiscal policy. These gaps to a great extent defined the new state's priorities with regard to institution building.

THE CONSTITUTION OF THE REPUBLIC OF SLOVENIA

On June 25, 1991, the Assembly of the Republic of Slovenia adopted the founding document of its independence, the Basic Constitutional Charter on the Independence and Sovereignty of the Republic of Slovenia (Uradni list Republike Slovenije 1992). This charter cited the following as established facts: the favorable outcome of the plebiscite on independence and sovereignty as of December 23, 1990; the fact that Slovenia had held the status of sovereign state within a previously existing constitutional order and had exercised a portion of its sovereign rights within SFR Yugoslavia; the fact that SFR Yugoslavia was not a state that observed the rule of law; the fact that SFR Yugoslavia's constitutional order was unable to resolve the mounting political and economic crises; the fact that the constituent republics had been unable to reach agreement on the restructuring of the federation into an alliance of sovereign states; and the fact that the Yugoslav federal constitution had ceased to be valid for Slovenia. On the basis of all these facts, the charter declared Slovenia to be an independent and sovereign state, assuming all the rights and obligations that, by the constitution of the Republic of Slovenia and the constitution of SFR Yugoslavia, had previously been transferred to the federal authorities of SFR Yugoslavia.

The new constitution of the independent state, the Constitution of the Republic of Slovenia, was accepted in December 1991 (Uradni list Republike Slovenije 1992). The constitutional system is that of a parliamentary democracy based on a social market economy. The preamble of the constitution states that the constitution is based on the charter of independence, on fundamental human rights and freedoms, on the right to national self-determination, and on the fact that Slovenia had proved, during the war for national liberation during World War II, its self-standing and had affirmed its statehood. The Republic of Slovenia is thus a democratic republic, based on the rule of law, respect for human rights, and fundamental freedoms, and is a social state. Supreme power is vested in the people of Slovenia, who exercise it directly during elections and in a manner consistent with the principle of the division of state power into three branches: legislative, executive, and judicial.

The Slovenian constitution is based on a combination of liberal, socialist, democratic, and corporative principles (Lukšič 2001). From the liberal tradition comes the principle of protecting human rights, the principle of separation of powers, the rule of law, the separation of church and state, and the protection of competition. The contribution of socialist doctrine can be traced in the definition of Slovenia as a welfare state, with the right to strike, the freedom of trade unions to exist and to organize, the rights of workers to participate in workplace decisions, and the duty of the state to provide suitable housing and a clean and healthy environment. From democratic principles comes the definition of Slovenia as a democratic republic, and the emphasis on the idea that power resides in the hands of the Slovenian people. Corporative elements are found in the definition of the

National Council, the second house of the legislature, as a corporative chamber, and in the right of citizens to associate in self-governed units. The constitution also grants special protection for two autochthonous ethnic minorities (Italians and Hungarians) as well as special rights for Roma (gypsy) communities.

To date, the Slovenian constitution has been amended on three occasions. In 1997 an article that forbade foreign ownership of land was revoked as required for membership in the European Union. The second amendment, in 2000, made changes to the Slovenian electoral system. In 2003 two changes were made. The first made it possible for foreigners to acquire full ownership rights to real estate, and the second defined the framework for transferring the exercise of part of the state's sovereign rights to international organizations and for application of their legal acts and decisions in Slovenia.

THE LEGISLATIVE BRANCH

Although the Slovenian legislature consists of two independent bodies or chambers, strictly speaking it is neither a bicameral nor a unicameral system. It could be referred to as a unicameral system with a second chamber, or, as it is often called, an incomplete bicameral system. The first chamber, the National Assembly, acts as the supreme legislative power, whereas the second, the National Council, performs solely an advisory or consultative function and has very limited powers. Both the National Assembly and the National Council engage in international activities.

The National Assembly, the representative chamber, consists of 90 deputies, who represent the citizens of Slovenia, elected in electoral units (11 deputies in each unit) organized on the principle that each deputy should represent approximately the same number of voters. Deputies are elected, by direct and secret ballot based on universal and equal suffrage, for a term of four years. The two autochthonous minorities—Italians and Hungarians—are each entitled to elect a single deputy. The president of the National Assembly is elected by a majority of the deputies' votes.

Only the National Assembly adopts laws (as well as declarations, resolutions, and national programs), passes amendments to the constitution, and makes certain other vital decisions; it ratifies international conventions and passes the budget as well. It is also empowered to proclaim a state of war or emergency and to decide upon the deployment of defense forces. Among its other powers is the power to call a referendum on its own initiative, although the assembly is afterward bound by its results. The National Assembly elects the prime minister and the other ministers of the cabinet, the president and vice president of the assembly, Constitutional Court judges, the governor of the central bank, the ombudsman, and other officials. In accordance with its control and enforcement functions, it may also establish parliamentary investigations into any matter of public importance; its powers of investigation and examination in these situations are similar to those of a court. Other mechanisms of control are the power to declare confidence or no confidence in the government and its work, and to pose questions to the government and initiate prosecutions of the president of the republic, the prime minister, or other ministers, in the Constitutional Court.

The National Assembly operates through committees, assigning legislative projects to these various working units for specific tasks. The number of working units is not fixed, although it is recognized that there are always too many for the number of deputies. Hence it is required that representatives of all political parties represented in the assembly be present in each working unit.

The National Council, founded on the principle of corporative representation, reflects the social structure of the Slovenian people. Various local, professional, economic, trade, and social interests (including employers, employees, the self-employed, local communities, and various autonomous associations and interest groups) are represented on the council. The council consists of 40 councilors, who are elected indirectly, by electoral bodies consisting of representatives of the various interest organizations, for a term of five years.

The National Council may initiate legislation by proposing the enactment of statutes and laws by the National Assembly, and it may transmit its opinion to the National Assembly on matters within its jurisdiction. Probably its greatest power in influencing the legislative process is its veto power. But thus far the veto power has not proved to be a real power. The National Assembly, as a rule, votes once more and overrules the veto.

The National Council is also entitled to require the National Assembly's reconsideration of statutes before their proclamation. Like the National Assembly, and under the same conditions, it is empowered to require a referendum. An important mechanism is its authority to call for a parliamentary investigation into matters of public importance. Because of these powers, the council exercises a special supervisory function.

The National Council works through six committees and five interest groups. It is bound and responsible to its voting base and therefore holds meetings, consultations, and lectures with the base and with professionals.

THE EXECUTIVE BRANCH

The Government

The Government of the Republic of Slovenia is the executive authority and the supreme body of civil administration. It is composed of the ministers of state and the prime minister, who are independent and accountable to the National Assembly. The prime minister is elected by secret ballot by the National Assembly on the proposal of the president of the republic. The political groups within the National Assembly may also propose candidates, if the first (president's) nominee has failed to win a majority. If, after all votes have been conducted, no candidate has received the required number of votes, the president of the republic dissolves the National Assembly and calls for new elections.

Ministers are appointed to and dismissed from office by the National Assembly on the proposal of the prime minister. Before being appointed, nominees must undergo a hearing before a constituted commission and must pledge the oath of office. The National Assembly must confirm, by simple majority, the complete list of ministers as well as individual ministers in cases of substitution.

The government determines, directs, and coordinates the implementation of state policy in accordance with the constitution, the laws, and other general acts of the National Assembly. The prime minister is accountable for the political unity, direction, and administrative program of the government. The prime minister also coordinates the work of the other ministers. Each minister is responsible for leading his or her own ministry and giving it political direction; the ministers collectively are responsible for the work of the government. In addition, secretaries appointed by the government perform expert work in individual areas of the ministries.

The term of office of all ministers, including the prime minister, expires when a new National Assembly is formed after an election. Ministers also cease to hold office when the prime minister's term runs out or he or she resigns or is dismissed. The prime minister and the other ministers continue to perform their duties until the new prime minister or other ministers are appointed.

Several mechanisms have evolved to supervise the work of the government. First, a vote of (constructive) no confidence can be called by the government or by the incumbent prime minister. This means that the National Assembly, upon the motion of at least 10 deputies and with a majority of all elected deputies voting for the no-confidence motion, must elect a new prime minister. Second, the prime minister may require a vote of confidence by the National Assembly upon a motion of confidence in the government or on a particular matter. The majority of elected deputies must express confidence or elect a new prime minister within three days; otherwise the president of the republic must dissolve the National Assembly and call for new elections. If a vote on a particular matter is lost, it is also regarded as a vote of no confidence in the government. The third mechanism of control is interpellation of an individual minister or with respect to the work of the government; it may be required by a minimum of 10 deputies of the National Assembly. Following an interpellation (which must be confirmed by the majority of elected deputies), a vote of no confidence may be carried against the government or an individual minister, in which case the National Assembly relieves the government or the minister of office. This mechanism provides a method by which the opposition can evaluate a minister's work. The final mechanism—impeachment, or the bringing of charges against any minister or the prime minister before the Constitutional Court—can be initiated by the National Assembly when it finds that the minister or ministers have committed a breach of the constitution, statutes, or other laws while performing their duties. The Constitutional Court has the authority to relieve such individuals of their position, by a two-thirds majority vote.

The President of the Republic

The constitution introduced elements of both a presidential and a pure parliamentary system, in a manner designed to ensure the fair distribution of power and lack of autocracy. The system can be described as essentially a parliamentary one, upgraded with the office of a state president.

The state president, the president of the republic, is the official representative of the state in foreign policy and foreign relations and exercises a highly integrative function. In addition, he or she is the commander-in-chief of the state's armed forces and is in charge of calling for elections of the National Assembly. Along with proposing a prime minister to form a government, the governor of the central bank, Constitutional Court judges, and others, the president is empowered to appoint and dismiss ambassadors and consuls. In addition, if the National Assembly fails to elect a prime minister, or in the case of a no-confidence vote, the president must dissolve the National Assembly. Other powers of the president include promulgating new laws; conferring state honors, decorations, and honorary titles; and deciding upon amnesties.

The president is elected by direct and secret ballot for a term of five years. If, in the first round of the election, no candidate receives an absolute majority of the vote, the two candidates with the highest number of votes enter a runoff election.

Upon being accused of violating the constitution, the president can be prosecuted by the National Assembly at the Constitutional Court, if no fewer than 30 deputies demand it. The court's decision must be made with a two-thirds majority of all the elected judges.

The Central Bank

After decades of monetary instability, inflation, and even hyperinflation, the design of an independent and accountable central bank was the main goal of institutional changes in the monetary and financial system. The Bank of Slovenia was established as a bank of issue and as the central bank of the Republic of Slovenia on June 25, 1991, when the legislature enacted the central bank act, the Law on the Bank of Slovenia (Republika Slovenija 1991). During the first several months following its establishment, the central bank continued to operate within the Yugoslav (dinar) monetary system. It took effective control of the monetary system on October 8, 1991, following the introduction of the new Slovenian currency, the tolar.

The primary objective of the Bank of Slovenia, as defined by the central bank act, is to maintain price stability (Republika Slovenija 2002). Consistent with the goal of price stability, the Bank of Slovenia is empowered to support the general economic policy of the state and to strive for financial stability in line with the principles of an open market economy and free competition.

The tasks of the Bank of Slovenia are to design and implement monetary policy, to put in place and implement appropriate monetary control mechanisms, to ensure the general liquidity of the banking system, to participate in transactions in foreign exchange and on the financial markets, to open accounts for and accept the deposits of banks and savings banks, and to regulate payments systems. In addition to these and other tasks, the Bank of Slovenia is engaged in the management of foreign exchange assets, as well as other assets entrusted to it; in acting as paying or fiscal agent for the state and as representative of the state in international financial institutions in accordance with the law; in opening and maintaining accounts for state bodies and public entities and for other participants in the money market; in accepting, when necessary, deposits from those entities; in setting up, implementing, and controlling a system of prudential rules for the safe and sound operation of banks and savings banks; in ensuring the implementation of an information system capable of performing all its functions without interruption; and in maintaining the accounts, on the basis of underlying contracts, of other financial institutions (clearing and depository corporations and stockbrokers).

The Slovenian constitution and subsequent laws grant the central bank full decision–making, operational, and financial independence and make it accountable to the National Assembly. It is the bank of banks, the lender of last resort, and the supervisor of the banking system. It is the banker to the government and conducts no business with corporate or natural persons. The bank is not allowed to take out loans abroad for its own account or for the accounts of third parties.

Decisionmaking authority in the central bank is exercised by the governor and the governing board. The competencies of the governing board are the determination of monetary policy and the adoption of measures for its implementation. The governor, who is also the chairman of the governing board, issues resolutions and other rules and regulations from the bank's operations and instructions for a uniform implementation of regulations, decrees, and measures passed by the governing board. In the implementation of its tasks as defined by law, the governor and the governing board are responsible to the National Assembly. The Bank of Slovenia is obliged to report to the National Assembly on its activities at least once every six months.

The governor of the Bank of Slovenia is nominated by the president of the republic and appointed by the National Assembly to a six-year term of office. Vice governors and other members of the governing board are also nominated by the president and appointed by the National Assembly for six-year terms. The governor, the vice governors, and the other board members may be reappointed at the end of their term.

The Bank of Slovenia is not allowed to grant overdrafts or any other type of credit facility in favor of state bodies of the Republic of Slovenia or of the European Union or its member states, or in favor of their regional or local authorities or other public entities. Further, the central bank is not allowed to issue guarantees for the liabilities of those entities or to purchase their debt instruments directly from them. These restrictions do not apply to banks, savings banks, and other financial institutions in public ownership, provided they are obliged to comply with the same conditions as other banks, savings banks, and financial institutions. Nor do they apply to the financing of Slovenia's liabilities to the International Monetary Fund, to operations related to the issue of coins not exceeding 10 percent of the value of coins in circulation, or to intraday bridging loans granted in favor of the public sector, provided that no extension to the following day is possible.

THE JUDICIARY BRANCH

On the principle of separation of powers, the Slovenian constitution defines the task of the judiciary branch as that of deciding upon the rights and obligations of every person within its jurisdiction through independent courts established by the law. Establishment of extraordinary courts or of military courts during peacetime is forbidden.

The constitution stipulates that judges shall independently exercise their duties according to the provisions of the constitution and the law. It defines the basic principles of the organization and jurisdiction of the courts, the participation of citizens in the performance of judiciary functions, the permanence of office of judges, the election of judges and the Judiciary Council, the termination and dismissal from office of a judge, and the incompatibility of the judiciary office with other offices and activities and judiciary immunity.

The judiciary system includes courts of general and specialized jurisdiction. There are four levels of courts of general jurisdiction: 44 county courts of the first instance, 11 district courts of the first instance, 4 higher courts of appellate jurisdiction (which also determine disputes of jurisdiction between the county and the district courts), and the Supreme Court, which is the highest court in the state. There are four specialized courts of the first instance, with competence in labor and social security disputes. They share a common court of appeal. Another specialized court, the Administrative Court, supervises the legality of documents and the operations of administrative bodies of the state. This court has the status of a higher court. The Supreme Court is a court of appellate jurisdiction in criminal and civil cases, in commercial lawsuits, and in labor and social security disputes; a court of second instance in cases of administrative review; and a court of third instance in almost all cases in its jurisdiction. Finally, the Constitutional Court is the highest authority of judicial power for the protection of constitutionality, legality, human rights, and fundamental freedoms.

SELECTED NATIONAL POLICIES

Public Finance

Slovenia inherited a rather sophisticated and decentralized public finance system developed over the decades within SFR Yugoslavia and under a socialist economy. Taking over sovereignty even before the formal declaration of independence meant stopping the outflow of resources to federal budgetary and extrabudgetary funds and reestablishing state control over the public finances, while building the institutions necessary to run an independent state. A smooth transition to establishing control over the fiscal and financial systems was achieved by giving a firm foundation to the restructuring and transformation of the economy, a sustainable social safety net, and the transformation of the systems themselves. During the decade-long reforms of the budget process, treasury, tax policy, and administration, internal control and external auditing measures were executed, resulting in powerful tools for the government and the legislature for the translation of policy decisions into budgetary allocations. As a result, from a system characterized by chronically late budgets and disruptive temporary financing, Slovenia advanced to a system where budgets are submitted and funds appropriated on time, with a focus on medium-term fiscal management (Republika Slovenija 1999–2002).

The government's tasks in the budget process are the following. It submits budget memoranda to the National Assembly. It proposes the central government budget, with explanations. It proposes sales of the central government's financial and physical assets for budgetary purposes for the subsequent year, with explanations. It proposes financial plans for the subsequent year with regard to the Health Insurance Institute of Slovenia and the Retirement and Disability Pension Insurance Institute of Slovenia, both in the area of compulsory insurance, public funds, and agencies founded by the central government, together with explanations. And it proposes laws required to implement the proposed central government budget.

The tax system initiated after independence was completed with the introduction of a value added tax and excise duties in 1999 (Ministry of Finance 2003). The new system, with the exception of a property tax, changes in which are currently under consideration, is similar in structure to the standard tax systems in OECD countries. The tax system consists of three main categories of taxes: direct taxes on income, direct taxes on property, and indirect taxes. The tax administration of the Republic of Slovenia is responsible for collection of all taxes, except for custom duties, excise duties, and the value added tax on imports, which are collected by the customs administration. Compulsory social security contributions are paid by both employers (currently 16.1 percent of gross wages) and employees (22.1 percent). Compulsory social security schemes (pension and disability schemes, health insurance, unemployment, and maternity leave) apply to the whole population, and contributions are paid to the Retirement and Disability Pension Insurance Institute of Slovenia, the Health Insurance Institute of Slovenia, and, for unemployment and maternity leave, directly to the central government.

Ultimate responsibility for auditing the state finances, the state budget, and monies expended for public purposes lies with the Office of the Auditor General. The office is independent in the performance of its functions.

Foreign Affairs

In the past decade Slovenia has proved itself an equal and respected member of the international community, making significant achievements in foreign affairs and in its relations with the world. Slovenia is currently in the process of becoming an equal member of the North

Atlantic Treaty Organization (NATO) and the European Union and thus being recognized as a modern democratic state (Rupel and others 2000).

The diplomatic activity of the Slovenian people began long before the establishment of an independent state with its own diplomacy. Slovenians' presence in diplomacy and international relations was constant and did not go unnoticed. It was an instrument for spreading the Slovenian people's history and knowledge around the world while also bringing home knowledge of the functioning of state institutions in other countries and direct diplomatic experience.

Within the framework of SFR Yugoslavia, Slovenia sought to make its borders more open, in order to improve the position of Slovenian minorities abroad and promote economic and technological development. Shortly after the new, democratically elected Slovenian government came to power, it became obvious that it would have to start from the beginning. The field of foreign affairs had to be formed from scratch, reconstructing the Slovene National Committee for International Cooperation into a real ministry of foreign affairs. It was clear at that moment that Slovenia had to separate from the federation, meaning that the new priority would become seeking international recognition and support. It was therefore crucial to maintain friendly relations with neighboring states, with other states sharing a similar destiny, and especially with those states playing decisive roles on the world political scene. Slovenia was recognized as an independent international subject on January 15, 1992, by the members of the European Community and other European countries. On May 22, 1992, Slovenia became the 176th member of the United Nations and soon thereafter gained the recognition of almost every country in the world. UN membership resulted in membership in a variety of other organizations, such as UNCTAD, ECE, UNDP, UNICEF, UNESCO, ILO, UNIDO, IAEA, and FAO. In 1993 Slovenia achieved full membership in the Council of Europe. Among other organizations in which Slovenia participates as a member are the Central European Initiative, the IMF, the GATT, and the WTO.

Slovenia has always been oriented toward Europe and has been striving for integration in European and Euro-Atlantic political security and economic structures, particularly the European Union and NATO. It has played an active and constructive part in various multilateral political and economic organizations (the UN, the Central European Free Trade Association, the Office on Security and Cooperation in Europe, and so on) and in ensuring better bilateral relations with partner countries and neighbors. In addition, Slovenia has always shown concern for Slovenians abroad. During the past several years of active participation in various important world multilateral organizations, Slovenia has been recognized as a reliable and constructive partner and member. Because of its activities in the United

Nations, Slovenia was accorded an unparalleled acknowledgment and confirmation in 1997 by being elected as a nonpermanent (presiding) member of the UN Security Council for the period 1998–99.

To summarize, Slovenia maintains close relations with the majority of European countries, particularly the members of the European Union, the central and southern European countries, the successor states of the former Soviet Union, and finally with the United States. Full membership in NATO is a strategic goal toward which Slovenia has been working hard ever since independence. NATO membership will help Slovenia consolidate its status as a safe and stable country, with a low level of business risk and safe conditions for investment. Membership in the European Union and NATO will also enable Slovenia to be included in technological, economic, scientific, multicultural, and information flows from the most developed countries in the world.

National Security Issues

The Resolution of the National Security Strategy of the Republic of Slovenia (Republika Slovenija 2001) defines the following national interests to be of paramount importance: preservation of national identity; preservation of the independence, territorial integrity, and sovereignty of the state; functioning of the democratic and parliamentary system; strengthening of the rule of law and the social state; consistent respect for human rights, including those of minorities; preservation and development of Slovenian minorities abroad; stable economic development; and strengthening of the competitiveness of the Slovenian economy as well as integration in the European Union and NATO. The Slovenian national security system consists of three parts, covering national defense, internal security, and protection against environmental and natural catastrophes.

Military and civil defense are the two constituent parts of the Slovenian defense system. The former represents the means by which Slovenia's safety and security are ensured; it encompasses military, technological, organizational, technical, normative, material, and other kinds of defense preparations (Vlada Republike Slovenije 2002). Its purpose lies in defending the state against external military aggression and other violent intrusions of beleaguering forces. When Slovenia becomes a NATO member, the national defense system will take on new responsibilities and tasks in the system of collective defense. The main task of the Slovenian army, apart from averting foreign aggression, is national defense. Its other tasks consist of implementing international contractual obligations, participating in peace-keeping and humanitarian missions, taking part in rescue operations with regard to environmental or other events of a catastrophic nature, and execution of any other duties as defined by law. Slovenia's civil defense system covers nonmilitary measures and activities that are complementary to military defense. The civil defense assists in ensuring the continuity of the government and the functioning of the economy in cases of emergency and, more generally, with the supply, protection, and survival of the nation. It entails measures for the functioning of governmental agencies, economic and psychological defense, and other kinds of nonmilitary resistance.

The *internal security system* (police, public prosecution, judiciary, and regulatory as well as investigating agencies) is responsible for ensuring the personal security of people, maintaining public order, guarding private property, protecting the national borders, implementing matters of an administrative nature, providing information, and executing regulatory and supervisory measures as well as those of the judiciary.

Finally, the *system of protection against environmental and natural catastrophes* comprises measures for the prevention of catastrophe; for detection, monitoring, and warning against potential dangers ensuing from them; as well as measures for putting into place preparations for protection and salvation, rescue and aid operations, and task forces for dealing with and mitigating the consequences of catastrophe.

REFERENCES

Lukšić, I. 2001. *The Political System of the Republic of Slovenia.* Ljubljana: Znanstveno in publicistično središče.

Ministry of Finance. 2003. "Taxation in Slovenia." Ljubljana.

Republika Slovenija. 1991. "Zakon o banki Slovenije" (Bank of Slovenia Act). Uradni list Republike Slovenije 1/1991.

————. 1999–2002. "Zakon o javnih financah" (Public Finance Act). Uradni list Republike Slovenije 79/1999, 124/2000, 79/2001, 30/2002.

————. 2001. "Resolucija o strategiji nacionalne varnosti Republike Slovenije" (Resolution on the Strategy of National Security of the Republic of Slovenia). Uradni list Republike Slovenije 56/2001.

————. 2002. "Zakon o Banki Slovenije" (Bank of Slovenia Act). Uradni list Republike Slovenije 58/2002.

Rupel, D., B. Trekman, M. Jazbec, and I. Golob. 2000. "Ten Years of Slovenia's Foreign Policy." Ministry of Foreign Affairs, Ljubljana (www.gov.si/mzz/eng/index.html).

Uradni list Republike Slovenije. 1992. *Constitution of the Republic of Slovenia.* Ljubljana.

Vlada Republike Slovenije. 2002. "Obrambna strategija Republike Slovenije" (Defence Strategy of the Republic of Slovenia). In B. Ferfila, ed., *Slovenia and European Union.* Ljubljana: Fakulteta za družbene vede.

Chapter 5
Transition to a National and a Market Economy: A Gradualist Approach

Jože Mencinger

The transition in Slovenia has been described as gradualist.[1] Indeed, gradualism was, in a sense, a natural heritage of previous systemic changes, embodied in the country's initial economic conditions and consistent with its political history. The transition process in Slovenia cannot be disentangled either from the legacy of the Yugoslav type of socialism or from the disintegration of SFR Yugoslavia. Although the reasons for that disintegration remain dominated by political and ethnic considerations, the prospects of transition and accession to the European Union were among the major real arguments for Slovenia's secession. The preoccupation of Slovenia's political leaders, government, and people with the disintegration of SFR Yugoslavia and the creation of a new country slowed and softened the transition measures undertaken as well.

This chapter is structured as follows. The first section describes the repeated failure of attempts at reform and transition in SFR Yugoslavia. The second deals with preindependence policy activities and systemic changes in Slovenia, which were characterized by cautious responses to uncertainty. The concluding section analyzes some of the dilemmas and controversies of Slovenia's transition.

THE FAILURE OF TRANSITION ATTEMPTS IN SFR YUGOSLAVIA

Economic reform in SFR Yugoslavia (including Slovenia) began in the 1950s, long before those in Central Europe. After 1945, four distinct "socialisms," defined in terms of the formal allocation of decision-making authority in the economy, can be distinguished in SFR Yugoslavia's history: "administrative socialism" (1945–52), "administrative market socialism" (1953–62), "market socialism" (1963–73), and "contractual socialism" (1974–88). The last of these rejected both the market as the basic mechanism of resource allocation and macroeconomic policy as the means of indirect regulation of economic activity. Instead it insisted that these be substituted by other mechanisms: social contracts, enterprise self-management agreements, and social planning. The concept was, however, never put into practice; the statutes regulating the behavior of economic units in accordance with contractual socialism either were abolished, explicitly or implicitly, soon after they appeared, or remained irrelevant to the actual functioning of the economy.

The breakdown of contractual socialism and the political vacuum after Tito's death in 1980, the rise in oil prices, and the tightening of world financial markets set in motion what, in the early 1980s, developed into a deep economic, social, and political crisis in SFR Yugoslavia. For the first time, and despite a proven ability of Yugoslav policymakers to adapt systems and redefine socialism to daily needs, SFR Yugoslavia found it impossible to move in any direction. The country reached a point at which economic reform could only increase the inconsistencies between the economic and the political system. A radical economic reform would require, above all, a separation of political and economic power, yet political considerations permitted only modest changes. The reform attempt of 1982, therefore, produced a long-lasting stalemate. The economic situation worsened and economic growth disappeared, while inflation and unemployment rose and the current account deficit grew.

In May 1988 Prime Minister Branko Mikulić introduced an economic stabilization program based on liberalization of prices, imports, and foreign exchange markets as well as on restrictive fiscal and monetary policy and wage controls. However, it soon became apparent that the government was unable to assert discipline over fiscal and monetary policy. In October the last of the anchors—the wage controls—slackened when urgent measures were added to ease social tensions. The government resigned and was succeeded by that of Ante Marković, which eagerly continued economic reform and launched a new stabilization program.

Also in 1988, while Party ideologists and economists continued to speculate about new types of socialism, the Mikulić government declared its inability to deal with the country's economic problems with the policy measures available within the existing system and established a commission to launch a new systemic reform. Contrary to expectations, the reform proposals of the Mikulić Commission were radical, although theoretically confused and inconsistent. They began with the premise that social ownership of the means of production was at the heart of the country's economic problems and urged that the so-called nonproperty concept of social property—whereby everyone and no one was the owner of property—be abandoned. The commission also proposed that the existing relationship between management and labor be replaced by the recognition that those who provide capital are entitled to management and profit sharing rights. But although the commission recognized the need for private property, its proposals formally insisted that social property remain the predominant form of ownership.

A general outline of economic reform, called "The Principles of the Economic System Reform," was adopted in October 1988, and the legal conditions necessary for the reform were created by amendments to the constitution the following month. Systemic laws regulating the economy and labor relations, adopted in 1988 and 1989, were even more radical than the proposals of the commission. The two most important laws, the Foreign Investment Act and the Enterprise Act, passed in late December 1988, formally abrogated the

existing economic system based on self-management and social property. They reestablished the company as a legal entity fully responsible for its own business operation and introduced four types of ownership: social, cooperative, mixed, and private. The Social Capital Act,
enacted in 1989, gave workers' councils the right to sell their enterprises to private owners.

In December 1989 the Marković government launched a new
"shock therapy" stabilization program. A fixed exchange rate, tight
monetary policy, and wage controls were to be its pillars. However,
overvaluation of the dinar, weakness of wage controls, and a fiscal
overhang existed from the very beginning. In the first two quarters of
1990, economic performance was satisfactory. In June, however, fatal
mistakes were added to those of the previous December, when the
government pumped money into the agricultural sector through selective credits and nearly doubled the salaries of federal employees. This
triggered a general race of wages upward. By the middle of 1990, the
program was left without any nominal anchor except for the fixed
exchange rate. Private and public sector spending increased dramatically during the summer and stayed high, while economic activity
plummeted. This made price stability unsustainable, and in the third
quarter of 1990, prices escalated. Severe monetary restrictions
imposed during the previous quarter pushed the economy into critical illiquidity, large-scale barter, and a recession without deflation.
Exports dropped, imports grew, and the trade deficit soared. October
1990 saw the beginning of a run on the banks, as depositors sought
to withdraw their deposits in foreign exchange, and foreign exchange
reserves, the last redoubt of the stabilization program, decreased
dramatically.

These attempts to change the economic system were accompanied
by political changes. The legalization of political parties in 1989 created the preconditions for free elections and parliamentary democracy
in the republics. The results of these elections in May 1990 further
divided the country; the emergence of nationalistic governments and
quickly growing animosity between Croats and Serbs accelerated the
country's disintegration. All attempts by the federal government to
halt the deterioration of the economy and the threatening political
developments were blocked by the republics. The country ceased to
exist as a functioning economic entity—taxes were not collected,
money was "printed" elsewhere (the required reserve ratios were
ignored), and special duties were assessed on "imports" from other
republics. In addition, the republics began to frame their own economic systems, which differed considerably. Under these circumstances the collapse of economic reform and of the stabilization program was unavoidable. In the autumn of 1990, SFR Yugoslavia began
to collapse as a country as well.

However, despite the failure of systemic changes and macroeconomic stabilization at the federal level, the former constituent republics retained advantages (compared with other former socialist countries) for a successful economic and social transition. Most of the preconditions for such a transition—decentralization, price liberalization, openness to the outside world, and diversification of ownership—were at least partly met before the political and ideological collapse of socialism and of the federation.

PREINDEPENDENCE POLICY ACTIVITIES AND SYSTEMIC CHANGES IN SLOVENIA: CAUTIOUS RESPONSES TO UNCERTAINTY

Slovenia proclaimed its independence on June 26, 1991. This proclamation coincided with unresolved disputes over customs duties. Yugoslav federal authorities intervened in an attempt to seize control of the borders. The federal army was, however, badly surprised by the Slovenian resistance. After a week of fighting, a cease-fire and an agreement, under which Slovenia postponed the implementation of independence for three months, were attained. On October 8, 1991, Slovenia became fully independent and introduced its own currency, the tolar.

Independence put an end to the tense and uncertain political and economic developments of the 1980s and, especially, of 1990. The economic policy of the Slovenian government elected in May 1990 was based on the supposition that both the prevailing economic policy and the existing economic system were inadequate and unstable and that the federation was facing political turmoil.[2] What remained unknown was the precise way in which SFR Yugoslavia would disintegrate and when. Consequently, the government decided to pursue an economic policy aimed at three major goals: the survival of the Slovenian economy in the period of stabilization and transformation, the construction of a market-oriented economic system, and the gradual takeover of economic policy tools from the federal government.[3] Pragmatism and gradualism were the pillars; they were the principles to be used to ascertain the socially bearable costs of transition, facilitate timely adaptation to highly uncertain political decisions, and generate suitable responses to the economic policies of the federal government.

From the very beginning, the government of Slovenia implicitly supported the federal stabilization program by imposing relatively efficient wage controls and by reducing (compared with the rest of SFR Yugoslavia) public consumption. However, increasing discrepancies in federal economic policies adversely affected the export sector and soon prompted demands for changes in the stabilization program.[4] These demands included devaluation of the dinar, reductions in federal taxes and spending, efficient control of wages, corrections to monetary policy, and redemption by the federal government of Iraqi debt to Yugoslav enterprises. Pleas for increased participation of the Slovenian government in federal economic policy were ignored. The Slovenian government therefore introduced measures to prevent bankruptcies, including postponing tax payments, issuing export subsidies, and redeeming part of the Iraqi debt from the budget of the republic by issuing government bonds. In January 1991, following the disintegration of the fiscal system (in September 1990 Serbia and Slovenia failed to transfer the proceeds of federal sales taxes to the federal budget), a trade war (in October 1990 Serbia imposed special deposits on all payments to Slovenia and Croatia), and Serbia's raid on the monetary system,[5] Slovenia demanded changes in economic policy, rejected federal proposals to enhance the power of the federal government, and, for the first time, proposed principles for the division of financial and non-financial assets and liabilities between Slovenia and the rest of SFR Yugoslavia.[6] The demands were again ignored. When the National Bank of Yugoslavia ceased to intervene on the foreign exchange market, Slovenia reacted by introducing its own quasi-foreign exchange market with a flexible exchange rate.

Systemic changes in Slovenia were made cautiously as well. Two types of statutes were introduced: the first facilitated the functioning of a normal market economy, and the second formed the basis for the transition to independence. In the first group, a system of direct taxation based on simple, transparent, uniform taxes was introduced in December 1990; the first normal budget of an independent Slovenia was presented to the National Assembly in February 1991; and a new system of indirect taxation was being prepared. The federal government did not object to these changes. In addition, statutes regulating the monetary and financial sector were prepared, and provisional notes were printed to enable swift adjustment toward what was then still an uncertain political independence. This policy of slow and pragmatic adjustment proved successful; within a year, Slovenia not only increased its relative competitiveness (as measured by unit labor costs) with the rest of SFR Yugoslavia by 35 percent, but also established sovereignty in the fiscal and foreign exchange systems and prepared the institutional arrangements for a "new" country.

Slovenia, as part of SFR Yugoslavia, shared the latter's advantages and disadvantages compared with other socialist countries in Eastern Europe, in particular a rather unique economic and political system based on ideas of social property and enterprise self-management. Owing to a decades-long series of reforms during SFR Yugoslavia's existence, many of the essentials for a successful transition were at least partly met before 1989: enterprises were autonomous, basic market

TABLE 5.1 SELECTED INDICATORS OF THE SLOVENIAN ECONOMY
          AT INDEPENDENCE
(millions of dollars unless stated otherwise)

Indicator	Value in 1991
Area (thousands of square kilometers)	20.2
Population (thousands)	1,996
Employment (thousands)	823
GDP per capita (dollars)	5,900
Foreign debt	1,955
Debt-to-exports ratio (percent)	31
Debt-to-GDP ratio (percent)	15
GDP at market prices	11,778
Exports of goods and services	5,828
Imports of goods and services	5,269
Private consumption	6,019
Public consumption	1,543
Gross domestic investment	2,238
Change in inventories	754

Source: Planning Office of the Government of Slovenia, 1991.

institutions existed, and the system of macroeconomic governance enabled the use of many standard economic policy tools. Slovenia itself had some specific advantages: it was the richest part of Eastern Europe, with an ethnically and socially homogeneous population, a diversified manufacturing sector, a predominantly private agriculture, a partly privately owned services sector, well-established economic links with Western markets, and a good geographic position. Furthermore, Slovenia was never fully integrated into SFR Yugoslavia; it was quite autonomous in terms of infrastructure, with its own access to the sea as well as its own pipelines, railways, telecommunications, and electrical grid, and its trade patterns with the rest of SFR Yugoslavia resembled its trade patterns with the rest of the world. Table 5.1 summarizes the basic statistics of the Slovenian economy at independence.

As the general public and many politicians continued to recite popular slogans about how badly Slovenia was being "exploited" within SFR Yugoslavia, the Slovenian government was already calculating what the true costs and benefits of independence would be. The liabilities included a reduction in the size of the domestic market (and thus reduced interest on the part of foreign investors, among other things), a diminished supply of raw materials from the rest of SFR Yugoslavia, the termination of foreign trade links that Slovenia had through Yugoslav enterprises (and vice versa), and a likely loss of property in other parts of SFR Yugoslavia. It was also evident that

TABLE 5.2 STRUCTURE OF SALES AND PURCHASES OF THE
         SLOVENIAN ECONOMY, 1990

(percent of total)

Item	Within Slovenia	To/from other Yugoslav republics	To/from other countries
Sales	57.3	24.8	17.9
Purchases	63.2	21.6	15.2

Source: Planning Office of the Government of Slovenia, 1991

issues such as how to apportion the Yugoslav foreign debt, the domestic debt denominated in foreign exchange, foreign exchange reserves, and the nonfinancial assets of the federation, and how to arrange the succession of the 2,500 different bilateral and multilateral agreements on export quotas, transport licenses, air controls, and so on, might take years to be resolved. The benefits, in contrast, were more potential than actual: as an independent state, Slovenia could steer clear of SFR Yugoslavia's continuing political turmoil, improve the prospects of its own transition, undertake appropriate economic policies, and ease its entry into the European Union. In the fall of 1990 the potential benefits of Slovenia's secession came to clearly exceed the economic and social costs, and independence became the "emergency exit" condition for democratic development and systemic transition.

Most of the potential benefits of independence listed above turned out to be real, whereas most of the costs proved to be overstated. It was the virtual disappearance of the Yugoslav market of 23 million people that has been by far the most important and difficult to overcome (Table 5.2).[7] Calculations intended to determine how much of Slovenia's trade with the other former Yugoslav republics would be lost because of new customs barriers and increased competition proved irrelevant; in the turmoil of war, trade simply disappeared.

Slovenia's quest for monetary independence began in June 1990 and concentrated on three issues. First, what would be the consequences of its unilateral decisions for the functioning of the financial system and for relations with other countries and international institutions? Second, what were the possibilities of a monetary system within a Yugoslav confederation (at the time still considered a viable solution)? Third, what were the prospects of eventual monetary independence? After the Serbian raid on the monetary system in December 1990, however, these questions became largely moot, and discussion shifted to the name, pattern, and most appropriate moment for the introduction of a Slovenian currency.[8]

Preparations on a functional level continued as well; before the end of 1990, for example, provisional notes were printed. At the same time, temporary solutions to handle the repercussions of a fixed, overvalued dinar and to cope with the advancing hyperinflation were explored. These efforts are best illustrated by the Law on the Introduction of a Parallel Currency, drafted on February 4, 1991. It envisaged a parallel currency pegged to the Austrian schilling; the new currency would enter circulation through foreign transactions and would float against the dinar. The concept of a parallel currency was abandoned, however, in favor of creating "certificates of import privileges," which involved a much simpler and less risky approach—in particular, it would not expose Slovenian banks to the likely wrath of the federal authorities. The system functioned in the following manner: an exporter who, for example, sold foreign exchange to a bank at the official exchange rate would get a certificate that was salable and would allow its buyer access to the foreign exchange. The fixed official exchange rate plus the price of the certificate equaled the flexible rate. At the same time, the black market in foreign exchange was abolished by its de facto legalization. Finally, the "Slovene ECU," a measure of account to which parties in economic transactions could adhere, was introduced in May 1991, less than two months before the proclamation of independence. Its value was to be determined by the average weekly price of the foreign exchange certificates on the Ljubljana stock exchange. Slovenia thus indirectly established an independent currency area with a floating exchange rate within the Yugoslav monetary system based on a fixed exchange rate.

Microeconomic restructuring has been considered, alongside privatization and macroeconomic stabilization, to be the third pillar of transition. A twofold transition, from a regional to a national economy and from a socialist to a market economy, was accompanied in Slovenia by structural changes from a manufacturing toward a services economy. Restructuring has likewise not been centrally organized; rather, it has been managed by enterprises themselves. In the first period of transition, that is, during the transformational depression, the essence of restructuring consisted of "firing and retiring," combined with ad hoc government interventions in cases of large troubled enterprises. This continued when the bottom of the recession had been passed, but at a slower pace.

POSTINDEPENDENCE TRANSITION DILEMMAS AND CONTROVERSIES

The fact that gradualism prevailed in Slovenia's macroeconomic policy and systemic restructuring does not imply that there was a general consensus. On the contrary. Gradualism implied that certain rather specific political, social, and economic features should be used in the transition. This became a disputed issue: the majority of domestic economists considered the legacy of the past an exploitable advantage; to many foreign and a minority of domestic economists, however, it would impede rather than assist the transition. The controversy over shock therapy versus gradualism also surfaced in the preparations for independence. The shock therapists, led by Slovenia's foreign advisers, proposed an overwhelming package that would encompass both the measures needed for independence and those needed for the transition. The gradualists, in contrast, suggested the separation of independence from transition.

Gradualism was consistent with soft changes occurring in the political sphere, the pillars of which can also be found in the process of pre-1989 democratization. Already in the 1970s, the League of Communists had evolved into a sort of conglomerate of the bureaucratic elite. Its members only pretended to believe in socialism and could easily adapt to any changes and to any system of values.[9] Indeed, the first steps toward transition were initiated by political "softness," which emerged in the early 1980s and became more evident in Slovenia than in other parts of SFR Yugoslavia. At the end of the 1980s, a basic consensus on democratization was achieved without any formal negotiations between the new political actors and the existing political elite. This development explains why the transition was smooth and peaceful, why the members of the former elite became an ally of the emerging civil society against the Yugoslav authorities, why no revenge was taken on them, and why they adapted so quickly and successfully to change. Also, the former economic elite (that is, the enterprise managers) retained or even strengthened their position in society. The coalition of the two elite groups ensured the exchange of economic and political support and enabled both to become the winners in the transition process.

One should not neglect, however, the impact that academic economists had on the Slovenian transition model, both indirectly, by participating in public and academic debates and often stubbornly rejecting foreign advice, and also through their direct involvement in the creation of the macroeconomic framework for the new country.[10] The reasons for the stubborn rejection of "Western" advice differed. Unlike other socialist countries, SFR Yugoslavia had been an open country; many economists had studied abroad, acquiring a solid understanding of mainstream Western economics, and were therefore not easily awed by foreign advisers. Most had participated in rather free debates on economic reform in the 1980s; thus they were not surprised by the breakup of socialism, and most shared a lack of ideology with the former political and economic elite of the country.

The privatization issue caused a major controversy within the government, divided politicians, and became the root of political instability. Two major approaches to privatization, embodied in what became known as the Korže-Mencinger-Simoneti Act and the Sachs-Peterle-Umek Act, competed for support. The former called for decentralized, gradual, and commercial privatization, which the government would only monitor; the latter advocated massive and speedy privatization administered by the government and relying on the free distribution of enterprise shares. Supporters of the decentralized approach believed that the legacy of the previous system of social property and enterprise self-management could and should be exploited in the transition, and that the adoption of the centralized method would nullify the advantages of the de facto independence of enterprises and decentralized decisionmaking that the previous economic system had securely established. They also argued that Slovenia had a relatively well-functioning economy, that unnecessary shocks should be avoided, and that enterprises themselves should be allowed the right to decide on the pace and method of privatization within the alternatives provided by law. The advocates of the centralized approach insisted that the socialist past was to be swiftly forgotten, and that speedy distributional privatization would immediately create the ownership structure of a Western economy and improve corporate governance in a way that would be fair to all citizens.

The controversy was a political rather than an economic one, the root of the matter being who should control the economy. Adoption of the decentralized approach would presumably allow control to remain in the hands of existing managers, and thus in the hands of the former political elite, whereas the centralized approach would transfer control to the government and thus to the new political elite. The controversy resulted in a stalemate. Although the National Assembly passed two out of three required drafts of the decentralized version of the privatization act, the political leaders of the coalition parties prevented the final draft from coming to a vote. After a year and a half of maneuvering and debate in the legislature and the mass media, the controversy was resolved by the adoption of a proposal that can be considered a compromise. The Ownership Transformation Act, passed in November 1992, combined the decentralization, gradualism, and diversity of privatization methods of the first approach with the free distribution of vouchers called for under the second.

Under the Ownership Transformation Act, privatization was to be achieved by a combination of several methods: restitution to former owners; debt-equity swaps; transfer of shares to the Restitution Fund, the Pension Fund, and the Development Fund; distribution of shares to employees; manager and worker buyouts; public sales of shares or of whole enterprises; and the raising of additional equity capital. The demand for enterprise capital was ensured predominantly by the distribution of voucher certificates to the population.[11]

Macroeconomic stabilization was another area of heated controversy.[12] The shock therapists, supported by the foreign advisers, proposed a package of sweeping reforms encompassing price stabilization, a fixed exchange rate, a balanced budget, and administrative restructuring of the manufacturing sector and of the banking system. All of this was to be part of the package of measures for independence, in the belief that the new country should start as a genuine market economy. The gradualists, in contrast, suggested that the issues surrounding macroeconomic independence, based on pragmatic economic policy and a floating exchange rate system for the new currency, be separated from those concerning the transition itself. It was hoped that such a policy would result in smaller output losses and lower unemployment by allowing some inflation.

The gradualists prevailed. The government document "P2" of April 15, 1991, dealing with the macroeconomic issues of independence, was also the key date in the creation of the new currency. It contemplated most of the provisions that were later applied: a rapid (within three to five days) conversion of dinars to a new currency, a 1:1 conversion rate, and a floating exchange rate.[13] Different solutions were proposed in the documents that followed during the summer of 1991.[14] These included a 10:1 rate for the conversion of dinars to the new currency and called for its pegging. The proposed changes emanated from the group led by Jeffrey Sachs, who had, in a document called "A Program for Economic Sovereignty and Restructuring of Slovenia" issued on March 21, 1991, proposed pegging to the German mark, the ECU, or a basket of currencies, to ensure a nominal anchor for a shock therapy stabilization program.[15]

Establishing a monetary system required choosing between a fixed and a floating exchange rate. Although economic theory does not provide a definitive answer to this question, the majority of experts either supported the view that a fixed exchange rate system suited the countries in transition better (Meltzer 1992) or proposed a crawling peg as an option (Bomhoff 1992). Slovenia, however, opted for floating after an abrupt drop in foreign exchange reserves in October 1990 revealed that a fixed exchange rate could not be defended. The debate over the proper exchange rate system nevertheless continued, encompassing the major theoretical quandaries familiar from the debate over optimum currency areas.

Two issues—the relationship between the real exchange rate and macroeconomic stability, and the anchoring role of the nominal exchange rate—divided participants. The theoretical pros and cons were used to defend different positions, and much less attention was addressed to actual arrangements in other countries. Also, the debate over pegging versus floating reflected the two opposite general approaches to the transition in Slovenia: the radical and the gradualist. The former suggested a formal "shock therapy" stabilization program encompassing a fixed exchange rate as an anchor, a monetary policy that would support it, a balanced budget, foreign financial assistance, and restructuring of manufacturing and banking by the government. The latter suggested that economic policy should remain founded on the gradual construction of market institutions, with no formal stabilization program and only an indirect role for the government in restructuring the economy. A firm but flexible wage policy, strong restrictions on government spending (enhanced by the fiscal deficit, if required), a monetary policy enabling tolerable liquidity, a flexible exchange rate, reliance on foreign equity capital, and concessions for investments in infrastructure were the preferred economic policy instruments under this approach.

The linkage between the monetary and exchange rate systems was ultimately defined by the Foreign Exchange System Act and the Bank of Slovenia Act. These provided for the independence of the monetary authorities and treated the supply of money as an exogenous variable to be determined by the central bank. The exchange rate would consequently be endogenous. Slovenia thus established a system of managed floating of the type exercised mainly by developed market economies. Subsequent experience proved that floating was the right solution. Fixing the new currency unit to the currency unit of a country with low inflation would have ensured financial discipline only if the exchange rate "never" changed. This would have turned out to be illusory, because the basic conditions for exchange rate stability were not met.

In short, gradualism prevailed. Indeed, the reality since independence has been an even more gradual transition than the most enthusiastic gradualists had suggested, both in terms of economic policy and in terms of changes in the economic system.

REFERENCES

Bomhoff, E. J. 1992. "Monetary Reform in Eastern Europe." *European Economic Review* 36(April): 454–58.

Hanke, S. H., and K. Schuler. 1991. "Monetary Reform and the Development of a Yugoslav Market Economy." New Series 3. Center for Research Into Communist Economies. London.

Meltzer, A. H. 1992. "Prices and Wages in Transition to a Market Economy." Paper presented at the 19th Karl Brunner Symposium on Liberty, Analysis, and Ideology, Interlaken, Switzerland, June 8–12.

Mencinger, J. 1991. "From Socialism to Capitalism and from Dependence to Independence (Double Transition of Slovenia)." *Est-Ovest* 22 (December): 57–92.

————. 1994. "The Birth and the Childhood of a Currency: The Experience of Slovenia." In J. Gacs, ed., *International Trade and Restructuring in Eastern Europe*. Vienna: International Institute for Applied Systems Analysis.

NOTES

1. The dichotomization of transition patterns into "shock therapy" and "gradualist" models is inadequate for the classification of transition economies for two reasons. First, the observed patterns of transition were rather chaotic mixtures of systemic changes and changes in economic policies, some of which could be considered elements of a gradualist approach whereas others could be viewed as elements of shock therapy. Second, what was a shock for one country, for example, price and trade liberalization, was an element of a gradualist approach or even of initial conditions in another. What really mattered for the choice of tools and for the outcomes of transition were initial conditions.

2. For more on Slovenia's economic policy after the May 1990 elections, see Mencinger (1991, 1994).

3. The greater part of the systemic framework for an efficient market economy was created in 1990 and 1991, that is, before political independence. A simple, transparent, and nondiscretionary system of direct taxes was introduced by the Income Tax Act and the Profit Tax Act. The statutes regulating the monetary and financial system, such as the Bank of Slovenia Act, the Banks and Saving Institutions Act, the Foreign Exchange Transactions Act, and the Rehabilitation of the Banks and Savings Institutions Act, were passed, together with the Declaration of Independence, in June 1991. After independence, the missing legal rules needed to guide economic behavior (company law), ensure a predictable bargaining framework (codes regulating business transactions), enforce rules, and resolve disputes (bankruptcy and competition) were added.

4. These demands were transmitted in a "Memorandum on Economic Policy in the Rest of 1990," sent to the federal government in August 1990.

5. The National Bank of Serbia, a branch of National Bank of Yugoslavia, allowed the banks in Serbia to ignore the required reserves ratio.

6. These proposals were communicated in a "Memorandum of the Executive Council of the Assembly of the Republic of Slovenia on its Standpoints about the Reorganization of Economic Relations in Yugoslavia."

7. In 1990 the sales of Slovenian enterprises to the rest of SFR Yugoslavia exceeded by almost 40 percent their exports to the rest of the world. Six years later, in 1996, trade with the successor countries of SFR Yugoslavia amounted to 11.8 percent of Slovenia's total foreign trade (16.7 percent of exports and only 7.5 percent of imports).

8. At the beginning of 1991, similar ideas appeared in other Yugoslav republics, notably Croatia, which at that time favored a monetary union among itself, Bosnia and Herzegovina, and Slovenia. The idea of establishing a Yugoslav currency board also circulated (see Hanke and Schuler 1991).

9. The liberalism of the Slovenian League of Communists in the 1980s made it possible for Slovenia to become a forerunner in political changes in SFR Yugoslavia. The stand of the Party on the issue of Kosovo, and the fact that its delegates left the Yugoslav League of Communists' Congress in 1989 and withdrew from it in 1990, characterize its behavior.

10. The creation of the monetary system remains so far an unchallenged success of the academic economists who commanded the first Board of Governors of the Bank of Slovenia, and who successfully rejected foreign advice and applied their own concepts. In addition, several academic economists have become ministers and state secretaries and taken other high positions in the new Slovenian government. Professor Marko Kranjec, the first finance minister of independent Slovenia, for example, introduced the new income tax system, created the first budget of an independent Slovenia even before its independence, and had an indispensable role in the creation of a monetary system. Another academic economist, Velimir Bole, has been for a decade the force behind practically all decisions involving monetary and fiscal policies.

11. Three laws added considerably to the scope of privatization. The Housing Act enabled the privatization of approximately 100,000 apartments; the Denationalization Act provided for the restitution of property nationalized under the Communist regime; the Cooperatives Act assigned 40 percent of shares in certain food processing enterprises to farmers' cooperatives.

12. The assessment of initial conditions by Western advisers and financial institutions was false from the very beginning. Although the so-called monetary overhang that had existed in the socialist countries disappeared practically overnight through hyperinflation, the basic tools for macroeconomic stabilization policies nevertheless evolved from the assumption that aggregate demand exceeded aggregate supply. Thus the advice of foreign advisers implied that the gap should be reduced by increasing supply and decreasing demand through restrictive fiscal and monetary policies and rapid liberalization of foreign trade and prices, while anchoring the exchange rate, wages, and government spending. Such policies could only augment János Kornai's "transformational depression" and push more domestically produced goods than necessary into the category of Leszek Balcerowicz's "pure socialist production goods," thus destroying domestic manufacturing and transforming many countries, notably Russia, into providers of raw materials, and most of the other countries of the former Soviet Union, lacking raw materials, into a hopeless situation.

13. The document also provided that the possibility of future pegging would depend upon the existence of foreign exchange reserves and settlement of Yugoslav foreign and domestic debt issues.

14. The author of this chapter, who was also the co-author of the document "P2," which was one of 17 documents dealing with independence issues, resigned the post of deputy prime minister in May 1991.

15. The Sachs group changed its views in favor of unrestricted floating in a memorandum on October 8, 1991, after the floating exchange rate system had already been introduced.

Chapter 6
Establishing Monetary Sovereignty

Andrej Rant

The process of establishing monetary sovereignty in the newly independent Republic of Slovenia cannot be understood without an understanding of the 1974 constitutional system of SFR Yugoslavia, its underlying economic components, and the position of the National Bank of Yugoslavia (NBY) in the central banking system of SFR Yugoslavia and within the constitutional system. This chapter describes the central banking system of the country after 1974 and the relevant NBY accountancy rules within the system of national banks of the republics and autonomous provinces. The chapter concludes by discussing some basic issues relevant to establishing Slovenian monetary sovereignty.

CENTRAL BANKING SYSTEM IN SFR YUGOSLAVIA AND ITS FUNCTIONING

The 1974 Yugoslav federal constitution brought significant changes in the organization of the central banking system. This new constitution established SFR Yugoslavia as a community of six republican states and two autonomous provinces, both within Serbia. The republics and provinces represented the constitutional elements of the federation, with equal rights in political and economic decisionmaking. These changes followed the internal political redistribution of power among the republics, under which the federative state was deprived of any centralized authority except that to which all constitutional elements specifically agreed. The 1974 constitution established such agreement for defense policy, foreign policy, trade policy, foreign exchange policy, foreign credit policy, fiscal policy, and monetary policy. This approach was also reflected in the organization of the Yugoslav federal assembly. It was composed of two chambers. The chamber of republics and autonomous provinces was the first chamber, in which each individual republic and province held veto power, established within the Yugoslav federal assembly to set commonly those policies under centralized authority. The second chamber, the federal chamber, dealt with other common federal issues relating to citizens, making decisions on the basis of majority vote.

As a consequence of these political arrangements, the central banking system was also reorganized. The central banks of the republics and the autonomous provinces (here called national banks) were established by laws for that purpose in each of them. Each of these banks was made responsible to its republican or provincial assembly. Their governors constituted the governing body of the National Bank of Yugoslavia (the board of governors) and of the system of republican and provincial national banks, which under federal law was empowered to decide a single monetary policy for the federation. The governors of the republican and provincial national banks each held veto power. Thus monetary measures undertaken by the NBY had to be accepted unanimously. Their implementation was a matter for the republican and provincial national banks.[1] This decentralized implementation of a single monetary policy respected the independence of the republican and provincial national banks in technical terms as well. The NBY was not in a position to technically impede money issuance by the republican and provincial national banks. This fact proved very important at the end of 1990, when the national bank of Serbia made illegal raids on the monetary system. The governors were granted veto power for a reason. The central bank in a one-party political system was the key institution to regulate and to manipulate the availability of funds disposable for financing the real sector.

Monetary policy in SFR Yugoslavia was not conceived as independent from the concrete financing needs of enterprises. Rather, it was designed to support two main economic sectors: agriculture and exports. The decisions of the NBY board therefore affected the basic ability of enterprises in those two sectors to operate. Commercial banks transmitted financial support by refinancing their real sector trade-based credit claims at the system of national banks. In the administratively governed system, commercial banks were conceived of as intermediaries that had to serve the needs of enterprises. The risks in their business were not under their own control. They were particularly exposed to currency risk as a consequence of raising funds in foreign currency and re-lending them at low interest rates in domestic currency. They were not allowed to lend in foreign currency and were restricted in their ability to keep foreign exchange reserves abroad. The investment activities of enterprises were largely based on foreign credits and domestic foreign currency savings, which were allowed in the domestic banking system. The commercial banks followed the planned priorities agreed to at the federal level for every 5-year period. According to a basic principle of the system, the end users of funds were liable for debt repayments. But the absorption capacity of enterprises in the prioritized sectors was low. SFR Yugoslavia was a net importer of capital, its investment needs exceeding the domestic saving available. But because of distorted relative prices, the efficiency of investment was low. Enterprises were not able to assume the real costs of their financing. To extend their absorption limits, schemes for subsidizing foreign currency-denominated debt were built into the system.

In 1977 a complicated system for "redepositing" foreign currency domestic savings by commercial banks with the NBY was introduced, and this system continued until 1988. With the redepositing scheme, exchange rate risk was formally removed from the banking system and transferred to the NBY and later to the federal budget. The ultimate beneficiaries of the redepositing system were the local enterprises that received low-cost investment loans in domestic currency. As of the end of 1990, outstanding NBY debt for the redepositing scheme amounted to $12.2 billion. On the asset side, the counterpart of this debt was a claim on the federation. The ultimate creditors on this debt to the banking system were the individual savers who had deposited hard currency in the banks.

In parallel with the redepositing scheme, foreign credits were also subsidized. A number of laws were adopted between 1983 and 1990 exposing, on the one hand, the NBY as a guarantor for new and old foreign debt and, on the other hand, subsidizing enterprises in priority sectors (predominantly in the less developed republics and regions) through debt repayments at historical exchange rates.

The establishment of the republican and provincial national banks coincided with the beginning of the period in which the external debt and the foreign currency-denominated domestic debt of SFR Yugoslavia began to accumulate. On the external account with the convertible currency area, this development provoked a growing current account deficit. Under the debt-subsidizing schemes, the NBY became the core federal institution to assume and finance the internal consequences of this deficit. Soon the veto power of the republican and provincial governors within the board became an obstacle to the reallocation of resources. As the debt problems grew, this veto power was abolished and replaced by two-thirds-majority voting. Moreover, the number of issues on which a two-thirds majority was required constantly diminished under systemic legal changes made up to 1990. All of these factors brought the NBY to the brink of insolvency. The result was hyperinflation and, after unsuccessful attempts at reform at the end of the 1980s, the dissolution of the state.

Debt repayment in such a system was highly dependent on the accessibility of federal sources rather than on the efforts of individual enterprises. Despite a formal request in the system that final beneficiaries should bear the debt burden, the enterprises receiving the funds were unable to repay their debts. Their position was aggravated following the oil crisis at the end of the 1970s. Bankruptcies were almost unknown in practice. Instead, in an attempt to resolve the growing threat of insolvency in the corporate and banking sectors in the last few years of the federation, the debt service due from the final beneficiaries of funds was increasingly socialized.[2] This socializing of debt repayments eroded the basic principle in the system according to which the end users of funds were responsible for repaying their debts. The republics, acting in the chamber of republics and autonomous provinces within the federal assembly, had to agree to any change to this principle. However, in case of disagreement, the Yugoslav presidency was authorized to decide on controversial issues and adopt interim laws with a validity of 1 year. The debtors, located mostly in the less developed republics and regions, were interested in having their debt burdens alleviated, whereas the more developed republics (Slovenia and Croatia) resisted. Their resistance was therefore circumvented by the adoption of interim laws by the Yugoslav presidency.

In addition, the NBY itself contributed to increased credit risk to its balance sheet with the placement of its foreign exchange reserves. A substantial part of these reserves was deposited in commercial banks with mixed capital abroad and used as collateral for the extension of credit by those banks to Yugoslav enterprises, mostly in Serbia. Such financing was a source of inflated foreign exchange reserves (foreign exchange from those credits was sold to the NBY and deposited again, mostly with the same banks), which gave the impression that the country enjoyed good foreign exchange liquidity, although the situation was in fact the opposite. Another element of risk was a long history of special bilateral trade and payment arrangements with certain countries (most importantly, the former Soviet Union), which involved the NBY in settling export claims from these arrangements. This type of trade accumulated claims on the asset side of the NBY's balance sheet in the amount of approximately $1.9 billion at the end of the 1980s. With the passage of time, these unfavorable developments culminated in the concentration of these various risks and in unsustainable pressures on the NBY's balance sheet. Only in 1990 was the system of payments in bilateral trade changed. At that time the obligation of the NBY to immediately pay exporters to nonconvertible areas was revoked and replaced with an arrangement linking export proceeds to import payments. In other words, exporters had to wait for import payments to be compensated for their trade. As those receipts were not well synchronized with the flow of exports, substantial arrears built up on the balance sheet of the NBY.[3]

At the end of 1990 the gap between the need for and the availability of financing triggered illegal raids by Serbia on the monetary system. Because the technical organization of money issuance in the monetary system was decentralized, the NBY could be circumvented. The national banks of Serbia and Vojvodina emitted a total of 13.3 billion dinars (equivalent to nearly $1.3 billion). The money thus emitted was used to finance pension payments in Serbia (5 billion dinars, or $472 million) and the liquidity needs of banks. This action by the two national banks was not simply a breach of the existing rules in the monetary system. It constituted a setting of new rules, a takeover of the federal monetary function by one republic, and an act of complete monetary independence within a still-functioning common system. It was based on a decision made by the assembly of the Republic of Serbia and published in the secret Serbian official gazette.[4]

ACCOUNTANCY IN THE CENTRAL BANKING SYSTEM OF
SFR YUGOSLAVIA

The hidden budget financing relationship between the NBY and the federal state, on the one hand, and the technical functioning of the central banking system, with the republican and provincial national banks, on the other, required a special system of accountancy. It had to reflect both the activities of the NBY at the federal level and those related to the system of republican national banks. The formal separation of financial statements became very important during Slovenia's process of gaining monetary independence. These statements therefore need to be explained in more detail.

The financial statements of the NBY consisted of two balance sheets. The first broadly represented the results of the special bilateral trade and payments arrangements, the intermediation of the NBY in foreign credits, as well as vault cash transactions in domestic and foreign currencies. The second represented foreign exchange reserves, the results of subsidy schemes for foreign and domestic foreign currency debt, and the financial relationship with the federal budget on the basis of those transactions. Both statements were subject to confirmation by the federal Yugoslav assembly.[5]

It would be too cumbersome and beyond the scope of this chapter to describe all the details necessary to understand the complicated arrangements that affected the individual elements of the financial statements of the NBY. A simplified approach is therefore used here instead. The statements for 1990, which the NBY board of governors examined in April 1991 (when the dissolution of SFR Yugoslavia was already foreseeable), are summarized in Table 6.1.

It is impossible to extract directly from these two balance sheets the regular monetary activities of the NBY in a strict sense. These activities were conducted via the accounts of the Social Accounting Service (SAS), organized in each republic and autonomous region as an independent payments system institution. Federal institutions such as the NBY were linked to the federal SAS, and, through the system of accounts, the republican and the federal SASs were linked together in a payments system network, which functioned independently from the NBY. The NBY had no direct control over the monetary activities executed in the republican central banks. However, it evidenced those activities through changes in its own account with the federal SAS. The principal recorded activity under the direct control of the NBY was the distribution of banknotes and coins. This is reported as a major item of monetary activity by the NBY in the first balance sheet in Table 6.1. On the assets side, the item for vault cash in domestic currency shows the claim corresponding to banknotes delivered to the republican national banks. On the liabilities side, the item "Banknotes

TABLE 6.1 BALANCE SHEET OF THE NATIONAL BANK OF
  YUGOSLAVIA, DECEMBER 31, 1990

Item	Billions of dollars[a]	Percent of total
First balance sheet		
Assets	29.4	100.0
Bilateral trade arrangements	2.1	7.1
Vault cash:	17.6	59.9
In foreign currency	0.0	0.0
In domestic currency	17.6	59.9
Intermediation of foreign credits	2.1	7.1
Other	7.6	25.9
Liabilities	29.4	100.0
Bilateral trade arrangements	0.6	2.0
Accounts of republican banks and other entities	2.9	9.9
Of which: required reserves	0.8	2.7
Banknotes and money issued	24.3	82.7
Of which: banknotes in circulation	5.0	17.2
Other	1.6	5.4
Second balance sheet		
Assets	17.9	100.0
Foreign currency reserves (including gold)	5.7	31.8
Claims on federation	12.2	68.2
Other	0.0	0.0
Liabilities	17.9	100.0
Foreign credits	4.0	22.3
"Redeposited" foreign currency savings	12.2	68.2
Other	1.7	9.5

a. At the time of the statement, $1 was equivalent to 10.6 dinars.
Source: National Bank of Yugoslavia (1991b).

and money issued" includes the liability of the NBY to the federal SAS for printed banknotes and coins as well as the balance of the NBY's account with the federal SAS, which evidenced monetary activities related to the accounts of the republican national banks with their republican SASs. Printed banknotes are by far the largest subitem within this item. The second balance sheet is dominated by the redepositing scheme and by the NBY's intermediation of foreign credits. It shows the size of the public debt arising from the redepositing scheme in the item "Claims on federation."

Only some of the elements in the NBY's statements of accounts represented monetary activities as usually presented in the balance sheet

TABLE 6.2 BALANCE SHEET OF THE NATIONAL BANK OF
YUGOSLAVIA AND THE SYSTEM OF NATIONAL BANKS,
DECEMBER 31, 1990

Item	Billions of dollars[a]	Percent of total
Assets	27.4	100.0
Foreign currency reserves		
(including gold)	6.4	23.4
Bilateral claims	2.3	8.4
Claims on federation	12.7	46.4
Monetary operations:	3.3	12.0
Selective credits	1.0	
Special-purpose credits	0.5	
Liquidity credits	1.8	
Other	2.8	10.2
Liabilities	27.4	100.0
"Redeposited" foreign currency		
savings	12.6	46.0
Foreign credits	4.0	14.6
Monetary operations:	6.6	24.1
Banknotes in circulation	5.0	
Required reserves	0.8	
NBY bills	0.5	
Bank accounts and banknotes	0.4	
Other	4.2	15.3

a. At the time of the statement, $1 was equivalent to 10.6 dinars.

Source: National Bank of Yugoslavia (1990).

of a central bank. An important part of such activities, executed by the national banks of the republics and autonomous provinces, does not appear in those statements. Because there was no formal connection between the NBY's statement of accounts and those of the republican national banks, the monetary survey for SFR Yugoslavia could only be established statistically, by joining together single elements from nine different statements without a formal consolidation of accounts. Only this statistically generated balance sheet of the system of national banks, published in the NBY's 1990 annual report (National Bank of Yugoslavia 1990) and summarized in Table 6.2, therefore gives a clear picture of monetary activities, abstracting from the "intrasystem" activities between the NBY and the republican national banks.[6]

The assets side in this statistically consolidated balance sheet shows that monetary financing was channeled predominantly to the federal state and on foreign exchange accounts. Only 12 percent of assets was used in other monetary operations. Within that 12 percent, 55 percent was used for liquidity purposes in 1990 connected with the outflow of savings and reflecting the deterioration of the Yugoslav financial system during that year. Fifteen percent of those operations was financed by foreign creditors and 64 percent by citizens (18 percent directly, by holdings of banknotes and coins, and 46 percent indirectly, through the redepositing system). Holdings of bank liquidity, obligatory reserve requirements, and obligatory investment in NBY bills (the last two were also used as a redistribution tool in monetary activities) amounted only to 6.2 percent of financing. External and domestic foreign exchange-denominated debt predominantly determined the NBY's monetary functioning. The main component of its activities on the assets side became the financing of a growing, but hidden, federal fiscal deficit. During the last quarter of 1990 and the first half of 1991, claims on the federation turned into nonperforming assets. Huge net withdrawals of foreign currency savings and reduced inflow of revenue to the federal budget made it impossible for the federal state to honor its debt.[7]

TOWARD MONETARY SOVEREIGNTY IN SLOVENIA

The structure of the financial statements of the NBY clearly exposes the economic and financial reasons that led to the dissolution of SFR Yugoslavia and paved the way toward the decisions of the different republics to opt for independence.[8] But to establish the elements relevant for monetary sovereignty of the states that emerged after June 1991, the incorporated NBY's activities have to be considered under three different aspects:

- Activities on the NBY's own behalf, without the participation of the republican and provincial national banks (that is, management of foreign exchange reserves, bilateral claims management, foreign credit arrangements and intermediation of foreign credits, the relationship with the federal budget and with the accounts of federal institutions, as well as some other activities) or with their participation as the NBY's agents (the redepositing system).
- The NBY's monetary activities involving the banking system (credits, required reserves, NBY bills) and the general public (banknotes in circulation), and its connection with the payment network of federal and republican SASs.
- The NBY's internal supply of banknotes and coins to the system of national banks for the disposal of the commercial bank's needs.[9]

These different aspects of the NBY's activities as reported in its financial statements are relevant to understanding the process of establishing monetary sovereignty in the new states that emerged from SFR Yugoslavia and the parallel approach to the treatment of related succession issues. The monetary activities of the NBY were relevant for the new states' transition to monetary sovereignty. Yet matters such as redepositing and foreign debt issues, bilateral claims, foreign exchange reserves, and the transactions of the NBY with federal institutions had no direct relationship with the balance sheet of the Bank of Slovenia. As one consequence, monetary independence was established without any foreign exchange reserves in the hands of the Bank of Slovenia. The only foreign exchange reserves available at that moment were those held by other commercial banks in Slovenia, which amounted to approximately $170 million. From that perspective, monetary sovereignty was indeed a risky exercise.

Moreover, the dissolution of SFR Yugoslavia was an extended process rather than a once-and-for-all event. It began at the end of 1990, continued throughout 1991, and ended in the first half of 1992. It was not peaceful, nor was it guided by common agreement.[10] From the beginning the position of Serbia was in complete conflict with that of the other republics.[11] A clear legal separation from the former federation occurred on June 26, 1991, when Slovenia proclaimed its independence (as did Croatia at the same time). But Slovenia did not introduce its own currency at that time. This was formally done only on October 8, 1991, after the Brioni moratorium expired.[12]

During the moratorium, the new Bank of Slovenia used the dinar as currency and followed the rules for monetary policy determined by the remainder of the board of governors of the former NBY.[13] But that was not an easy task. On June 27, 1991, the Serbian-dominated remainder of the NBY board of governors accepted a decree on the protection of the interests of SFR Yugoslavia in the functioning of the monetary and foreign exchange system and policy (National Bank of Yugoslavia 1991a). The decree excluded banks from Slovenia and Croatia from the NBY's monetary supply, from the supply of banknotes and coins, from access to the foreign exchange market, and from access to foreign credits. In these circumstances the Bank of Slovenia had to reactivate its account with the republican SAS to satisfy the liquidity needs of banks, and to use dinar banknotes and coins already withdrawn from circulation. Central banks abroad and the international financial institutions were notified about the conditions under which the banking system in Slovenia had to function during the Brioni moratorium. Despite the recommendations of the federal government, the NBY decree was never revoked during this period, and meanwhile the Bank of Slovenia was exposed to several federal controls, especially with regard to vault cash transactions. The expulsion of Slovenia and Croatia from the monetary system was a clear breach of the Brioni agreement. It reflected the Serbian view that federal institutions could function without their constitutional elements. Under the Badinter opinions, issued during the International Conference on Former Yugoslavia, this view proved to be wrong. But it took 10 years and a change of political regime for Serbia to recognize and accept that fact.

Meanwhile the existing stock of banknotes and coins became one of the major issues of monetary sovereignty in discussions between the former NBY and the Bank of Slovenia. The amount of dinar banknotes and coins in circulation in the territory of Slovenia was unknown at the moment of independence on June 26, 1991. Only on October 8, 1991—the date of the actual changeover—did the amount of converted dinar banknotes show that the previous estimates of 15 billion to 20 billion dinars were overstated: the actual figure turned out to be 8.6 billion. Dinar banknotes and coins in the hands of the general public constituted a claim on the NBY. With the changeover, this claim passed on to the Bank of Slovenia. It would have to be taken into account in the distribution of the NBY's assets and liabilities as part of the succession. But the Serbian-dominated NBY did not acknowledge the dissolution of federal institutions. Presuming their continued existence, it converted its internal claims on the system of republican national banks into an external claim on the new central banks. After October 8, 1991, it demanded from the Bank of Slovenia that 27.3 billion dinars in banknotes and coins be returned to the NBY or the equivalent (about $1.25 billion) paid in hard currency. Only in 2001, with the Agreement on Succession Issues in Vienna, was this claim abandoned.[14] Other monetary activities in Slovenia showed equal amounts of claims (bank accounts, required reserves, NBY bills) on and liabilities (liquidity and other credits) to the NBY. Their net outcome therefore was neutral.

On October 8, 1991, the Brioni moratorium expired, and the actual changeover took place, but with one complication. On the day of independence, Slovenia did not yet have any Slovenian currency banknotes. The new monetary unit had not yet been determined. Substitute coupons in different denominations, with no currency name on them, were prepared in secret instead of real banknotes and coins. Anonymous coupons were needed to avoid accusations of a breach of federal laws on the monetary unit during the preparation period before June 26. In case their existence was discovered, they would be presented as a type of republican security, which the Slovenian state was authorized to issue. The issuer of the coupons was indeed the Slovenian state, and they were signed by the Slovenian finance minister (for more on that subject, see Majce 2001). No coins were minted at that time. On October 7, 1991, therefore, the Slovenian legislature adopted two laws: the Monetary Unit Act and the Implementation of Monetary Unit Act. The first established the tolar as the new Slovenian currency, and the second called for the prepared coupons to be used as an interim substitute for the tolar banknotes and coins still to be issued. At the same time, a public bid was opened for the design of new currency banknotes and coins. These replaced the coupons on the first anniversary of the tolar.

On the basis of these two laws, the Bank of Slovenia accepted the by-laws necessary for the changeover. The changeover took place over 4 days, from October 8 to October 11, 1991. As the amount of dinar banknotes and coins in circulation within the territory of Slovenia was not known, special rules were applied to avoid any shortage of new currency banknotes or speculation using dinar banknotes from the territories of other republics. A 20,000-dinar limit was set for direct cash conversion; amounts between 20,000 and 50,000 dinars could be converted and deposited in bank and savings accounts without checking the origin of the banknotes; amounts over 50,000 dinars could be converted only after detailed checking of the banknotes' origin. The identity of the bearer was also checked in all cases. A 1:1 exchange rate was applied during the period of the changeover. From then until October 31, it was still possible to exchange dinars for tolars, but at a less favorable rate (1:0.875) and under additional limitations in value, to prevent speculative inflows from other parts of SFR Yugoslavia.

Any dinar balances on bank accounts were automatically transformed into tolars at a rate of 1:1 on October 8, 1991. A minor float from other republics in the payments system on that date was channeled to special accounts opened for each individual republic and was kept in dinars.

Immediately after the conversion, the NBY requested that foreign banks block the accounts of Slovenian banks abroad, and, as mentioned previously, it issued a decree requesting the restitution of 27.3 billion in dinar banknotes (or payment of $1.25 billion equivalent in hard currency) to the Bank of Slovenia (Official Gazette of SFRY 1991a, 1991b). Foreign banks did not honor the request, however. The monetary sovereignty of Slovenia was internationally acknowledged and recognized.

CONCLUSIONS

The process of monetary sovereignty of the Republic of Slovenia came as a consequence of a long period of systemic economic mismanagement, which in the end led the SFR Yugoslavia to the edge of bankruptcy. The degradation of the Yugoslav economy, attributable to systemic deficiencies that could not be repaired under the then-existing political system, ended with the disintegration of the state. The 1974 constitutional system with its decentralized organization of the central banking system facilitated the process of establishing monetary sovereignty and enabled Slovenia to more smoothly separate daily monetary and financial operations from succession-related issues, as well as to convince the international financial community of the necessity of the steps it was taking.

REFERENCES

Bank of Slovenia. 1991. *Annual Report 1991*. Ljubljana.

Majce, J. 2001. "Slovenian Money." Bank of Slovenia, Ljubljana. Processed.

National Bank of Yugoslavia. 1990. *NBY Annual Report 1990*. Belgrade.

————. 1991a. "Decree on Protection of Interest of SFRY in Domains Relating to the Functioning of the Single Yugoslav Monetary and Foreign Exchange System." Belgrade (June 27).

————. 1991b. *NBY Annual Statement of Accounts for 1990*. Belgrade.

Official Gazette of SFRY. 1991a. "Decree on Liability of Bank of Slovenia for Banknotes and Coins Issued by NBY." *Official Gazette of SFRY* 74/91 (October 16).

————. 1991b. "Decree on Restriction of Activities Abroad of the Banks from the Territory of Republic of Slovenia and of Republic of Croatia." *Official Gazette of SFRY* 74/91 (October 16).

NOTES

1. The republican and provincial national banks participated in the distribution of monetary income on the basis of rules established by the board of governors. Those rules envisaged different treatment of the more developed and less developed republics and autonomous provinces. As a consequence, the national banks of Slovenia and of Croatia each received 20 percent of the income from the NBY's monetary operations, whereas the shares of the other national banks were much higher.

2. The NBY not only was a guarantor for the foreign Yugoslav debt, but also became, as a participant in the 1988 New Financing Agreement with London Club creditors, jointly and severally liable, without sovereign immunity, for any individual debt under this agreement. With the NBY thus made jointly and severally liable, the agreement also allowed internal trade of London Club debt among different Yugoslav debtors, the NBY becoming a supervisory institution for such trade. This later complicated negotiations with London Club creditors on the distribution of that debt among the successor states of SFR Yugoslavia.

3. Bilateral trade and payments agreements provided for immediate and complete payment for exported goods by the NBY to the exporters. In the case of hard currency payments, exporters were exposed to the credit risk of

the individual purchasers of their goods. Under the bilateral trade and payments agreements, this individual credit risk was eliminated by the involvement of the state. Central banks on both sides were responsible for executing
payments immediately after exports were shipped. The terms of commercial
credit were established at the state level and regulated through the agreement
between the two central banks. Those terms were not respected in practice,
however. As long as the financial strength of the central bank enabled the
financing of a growing surplus, which under market terms would be unbear-
able for individual exporters, the credit risk was accumulated on the NBY's
balance sheet. At the end of the 1980s, when the financial strength of SFR
Yugoslavia weakened, changes were introduced in the system of bilateral payments. The NBY was no longer obliged to execute payments to the exporters
without being compensated by the importers. But even with these adjustments, the system was unable to survive. In 1991 the system of bilateral trade
and payment arrangements was abolished and replaced with a convertible
system of payments.

4. As a response, Slovenia protected its interests by issuing a constitutionally based Decree of the Slovenian Government in January 1991, regulating the interim conditions for liquidity management in the banking system in
Slovenia. The decree was removed in February 1991, when the board of governors of the NBY accepted the appropriate countermeasures. One of the consequences of illegal raids on the monetary system was the reshaping of the
technical conditions for money issuance. It was centralized on the federal
level, and the republican central banks had to open their accounts and present payment orders related to the implementation of monetary policy to the
federal Social Accounting Service (the SAS was an independent payment system institution; see the text below) and not to the republican SASs, as had
been systemically done until then. Accounts with the republican SASs had to
be abolished.

5. The statements for 1990 were examined and accepted by the NBY board
of governors but were not confirmed by the federal assembly. The National
Bank of Slovenia did not give its consent to these statements.

6. Figures for some items differ between the NBY's 1990 financial statements and the balance sheet of the NBY and the system of national banks
from the NBY's 1990 annual report (National Bank of Yugoslavia 1990).
Because the methodology for aggregating and consolidating the accounts
within specific items is not explained in the documents available, and because
the purpose of this chapter demands certain restructuring of the published
items, the result cannot be a perfect match. The main purpose of the tables is
to show the main elements to be dealt with at the time of Slovenian independence during the process of dissolution of SFR Yugoslavia and the succession negotiations that followed. It must also be emphasized that the
balance sheet of the NBY and the system of national banks was consolidated
for statistical purposes only and not in the accounting exercise. The accounting of the republican national banks was separate from that of the NBY,

because the former were independent parties, each established by its own republic's laws and responsible to its assembly.

7. The reduced flow of revenue to the federal budget in that period reflects the changes in the relationship between the federation and the individual republics that had already occurred as a result of political changes implemented in the different republics.

8. Unless stated otherwise, data in this section are from the Bank of Slovenia's 1991 annual report (Bank of Slovenia 1991) and internal Bank of Slovenia documents.

9. The accounting for this supply should include the quantity of banknotes and coins in the vaults of the republican and provincial national banks not yet put into circulation. However, because the actual entries in the books were made on a cumulative basis, at the face value of banknotes and coins, without deducting the quantity of banknotes and coins sold to banks as they were put into circulation and without deducting banknotes and coins destroyed, the actual balances in the vaults were in complete disagreement with the accounting figures. These deficiencies remained a major issue in the succession negotiations for a long time.

10. For 10 years there had been disagreement in principle over whether SFR Yugoslavia had dissolved (the position of Slovenia, Croatia, Bosnia and Herzegovina, and FYR Macedonia) or whether the four republics seeking dissolution had seceded (the position of what became the Federal Republic of Yugoslavia, that is, Serbia and Montenegro). Only in 2001, after the removal of the political regime of Slobodan Milošević, did the Agreement on Succession Issues in Vienna confirm the dissolution.

11. After constitutional changes in Serbia in 1989, the autonomous status of the two provinces (Vojvodina and Kosovo) within Serbia was unilaterally abolished. This was in clear conflict with the federal constitution, which continued to preserve an autonomous status for those two provinces, assuring them equal rights in decisionmaking within federal institutions. With the loss of the provinces' independence, Serbia acquired two more votes in these federal institutions. This allowed Serbia to dominate decisionmaking at the federal level without changing the federal constitution.

12. During the short war in Slovenia after the proclamation of its independence, on the basis of the intermediation of the European Union on the Croatian island of Brioni, it was decided that Slovenia would postpone the implementation of its independence legislation for 3 months. The term expired on October 8, 1991.

13. After June 26, 1991, the board functioned without the participation of the Bank of Slovenia and of the National Bank of Croatia.

14. Interestingly, the NBY did not recognize its debt on the same basis to the national bank of FYR Macedonia, where the actual balance of banknotes and coins in the vaults exceeded the amount claimed from FYR Macedonia by the NBY. This was the result of the bookkeeping deficiencies mentioned above. But the acceptance of the dissolution of SFR Yugoslavia as a general

principle in succession issues eliminated all such peculiarities from the discussion. Annex C, article 10, of the Agreement on Succession Issues states that "no successor State shall pursue financial claims or legal proceedings against any other successor State related to the introduction of its new currency or the establishment of its monetary independence."

Chapter 7
Succession Issues in Allocating the External Debt of SFR Yugoslavia and Achieving Slovenia's Financial Independence

Mojmir Mrak and France Arhar

Less than 1 year after its June 1991 declaration of independence, Slovenia became a full-fledged member of the international political community. Not only has the country been recognized by more than 100 states, including the most important, but it has also become a member of the United Nations.

Political recognition of Slovenia was a precondition for intensifying the country's efforts toward another strategic objective, namely, to constitute its independent financial position and to delink it from the country risk of what used to be Yugoslavia. Meeting this objective was essential if Slovenia was to normalize its relations with international capital markets and, as a result, to create conditions for the normal access of Slovenian entities to these markets.

This chapter presents the main features of Slovenia's process of normalizing its relations with foreign creditors as the key element for constituting an internationally independent financial position. The chapter has five main parts. The first profiles the external debt of SFR Yugoslavia at the time of its dissolution and the position of Slovenia within this framework. The second briefly describes the foundation constructed by Slovenia for the normalization of relations with its foreign creditors. The third analyzes various issues related to Slovenia's becoming a member in major international financial institutions, including the principles applied by these institutions for apportionment of their credits to SFR Yugoslavia among the five successor states. The fourth part discusses the evolution of the institutional setting for Slovenia's external debt negotiations, and the fifth explains the main features of Slovenia's negotiations with its official bilateral creditors (the Paris Club) and commercial bank creditors (the London Club).

EXTERNAL DEBT PROFILE OF SFR YUGOSLAVIA AT THE TIME OF ITS DISSOLUTION

One of the dominant features of SFR Yugoslavia's economy during the last two decades of its existence was the ever-deepening economic crisis. In the 1970s the country came increasingly to rely on foreign borrowing. In the period 1972–82 the external debt of SFR Yugoslavia grew from $2.1 billion to $16.9 billion (World Bank 1988). This eight-fold increase was partly due to internal factors, such as deficiencies in the country's economic policies that led to a growing current account deficit, and partly the result of external factors, including the two oil shocks, interest rate increases, and recession in the industrialized world.

In the early 1980s SFR Yugoslavia was faced with growing debt-servicing problems, and finally, in 1982, the government was forced to ask its foreign creditors to restructure the country's external debt

TABLE 7.1 MEDIUM- AND LONG-TERM CONVERTIBLE CURRENCY
EXTERNAL DEBT OF SFR YUGOSLAVIA, END 1991
(Millions of Dollars)

Type of debt and republic	Multilateral debt	Commercial bank debt[a]	Bilateral official debt and other[b]	Total
Allocated debt	3,093	3,335	5,572	12,000
Bosnia and Herzegovina	550	517	420	1,487
Croatia	299	800	1,584	2,683
Macedonia	235	228	201	664
Slovenia	525	402	864	1,791
Serbia and Montenegro	1,484	1,388	2,503	5,375[c]
Nonallocated debt	683	1,070	1,392	3,145
Total	3,776	4,405	6,964	15,145

a. Includes commercial bank debt restructured under the 1988 New Financing Agreement.
b. Calculated as a residual; includes bilateral official debt restructured under the 1988 arrangement with the Paris Club, commercial bank debt under the 1988 Trade and Deposit Facility Agreement, and private nonguaranteed debt (mainly commercial bank debt).
c. Includes $4,793 million for Serbia and $582 million for Montenegro.
Sources: Cvikl and Mrak (1996); National Bank of Yugoslavia, internal documents.

obligations. On the basis of several arrangements with the International Monetary Fund (IMF), SFR Yugoslavia entered into a number of restructuring agreements both with official creditors and with commercial banks. The first of these occurred in 1983 and the last in 1988. Although the terms of these agreements were similar to those reached by other debtor countries at that time, two specific conditions accepted during the 1983 negotiations have had a major impact on Slovenia's negotiations with foreign creditors since independence (Mrak 1999b). First, SFR Yugoslavia provided a guarantee not only for public and publicly guaranteed debt, but also for restructured private debt previously not guaranteed by the state. Second, SFR Yugoslavia accepted a joint and several liability clause in its restructuring agreement with commercial banks. According to this clause, each debtor under the contract was formally liable for the total amount of debt under the contract.

Because SFR Yugoslavia was completely denied access to finance in the international capital markets, its external debt did not increase further after the eruption of the international debt crisis. Between 1982 and the dissolution of the country in 1991, its external debt in fact declined, mainly as a result of debt conversion transactions on the secondary market.

Table 7.1 shows that the medium- and long-term convertible currency debt of SFR Yugoslavia was estimated at $15.1 billion at the end of 1991 (soft currency debt amounted to an additional $0.8 billion). Because the country was constitutionally defined as a federative state, in which the republics had significant economic autonomy, its external debt was internally divided into two categories. The first, called "allocated debt," included debt incurred for the use of individual republics and autonomous provinces and whose final beneficiaries were enterprises and other entities of those republics and provinces. Table 7.1 indicates that total debt in this category amounted to $12.0 billion at the end of 1991, with Slovenia's share approximately $1.8 billion.[1] The second category, called "nonallocated debt," included debt incurred by the federation mainly for balance of payments purposes and whose immediate beneficiary is therefore not ascertainable. Total debt in this category amounted to $3.1 billion at the end of 1991.

FOUNDATION FOR NORMALIZING RELATIONS WITH FOREIGN CREDITORS

SFR Yugoslavia's large volume of external debt at the time of the country's dissolution and its complete exclusion from international capital markets for more than a decade created strongly unfavorable conditions for Slovenia's efforts to become a normal partner in the international financial community. These efforts were further hampered by the fact that the dissolution took place in a hostile environment, where hopes for a constructive dialogue among the successor states about the allocation of assets and liabilities of the predecessor state were completely unrealistic.

Slovenia inherited yet another unfavorable legacy in the area of external finance and relations with foreign creditors. Under the federated Yugoslav state, its republics, including Slovenia, were for all practical purposes unable to establish their own financial identity within the international financial community. They had always been considered an integral part of the state's country risk, and any transactions with the republics had always been effected within the framework of country risk ceilings set for SFR Yugoslavia.

Although the external financial position of the country was thus extremely vulnerable at the time Slovenia declared independence, the Constitutional Law of the Republic of Slovenia—enacted at that time—provided a clear political foundation for the future relationship with foreign creditors. According to this document, "the Republic of Slovenia shall, on the basis of an agreement on the legal succession of SFR Yugoslavia, take over that part of SFR Yugoslavia's national debt that refers to the Republic of Slovenia and that part of SFR Yugoslavia-guaranteed debtor obligations whose beneficiaries are legal entities based on the territory of the Republic of Slovenia." Slovenia's clear political commitment to take over its entire allocated debt was accompanied by a commitment to assume a portion of SFR Yugoslavia's nonallocated debt: the Constitutional Law says that "the Republic of Slovenia shall take over the corresponding part of the SFRY national debt whose immediate beneficiary is not ascertainable."

Building on these political premises, the government of the Republic of Slovenia laid down some basic parameters for negotiations with foreign creditors in July 1992. The most important among these were the following: First, Slovenia would take over its whole allocated debt of SFR Yugoslavia based on the territorial principle. Second, Slovenia would take over an agreed share, or one established through arbitration, of the nonallocated debt, but that share had to correspond to the distribution of the federation's assets. Third, Slovenia would do its utmost to ensure that as much as possible of the external debt of SFR Yugoslavia would be allocated to individual republics. Fourth, for the external debt obligations it assumed, Slovenia would not request new external debt restructuring from its creditors but stood ready to honor those obligations on the terms laid out in previous agreements between the Paris Club and the commercial banks, on the one hand, and SFR Yugoslavia, on the other.

MEMBERSHIP IN INTERNATIONAL FINANCIAL INSTITUTIONS AND PRINCIPLES OF EXTERNAL DEBT APPORTIONMENT

In 1992 Slovenia faced two major preconditions to becoming a recognized partner in the international financial community: admission to membership in the major international financial institutions, especially the two Bretton Woods institutions, and regularization of the country's relationship with its foreign creditors. For several reasons, membership in the international financial institutions was considered at the time to be the more pressing issue and therefore given clear priority over resolving the external debt problem. First, admission to membership in the most important international financial institutions represents by itself an important step toward international financial recognition of a newly independent state. Second, membership was also a precondition for renewed access of Slovenia and its entities to the financial resources of these institutions, of which the former Yugoslavia had been a founding member. Third, and most important, it was believed that, through the membership procedures, an important precedent would be set with regard to the legal status of the states on the territory of the former Yugoslavia, and consequently with regard to the apportionment of its external debt obligations. It was further believed that this precedent would be applied in the negotiations that would follow with other groups of foreign creditors (Mrak 1999a).

Slovenia became a member of the IMF in January 1993, but the membership procedure was politically difficult and extremely contentious. The IMF Board of Governors was put in a situation where it had to decide about the legal status of SFR Yugoslavia as a predecessor state. If the IMF decided that FR Yugoslavia (Serbia and Montenegro) was the continuation of SFR Yugoslavia, retaining the predecessor country's quota as well as its liabilities in the IMF, then all other new states in the territory of SFR Yugoslavia, including Slovenia, would be considered seceding states. As such, they would have to join the organization as completely new members by way of the normal admission procedures. In this case, which FR Yugoslavia favored, Slovenia and the other seceding states would be offered their own quotas and would not participate in the quota and liabilities of SFR Yugoslavia in the IMF. If, on the other hand, the IMF decided that the former Yugoslavia had been dissolved, then all five successor states would seek membership by the succession-to-membership procedure, meaning that each of these states would take its share in the quota and liabilities of the dissolved state in the IMF.

Taking into account the position of the international community (the July 1992 opinion of the Badinter Commission and the United Nations' position on the membership of FR Yugoslavia in this organization, announced in September 1992), the IMF decided in December 1992 that SFR Yugoslavia had ceased to exist and had therefore ceased to be a member of the IMF (IMF 1992). This position was shared by all of the states on the territory of the former Yugoslavia, except FR Yugoslavia.

The choice of IMF membership procedure was not only crucially important for reaching a fundamental decision on the succession principle in the case of the former Yugoslavia (with five equal successors as opposed to one continuing and four seceding states). Together with the procedure for membership in the World Bank Group, it was also instrumental for setting important principles with regard to the apportionment of the predecessor state's external debt.

For the apportionment of the nonallocated debt, the precedent was set by a formula proposed by the IMF board, according to which the quota and liabilities of the dissolved Yugoslavia were distributed among the five successor states based on their economic power. According to this formula, the quota of the former Yugoslavia as well as its obligations to the IMF (because IMF loans are used exclusively for balance of payments support of a member country, they are a clear example of nonallocated debt) were allocated as follows: Bosnia and Herzegovina, 13.20 percent; Croatia, 28.49 percent; FYR Macedonia, 5.40 percent; Slovenia, 16.39 percent; and FR Yugoslavia, 36.52 percent.

This formula was accepted by all the successor states, including FR Yugoslavia, and was applied to the actual succession to membership of the other four successor states to the IMF (IMF 1992).

With respect to apportionment of the allocated debt, the precedent was established in February 1993 when the board of the International Bank for Reconstruction and Development (IBRD), as part of the World Bank membership procedure, confirmed the interim bilateral agreements reached with Slovenia and some of the other successor states a year earlier. According to these agreements, each of the successor states would take over and service those IBRD loans used by the final beneficiaries on their respective territories (World Bank 1993).

INSTITUTIONAL FRAMEWORK FOR EXTERNAL DEBT NEGOTIATIONS

In the early period following the break-up of SFR Yugoslavia, it was generally believed that its assets and liabilities would be apportioned among its successors through a general solution reached within the framework of an international conference. All three international peace conferences on SFR Yugoslavia—the Peace Conference on Yugoslavia (August 1991 to August 1992), the International Conference on the Former Yugoslavia (August 1992 to December 1995), and the Peace Implementation Conference (begun in December 1995)—have adopted succession as an integral part of their mandate.

With the significant exception of the Badinter Commission's opinions, the results of all three conferences have been very disappointing with respect to succession issues in general, and therefore also with respect to the apportionment of SFR Yugoslavia's external debt obligations. The primary cause has been the hostilities on the territory of SFR Yugoslavia and the opposing positions of FR Yugoslavia, on the one hand, and the other four successor states, on the other, with respect to certain important issues of succession.

With succession negotiations within the framework of international peace conferences on SFR Yugoslavia thus paralyzed, Slovenia had practically no hope that its relationships with foreign creditors would be regularized in the foreseeable future if it relied exclusively on the international conference route. Because Slovenia's vital interests depended on normalizing relations with foreign creditors and securing normal access to international capital markets, Slovenia started to pay growing attention to the alternative route of direct negotiations (Mrak 1996).

There were also at least three additional reasons why, over time, Slovenia came to prefer the route of direct negotiations for resolving its problems with foreign creditors. First, by February 1993 the IMF and the World Bank had already made their determinations not only with respect to SFR Yugoslavia's continuity versus dissolution, but also on the principles for apportioning SFR Yugoslavia's assets and liabilities in their respective institutions. Second, with regard to restructured commercial bank debt, the Badinter Commission issued its Opinion No. 15, stating that problems arising from the rights and obligations under the 1988 New Financing Agreement (NFA) were to be resolved by reference to the terms of the agreement and were not to be dealt with within the framework of the international conference negotiations on succession. Third, the commercial banks made it clear that inclusion of their claims under the NFA in any eventual succession treaty would not be binding on NFA creditors (Mrak 1996).

NEGOTIATIONS WITH BILATERAL OFFICIAL CREDITORS AND COMMERCIAL BANKS: PROCESS AND RESULTS

The membership procedures of the IMF and the World Bank, discussed above, were instrumental in establishing principles for the apportionment of SFR Yugoslavia's allocated and nonallocated debt. In so doing they created the necessary background for effective negotiations between Slovenia and the other two groups of its foreign creditors, namely, the bilateral official creditors (the Paris Club) and the commercial banks (the London Club).

Bilateral Official Creditors: The Paris Club

Based on the parameters discussed above, Slovenia established its first contacts with the Paris Club in mid-1992. In his October 1992 reply to Slovenia, the chairman of the Paris Club indicated that the creditor countries were willing to conclude bilateral agreements with Slovenia.

In February 1993, immediately after Slovenia became a member of the IMF and the World Bank, negotiations with the Paris Club intensified, and already by June of that year an agreement in principle had been reached with this group of creditors. Its main provisions were the following (Cvikl and Mrak 1996): First, Slovenia would take over the entire debt owed to Paris Club members that was allocated to Slovenia on a final beneficiary basis, as well as 16.39 percent of SFR Yugoslavia's nonallocated debt to this group of creditors. Second, because Slovenia did not ask for any rescheduling of its external debt obligations, the terms and conditions of the existing bilateral agreements signed by the authorities of SFR Yugoslavia in 1988 were to remain unchanged. Third, Slovenia would take over those Paris Club debts of Slovenian entities that had been, on the basis of SFR Yugoslavia's legislation and without the consent of the foreign creditors, transferred to the country's central bank for further servicing. Fourth, Slovenia would repay, within a reasonable period of time, all principal arrears on its Paris Club debt arising from Slovenia's preindependence period.

On the basis of the June 1993 agreement in principle, Slovenia started technical reconciliation discussions with each of the 16 Paris Club members; it took several years before final bilateral agreements were reached between Slovenia and each of these countries. Under these agreements Slovenia assumed approximately $250 million of SFR Yugoslavia's nonallocated debt to this group of creditors.

The case of Slovenia has set the model for the apportionment of SFR Yugoslavia's Paris Club debt among the successor states. The "Slovenian model," whereby a successor assumes all debt owed to this group of creditors that is allocated to it, plus the IMF-determined share of SFR Yugoslavia's nonallocated debt toward this group, was applied in the Paris Club agreements in principle signed with all the other states created from the predecessor state: with Croatia and FYR Macedonia in 1995, with Bosnia and Herzegovina in 1998, and with FR Yugoslavia after the fall of the Milošević regime. The financial terms of these agreements differ, both from that of Slovenia and among themselves, depending on the capacity of each state to service the assumed external debt obligations.

Commercial Banks: The London Club

The third group of SFR Yugoslavia's foreign creditors with whom Slovenia has had to formally settle its relationships is the group of commercial banks known as the London Club. The main subject of the negotiations was the NFA of 1988, the last commercial debt restructuring undertaken by SFR Yugoslavia before its collapse. The obligors under this agreement were the National Bank of Yugoslavia (the central bank of SFR Yugoslavia) and 10 commercial banks from all six republics—two of them, Ljubljanska Banka and Kreditna Banka Maribor, from Slovenia. SFR Yugoslavia's federal guarantee was also provided for this agreement, and the Republic of Slovenia was liable, as one of the successor states, for a part of the guarantee. Under the NFA $7.3 billion was restructured, but by the end of 1991 this amount was reduced to about $4.2 billion, mainly as a result of market-based debt transactions, such as debt-for-export swaps and debt buybacks.

As in the case of the Paris Club, Slovenia was a forerunner among the successor states in negotiations with the London Club. In mid-1993, immediately after reaching the agreement in principle with the Paris Club, the country initiated formal negotiations with the International Co-ordinating Committee (ICC), which served as a negotiating team for the London Club.[2] Slovenia had two reasons for choosing to negotiate with the commercial banks only after agreements with the other two groups of foreign creditors had been reached. First, it was expected that arrangements with the international financial institutions and with the Paris Club would establish some useful precedents that could be used in negotiations with the London Club. Second, the NFA contained some clauses that were extremely unfavorable to debtors and their guarantors. It was the only arrangement between foreign creditors and SFR Yugoslavia that held all obligors "jointly and severally liable" for the total amount under the contract. It therefore provided no legal grounds for distinguishing between allocated and nonallocated debt. Slovenia's main objective in its negotiations with the London Club was to conclude a separate agreement whereby Slovenian debt under the NFA would be clearly identified and formally separated from other debts under this agreement, and whereby Slovenian obligors under the NFA would be released from the joint and several liability obligations as well as from any other obligation under this contract.

In the first round of negotiations that took place in June 1993, Slovenia made an offer to the ICC based on the same principles used in negotiations with the other groups of foreign creditors. Under this proposal, Slovenian obligors would assume the equivalent of about 14 percent of the total debt under the NFA. This amount was calculated by summing the roughly $410 million that Slovenia considered as its total allocated debt under the NFA and the $170 million that Slovenia considered to be equal to 16.39 percent (the IMF-determined share) of the total nonallocated debt under the NFA.

Citing the contractual provisions, however, the ICC rejected the distinction between allocated and nonallocated debt and proposed that Slovenia take on $1.2 billion of NFA debt, an amount equivalent to about 28 percent of the total. This proposal, although completely financially unacceptable to Slovenia, was the first formal indication that the commercial banks were ready to allow a legal arrangement releasing Slovenian obligors from part of their obligation under the NFA. But at the same time it was a clear indication that the banks were ready to do so only if Slovenia paid a certain "price" for such a release.

Negotiations continued in the second half of 1993, throughout 1994, and into the first half of 1995, with two issues being the most contentious. The first was the share of total NFA debt to be assumed by Slovenia. The ICC insisted that Slovenia take over a share of the NFA debt amounting to at least 4 to 5 percentage points more than the 16.39 percent determined as Slovenia's share by the IMF. The second issue was Slovenia's insistence that so-called controlled Yugoslav persons, that is, entities from FR Yugoslavia holding NFA loans as well as entities holding these loans on behalf of their interests, be excluded from the final agreement with the London Club. The reason for their exclusion was that at least some of them had bought up NFA loans on the secondary market at a large discount, using SFR Yugoslavia's foreign exchange reserves to which Slovenia, like all the other successor republics, had a claim. This debt had not been retired, since it was anticipated that Slovenia, and later the other republics, would start to service it. It was unacceptable for Slovenia to treat these "creditors" in the same way as regular creditors (which the final agreement refers to as "participating creditors"), and therefore Slovenia insisted that these controlled Yugoslav persons be excluded from the arrangement (in the final agreement they have the status of "nonparticipating creditors").

An agreement in principle was finally reached in June 1995, and the transaction was formally completed 1 year later, when Slovenia issued bonds equivalent to $812 million (15.4 percent of total outstanding obligations under the NFA, or 18.0 percent of the obligations to "participating creditors") in exchange for the release of Slovenian obligors from joint and several liability under the contract.[3]

Slovenia's agreement with the London Club was important not only for the negotiating partners, but also because of its broader relevance in setting, de facto, a model for the overall resolution of SFR Yugoslavia's commercial bank debt. This was confirmed by a number of events that took place in the first half of 1996, that is, immediately before the issuance of Slovenia's bonds. One of these was the bitter opposition of FR Yugoslavia to the completion of the transaction. FR Yugoslavia even initiated a lawsuit against the commercial bank creditors and Slovenia, seeking to prevent the transaction from being consummated. There seem to have been at least two reasons for this reaction: one political and the other economic. The political reason is that the transaction undermined FR Yugoslavia's contention that it was the sole successor to the former SFR Yugoslavia and therefore the party that should negotiate with the London Club over the entire Yugoslav commercial bank debt. Had this happened, upon reaching agreement with the banks, FR Yugoslavia would, of course, have initiated negotiations with each of the "separatist" republics (which would still be jointly and severally liable) on how the debt would actually be serviced. Given the weakened status of FR Yugoslavia's economy, it was very reasonable to expect that the wealthier republics would have been asked to assume larger shares. With the Slovenian transaction with the London Club completed, FR Yugoslavia therefore lost an important political argument in its claim to sole successorship as well as a powerful vehicle for keeping the "separatist" republics under its further financial control.

In contrast, the Slovenian transaction with commercial bank creditors was welcomed by the other successor states, especially Croatia, because the deal established a model for their own negotiations with the London Club. It was interesting to see how June 11, 1996—the date when the Slovenian transaction was completed—became a deadline for all of them to get the required consent of creditors either for their already-negotiated transactions (in the case of Croatia) or for negotiations scheduled for the second half of 1996 (in the case of FYR Macedonia) or the first half of 1997 (in the case of Bosnia and Herzegovina).

The agreements of these three states with the London Club shadowed the "Slovenian model" in several ways. First, in each case the successor country assumed a share of NFA obligations (principal and past-due interest) that was close to that determined by the IMF. Second, in exchange for doing so, all three successor states were released from any further obligations under the NFA. Third, in all three agreements, controlled Yugoslav persons were not allowed to participate. Fourth, all three successor states have issued bonds in exchange for their assumed portion of NFA debt.

CONCLUSIONS

Over the 5 years between mid-1991 and mid-1996, Slovenia managed to constitute its international financial position as a fully independent state and to establish the conditions required for normal access of the country and its economic entities to international capital markets. Two main areas of activity were crucial in reaching this strategic objective. The first was the admission of Slovenia to membership in the international financial institutions, especially the IMF and the World Bank, as discussed above, but also the European Bank for Reconstruction and Development. Successful completion of membership procedures in these institutions not only opened the way for Slovenia's renewed access to the financial resources of these institutions, but also established two key principles for apportioning among the successor states SFR Yugoslavia's external debt to other groups of foreign creditors. First, the principle governing the apportionment of nonallocated debt was based on the IMF-determined formula reflecting each successor state's economic size relative to the others. Second, the principle governing the apportionment of the allocated debt of SFR Yugoslavia was based on the World Bank's final beneficiary concept, which it applied in allocating its credits among the five successor states.

Following the principle that Slovenia was one of five equal successors to SFR Yugoslavia, and applying both of the above debt apportionment principles, Slovenia had completely regularized its relationship with foreign creditors by mid-1996. As part of this process, the country took over its total allocated debt as well as about

16 percent—in nominal terms, about $500 million—of SFR Yugoslavia's nonallocated debt.

Throughout the 1991–96 period, Slovenia was by far the most active among the successor states in dealing with the legacy of SFR Yugoslavia's external debt. As the forerunner in this process, Slovenia was exposed to a number of problems in its negotiations with the various groups of foreign creditors. At the same time, Slovenia was also the only successor state of SFR Yugoslavia that actively participated in the design of the model arrangements for the apportionment of its debts to the Paris and London Clubs. The "Slovenian model" of debt apportionment was reconfirmed de facto by the Agreement on Succession Issues signed in May 2001 by representatives of all five successor states.

The stabilization of Slovenia's economy, accompanied by accession to the key international financial institutions and by an active strategy aimed at resolving the external debt problems caused by the dissolution of SFR Yugoslavia, was reflected in the country's improved creditworthiness. In 1993 the country arranged its first syndicated credit, although the terms were unfavorable. In the following 2 years, the terms offered to Slovenian borrowers improved steadily, reflecting both the sound economic position of the country and the progress achieved in external debt negotiations. It was the agreement with the London Club creditors in mid-1996 that enabled Slovenia to complete the process of establishing its fully independent international position and that of creating conditions for the country's full access to international capital markets. The completion of negotiations with foreign creditors, followed by the achievement of investment grade ratings by the three major international rating agencies, has allowed Slovenia not only to tap new funding sources on the international capital markets but also to further reduce its funding costs.

REFERENCES

Cvikl, M., and M. Mrak. 1996. "Former Yugoslavia's Debt Apportionment." Internal Discussion Paper, World Bank, Europe and Central Asia Region, Washington, D.C. Processed.

International Monetary Fund. 1992. "Decision Taken by the IMF Executive Board on 14 December 1992." Press Release 92/92, December 15. Washington, D.C.

Mrak, M. 1993. "Slovenia: Creating Its Own Identity in the International Financial Community." Government of the Republic of Slovenia, Ljubljana. Processed.

_____. 1996. "Succession of the Former Yugoslavia's External Debt: The Case of Slovenia." *Development and International Cooperation* 12(23): 167–82.

_____. 1999a. "Succession to the Former Yugoslavia's External Debt." In M. Mrak, ed., *Succession of States*. The Hague: Kluwer Law International.

_____. 1999b. "Apportionment and Succession of External Debts: The Case of the SFR Yugoslavia." Research Report 259. Wiener Institut für Internationale Wirtschaftsvergleiche, Vienna.

World Bank. 1988. *World Debt Tables 1988–89*. Washington, D.C.

_____. 1993. "Decision Taken by the Board of Directors of the World Bank on 25 February 1993." Press Release 93/S43, February 26. Washington, D.C.

NOTES

1. This figure for Slovenia's allocated debt is from the National Bank of Yugoslavia (which was the central bank of SFR Yugoslavia) and differs by less than 2 percent from that reported by the Bank of Slovenia in its *Monthly Bulletin* of December 2001.

2. The first informal discussions between Slovenia and the ICC started already in July 1992, soon after the Slovenian government suspended interest payments under the NFA. This decision was made because obligors from some other republics of the former SFR Yugoslavia had stopped honoring their obligations under the NFA at that time. Given that all obligors under the agreement were "jointly and severally liable," any further payment made by the Slovenian obligors would not be considered as full servicing of the Slovenian obligations, but only as partial servicing of the overall Yugoslav obligations. At the official meeting in October 1992, the two parties reached the following interim agreement: Slovenian obligors would resume interest payments on the NFA on the same principle as before the suspension (this was, de facto, allocated debt), and payments made by Slovenian obligors would be acknowledged in the new agreement reached with the London Club (Mrak 1993).

3. This total is analytically composed of three parts: $425 million in allocated debt, $245 million as Slovenia's portion of the former SFR Yugoslavia's nonallocated debt to the London Club, and $142 million in past-due interest on both the allocated and the nonallocated debt (Mrak 1996).

Part II: Socioeconomic Transformation—The Slovenian Way

Chapter 8
Macroeconomic Stabilization and Sustainable Growth

Carlos Silva-Jáuregui

During the second half of the 1980s, the deterioration of the economic and political situation in SFR Yugoslavia accelerated. Declining output growth in the 1980s (with recession in the later years of the decade), high public debt, and hyperinflation marked the end of the decade and precipitated the disintegration of the federation. At the time, Slovenia was in a privileged position relative to the other members of the federation. It was the wealthiest and most Western-oriented member of SFR Yugoslavia, generating 18 percent of the federation's social product and 20 percent of its industrial production with only 8 percent of the population. Its unemployment rate, at 3.2 percent, was about one-fifth that of SFR Yugoslavia as a whole, and productivity was at least twice the national average. Slovenia was also SFR Yugoslavia's window to the Western world.

The crisis that engulfed the federation at the end of the 1980s, however, had a significant impact on Slovenia's production capacity. The loss of markets, both in the other former Yugoslav republics and in the countries of the Council of Mutual Economic Assistance (the economic organization of the former Soviet bloc), aggravated the recession of the late 1980s and early 1990s. In addition, regional political instability reduced Slovenia's income from tourism and freight services. As a result of these factors, Slovenia's GDP dropped by about 9 percent in 1991, the year of its independence, and 5.5 percent in 1992. Slovenia also inherited from SFR Yugoslavia a large public debt burden and hyperinflation.

Following its declaration of independence in June 1991 and its recognition by the international community in early 1992, Slovenia moved quickly to establish macroeconomic stability, to launch a program of structural reforms aimed at the systemic transformation of the economy, and to normalize relationships with the international financial community. With the resolution of its external debt problem (discussed in Chapter 7) and the signing of the European Association Agreement in June 1996, Slovenia signaled its commitment to complete the systemic transformation of its economy and achieve membership in an enlarged European Union. Today Slovenia is ready to take on the opportunities and challenges of the single European market. Prudent and well-executed economic policies have helped Slovenia set its economy on the right path, advance its real convergence with the Western industrial economies, and avoid the imbalances and crises experienced by other transition economies.

This chapter evaluates Slovenia's experience in stabilizing its economy, generating sustainable growth, and qualifying for membership in the enlarged European Union. Macroeconomic stabilization was the backbone of Slovenia's rapid economic recovery after independence. It was based on a set of prudent fiscal and monetary policies that helped Slovenia return to the path of sustainable growth and development. But whereas stabilization proceeded relatively quickly, the traditional Slovenian consensus-building approach to policy formulation slowed the pace of needed structural reforms. Gradualism prevailed in the structural reform agenda, but reforms nevertheless moved forward (as described in Chapters 5 and 24). As Slovenia looked forward to accession to the European Union, its overarching development objective was to achieve sustainable growth and enhance the welfare of its population (World Bank 1999a). The policies and institutional reforms that are conducive to sustainable growth coincide with those required for the adoption of the EU *acquis communautaire*. This gave Slovenia the incentives to adopt win-win policies that would contribute to achieving its objectives.

STABILIZATION AND RECOVERY IN THE EARLY YEARS OF INDEPENDENCE

Slovenia responded to the challenges of transition and independence with a strong adjustment program aimed at retaking control of its economy. Implementation of the macroeconomic stabilization program was among the most important economic tasks of the newly established state. A new currency, the tolar, was introduced on October 8, 1991, delinking Slovenia's monetary policy from that of the federation and thus breaking with the hyperinflationary trends of the past. Reforms touched many sectors of the economy, as Slovenia needed to move from a crisis situation to stability, and from the Yugoslav model of socialism to a market economy. The overall impact of this adjustment program was remarkable, and the beginning of the economic turnaround, after the initial adjustment shock, was visible already by early 1993. Despite this rapid success, the independence of Slovenia and the transformation of its economic structures during the early transition period were not painless, and Slovenia, like the other transition economies of Central and Eastern Europe (CEE), suffered from the severe economic shock that these two events produced (World Bank 2002; Svejnar 2002).

Real Output

Real output, which was already declining before independence (it fell by 4.7 percent in 1989), fell significantly further in the early years of the transition, as noted previously. But growth resumed in 1993 and had picked up momentum by 1994. As a result, since 1993 Slovenia has maintained a robust growth rate of about 4 percent a year on average, substantially narrowing the income gap with the European Union (Table 8.1). Moreover, the success of its adjustment program made

TABLE 8.1 GDP PER CAPITA IN SLOVENIA AND FOUR CENTRAL
           EUROPEAN COUNTRIES RELATIVE TO EU AVERAGE,
           1995 AND 2001

(EU average = 100)[a]

Country	1995	2001
Czech Republic	62	59
Hungary	46	53
Poland	34	40
Slovakia	46	48
Slovenia	63	70

a. At purchasing power standards.

Sources: International Monetary Fund and Eurostat data.

Slovenia the second CEE economy, after Poland, to recover from the severe initial real output shock of the transition and to achieve production levels above those observed before the transition—in Slovenia's case by 1996 (World Bank 1999b; Figure 8.1). Much of this recovery has come through gains in productivity, as employment has remained flat (see the discussion of unemployment below).

Inflation

After the hyperinflation of the period immediately before independence, Slovenia's policymakers took a gradual approach to disinflation.

FIGURE 8.1 REAL GDP IN EU ACCESSION COUNTRIES

(index, 1990 = 100)

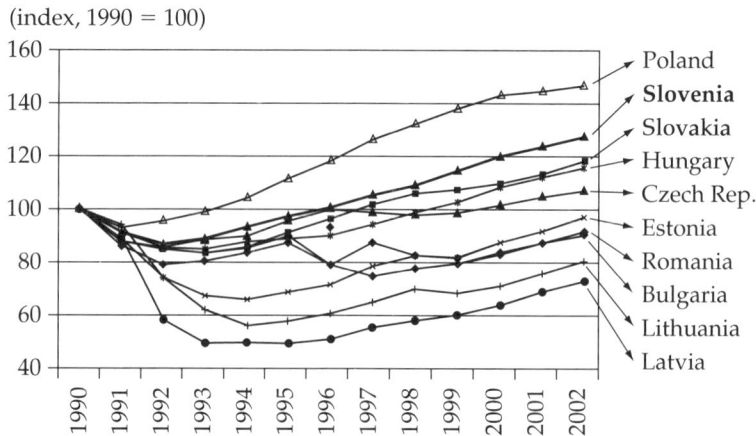

Source: World Bank data.

FIGURE 8.2 INFLATION RATE, 1987–96

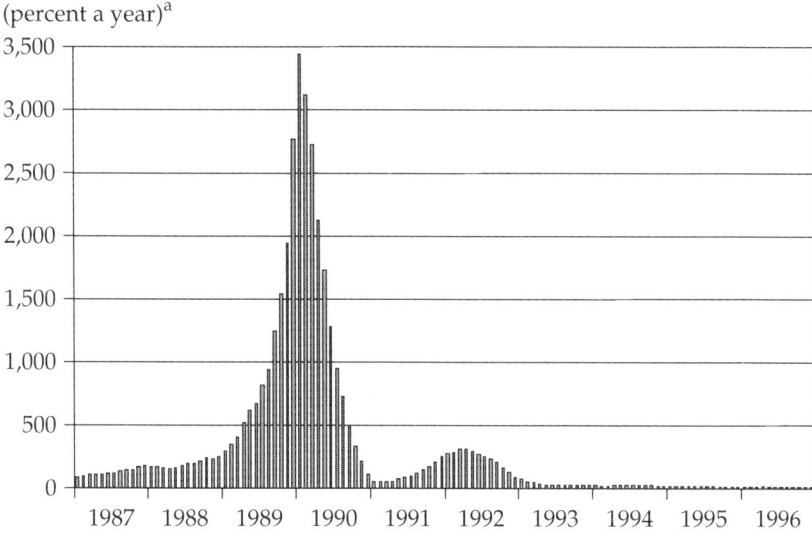

(percent a year)[a]

a. Monthly data at annualized rate.
Source: Bank of Slovenia.

The Bank of Slovenia, together with the government, succeeded in lowering inflation gradually over a period of several years, under a managed floating exchange rate regime rather than under a more orthodox exchange rate anchor policy. This unorthodox stabilization policy eventually proved to be efficient at braking hyperinflation without compromising the recovery of real output. Inflation, which had reached 1,306 percent annually in the last quarter of 1989 and peaked at an annualized rate of just under 3,500 percent in January 1990, was reduced to 201 percent by 1992 (at an average annual rate) and then declined gradually to the upper single digits (8.6 percent) by the end of 1995 (Figure 8.2). This level of inflation was the lowest Slovenia had witnessed since the mid-1970s.

Inflation continued to decline, but at a slower pace, until 1999, and it has for all practical purposes remained in the vicinity of 6 to 9 percent a year since 1997 (Figure 8.3). Recent progress with the government's disinflation efforts, however, has been less than anticipated by the Bank of Slovenia's own targets and projections. Factors contributing to higher than desirable inflation included the introduction of the value added tax and needed increases in indirect taxes and administered prices (oil, telephone, electricity, and municipal services

FIGURE 8.3 INFLATION RATE, 1997–2003

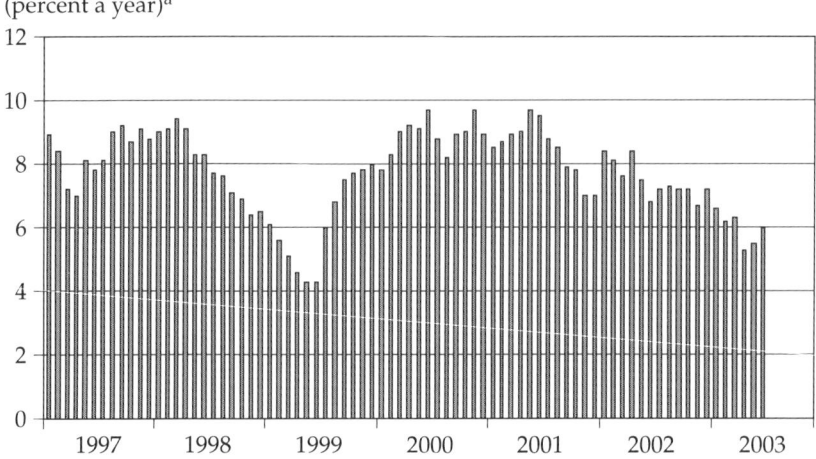

(percent a year)[a]

a. Monthly data at annualized rate.
Source: Bank of Slovenia.

charges). But, most important, the underlying inflation rate continues to be in the neighborhood of 4.2 percent a year.

Disinflation remains among the principal challenges for Slovenian policymakers. Annual inflation needs to be brought down to about 3 to 4 percent in preparation for adoption of the Exchange Rate Mechanism II (ERM-II), slated for the first half of 2005, and the eventual adoption of the euro. As of 2002 Slovenia had the second-highest inflation rate of all 10 CEE countries seeking EU accession (Figure 8.4). To meet this important challenge, the central bank has adopted a policy of inflation targeting and moved away from targeting money growth. Financial contracts are being deindexed as well. This policy should help Slovenia reach its inflation goals and bring annual inflation closer to EU levels.

External Sector

External vulnerability was an important risk during the early years of transition and independence, but the Slovenian authorities have been able to manage this risk very well. A critical challenge was to build up a strong foreign exchange position. Foreign exchange reserves were built up from virtually zero at independence to a comfortable $4.2 billion by 1996 (equivalent to about 4.5 months of imports) and

FIGURE 8.4 INFLATION IN EU ACCESSION COUNTRIES, 2002

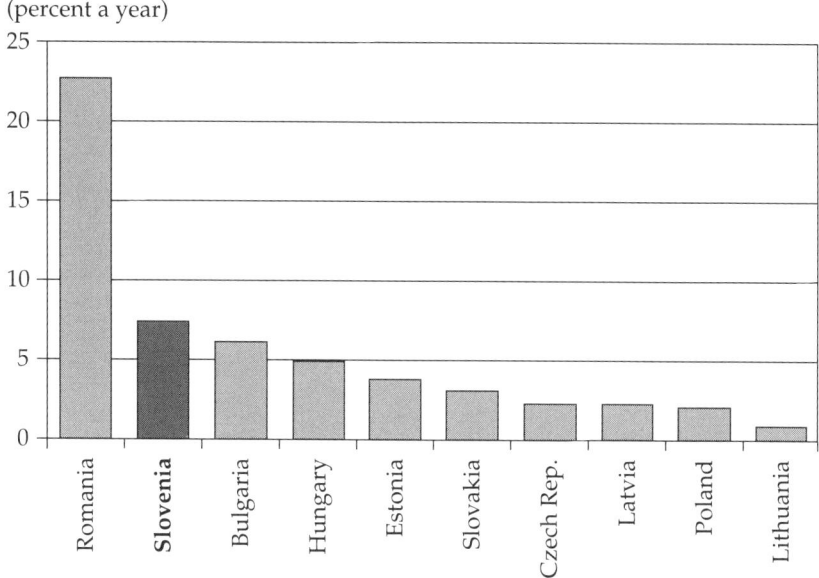

(percent a year)

Source: European Bank for Reconstruction and Development.

to $7 billion in 2002 (6.8 months of imports). This reserve accumulation gradually gave greater security to the new currency. The current account surpluses recorded until 1994, and the capital inflows of the years thereafter, helped in building up reserves. The improvement in the current account reflected a revival in exports of goods and services, especially tourism.

By 1995, however, exports of goods had slowed while imports were rising significantly, producing the first trade deficit since independence (Figure 8.5). An important component of the import boom was much-needed capital goods to modernize the productive sector. This early behavior of exports and imports was consistent with the real appreciation of the tolar, which continued for 1½ years during the early transition. This, combined with an increase in labor costs in real terms, resulted in a decline in the competitiveness of Slovenian exports in 1995 (World Bank 1998b).

A further deterioration of the current account took place in 1998–2000, in part due to the introduction of the value added tax, which prompted a rise in imports in anticipation of the tax. Corrective policy measures were introduced, however, and the trade deficit started to turn around by 2000. Since 2001, current account surpluses

FIGURE 8.5 CURRENT ACCOUNT BALANCE

(percent of GDP)

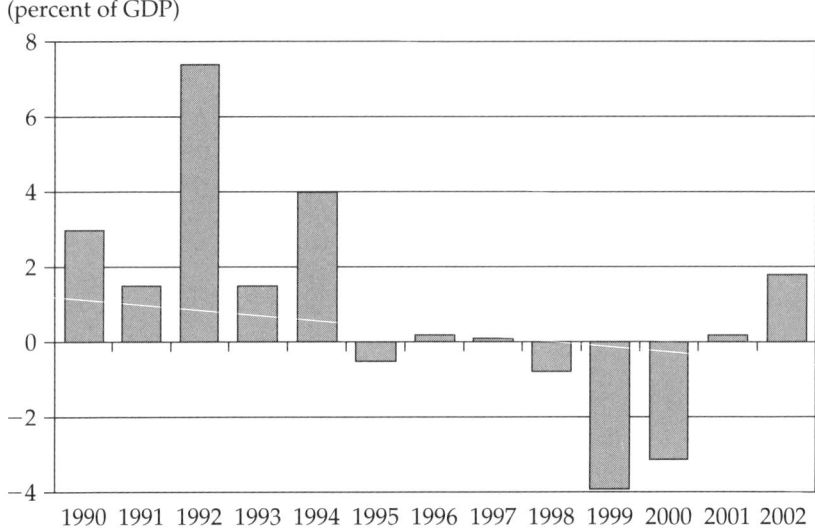

Source: World Bank data.

have returned, and with the widening of the surplus in 2002 and large inflows of foreign direct investment during the same year, foreign reserves rose to five times the monetary base. This gives more comfort to Slovenia as it tackles the challenges of ERM-II and eventual adoption of the euro.

Slovenia has also regained its lost export market share. There has been a successful effort to increase the presence of Slovenian firms in the markets of the other former Yugoslav republics, as well as in those of other non-EU countries. Moreover, external vulnerabilities have been reduced with the introduction of an exchange rate policy that has been able to keep the real effective exchange rate broadly stable since 1998. This policy has helped Slovenia maintain external competitiveness and win back access to export markets.

Foreign Direct Investment

Unlike in some other leading transition economies, foreign direct investment (FDI) did not play an important role in Slovenia's transition until recently, in part because the privatization policy adopted by Slovenia gave preference to insiders rather than potential foreign investors. Capital controls during the transition also played a role in diminishing the interest of foreign investors in the 1990s.

FIGURE 8.6 INWARD FOREIGN DIRECT INVESTMENT

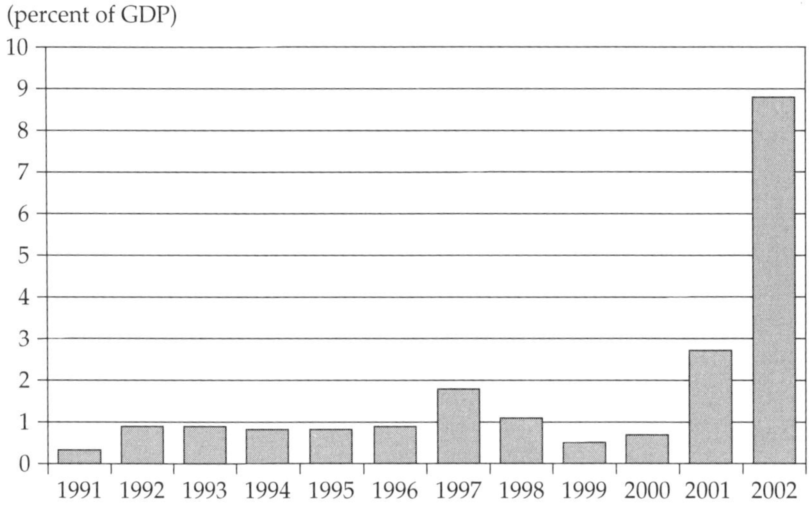

(percent of GDP)

Sources: Bank of Slovenia and International Monetary Fund.

With the gradual reduction in capital account restrictions since 1999, the removal of restrictions on foreign investment in Slovenian long-term securities in 2001, and clearer prospects for EU membership in 2004, Slovenia has become a more attractive destination for foreign investors. FDI flows increased substantially in 2001 and 2002 (Figure 8.6). This sudden increase was the result of a number of factors and included several large privatization transactions and foreign acquisitions of private enterprises.

On the privatization front, in May 2002 the government sold the equivalent of 34 percent of Nova Ljubljanska Banka (NLB), the largest bank in Slovenia, to KBC of Belgium for about €435 million. In 2001 NLB had a 34 percent market share as measured by assets. In June 2002 an additional 5 percent of NLB was sold to the European Bank for Reconstruction and Development for €64 million, for a total of almost half a billion euros in these two transactions alone. The privatization of NLB is also helping to increase competition in the financial sector.

Foreign acquisitions of previously privatized Slovenian companies have also taken place in recent years in sectors where European firms are seeking a strategic presence. The Swiss firm Novartis acquired the pharmaceutical company Lek for about $860 million; this was by far the largest single foreign investment transaction in Slovenia to date.

Austria's cellular telephone company Mobilkom bought Simobil, and Austria's Lafarge Perlmooser bought the cement milling company Cementarna Trbovlje. In the banking sector, France's Société Générale made an additional investment in SKB, the second-largest bank in Slovenia; Banka Koper was acquired by Italy's San Paolo IMI, and Krekova Banka by Austria's Raiffeisen. The pace of FDI inflows slowed in 2003, however, with only $33.7 million in transactions recorded during the first 8 months of the year.

External Debt

Slovenia inherited a large debt burden upon independence, but early negotiations with the Paris and London Clubs solved the immediate problems associated with debt succession. That experience made policymakers quite conservative in managing the country's external debt: throughout the past decade, Slovenia's foreign debt has been kept at manageable levels. Total external debt reached 41.5 percent of GDP in 2002, of which public and publicly guaranteed debt represented less than a third (15.3 percent of GDP). These levels are in the midrange of comparable leading EU accession countries (Figure 8.7).

FIGURE 8.7 EXTERNAL DEBT IN EU ACCESSION COUNTRIES, 2002

(percent of GDP)

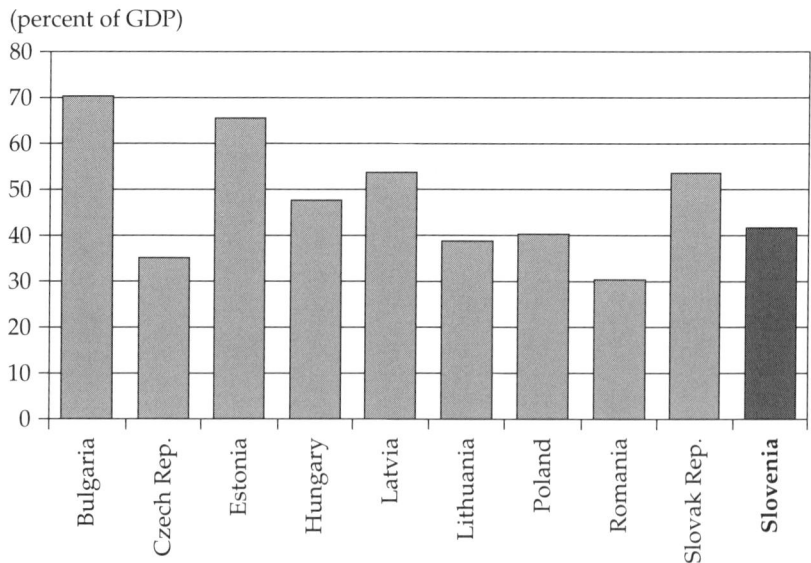

Source: World Bank data.

Unemployment

The rate of unemployment in Slovenia has remained relatively low and on a declining trend during the transition, largely thanks to the Slovenian privatization model, which maintained the status quo and avoided large layoffs at the beginning of the transition (World Bank 1998a). As measured by surveys similar in nature to those of the International Labour Organisation, unemployment has declined gradually. From 1993 to 2002 the unemployment rate fell by about one-third, to 6.3 percent (Figure 8.8).[1] These levels of unemployment are low in comparison with other transition economies and lower than those of many EU members (Riboud, Sanchez-Paramo, and Silva-Jáuregui 2002).

Although Slovenia's economy proved itself capable of a fast output turnaround, this has not led to significant employment growth. The labor force declined by 2 percent during the first 6 years of the transition (1992–97). During the same period employment declined by 5 percent, even as real output increased by 21 percent. For the decade 1992–2002 as a whole, employment and the labor force have remained practically flat, while real output has increased by 48 percent. This dramatic output growth without a recovery in employment essentially reflects significant productivity gains. Some of the labor shed by manufacturing has been absorbed by the services sector, which now

FIGURE 8.8 UNEMPLOYMENT RATE

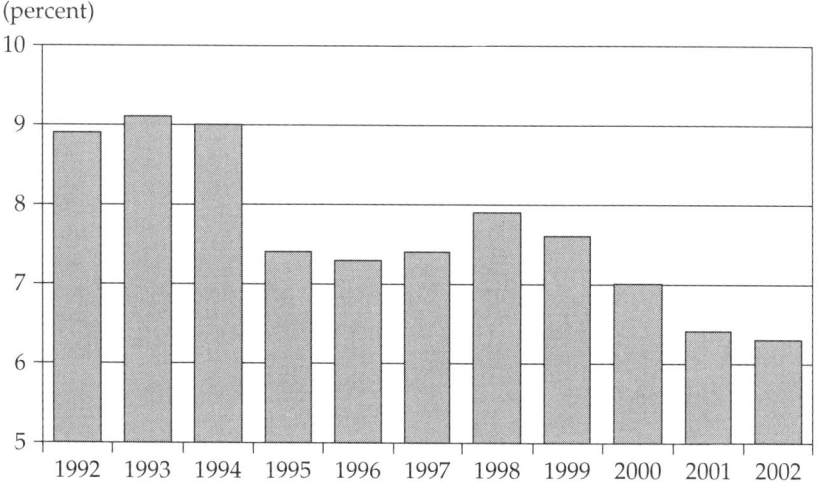

Source: Bank of Slovenia.

accounts for more than half of GDP. In addition, the low overall unemployment rate masks large regional disparities, and unemployment remains highly concentrated among unskilled and older workers. Moreover, the average duration of unemployment has been increasing, suggesting that the bulk of unemployment is structural.

Real Wages

In the early years of the transition, real wages grew at a rate above the targets agreed to by the social partners, and above productivity increases. This was particularly true for the government sector, and higher wages there spilled over to increase wage demands throughout the economy. The outcome of these wage pressures was lower competitiveness in the real sector as well as higher expenditure for social payments linked to wage increases, such as pension payments. The need to establish wage discipline in the government sector was reflected in the wage adjustment law enacted in mid-1997, which helped moderate real wage growth, ease wage indexation, and reverse the trend toward real wage increases exceeding productivity gains. As a result of these policies, unit labor costs started to fall. Although real gross wage growth moderated from 4.4 percent in 1996 to 2.1 percent in 2002 (Table 8.2), wage growth in the government sector continued to outpace that in the private sector, despite efforts to curtail wage growth in the public administration. Further efforts are thus required to avoid wage escalation in the future that could damage the prospects for growth and integration.

Fiscal Policy

Most economies in transition undertook price liberalization and privatization, albeit at different paces and using a variety of methods. As a result, all of them went through a cycle of sharp recession followed, in most cases, by private sector-led recovery. A central feature of the

TABLE 8.2 REAL NET WAGES, 1992–2002

Item	1993	1994	1995	1996	1997	1998	1999	2000	2001	2002
Real net wages (1992 = 100)	116.4	123.3	129.1	134.8	138.7	140.8	145.0	147.1	151.6	154.7
Change from previous year (percent)	16.4	6.0	4.7	4.4	2.9	1.5	3.0	1.4	3.1	2.1

Source: Bank of Slovenia (2003).

FIGURE 8.9 GENERAL GOVERNMENT FISCAL BALANCE

(percent of GDP)

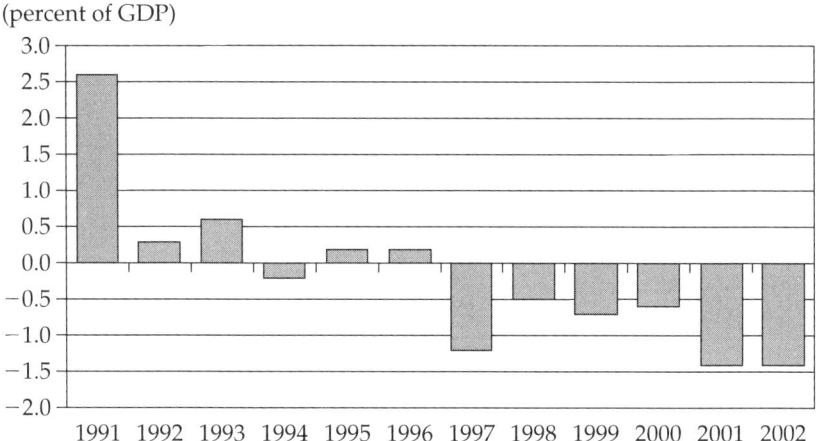

Sources: World Bank, International Monetary Fund, and Bank of Slovenia.

liberalization packages introduced by the transition economies was a set of policies intended to affect the fiscal accounts but that, in many cases, led to fiscal crises, which had been a rare phenomenon under socialism.

Slovenia's public finances, however, did not deteriorate during the initial stages of the transition.[2] Rather, Slovenia was able to keep its general government budget virtually balanced during the first 5 years of independence (Figure 8.9). The policy of maintaining overall fiscal balance was indeed one of the cornerstones of Slovenia's transition and an important support to its monetary policy during the initial macroeconomic stabilization efforts. In 1997 the general government slipped into deficit by 1.1 percent of GDP, still small in comparison with those of other transition economies.

The 1997 deficit was mainly the result of reductions in social security contributions; diminished border trade and lower customs duties in accordance with EU and CEFTA agreements; and increases in social transfers, wages, and subsidies. The size of the fiscal deficit in that year did not by itself raise concerns, but it did reflect a changing trend in Slovenia's fiscal position, which has continued since then.

The general government deficit has remained below 1.5 percent of GDP during the transition, with primary surpluses recorded virtually throughout the decade (exceptions occurred in 1997 and 2000, when Slovenia experienced small primary deficits). This record of fiscal conservatism has been a remarkable achievement and has placed

FIGURE 8.10 FISCAL BALANCE IN SELECTED EU ACCESSION
              COUNTRIES AND THE EUROPEAN UNION, 2002

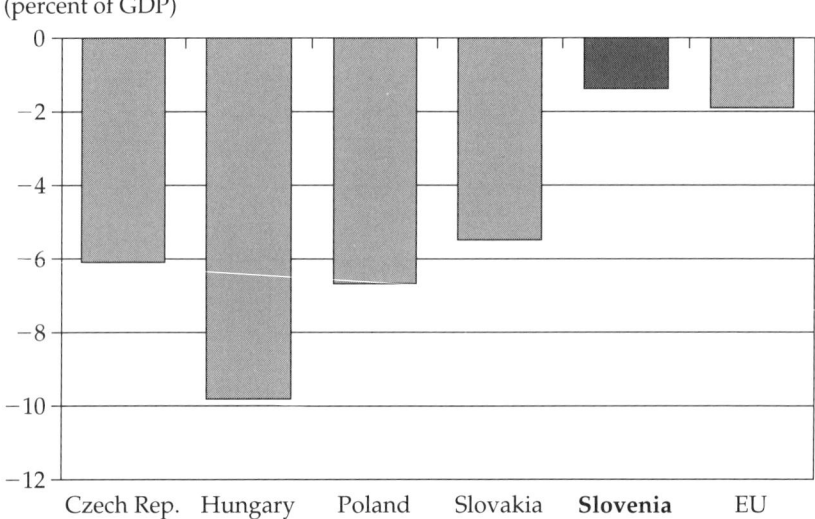

Source: International Monetary Fund.

Slovenia in a much better position than other leading EU accession
countries; indeed, Slovenia's fiscal performance has been better than
the EU average (Figure 8.10).

An additional fiscal challenge for Slovenia is to bring the level of
public expenditure down: spending has remained in the vicinity of 43
to 45 percent of GDP in recent years. At that level the size of the public sector puts Slovenia in the company of some of the more advanced
OECD countries, but well above countries with similar incomes per
capita, such as Portugal and Spain. Although Slovenia is likely to be
a net recipient of EU funds, the EU accession process will exert additional spending pressure.

SLOVENIA AND THE MAASTRICHT
CONVERGENCE CRITERIA

Slovenia is favorably positioned to meet some, but not all, of the convergence criteria laid out in the 1992 Maastricht Treaty, which set,
among other things, prudential guidelines and ceilings for fiscal
deficits and total debt in the EU countries (Figure 8.11).[3] The treaty
also defined the convergence criteria for economies seeking to join

FIGURE 8.11 EU ACCESSION COUNTRIES AND
MAASTRICHT PARAMETERS, 2002

Source: World Bank data.

European Monetary Union (EMU). Those criteria included the following five conditions: annual inflation should be no more than 1.5 percentage points above the average inflation rate of the three EU countries with the lowest inflation; long-term interest rates should be no more than 2 percent above the average of the three countries with the lowest inflation; budget deficits should be no higher than 3 percent of GDP; the national debt should be no more than 60 percent of GDP; and exchange rates should be within the normal bands of the ERM and should have undergone no realignments for at least 2 years. These elements of the Maastricht convergence criteria are essential to guarantee the functioning of the European single currency. New EU members are required to join EMU.

Slovenia fares well against these criteria with respect to its total debt and its fiscal deficit—a result of the prudent economic policies of the past decade. However, the inflation target and, as a result, the interest rate target are still to be attained, and exchange rate policy should guarantee that the value of the currency is set correctly upon entry into ERM-II in the near future. This will ensure a smooth convergence and entry into EMU. Lowering inflation before entry into the ERM-II will require a sustained effort, however.

CONCLUSIONS

Slovenia embarked on its transition with some of the most favorable initial conditions of all the transition economies, including a good geographical location, skilled human capital, and significant trade links with the West, established in the 1970s and 1980s through the development of long-run contracts with Western firms. As a result of these links, during the breakup of SFR Yugoslavia, Slovenia was able to quickly redirect its vanishing interrepublic trade, thus boosting its chances for a fast economic turnaround. But the quick turnaround that did occur was not only the result of location and favorable initial conditions. Prudent economic policies played a critical role during the transition to independence and a market economy and helped to quickly build confidence in the new state and its economy.

Slovenia has a functioning market economy, one that will be capable of facing the competitive pressures within the European Union. The country has made good progress in the adoption and implementation of the *acquis communautaire*, as well as in the development of the institutions necessary for its implementation (World Bank 2000).

Slovenia is today one of the most successful EU accession candidates. Its economy has shown considerable resilience to EU business cycles. The success of the transition years is the result of prudent economic policies and a gradualist approach to structural reforms, which have served the country well in many ways. Income per capita is the highest among the accession countries, and convergence toward the EU average real income has taken place during the past decade. In the future, economic policy will need to continue to provide support for sustainable growth, furthering income convergence and development.

REFERENCES

Bank of Slovenia. 2003. *Monthly Bulletin* 12(5). Ljubljana.

European Bank for Reconstruction and Development. Various years. *Transition Report*. London.

International Monetary Fund. Various years. "Republic of Slovenia: Article IV Consultation." Washington, D.C.

Riboud, M., Sanchez-Paramo, C., and Silva-Jáuregui, C. 2002. "Does Eurosclerosis Matter? Institutional Reform and Labor Market Performance in Central and Eastern European Countries." World Bank Technical Paper 519. Washington, D.C.

Svejnar, J. 2002. "Transition Economies: Performance and Challenges." *Journal of Economic Perspectives* 16: 3–28.

World Bank. 1998a. *Slovenia: Labor Market Issues.* Washington, D.C.

_____. 1998b. *Slovenia: Trade Sector Issues.* Washington, D.C.

_____. 1999a. *Slovenia: Economic Transformation and EU Accession.* Washington, D.C.

_____. 1999b. *Czech Republic: Toward EU Accession.* Washington, D.C.

_____. 2000. *Progress Toward the Unification of Europe.* Washington, D.C.

_____. 2002. *Transition—The First Ten Years: Analysis and Lessons for Eastern Europe and the Former Soviet Union.* Washington, D.C.

NOTES

1. Labor force survey unemployment measures more accurately characterize unemployment in Slovenia. Unemployment rates measured by the registry of the National Employment Office, although also declining, are significantly higher (11.6 percent in 2002), but the data are contaminated by a number of factors, including pervasive incentives and distortions due to active labor market policies (see World Bank 1998a).

2. See Chapter 12 for a further analysis of fiscal policies and public finance during the transition.

3. In December 1991 the leaders of the member countries of the European Community met at Maastricht, the Netherlands, to negotiate a treaty on the European Union. Finally signed in February 1992, the treaty advanced the European agenda significantly toward economic, political, and social union and set out a detailed timetable for EMU.

Chapter 9
Trade Policy in the Transition Process

Boris Majcen and Bartlomiej Kaminski

Independent Slovenia has inherited a process of foreign trade liberalization that had already begun in SFR Yugoslavia. This was the first radical step in the liberalization of import regimes in Slovenia and was accompanied by the removal of certain import charges and numerous tariff exemptions.[1] Undoubtedly, the need to redirect sales to foreign markets and to open up the domestic market to foreign competition, especially through integration in the rest of Europe as well as in the world economy, accounts for Slovenia's determination to continue the process of foreign trade liberalization and to participate in various multilateral, regional, and bilateral trade initiatives. Slovenia made extensive commitments upon its accession to the General Agreement on Tariffs and Trade (GATT) and the World Trade Organization (WTO); these included binding 100 percent of its tariff lines, dismantling remaining nontariff barriers, making specific commitments in two-thirds of the issues covered by the General Agreement on Trade in Services (GATS), and signing free trade agreements with 33 other European countries.

This quite radical approach to multilateral and bilateral trade liberalization was in stark contrast to the gradual approach adopted in many other aspects of the transition, which in Slovenia's case has been viewed as unique and admittedly very successful (Bernard 1997). The gradualism of the Slovenian transition was the outcome of certain specific initial conditions, which differed markedly from those in other Central and Eastern European (CEE) countries. These included a unique economic and political system; systemic changes and developments in the political sphere; established economic links with Western markets, with very liberal access to the EU market for most manufacturing exports under the 1993 Cooperation Agreement; and the transition to independence. Nevertheless, the slow pace of privatization and a reluctance to open up to foreign direct investment before the 1999 acceleration in structural reforms probably contributed to a foreign trade performance that is less impressive than those of many other CEE economies, especially Hungary (Kaminski 1998, World Bank 1999).

During the transition, and with the final aim of accession to the European Union, Slovenia's trade policy has been largely oriented toward harmonization with the EU Common External Tariff (CET) and with EU regulations on customs, standards, competition policy, and other trade-related areas. Since 2001, Slovenia's trade in manufactures with its largest trading partners has been duty free, and agricultural goods are granted a wide variety of product- and country-specific preferences. Last but not least, Slovenia's trade regime is largely compatible with the *acquis communautaire* of the European Union.

Hence it appears that accession to the European Union, or, more precisely, the influence of EU policies aimed at building the economic foundations for its "Eastern enlargement," has been the major incentive for Slovenia's as well as other EU candidates' choice of economic policies, not just in trade but in a number of other areas. The process of aligning Slovenia's institutions with the requirements of the *acquis* has served as a basis for the domestic transition in Slovenia to a market-based economy. With the progress already realized, both in the integration process and in the harmonization of economic regimes with the *acquis*, the integration framework's impact on foreign trade institutions and policies has increased.

This chapter is organized as follows. The first section focuses on the dismantling of SFR Yugoslavia's protectionist foreign trade system and the pursuit of multilateral liberalization in the context of WTO membership. The second section reviews the bilateral liberalization track of Slovenia's trade policy. The last section concludes.

THE LEGACY OF IMPORT SUBSTITUTION AND MULTILATERAL TRADE POLICY

The development strategy of SFR Yugoslavia (and hence of Slovenia) before 1990 was oriented toward import substitution, using a complicated system of various interventionist measures. The system of tariff protection followed the principle that the degree of processing undergone by a product determined the protection it enjoyed. This system was further complemented by a complicated "system" of other import charges. Various schemes of relieves and exemptions (including some that were of a confidential nature) resulted in a marked increase in the variability of nominal protection and proved counterproductive to the fundamental objectives of tariff protection itself.

Besides tariffs, another very important aspect of import protection came in the form of restrictive import regimes: quotas, licenses, special import licenses, and conditionally free imports, together with a complicated system of payment for imported goods, were to be found in almost all industrial sectors—imports of investment and consumer goods were further restricted by annual global quotas. In 1986, 42 percent of the value of production of Slovenian industry and mining was additionally protected by import restrictions such as quantity quotas, value quotas, and licenses, as well as by special import licenses (Table 9.1). Undoubtedly, the import regimes together with foreign exchange restrictions contributed significantly to the level of protection, with a profoundly negative impact on the allocation of resources and the competitiveness of domestic firms in international markets.

All these factors led to a nontransparent "system" of protection policy, which also gave rise to a number of unintended effects. Among these were a strong bias against agriculture and exports, undesirable

TABLE 9.1 SHARES OF INDUSTRY AND MINING SUBJECT TO
          IMPORT REGIMES, 1986

(percent)

Regime	Share of imports	Share of production
Free[a]	3	}58
Conditionally free[b]	53	
Free under agreement or permission[c]	1	1
Special import licenses	5	4
Quotas	37	32
Licenses	1	0
Others[d]	. . .	4

a. Imports allowed without any restrictions regarding the quantity, value, or form of payment.
b. Imports conditionally free within the specified amount of payments. Investment and consumer goods were further restricted by annual global quotas.
c. Imports allowed under agreement or permission that certain specific conditions were fulfilled.
d. Groups of products with mixed import regimes.
Source: Majcen (1993, Table 3).

economic rents, and, as a consequence, inefficient use of the factors of production, inappropriate development of the structure of the economy, and a reduction in the economy's flexibility and ability to adjust to changes in the global economy.[2]

Estimates of the nominal and effective rates of protection in various sectors during that period clearly confirm that Slovenian producers enjoyed high levels of protection. Even more clearly, they confirm the extreme importance of nonprice protective measures. However, this protection was not the result of a carefully designed trade policy, but rather the cumulative effect of numerous ad hoc measures taken over decades. To an increasingly obvious degree, the accumulated problems and the external pressures that accompanied them required a fundamental change of strategy.

After pursuing an import-substitution development strategy for many years, SFR Yugoslavia began to open up to foreign competition at the end of the 1980s. Restrictive import regimes were dismantled, certain import charges were removed, and numerous duty exemptions were extended. Unfortunately, this was done without the necessary preliminary analysis of the existing degree of protection and the possible effects of the proposed liberalizations. The shift in policy was primarily a response to the crisis into which the economy had fallen. The process of trade liberalization continued in independent Slovenia after 1991, beginning with the elimination of a special tax on imported goods and many of the remaining quantitative import restrictions (with the exception of the agriculture, food processing, and textile industries).

The result of this first stage of trade liberalization was an almost complete elimination of nontariff forms of protection, which was not offset by a higher rate of price-based forms of protection (tariffs and other import charges). The result was a more transparent and less distortive system (Table 9.2). The removal of direct import controls, combined with the convertibility of domestic currency for current account transactions and a dramatic decline in additional import charges, made tariffs the most important tool of foreign trade policy in industrial products.

Throughout the period of foreign trade liberalization, the previous Tariff Schedule Act remained in force. Slovenia tried to correct the inadequate tariff protection structure by introducing a series of individual amendments (including reductions of tariff rates for imports of raw materials and intermediate and capital goods not domestically produced, and allowing duty-free imports of raw materials and intermediate goods for export-oriented production). This caused a substantial reduction in tariff protection, the only exception being those aimed at the production of consumer goods.[3]

The inadequate and opaque structure of protection, the need for new foreign trade legislation, Slovenia's accession to the GATT and the WTO, and the need to join the European integration process urged Slovenia to adopt a new Tariff Schedule Act on the basis of the coding system used in the European Union. Upon accession to the WTO, Slovenia made some quite substantial commitments. As already noted, it has bound 100 percent of its tariff lines and abolished almost all import charges other than tariffs.[4] It has made specific commitments in two-thirds of the activities covered by the GATS.[5] It has also lowered most-favored-nation (MFN) applied tariff rates: the simple applied average MFN tariff rate fell from 15 percent in 1994 to 11 percent in 2001 (Table 9.3).[6] Ninety-six percent of all 10,300 tariff lines are ad valorem tariffs, and about 400 tariff lines in agriculture are subject to a compound tariff. The number of tariff rates has been reduced, with two-thirds of tariff lines subject to tariffs of between 0 and 10 percent.

Although the WTO has praised Slovenia for its strong commitment to the multilateral trading system, its MFN tariffs have fallen less rapidly than its preferential rates, thus increasing preferential margins. Slovenia's tariff structure continues to suffer from four other weaknesses. First, there is a significant dispersion of tariff rates, leading to tariff escalation. Applied tariff rates are significantly lower for imports of raw materials than for those of processed goods and intermediate products (Table 9.4).

Second, a large gap (13 percent on average) between bound and applied rates (see Table 9.3) undermines the predictability of Slovenia's

TABLE 9.2 SHARES OF IMPORT VALUE AND FOREIGN TRADE CLASSIFICATION CODES BY IMPORT REGIME, AND TARIFFS AND CHARGES PAID, 1986–96

Import regime	Share of import value (percent)				Share of codes (percent)			
	1986	1990	1993	1996	1986	1990	1993	1996
Free imports	3	78	97	98	8	85	95	93
Conditionally free imports	58	8	0	0	74	2	0	0
Quotas	37	12	1	0	17	11	1	3
Licenses	2	2	2	2	2	3	2	4

Import charge	1986	1990	1993	1996
Official tariffs[a]	11.0	12.0	12.3	10.7
Other official import charges[b]	17.5	16.0	2.0[c]	0.0
Tariffs actually paid	7.4	7.1	...	5.6
Other import charges actually paid	4.8	9.3	...	0.0

a. Unweighted averages; differences are due to the introduction of the harmonized coding system in 1988, code changes in 1993, and the new tariff schedule in 1996.

b. Unweighted averages; numerous exemptions apply; special import duty on agricultural products not included.

c. Charges on alcohol and cigarettes were 17.0 percent of import value.

Source: Majcen (1995, Tables 2.1 and 2.2).

TABLE 9.3 APPLIED TARIFF RATES IN 1994 AND 2001 AND WTO
         BOUND TARIFF RATES

(percent ad valorem)

Sector	Applied tariff rate			WTO bound tariff rate	Difference between bound and applied tariff rates, 2001
	1994	2001	Change, 1994–2001		
Total	14.6	10.8	−26.0	23.8	13.0
Agriculture	6.8	15.3	125.0	25.4	10.1
Mining	6.7	1.7	−74.6	23.9	22.2
Manufacturing	15.3	11.1	−27.5	23.9	12.8
Consumer goods	17.5	16.3	−6.9	26.2	9.9
Intermediate goods	12.6	8.1	−35.7	23.1	15.0
Capital goods	16.3	9.1	−44.2	20.6	11.5

Sources: Majcen (1995), WTO (2002).

tariff regime (WTO 2002). This largely results from the binding of a large number of tariff lines at a uniform rate of 27 percent (with peaks well beyond 100 percent for lines subject to tariff quotas) and the rapid reduction of applied rates (WTO 2002, p. 34).

Third, the increasing gap between average weighted tariff rates and customs-collected rates (calculated as revenue from tariffs and other import charges, divided by the value of total imports) after Slovenia's adoption of its own tariff schedule can be attributed to numerous tariff exemptions as well as to a number of preferential trade agreements that Slovenia has signed with its most important trading partners. To reduce the disadvantages of such arrangements for third countries, in 1999 the Slovenian authorities adopted a plan of gradual alignment of the country's applied MFN tariffs with the EU CET.

Fourth, although a thorough examination would be beyond the scope of this chapter, Slovenian MFN tariff rates are significantly higher and more dispersed than those of the EU CET. As Table 9.5 shows, the simple average MFN applied tariff rate in 2001 was more than twice as high as that in the European Union.

TABLE 9.4 SIMPLE AVERAGE OF MFN TARIFFS BY STAGE
         OF PROCESSING, 2001

(percent)

Product category	Applied rate	Bound rate
Raw materials	5.6	20.9
Intermediate goods	8.3	24.6
Processed goods	13.1	24.0

Source: WTO (2002).

TABLE 9.5 EU AND SLOVENIAN MFN AVERAGE TARIFF RATES, 2001[a]

(percent ad valorem)

Product category	European Union	Slovenia
All products (Harmonized System [HS] 0–97)		
Simple average	4.7	10.8
Standard deviation	4.6	9.1
Maximum tariff rates	74.9	293.1
Agricultural products (HS 0–24)		
Simple average	8.9	15.3
Industrial products (HS Chapters 25–97)		
Simple average	4.3	9.5

a. EU values are for the common external tariff.

Sources: Authors' calculations; WTO (2002).

None of these weaknesses represents a threat to Slovenia's economic welfare. One reason is that the current import regime will cease to exist once Slovenia accedes to the European Union, which, barring unforeseen developments, will occur in May 2004. But the crux of the matter is that, because of various bilateral liberalization initiatives (discussed below), the MFN import regime has affected only an insignificant portion of Slovenia's total imports. The large share of duty-free imports (85 percent) understates the degree of openness to foreign competition for at least two reasons. First, Slovenia has granted tariff exemptions to a number of imported products, effectively lowering the implicit tariff rate. Second, and more important, imports from nonpreferential trade partners tend to concentrate in raw materials and in intermediate products with little processing. More-protected processed goods come mainly from trade partners enjoying duty-free status (probably exacerbating the trade diversion effect).

Some insights into the effects of these two factors on both historical levels of protection as well as the year of full implementation of the European Association Agreement and other free trade agreements (FTAs) can be gained from estimates of the rates of effective protection based on customs collection rather than legislated tariff rates. Comparison of the effective rates of protection estimated for 1993 with those estimated for 1986 (Table 9.6) reveals that the main reductions came at the end of the 1980s (during the last years of SFR Yugoslavia) and in the first years of Slovenia's independence. Producers in the manufacturing, energy, and mining sectors had already experienced the main shock of foreign trade liberalization and reorientation from domestic to foreign markets by 1993; the estimated rate of effective protection for manufacturing decreased from 37 percent in 1986 to only 4 percent in 1993.

TABLE 9.6 EFFECTIVE RATES OF PROTECTION, 1986–2001
(percent)

Sector	1986	1993	1996	1997	1998	1999	2000	2001
Energy and mining	25.6	5.0	2.4	1.8	1.6	1.4	1.3	1.3
Manufacturing	36.7	4.2	3.9	2.7	2.1	1.7	1.3	0.9
Capital goods	23.7	2.3	2.5	1.6	1.1	0.9	0.6	0.3
Intermediate goods	45.4	4.4	3.9	2.8	2.1	1.7	1.3	0.8
Consumer goods	32.7	4.7	4.6	3.1	2.4	2.0	1.5	1.1
Agriculture	8.7	18.2	25.9	26.3	26.5	26.6	26.7	26.7
Unprocessed goods	–5.7	9.8	9.0	9.6	9.8	9.9	10.1	10.1
Processed goods	47.2	26.9	42.5	42.8	42.9	42.9	43.0	43.0
All goods	30.9	7.0	7.9	7.1	6.6	6.4	6.1	5.9

Source: Majcen (1995).

One can conclude from this review of Slovenia's entry into the multilateral trading system that Slovenia inherited the first stage of foreign trade liberalization, which had already been initiated in SFR Yugoslavia, starting with a radical removal of nontariff barriers. After independence, Slovenia continued with the further elimination of the remaining nontariff barriers and adopted a new tariff schedule, ultimately abolishing almost all other import charges except tariffs. Tariffs were set in line with the perceived need to protect various industrial sectors deemed vulnerable to competition from imports. The fact is that protection was mainly reduced at the end of the 1980s, while Slovenia was still part of SFR Yugoslavia, and in the first years of Slovenia's independence. From that point, with levels of protection already low compared with the situation before the end of the 1980s, liberalization proceeded through accession to the WTO and the implementation of FTAs.

BILATERAL REGIONAL LIBERALIZATION: THE EU FACTOR

After the important opening of the domestic market through unilateral measures during the first phase of liberalization, which evolved into the multilateral phase with accession to the WTO, Slovenia opted for bilateral liberalization of its foreign trade policy driven almost exclusively by the goal of joining the European Union. Not unlike the other candidates for EU accession, Slovenia has followed very closely the vision and policies designed by the European Union to carry out its Eastern enlargement. EU policy has evolved over time: it began with the "Europe Agreements" (EAs) modeled after earlier agreements among the founding countries of the European Communities.[7] Soon thereafter, the European Union moved to push for greater

integration among the agreements' signatories through FTAs and subsequently through diagonal cumulation of the rules of origin, which
culminated with the Pan-European Cumulating of Origin Agreement
on January 1, 1997.[8] This agreement established a single territory for
purposes of rules of origin and set the stage for a single European
trading bloc for industrial products, which was fully implemented on
January 1, 2002 (Kaminski 2001).

Although the trade components of the EAs with some CEE countries went into effect on different dates, ranging from 1992 (former
Czechoslovakia, Hungary, and Poland) to 1997 (Slovenia), schedules
for the elimination of duties and nontariff trade barriers on industrial
products had one important element in common: all set January 1,
2002, as the date for completing the liberalization process. Similarly,
the elimination of duties on industrial products did not go beyond
these dates in all the other bilateral FTAs signed among CEE countries. The pace of liberalization has been harmonized in terms of the
date of the emergence of a pan-European FTA in industrial products,
and a single framework has shaped the external commercial activities
of all current accession candidates. The prospect of accession has
shaped the trade policies of all these countries.

Slovenia has been no exception to this pattern. Indeed, it has pursued this path with greater zeal and determination than many other
candidate countries, not only for economic but also for national security reasons. Immediately after independence, the government
declared full membership in the European Union as the main strategic goal. The first step was to sign an EA, which was similar to that
signed between the European Union and the Central European countries (former Czechoslovakia, Hungary, and Poland) on December 15,
1991. In the meantime, the European Union "reactivated" the old
Cooperation Agreement that was signed with SFR Yugoslavia in 1980,
but with some extra provisions (Table 9.7). That agreement gave
Slovenian exporters almost unlimited duty-free access to most EU markets for industrial products they already had within SFR Yugoslavia,
thus reducing the sense of urgency to replace it with the EA.

Indeed, negotiations on the EA were lengthy. The European Union
objected to Slovenia's real estate legislation banning foreigners from
owning property. Once the required amendments were enacted, however, this major stumbling block disappeared. Pending ratification of
the EA by Slovenia's legislature and the legislatures of the EU members, its interim trade component went into effect on January 1, 1997,
replacing the Cooperation Agreement, which until then had provided
a framework for Slovenian-EU trade relations.

However, in contrast to the Cooperation Agreement, which offered
Slovenia trade preferences on an autonomous basis, the interim trade
agreement, albeit initially asymmetrical, compelled Slovenia to open

TABLE 9.7 MAJOR EVENTS IN BILATERAL TRADE RELATIONS
BETWEEN THE EUROPEAN UNION AND SLOVENIA

Date	Event
April 1992	Diplomatic relations established.
September 1993	Cooperation Agreement modeled on the 1980 agreement with SFR Yugoslavia, with supplements on transport, textiles, and financial cooperation, enters into force.
June 1996	European Association Agreement signed.
June 1996	Slovenia requests full membership in European Union.
January 1997	Interim Agreement on Trade enters into force, replacing Cooperation Agreement.
July 1997	European Union declares Slovenia eligible to start negotiations on full membership.
March 1998	Accession negotiations begin.
December 2002	Accession negotiations concluded.
May 2004	Scheduled accession to the European Union.

Sources: European Union (1997, 1998–2002).

its markets to EU exporters on preferential conditions. Customs duties on imports into Slovenia of products originating in the European Union were immediately abolished for 41 percent of total imports (those on list A). For sensitive goods (list B, with 28 percent of total imports, and list C, with 32 percent), customs duties were reduced to 55 percent or 70 percent of the basic rates (MFN applied tariff rates in 1996), respectively. They were to be progressively reduced by the end of 2000. As Table 9.8 shows, the trade component of the EA has played an important role in further opening the Slovenian economy to external competition.[9] Note first that list A contained those products subject to the lowest applied MFN tariff rates. In general, the period of elimination of duties was longer for those products with higher tariff rates. List B reached its goal of zero tariffs by the end of 1999, and list C was put to rest at the end of 2000.

Multilateral liberalization is always more effective than bilateral liberalization at increasing competitive pressure on domestic producers and reaping the associated economic efficiencies. But the European Union is both an economic superpower and Slovenia's natural trading partner for reasons of both geography and economic potential. Although it does not necessarily produce all industrial products at the lowest cost worldwide, it does produce most of them. Hence, although in some cases Slovenian importers probably chose EU suppliers not because their products were the cheapest, but only thanks to trade preferences (the difference between the applied MFN tariff rate and the preferential rate), one suspects that, for the majority of imports, internal competition within the European Union prevented

TABLE 9.8 SHARES OF EU IMPORTS IN TOTAL IMPORTS BY PRODUCT LIST, AND ESTIMATED CUSTOMS DUTIES LEVIED, 1994–2001[a]

(percent)

| List | No. of codes | 1994 | | 1996 | | Customs duties, ad valorem | | | | |
		Share of total imports from EU	Customs duties and other charges, ad valorem	Share in total imports from EU	Customs duties and other charges, ad valorem	1997	1998	1999	2000	2001
A	3,964	41.1	4.6	41.0	2.5	0.0	0.0	0.0	0.0	0.0
B	2,337	28.5	7.6	26.6	6.3	3.2	2.3	1.1	0.0	0.0
C	2,092	30.3	13.1	32.4	10.5	7.2	5.9	2.0	2.1	0.0
Total	8,393	100.0	8.1	100.0	6.1	3.2	2.5	0.9	0.7	0.0

a. Customs data are averages weighted by 1996 imports; inward and outward processing, basic agricultural products, and processed foods are excluded.

Source: Authors' estimates based on data in Majcen (1997).

143

EU exporters from extracting rents at the expense of their Slovenian customers. After May 1, 2004, when Slovenia adopts the EU CET, the extent of reverse discrimination, that is, of discrimination against MFN suppliers, will fall dramatically, because EU applied MFN tariff rates are much lower. The assessment of rents collected by EU firms will then become an exercise in economic history.

A series of bilateral FTAs that Slovenia signed with other "enlargement" countries (those of the European Free Trade Association [EFTA], the Central European Free Trade Agreement [CEFTA], and FTAs with the Baltic states, Israel, and Turkey) and with the successor countries of SFR Yugoslavia (Croatia, FYR Macedonia, and Bosnia and Herzegovina) has somewhat weakened the potential for trade diversion inherent in the trade component of the EA, or, for that matter, in any FTA (Table 9.9). None of these countries is an economic powerhouse, but taken together they represent a significant economic potential, with a clear advantage over Slovenia's other trade partners due to geographic proximity and historical economic ties.

Slovenia's trade structure after independence indicates a rapid reorientation toward the European Union between 1992 and 1999, when both exports to and imports from the European Union grew on average by 9 and 13 percent, respectively, and increased from 55 percent

TABLE 9.9 BILATERAL FREE TRADE AGREEMENTS, 2001

Country or group	No. of countries	Signed	In effect since	Share of total Slovenian trade, 2001 (percent) Exports	Imports
European Union	15	June 10, 1996	January 1, 1997	62.2	67.6
EFTA	4	June 13, 1995	January 1, 1996	1.3	1.7
CEFTA	6	November 25, 1995	January 1, 1996	8.0	9.5
Croatia	1	December 12 1997	January 1, 1998	8.6	4.0
FYR Macedonia	1	July 1, 1996	September 1, 1996	1.4	0.3
Estonia	1	November 26, 1996	January 1, 1997	0.1	0.0
Latvia	1	April 22, 1996	August 1, 1996	0.1	0.0
Lithuania	1	October 4, 1996	March 1, 1997	0.3	0.0
Israel	1	May 13, 1998	September 1, 1998	0.1	0.8
Turkey	1	May 5, 1998	January 1, 1999	0.4	0.8
Bosnia and Herzegovina	1	October 1, 2001	January 1, 1902	4.3	0.6
Total	33			86.9	85.4

Source: Damijan (2002).

to 66 and 69 percent of total trade. Trade with the European Union has stagnated since 1999. However, exports to the CEFTA countries and the other former Yugoslav markets are rapidly increasing, not only because of preferential arrangements but also because trade has recovered with the cessation of conflict in the Balkans. Preferential trade, including that with the European Union, accounted for more than 85 percent of Slovenia's total trade in 2001 (Table 9.9).

Slovenia did not choose its FTA partners at random. Their choice reflected both the country's determination to participate in the EU enlargement project as well as its own economic interests. The insistence on FTAs with the successor countries of SFR Yugoslavia was driven by the desire to salvage the buoyant trade that had existed before the collapse of SFR Yugoslavia. All of the other partners had, at the time the FTA was signed, preferential arrangements with the European Union. The FTA with EFTA has been viewed as a preparatory stage for full EU membership, but it was very soon thereafter complemented with the CEFTA agreement. That agreement was established in response to pressure from the European Union for cooperation among the transition countries, which marked the beginning of Slovenia's venture into regional trade liberalization.

Tariff preferences were negotiated primarily for industrial products, resulting in duty-free imports in 2001. However, the average collected tariff for countries without FTAs was 3.8 percent (Table 9.10). Relatively low levels of collected tariff rates do not necessarily imply low tariff barriers for MFN exporters. If anything, this may suggest significant levels of trade diversion in the more protected sectors and concentration of MFN exports on products subject to lower MFN applied tariff rates.

Outstanding results were found for agricultural products. In the case of the Europe Agreement and the other FTAs, they reveal the fact that these products are subject to concessions only to a certain extent, resulting in a wide variety of restrictions and decreased transparency

TABLE 9.10 COLLECTED TARIFF RATES AND VARIABLE LEVIES, 2001

(percent ad valorem)

Sector	Total	EU-15	EU candidate countries	Other countries with FTAs	Rest of world
Agriculture	8.01	10.18	7.59	7.38	3.47
Other sectors	0.61	0.13	0.12	0.22	3.82
Total	1.15	0.68	1.15	1.06	3.86

Sources: Customs declarations for 2001, from the Statistical Office of the Republic of Slovenia; authors' calculations.

of the tariff regime.[10] These are also the products for which one can expect the highest negative effects of the abolishment of protection after Slovenia enters the European Union.

Leaving aside the interesting question of what considerations of political economy prompted Slovenia not to align its MFN tariff rates more closely with those of the EU CET, one should note that the Slovenian manufacturing sector has been almost completely exposed to fierce foreign competition from EU and other preferential trade partners. Although many highly competitive firms, especially in sectors where two or three companies dominate, may have been able to collect rents by charging higher prices than in the absence of tariffs, keeping MFN competitors at bay, Slovenian domestic markets have become as competitive as those in the most competitive industrial countries. This augurs well for their capacity to withstand competitive pressures from the single market once Slovenia joins the European Union.

CONCLUSIONS

Slovenia is a stable democracy with an economy based on competitive markets. It is ready to take advantage of the unique opportunities offered by integration into the global economy through its imminent membership in the European Union. One might argue that a stable democracy and a prosperous economy, capable of taking advantage of the opportunities offered by a contemporary global economy, could also be achieved through multilateral rather than regional integration. But for both domestic and external reasons, accession to the European Union was deemed the best policy option. Domestically, the accession process has provided clear guidance to Slovenia's institutional transformation and liberalization of trade.

Domestically, the loss of the former Yugoslav market, together with the EU accession process, has spurred the opening of the Slovenian economy to external competition, which is the necessary condition for the prosperity and survival of a small economy critically dependent on foreign trade. Accession to the WTO has failed to achieve this goal completely, as Slovenia's relatively high MFN applied tariff rates, which have not yet been aligned with the EU CET, clearly demonstrate. These high rates are still in place despite the fact that they offer little or no protection. The government has abandoned its attempts to align tariff rates with the EU CET, revealing strong internal opposition to liberalization, even though MFN tariffs have little relevance for domestic producers already facing strong competition from duty-free imports. Indeed, it is hard to find an economic justification for high MFN rates applicable to only 15 percent of imports. Without the EU enlargement project, liberalization and rapid integration into global markets would have probably still occurred, but with huge delays and high adjustment costs.

Externally, the EU accession process has offered both political and economic opportunities. It has offered preferential access to EU markets as well as significant technical assistance under the PHARE program. Although Slovenia enjoyed preferential access under the revived Yugoslav Autonomous Trade Preferences, these had to be renewed annually and were probably unsustainable under WTO rules requiring reciprocity. Furthermore, it is rather unlikely that, under these arrangements, Slovenia would have become part of the Pan-European Cumulation Agreement and, by the same token, part of a single European free market for industrial products encompassing almost 500 million consumers from 29 countries.

Hence, in retrospect, the EA was the starting point of a process that has put in place a new framework providing strong incentives for economic integration on the European continent. This seems to be a huge, even if originally unanticipated, return from regional integration, both for the European Union and for its European associates that are soon to become members.

REFERENCES

Bernard, L. D. 1997. "Transition économique atypique. Le cas de Slovénie." *Reflets et Perspectives* 2: 75–87.

Buehrer, T., and B. Majcen. 2001. "Izračunljivi model splošnega ravnotežja za Slovenijo [Computable General Equilibrium Model for Slovenia]." Institute for Economic Research, Ljubljana. Processed

Damijan, J. P. 2002. "International Trade." University of Ljubljana, Ljubljana. Processed.

European Union. 1997. "Agenda 2000—Commission Opinion on Slovenia's Application for Membership of the European Union." DOC 97/19. European Commission, Brussels.

————. 1998–2002. "Regular Report on Slovenia's Progress Toward Accession" (annual reports). European Commission, Brussels.

Kaminski, B. 1998. "Foreign Trade and FDI in Hungary and Slovenia: Different Paths—Different Outcomes." *Transition* 8 (6): 15–20.

————. 2001. "How Accession to the European Union Has Affected External Trade and Foreign Direct Investment in Central European Economies." Policy Research Working Paper 2578. World Bank, Development Research Group-Trade, Washington, D.C.

Majcen, B. 1993. "Temeljna izhodišča za pripravo osnov zaščitne politike R Slovenije [Basic Starting Points of the Protection Policy in the Republic of Slovenia]." Institute for Economic Research, Ljubljana. Processed.

————. 1994. "Zunanjetrgovinska zaščita gospodarstva Republike Slovenije–analiza stanja po osamosvojitvi [Slovene Foreign Trade Protection after Independence]." *Slovenska ekonomska revija* 45(1–3): 214–22.

————. 1995. "Zunanjetrgovinska liberalizacija industrijskih in kmetijskih proizvodov [Foreign Trade Liberalization of Industrial and Agriculture Products]." Institute for Economic Research, Ljubljana. Processed.

————. 1997. "Approaching the European Union—Effects on Slovenian Economy." Paper presented at a conference on the Economic System of the European Economy and Adjustment of the Republic of Croatia, Rijeka, Croatia, April 24–25.

Majcen, B., and M. Lapornik. 1989. "Efektivna zaščita panog gospodarstva SR Slovenije v letu 1986 [Effective Protection of Individual Sectors of the Economy of SR of Slovenia in 1986]." Institute for Economic Research, Ljubljana. Processed.

Potočnik, J., and B. Majcen. 1996. "Possible Effects of Slovenian Integration into the EU—CGE Approach." Analysis, Research and Development series. Institute for Macroeconomic Analysis and Development, Ljubljana.

World Bank. 1999. "Foreign Trade Sector." In *Slovenia: Economic Transformation and EU Accession,* Volume II: *Main Report.* World Bank Country Economic Study. Washington, D.C.: World Bank.

World Trade Organization. 2002. "Trade Policy Review—Slovenia 2002." World Trade Organization, Geneva.

NOTES

1. Compared with other former socialist countries, Slovenia and the other successor countries of SFR Yugoslavia retained the advantages for a successful economic and social transition of stabilization programs launched in SFR Yugoslavia in May 1988 and December 1989 (see also Chapter 5). Trade liberalization was one of several transition processes (decentralization, price liberalization, and diversification of ownership being others) that had been at least partly initiated before the disintegration of SFR Yugoslavia.

2. Estimated implicit effective protection rates for domestic sales, agriculture, and exports to industrial countries in 1986 were 35.5 percent, –6.2 percent, and –31.9 percent, respectively (Majcen and Lapornik 1989).

3. In 1993, Slovenian importers thus actually on average paid only 50 percent of applied tariffs and other import charges. The main contributors to this reduction were duty-free imports of raw materials and intermediate goods for export-oriented production (69 percent), as well as reduced tariff rates for the imports of raw materials, and intermediate and capital goods (19 percent). Importers paid the full amount of applied tariffs and other import charges for only 21 percent of the capital goods imported, 21 percent of the intermediate goods imported, and 91 percent of the consumer goods imported (Majcen 1994).

4. Only a few nontariff barriers remain. These include nonautomatic licensing requirements to control specific imports affecting public security, safety, health, and the environment; administered tariff quotas in agriculture; and the remaining quantitative restrictions on textiles and clothing, which are to be phased out under the WTO Agreement on Textiles and Clothing.

5. Given that services account for about one-half of Slovenia's GDP, Slovenia's GATS commitments were bound to have a significant, positive economic impact. It appears that the serious effort at second-generation reforms since 1998 can be traced to these commitments, although the goal of EU accession has also driven these reforms.

6. In 2001, Slovenia's simple average applied MFN rate was 9.5 percent for nonagricultural goods (WTO definition) and 16 percent for agricultural products (WTO 2002).

7. The European Agreement went beyond trade per se to include provisions on liberalization of services, movement of workers, customs, public procurement, right of establishment, standardization of norms, competition, and other trade-related matters. It has provided a basis for the approximation of legislation, with the final aim of successful adoption of the *acquis communautaire* as one of the three main eligibility conditions for EU membership.

8. Diagonal cumulation allows inputs from countries participating in the agreement to be treated as domestic input in terms of domestic content requirements, so as to qualify for preferential treatment in the markets of other countries participating in the agreement.

9. First assessments of the complex effects of the full implementation of the EA pointed out that trade liberalization under the agreement will give rise not only to substitution of domestic products by imports, but also to an increase in GDP, employment, and exports (Potočnik and Majcen 1996). Sectoral results revealed that those producers who still produce primarily for the domestic market and have higher protection would face the greatest problems. Conversely, trade liberalization due to the EA would have positive effects on producers that were already highly export oriented. Later estimates of the relative importance of the three stages of foreign trade liberalization revealed that the most important has been full implementation of the EA (accounting for 50 percent of the total effect), followed by the implementation of the new customs system (30–40 percent), and only then by the trade liberalization due to accession to the European Union (10–20 percent; see Buehrer and Majcen 2001). These results were expected and confirmed the findings based on partial-equilibrium calculations of changes in applied and collected implicit rates due to the trade liberalization process.

10. Lower average rates of import duties for the imports from third countries are primarily the outcome of the different structure of imports of agricultural products.

Chapter 10
Monetary System and Monetary Policy

Ivan Ribnikar and Tomaž Košak

This chapter begins by discussing the functioning of the Slovenian monetary system during the rather brief period from the foundation of the Bank of Slovenia to its integration into the euro system, which will probably happen in the not-too-distant future. The second part of the chapter discusses the instruments of monetary policy that follow from the structural position of the money market, which has been one of large surpluses. Interest rates and some key data about monetary development are the topic of the third part, and the connections between monetary policy and the exchange rate regime and exchange rate policy are considered in the fourth part. The chapter ends with a discussion of how the Bank of Slovenia should adapt itself to membership in the euro system.

A SHORT HISTORY OF THE SLOVENIAN MONETARY SYSTEM

October 8, 1991, is the official date of birth not only of Slovenia's central bank, the Bank of Slovenia, but of its currency, the tolar, and of its independent monetary system. The origins of today's Bank of Slovenia lie not far back in time: the National Bank of Slovenia was founded in 1976, while Slovenia was still a republic of SFR Yugoslavia.

Apart from whether the National Bank of Slovenia had any influence on the monetary policy of the National Bank of Yugoslavia (NBY), the year 1976 is important because it was from that time forward that nearly all traditional relationships of banks and other entities in Slovenia vis-à-vis the Yugoslav central banking system started to show up on the books of the National Bank of Slovenia. The exceptions are the claims of legal entities and individuals in Slovenia on the NBY and, through the latter, on the national central banks of the seven other republics and autonomous provinces, on the basis of the currency they held in their vaults. These very peculiar aspects of the decentralization of the Yugoslav central banking system turned out to be quite important on October 8, 1991. Shortly after introducing its new currency, the Bank of Slovenia was able to prepare its opening balance sheet.

Slovenia's relationships with the NBY involve the claims on and debts to the NBY of banks and other entities in Slovenia. It was to be expected that these claims and debts would not balance. In fact, the claims (bank reserves, deposits, securities, notes in circulation) amounted to SIT 21,231 million, whereas the debts amounted to only SIT 12,581 million. Had there been an agreement on the separation of the monetary system, the difference of SIT 8,650 million would have been paid in foreign currency by the NBY, or through it by the other newly independent states of the former SFR Yugoslavia, to entities in

Slovenia. Given that Slovenia had more claims than obligations, all other entities in other parts of the former SFR Yugoslavia must have had exactly the same amount or more in debts (or net debts). Since the separation or disintegration of the Yugoslav monetary system was far from amicable, the Bank of Slovenia showed, among the assets in its balance sheet, these net claims on the Republic of Slovenia, and through it on the other former republics of Yugoslavia. Obviously, the Bank of Slovenia could not start a balance sheet with more debts than claims.

The most important items among the Bank of Slovenia's assets were claims on other banks (56 percent) and claims on the Republic of Slovenia (40 percent). Among its liabilities, the largest share consisted of notes in circulation (40 percent), followed by deposits by banks and others (29 percent) and securities (24 percent).

There was another category of unusual relationships among banks and the NBY that was not recorded in the Bank of Slovenia's books. From the early 1960s onward, banks were obliged to accept foreign currency deposits but were prohibited from extending foreign currency loans or to take other measures to protect themselves from exchange rate risk. Consequently, banks had been recording losses on these foreign currency deposits, which showed up on their books as "negative exchange rate differences." Eventually, these banks would have become insolvent if these had not been classified as "good" assets. The bank owners had unlimited liability. This fact, however, was not remembered at that time or, more important, when the banks were corporatized.

The insolvency problem was resolved by the NBY, which, through a sophisticated system of actual and fictitious foreign currency deposits by banks with the NBY and interest-free loans by the NBY to these same banks, took over the "negative exchange rate differences." In fact, the NBY acknowledged these as its own debt, which constituted an additional claim by the banks on the NBY. But, in contrast to the net claims of SIT 8,650 million, corresponding to which there had to exist a net debt owed by the other national banks, the claims based on "negative exchange rate differences" were claims on the NBY and eventually on the republics of SFR Yugoslavia. This is a crucial difference. Even if the disintegration of the monetary system had been peaceful, the NBY would still not have had sufficient assets to settle these debts. They would simply have been passed on to the republics of SFR Yugoslavia and thus to today's independent states. The Republic of Slovenia issued state bonds to all banks in its territory to cover the "negative exchange rate differences." By doing so, Slovenia anticipated that the only realistic and economically reasonable solution would be for it to take over all the liabilities of SFR Yugoslavia toward banks on Slovenian territory. The banks lost assets when loans to their clients, mostly local companies, depreciated or when their clients went bankrupt. At that time, "globalization" in the banking sector was limited to the local community, as this was the area where the banks operated, and it would have been unusual to look to the NBY for assets to cover these "negative exchange rate differences" when these assets were to be found locally.

STRUCTURAL POSITION OF THE MONEY MARKET AND INSTRUMENTS OF MONETARY POLICY

From a starting point of almost zero, international reserves had become almost the only assets on the balance sheet of the Bank of Slovenia within a few years. Indeed, one of two striking characteristics of the central bank's balance sheet has been that its assets have been 90 percent foreign. The other is that usually more than half of its liabilities have been in the form of its short-term bills, in either domestic or foreign currency. To understand how this came about and what the Bank of Slovenia has been doing, one can either divide the bank's balance sheet into three parts (as is done in Ribnikar 1999a, 2001) or take into account the structural position of the money market in Slovenia.

There is, of course, a surplus in the structural position of the money market, even if we make some changes in its definition to adapt it to Slovenia's situation (Ribnikar 1999b). Net foreign assets, usually the most important autonomous item on the central bank's balance sheet, should mean, in the case of Slovenia or its central bank, net foreign currency assets. In this way its liabilities in the form of short-term bills denominated in foreign currency (euros) disappear. Banks are obliged to hold these bills as short-term foreign currency liquid assets against their short-term foreign currency liabilities—at present, in the amount of at least 36 percent of foreign currency liabilities with a remaining maturity of up to 180 days.

By eliminating those foreign currency liabilities and thus reducing the structural surplus of the money market, those items that are somehow strange, and not necessarily a part of the central bank balance sheet at all, disappear (the same goal, as will be seen later, could have been achieved by other means). More important for the absorption of excessive liquidity from banks, the result is a situation where the usual or at least almost usual instruments of monetary policy are being used.

Figure 10.1 shows what has been happening with the structural surplus in the money market. There has been much volatility, and since 2000 that volatility has been increasing. The fluctuations have

FIGURE 10.1 STRUCTURAL POSITION OF THE MONEY MARKET AND
            NET FOREIGN CURRENCY ASSETS OF THE
            CENTRAL BANK

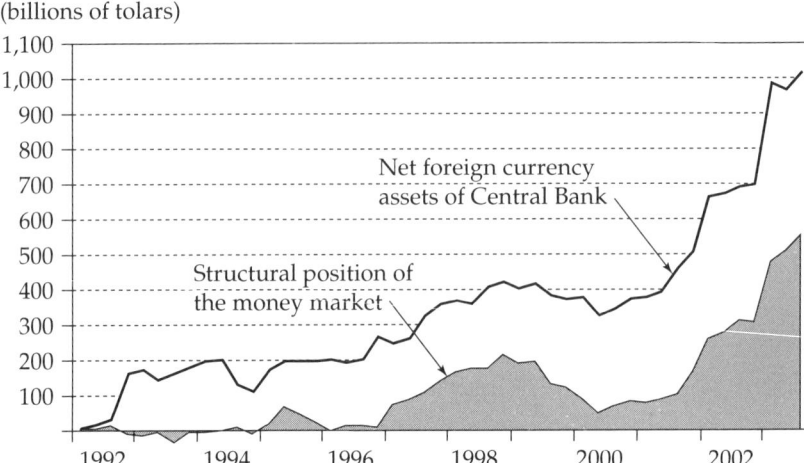

Source: Bank of Slovenia.

closely tracked those in net foreign currency assets, which in turn depend on the current account and international financial flows, primarily inflows of foreign capital.

Figure 10.2 shows that the primary goal of the Bank of Slovenia has been to extract from the banks the surplus liquidity created autonomously through its purchases of foreign exchange. Required reserves have usually not been enough. The Bank of Slovenia has relied mostly on its short-term bills, denominated in tolars, and therefore the most important instrument of monetary policy has been the issue and sale of these bills to the banks.

By extracting from the banks more liquidity than it was obliged to, the Bank of Slovenia put the banks in a position where they did not have enough liquidity. Only in this way was it able to make space for the ordinary instruments of monetary policy, through which it provides liquidity to banks. Figure 10.2 shows that, since 1996, this space has been shrinking, and since 2000 it has almost disappeared.

By adapting the definition of the structural position of the money market to Slovenia's circumstances, one can arrive at three kinds of instruments of monetary policy: required reserves; the issue or sale of short-term, tolar-denominated bills to banks; and various instruments through which liquidity is provided to banks. The following subsections discuss each of these in turn.

FIGURE 10.2 STRUCTURAL POSITION OF THE MONEY MARKET,
             REQUIRED RESERVES, AND NET LIQUIDITY SUPPLY
             VIA MONETARY POLICY INSTRUMENTS

(billions of tolars)

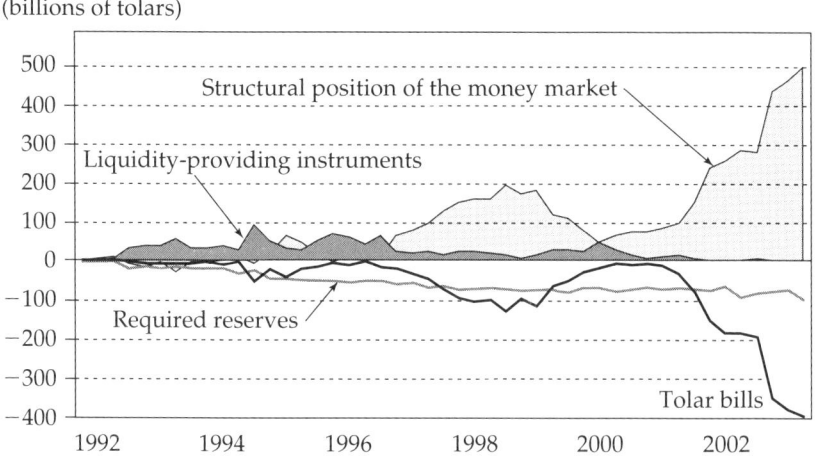

Source: Bank of Slovenia.

Required Reserves

In Slovenia, as in many other countries where a structural surplus prevails, a system of reserve requirements is in place. One of the important functions assigned to the reserve requirement system was to
enhance the structural liquidity shortage of the Slovenian banking system, or at least reduce the liquidity surplus that has prevailed in
recent years. Therefore, in 1998 required reserves amounted to 2 percent of GDP, after which they fell to 1.6 percent in 2002. Reserves have
varied between 5 and 12 percent of the central bank's total assets
(Table 10.1).

The methodology of the required reserve calculation was established in 1992, when reserve requirements were the main instrument
for absorbing liquidity from the banking system. The methodology
remained basically unchanged until April 1995, when the reserve
ratios for short- and long-term liabilities in domestic currency were
reduced. The Bank of Slovenia did not set a minimum reserve for liabilities denominated in foreign currency until 2002, but instead used
a special instrument called a "foreign currency minimum," which was
a minimum amount of foreign currency assets that each bank with
foreign currency liabilities was required to hold in a highly liquid
form. In 1995 reserve ratios were set at 12 percent for demand deposits

TABLE 10.1 SHARES OF MONETARY POLICY INSTRUMENTS ON THE BALANCE SHEET OF THE BANK OF SLOVENIA, 1992–2002

(percent)

Instrument	1992	1993	1994	1995	1996	1997	1998	1999	2000	2001	2002
Liquidity-providing instruments	16	11	12	14	4	3	1	3	1	0	0.1
Liquidity loans	1	2	7	11	4	3	1	3	1	0	0.1
Repurchase agreements	15	10	6	2	0.3	0	0	0.3	0	0	0
Required reserves	7	8	12	11	12	10	10	9	9	7	5
Short-term bills	2	2	5	2	4	13	13	4	1	11	23
Overnight deposits	0	0	0	0	0	0	0	0	0	3	1

Source: Bank of Slovenia.

and other liabilities with a maturity of up to 30 days; at 6 percent for liabilities maturing between 31 days and 90 days; at 2 percent for liabilities maturing between 91 and 180 days; and at 1 percent for liabilities maturing between 181 days and 1 year. By adopting such a gradually decreasing schedule of reserve ratios, the Bank of Slovenia tried to stimulate deposits of long-term savings with banks and to reduce the opportunity cost burden arising from the below-market rate of remuneration on banking assets.

In 2002 the Bank of Slovenia started to gradually adopt the euro system's reserve requirement in principle. In January 2002 the treatment of repurchase agreement transactions was changed so that those repos based on short-term government securities were no longer a part of a bank's reserve base. Further, in September 2002 the required reserve base was extended to include liabilities denominated in foreign currency with a maturity of up to 2 years as well as liabilities in domestic currency. The main reserve ratio was set at 2 percent; meanwhile a 7 percent reserve ratio was used for liabilities in domestic currency with a maturity of up to 3 months. However, the Bank of Slovenia still did not remunerate compulsory deposits with the central bank at an interest rate comparable to rates in the money market, although this is also the practice in the European Central Bank system.

Bank of Slovenia Short-Term Bills and Sterilized Purchases of Foreign Exchange

The structural surplus in the Slovenian money market, which has been as large as 30 percent of the Bank of Slovenia's total assets, required either a net withdrawal of liquidity from the banking system or a more intensive use of those instruments by which the structural surplus could be converted into a short position (Košak 1997). As already mentioned, from 1992 until 1994, required reserves were the most important instrument for shifting the structural liquidity position from a surplus to a deficit. However, already in 1994 this instrument was proving insufficient to withdraw the excess liquidity from the banking system. The Bank of Slovenia was constrained to issue tolar bills with warrants due to the sterilization of a foreign exchange surplus in the market. The current account surplus reached 4.2 percent of GDP in 1994, well above that of the previous year. The supply of tolar bills with warrants only supplemented the already well-accepted foreign exchange bills that the central bank had supplied since the spring of 1992. Tolar bills with warrants (or, more precisely, the coupons attached to the bills) stimulated market participants to buy foreign exchange bills at a discount if the rate of change in the exchange rate was well below the officially projected inflation rate, and to sell foreign exchange bills otherwise. They also stimulated banks and other holders of warrants to buy tolar bills at a discount, if the current inflation rate was above the officially projected one. In the middle of 1994, tolar bills for the first time amounted to more than 27 percent of all bills sold by the Bank of Slovenia, or 14 percent of the central bank's total assets. Until 1994 the Bank of Slovenia had sold only four types of tolar bills, all with very short maturities (from 2 to 14 days), to which only banks and savings banks were allowed to subscribe. At the end of 1994, when the first issue of bills with warrants reached maturity, the Bank of Slovenia introduced a 60-day bill in order to neutralize the creation of base money.

From the last quarter of 1997 until the middle of 1999, when net capital inflows increased to 3.5 percent of GDP, tolar bills played a crucial role in withdrawing excess liquidity. The amount of tolar bills reached a peak of 13 percent of the assets of the central bank (Table 10.1). In 1997 another tolar bill was introduced with a maturity of 270 days, which was otherwise similar to the 60-day bill in the series. Thus, at the end of 1998, the Bank of Slovenia was offering nine different types of tolar bills, with maturities of 2, 7, 12, 14, 30, 60, and 270 days, as well as tolar bills with warrants and so-called twin bills. The twin bills, first issued in 1992, were split into a tolar part and a foreign currency part. Technically, they were bought in domestic currency at a discount and were redeemed, at maturity, half in tolars and half in foreign currency. However, they have never played a notable role in the withdrawal of base money from circulation. Until the end of 2002, the central bank gradually ceased to offer most of the varieties of tolar bills, and today banks can subscribe only to the 60- and 270-day bills. The 270-day tolar bills have been sold at regular weekly auctions, whereas the 60-day bills have been offered under a standing facility.

The latest change in the tolar bills offered by the Bank of Slovenia was made in 2002. From November 2002 to January 2003, some banks were eligible to subscribe to 360-day tolar bills aimed at absorbing the liquidity then flooding the money market. The excess liquidity stemmed from foreign currency transactions related to some large foreign takeovers in the pharmaceutical and banking sectors at that time. The dimensions of the phenomenon can be seen in Figure 10.2 and Table 10.1.

Liquidity-Providing Instruments

The shape and magnitude of the structural position of the money market have not allowed the intensive use of liquidity-providing instruments. These instruments have varied between zero and 14 percent of the Bank of Slovenia's total assets, depending on the volume of foreign exchange inflow (Table 10.1). However, a clear decreasing trend of necessary additional liquidity supply through that channel can be noted since 1995.

Standing facilities and open market operations can also be found among liquidity-providing instruments. The rest of this section describes only those instruments that have been predominantly involved in the conduct of monetary policy rather than foreign exchange policy.

Open Market Operations

The repurchase agreement has been the most frequently applied instrument of monetary policy since 1994. With this instrument, the Bank of Slovenia has ensured a stable and reliable source of liquidity for banks, especially in periods of low supply of foreign currency in the market. From 1995 until 2000, the central bank intervened daily with auction sales of 28-day repos of Bank of Slovenia foreign currency bills. At the beginning of 1995, banks auctioned the amount of foreign currency inflows to be purchased from enterprises; thereafter they auctioned the exchange rate for the repurchase of bills. The repo interest rate was calculated indirectly from the banks' auctioned exchange rate. Commonly, the auction at the Bank of Slovenia included the additional requirement that a specific amount of foreign currency be purchased from enterprises.

In 2000 two new instruments for the temporary purchase of foreign currency bills were introduced. The first instrument was a seven-day repo, which enabled banks to manage their intramonth liquidity. It also enabled the Bank of Slovenia to react more quickly to current developments in the money market by changing the daily quote at the auction. The second instrument was a 60-day repo of foreign currency bills, which the Bank of Slovenia used to steer part of base money growth into longer-term instruments. It remained in place until 2001.

Standing Facilities

Lombard loans were introduced already at the end of 1991 as one of the first standing facility instruments offered by the Bank of Slovenia. Although the interest rate on these loans was relatively low compared with those on other lending facilities (1 percentage point above the discount rate), it was not the whole price. There were also additional conditions that banks taking the loans had to implement. Five-day Lombard loans were available to banks at any time, in an amount not higher than 2.5 percent of foreign currency bills or treasury bonds submitted to the Bank of Slovenia as collateral. Until the end of 1995, there was an additional condition whereby banks had to purchase foreign exchange from enterprises at an exchange rate determined by the central bank. Therefore the Lombard loans actually functioned as marginal refinancing instruments in spite of their low interest rate. In 1992 and 1993 they were the second most frequently used instrument for regulating the amount of money in circulation (during this period these loans were acquired by banks through auction or at a permanently open Lombard loan window, that is, a standing facility); otherwise they have not been used intensively.

Standing facilities also include various liquidity loans that primarily serve as instruments for balancing short-term liquidity in the domestic currency of the banking system. Because different types of short-term liquidity loans have been in place, this chapter will describe only their common characteristics.

After the abolition of rediscount quotas in the first quarter of 1992, the Bank of Slovenia sought to maintain the general liquidity of the banking system through the liquidity loans window. All liquidity loans were granted by banks against collateral in the form of Bank of Slovenia bills or government bonds.

For banks undergoing the prerehabilitation and rehabilitation processes from 1993 until 1997, special liquidity loans with maturities of up to 2 weeks or, in exceptional cases, up to one month were available. These loans were used intensively in the first years of the rehabilitation process, and their extension ceased in 1996. Also, in 1992 the Bank of Slovenia began to offer overnight liquidity loans. These were available to all banks that were net debtors in the interbank money market, and banks taking the loans were obliged to use the funds to meet those obligations. Through its presence in the money market with these overnight liquidity loans, the Bank of Slovenia limited interest rate fluctuations.

After 1995 the volume of liquidity loans extended decreased substantially, from 11 percent of the central bank's assets to 4 percent. At the end of 1996, liquidity facilities of last resort and a special facility for banks with liquidity problems were introduced; these carried the highest interest rates among the Bank of Slovenia's monetary policy instruments. They were available to banks in the event of unexpected liquidity constraints for performance of payments due or fulfillment of required reserves.

INTEREST RATES AND MONETARY DEVELOPMENT

As a small, open transition economy, Slovenia's economic performance has been rather different from that of the more developed EU countries. One can identify certain important institutional and other factors that have largely determined the evolution of the role of interest rates in the monetary transmission mechanism since independence.

In October 1991, when Slovenia introduced its new currency, the economy was facing galloping inflation of about 22 percent a month. Besides the tremendous need to build up appropriate foreign exchange reserves, which amounted to only 4 days of imports at that time, the Bank of Slovenia was obliged to reduce the inflation rate. Because the banking system was highly liquid at the end of 1991, the central bank shrank base money in stepwise fashion toward the amount estimated to be sufficient to meet demand. Liquidity loans of the Bank of Slovenia to banks were reduced to a minimum until the beginning of 1992. The governing board of the central bank set the discount rate at 24 percent a year, with an explicit target for inflation of 2 percent a month for the first half of 1992.

The harmful effects of increasing real interest rates at a time of falling inflation were mitigated by rescaling interest rates in the financial sector. In 1991 a conversion table was used to determine a conversion scale between interest rates in financial contracts in the former Yugoslav currency and those in Slovenian tolars. This rescaling made the shrinking of liquidity less harmful for economic activity than would have been the case in a straightforward money supply contraction (Bole 1995). The Bank of Slovenia conducted monetary policy in accordance with an exogenous money supply and a floating exchange rate at that time. To reduce the high nominal interest rates paid by banks on demand deposits, reserve requirements on these deposits were increased to 13 percent while those on savings deposits were lowered. In the second half of 1992, the Bank of Slovenia started to sterilize the increasing inflow of foreign exchange by offering bills denominated in foreign currency as well as the twin bills described above. At the same time, the central bank consistently limited access to the rediscount window to banks only, which significantly contributed to the absorption of excess foreign exchange inflows.

The success of this approach to monetary policy in the period immediately after independence contributed to a rapid fall of inflation from 22 percent a month in October 1991 to 2 percent a month by the middle of 1992. Lower inflation allowed a sustained decrease in banking interest rates, which still were quite high in real terms. Foreign capital inflows started to grow in 1993, partly because of the high interest rates and partly because of reduced exchange rate risk premiums for borrowing abroad.

It took 2 years to calm inflation down further from 2 percent a month to around 1 percent, and another year and a half for inflation to drop to 0.5 percent a month. At the beginning of 1995, price competition among banks for large depositors halted the fall in interest rates. At that time the Bank of Slovenia intervened administratively to prevent such unhealthy and uncontrolled competition, penalizing those banks with exceptionally high deposit rates.

This intervention led to an interbank agreement on deposit interest rates, which determined their maximum level in the banking sector. The agreement was in force from 1995 to 1999, after which it was replaced by a "recommendation" on deposit interest rates, prepared by the Bank Association of Slovenia. This remained in force until the end of 2000. Under the agreement, and later the recommendation, commercial banks committed themselves not to exceed the agreed maximum deposit interest rates, in order to prevent unfair and uncontrolled price competition among banks for large clients. Although the agreement contributed to the reduction of real interest rates, it also hampered the normal development of the interest rate channel of the transmission mechanism.

The transmission of monetary policy changes through the interest rate channel has proved empirically to be weak and long lasting in the Slovenian economy in the entire period until recent years. Its effectiveness was diminished by the widespread use of indexation mechanisms in financial contracts, the consequence of the high inflation experienced in the last days of SFR Yugoslavia. For the indexation factor, the last-reported monthly inflation rate, annualized, was used until May 1995. However, after the first recorded monthly deflation occurred in April 1995, the indexation rate was calculated as a three-month average inflation rate. The methodology for calculating the indexation factor was gradually changed with the intention of reducing its variability. The extensive use of indexation in almost every form of commercial bank financial instrument until July 2002 hampered the ability of economic agents to correctly understand the changes in the policy rate. The indexation factor for short-term financial instruments was abolished in July 2002; long-term instruments continue to be indexed by the average inflation rate over the past 12 months. Although the indexation mechanism in financial contracts has had a negative impact on the transmission of monetary policy activities, it enabled financial intermediation through the banking sector to proceed more or less normally during the period of high inflation.

A well-known problem in transition economies has been the underdevelopment of capital markets. In Slovenia's case this was accompanied by the problem of a very slowly developing money market. The government issued its first treasury bills, of three-month maturity, only in 1998, and the depth and liquidity of the secondary market in these bills have not been sufficient to allow their use in active management of banking sector liquidity. In 1999 and 2000, treasury bills of 6- and 12-month maturities were also issued. In 2001 the Bank of Slovenia and the Ministry of Finance undertook some coordinated action (for example, by creating information infrastructure) to promote trading in treasury bills on the secondary money market among banks and other market participants. In the past there had been only a well-functioning interbank loan money market with regularly quoted interest rates, which reflected liquidity changes in the banking sector quite well.

During the 1990s the Bank of Slovenia focused on a reserve money-based anchor to achieve its overall goal of price stability. In 1997 the central bank judged that there was a closer relationship between its final objective of price stability and the broader M3 monetary aggregate, leading it to change the monetary policy framework accordingly (Košak 2002). This change increased the transparency of monetary policy. In line with Slovenia's convergence to conditions in the European Union, in November 2001 the Bank of Slovenia framed its strategy of steering monetary policy during the period before entering European Monetary Union. The new strategy establishes that the implementation of monetary policy rests on two pillars. The first takes into account the quantity of money in circulation, and the second takes into consideration indicators that supplement information about the economic stance in general.

MONETARY POLICY, THE EXCHANGE RATE REGIME, AND EXCHANGE RATE POLICY

Because almost all of the Bank of Slovenia's assets are foreign assets, acquired through purchases of foreign currency from banks on the foreign exchange market, connections between the foreign exchange market and Slovenia's monetary development clearly have been very tight. One cannot explain or analyze the monetary sector without understanding the exchange rate regime and exchange rate policy, which have importantly determined conditions in the foreign exchange market. Their interdependence has become even more pronounced as Slovenia has been preparing for entry into the European Union, and therefore will soon be entering European Monetary Union through Exchange Rate Mechanism II. Although this chapter is primarily concerned with the monetary system and monetary policy, the discussion must necessarily touch on the exchange rate regime and policy.

Since 1991 the exchange rate regime has been classified as a pure float at the very beginning followed by a managed float without a pre-announced exchange rate path. Predominantly because of changes in the current account and in inflows of foreign capital, the Bank of Slovenia has practiced managed floating, with at least a few changes in its methods and with some difficulties. Before describing the present, much tighter connections between monetary and exchange rate policy, we must explain three almost permanent mechanisms that have been in place. These are nonsterilized purchases of foreign exchange, sterilized purchases, and the requirement that banks hold a minimum amount of liquid foreign currency assets against their foreign currency liabilities.

Initially the only assets available for the Bank of Slovenia to purchase or monetize were foreign currencies. There were no treasury bills and no short-term debt securities of the business sector of adequate quality. This situation has remained almost unchanged, although there are now some treasury bills and some adequate short-term debt securities of the business sector. Nevertheless, one can see that base money in Slovenia has been predominantly created through monetization of foreign currencies. Thus there has been a permanent demand for foreign exchange on the part of the Bank of Slovenia that is almost one for one with increases in base money.

Sterilized purchases of foreign exchange have been much more volatile than nonsterilized purchases, for obvious reasons. These purchases change the levels of the current account and of capital inflows. The Bank of Slovenia has been trying to prevent a real appreciation of the tolar (or monetary expansion) resulting from the inflow of capital, which in many cases has originated from the sale of existing business enterprises to foreigners. These were predominant originally, before the abolition of social ownership of business enterprises had been completed in social ownership. Because this inflow of capital was largely a transitional phenomenon, lasting until all enterprises to be sold to foreigners had been sold, it probably would not have been wise to let the exchange rate adapt in permanent fashion to these inflows.

The compensating operation on the part of the Bank of Slovenia for its sterilized purchases of foreign assets or currencies has been the issue or sale of its short-term bills. The central bank has had no domestic assets to sell as a means of compensating for its purchases of foreign assets. In the first years of its existence, the Bank of Slovenia used for this purpose its own bills, denominated in tolars and in foreign currencies (deutsche marks and U.S. dollars) with maturities longer than 120 days. Since 2001 it has predominantly been using tolar-denominated bills with 60- and 270-day maturities for these compensating operations.

The third demand for foreign currencies that has been ascribed to the Bank of Slovenia has originated with the banks. A large share of bank liabilities and assets is in foreign currencies. The most important part of their foreign currency liabilities has been the foreign currency deposits of residents. To preempt bank runs, the Bank of Slovenia has required that banks hold a substantial portion of their foreign currency assets in liquid form, as the counterpart of their foreign currency deposits or other foreign currency liabilities. Among these liquid foreign currency assets, a substantial part has had to be Bank of

Slovenia short-term bills denominated in foreign currencies (nowadays in euros). Until some time ago, the requirement was 60 percent of the minimum amount of liquid foreign currency assets; since December 2001, as noted previously, it has been 36 percent of foreign currency liabilities with a remaining maturity of up to 180 days.

The requirement that banks hold liquid foreign currency assets, either in deposits with foreign banks or in foreign short-term securities or Bank of Slovenia short-term bills denominated in euros, has meant additional demand in the country for foreign exchange. Without this prudential regulation, banks would probably have put their money mostly into foreign currency loans to residents. By not allowing banks to do that, the Bank of Slovenia has achieved more or less the same result with regard to the exchange rate as would have been achieved by sterilized purchases of foreign currencies. This demand from banks for foreign exchange or liquid foreign currency assets has thus been a kind of substitute for sterilized purchases of foreign exchange or the issue of short-term bills denominated in tolars.

The demand for foreign exchange on the part of banks has been substantial and relatively stable. If one adds together all three sources of demand for foreign exchange or foreign assets—demand for monetization, demand on the basis of sterilized purchases of foreign exchange, and demand from banks—it is clear that the influence of the Bank of Slovenia on the exchange rate, on the basis of its purchases (and sometimes sales) or purchases induced by it (that is, by the banks) on the foreign exchange market, is significant.

But the Bank of Slovenia has exercised its influence on the exchange rate not only through its changing presence on the foreign exchange market, but also in a more idiosyncratic way. At the end of 1997, the Bank of Slovenia proposed to the banks an agreement on their participation in the central bank's foreign exchange market interventions. The contract regulated the participation of banks in this intervention, and meanwhile the Bank of Slovenia provided to the signatory banks a temporary purchase of foreign exchange, which enabled banks to manage the open foreign exchange position (Bank of Slovenia 1999).

But both the Bank of Slovenia's own (and induced) purchases and sales on the foreign exchange market and its actions on the foreign exchange market in cooperation with banks have been constrained or influenced by monetary policy targets. As international capital flows become more liberalized, monetary and exchange rate policy are becoming more and more interdependent.

Only some combinations of monetary policy (as indicated by, for instance, the interest rate for 60-day Bank of Slovenia bills, denominated in tolars) and exchange rate policy (as indicated by, for instance, the rate of nominal appreciation of the euro) are possible, of course, if the central bank is to maintain control over monetary expansion and over the exchange rate against the euro. The Bank of Slovenia has been trying, through its monetary and exchange rate policy, to prevent the difference between the expected returns on domestic and foreign currency (euro) assets from becoming greater (or smaller) than the risk premium on domestic currency assets.

The risk premium on domestic currency assets relative to euro-denominated assets is not only difficult to determine but variable as well. Therefore the Bank of Slovenia must continuously monitor short-term capital flows and, if necessary, make changes either in monetary policy (through the interest rate on 60-day bills denominated in tolars) or in exchange rate policy (the nominal rate of change in the euro exchange rate).

HOW THE BANK OF SLOVENIA SHOULD ENTER THE EURO SYSTEM

Since 1992, when the Bank of Slovenia first started issuing short-term bills denominated in domestic currency and twin bills (and, until February 2001, its longer-term bills denominated in foreign currencies) as the counterpart of its sterilized purchases of foreign exchange, and since it started issuing bills denominated exclusively in foreign currencies, which banks have been obliged to buy and hold against their foreign currency liabilities, the amount of those bills outstanding has been increasing. Amounts outstanding of the first type of bill have alternately risen and fallen, and their amount came to almost nil at the end of 2000. The second type has been consistently increasing as foreign banks' currency liabilities have increased.

The amount of these bills outstanding shows the importance of the Bank of Slovenia's role in absorbing foreign exchange in the market and thus preventing an undesired real appreciation of the tolar. But before Slovenia enters the euro zone, such bills, whether denominated in tolars or in euros, must disappear from the Bank of Slovenia's balance sheet. If this is accomplished by the Bank of Slovenia simply paying off its bills in euros and tolars upon maturity, the result would be an excess supply of both. Because it is not realistic that the Bank of Slovenia would allow such an extraordinary monetary expansion, all of the impact would fall on the euro exchange rate. The Bank of Slovenia would, in other words, sterilize its repayment of the tolar bills by selling euros on the foreign exchange market. There would be an additional supply of euros from the Bank of Slovenia in the amount of the repayment of tolar bills at their maturity.

If the Bank of Slovenia were to adapt to entry into the euro zone by simply paying its bills to banks at their maturity, then its sterilized purchases of foreign exchange, and the regulation that requires banks to keep liquid foreign currency assets (including euro-denominated Bank of Slovenia bills) against their foreign currency liabilities, would be largely transitory—a temporary postponement of the necessary real appreciation of the tolar. Therefore the central bank's task is to try to do the right thing in the near future and to choose the right time to join the euro zone, if it wants to prevent, without help from the government, a substantial real appreciation of the tolar as a delayed effect of what the Bank of Slovenia has been doing since 1992. What the central bank must take into account, and when it would be appropriate to join the euro zone, can be explained with reference to Figure 10.3.

The x axis in Figure 10.3 indicates the required decrease in Bank of Slovenia bills (and changes in the assets of banks), relative to the

FIGURE 10.3   RELATIONSHIP OF CHANGE IN CENTRAL BANK
              BILLS OUTSTANDING TO NECESSARY PURCHASES OR
              SALES OF FOREIGN EXCHANGE

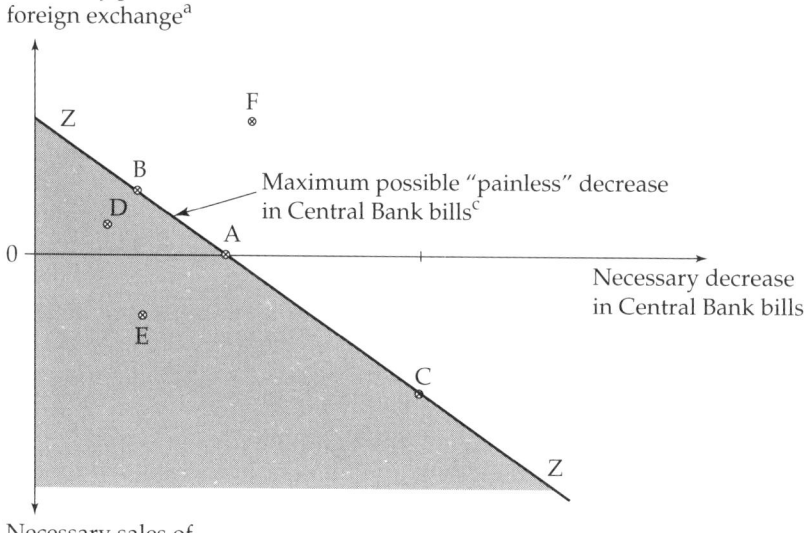

a. Purchases that must be undertaken to prevent an undesired real appreciation of the currency.
b. Sales that must be undertaken to prevent an undesired real depreciation of the currency.
c. Largest possible decrease in Central Bank bills that can be accomplished without undesired changes in the exchange rate.
Source: Authors' model.

necessary annual increase in base money. The part of the y axis above zero indicates the amount of necessary purchases of foreign exchange, and that below zero the necessary sales of foreign exchange, both also expressed relative to the necessary annual increase in the base money. Necessary purchases of foreign exchange are those that must be undertaken to prevent an undesired real appreciation of the tolar, and necessary sales are those required to prevent an undesired real depreciation. Line ZZ shows the maximum possible decrease in Bank of Slovenia bills that can be accomplished painlessly, that is, without undesired changes in the tolar exchange rate; this depends on the balance of payments situation. All points within the shaded area of the figure are painless: in this area the necessary decrease in Bank of Slovenia bills does not exceed the required increase in base money. Points above or to the right of ZZ are not painless.

The maximum possible decrease in Bank of Slovenia bills is equal to the necessary increase in base money (point A) if the central bank is not required to intervene in the foreign exchange market. This amount is smaller if the Bank of Slovenia must intervene in the foreign exchange market as a buyer (point B), and greater (for instance, point C) if it must intervene as a seller. At points D and E the possible decrease in bills is greater than required, by the horizontal distance to line ZZ. A decrease in the amount of bills represented by point F cannot be accomplished painlessly.

Several conclusions can be drawn from this analysis. First, the smaller the amount of Bank of Slovenia bills (and other foreign currency assets that banks are required to hold instead of loans to residents or their securities), the greater the possibilities for their painless decrease. The second concerns the balance of payments. The Bank of Slovenia is in a good position if it does not need to buy foreign exchange, and in an even better position if it must sell foreign exchange. The third factor is the amount of necessary increase in base money. The greater that amount, the better the possibilities for a painless decrease in Bank of Slovenia bills outstanding.

If the Bank of Slovenia chooses the right time to join the euro zone (and the chances are great that it will remain in the shaded area of Figure 10.3), sterilized purchases of foreign exchange and the regulation on banks to hold foreign assets that they would not have held otherwise would not only postpone the real appreciation of the tolar. The importance of what the Bank of Slovenia has been doing is that, in the longer run, sterilized purchases of foreign exchange (and of foreign assets by banks) may be replaced by unsterilized (and desired) purchases, and that sterilized purchases may exist because of changes in the balance of payments counterbalanced by sterilized sales. If there is no further inflow of capital that the Bank of Slovenia is trying to neutralize, it may monetize foreign exchange by the amount of necessary increase in base money. In this way sterilized purchases change into unsterilized purchases. If the balance of payments shifts into deficit, in the longer run the Bank of Slovenia would probably be obliged to neutralize the monetary consequences with sterilized sales of foreign exchange. Therefore sterilized purchases would be neutralized by sterilized sales.

If the Bank of Slovenia is not to end up spoiling almost everything it has accomplished since 1992, it must choose carefully the timing of its entry into the euro zone and then behave accordingly. Sterilization and purchases of foreign assets by banks that had been required by the Bank of Slovenia should lead as little as possible to postponement of the real appreciation of the tolar. During its transition to a national central bank within the euro system, the Bank of Slovenia should try to stay most of the time within the shaded area of Figure 10.3.

REFERENCES

Bank of Slovenia. 1999. *Annual Report*. Ljubljana.

Bole, V. 1995. "Stabilization in Slovenia: From High Inflation to Excessive Inflow of Foreign Capital." Working Paper 1. Economics Institute of the Faculty of Law, Ljubljana.

Košak, T. 1997. "What Tell Us the Structure Position of the Money Market about Monetary Policy in Slovenia." *Prikazi in analize* (Bank of Slovenia) 5(3).

————. 2002. "Searching for the Liquidity Effect in Slovenia." Paper presented at a research meeting at the European Central Bank on Monetary Policy Transmission in the Euro Area and in Accession Countries, Frankfurt am Main, October.

Ribnikar, I. 1999a. "Monetary Arrangements and Exchange Rate Regime in a Small Transitional Economy (Slovenia)." In P. De Grauwe and V. Lavrač, eds., *Inclusion of Central European Countries in the European Monetary Union*. Boston: Kluwer Academic Publishers.

————. 1999b. "Structural Position of the Money Market in Slovenia." *Bančni vestnik* 48(6), pp. 47–49.

————. 2001. "A Small Country's Monetary System in a Globalised World." In L. Božina and D. Krbec, eds., *Ekonomska globalizacija u malim zemljama Evrope*. Pula, Croatia: Fakultet ekonomije i turizma 'Dr. Mijo Mirković.'

Chapter 11
Exchange Rate Policy and Management of Capital Flows

Velimir Bole

During the transition, the Slovenian economy went through a decade-long intensive real restructuring and a reshuffling of the institutional infrastructure. At the same time, Slovenia faced a highly volatile external environment. Changes in economic structure and in the external environment influenced both the choice of exchange rate policy and subsequent adjustments to that policy. At different times during the transition, both the type of variables to be considered, and their quantity, differed in the tightness of the constraints they set on the choice of exchange rate regime. Slovenia is therefore one country for which the assertion that "no single currency regime is right for all time" (Frankel 1999) obviously makes sense.

To analyze the decisions of policymakers in transition economies, one has to know what their objectives were as well as the basic constraints they took into account. It is possible to discover something about policymakers' preferences from their actions. But to reveal policymakers' preferences regarding changes in the exchange rate regime and related policy measures using available evidence on their actions alone would be impossible. At least some sketchy information (or suppositions) about their longer-term goals and the basic constraints that they considered is necessary. Assuming that restoring sustainable internal and external equilibrium was a longer-term goal of monetary policy in Slovenia, the question is which constraints were crucial for the choice of a specific exchange rate policy or regime, how changes in policy were timed, and how policy measures were implemented.

This chapter provides some evidence to help answer these questions. The chapter is structured as follows. In the first section, two basic constraints on the choice of monetary and exchange rate policy are briefly described. In the second an overview of the actions of the Slovenian monetary authorities is presented; in the same section the timing of changes in monetary and exchange rate policy is pinpointed as well. The last two sections describe the implementation of the exchange rate regime in the initial, "emergency" period and in the period after policymakers gained control over the economy.

CONSTRAINTS ON EXCHANGE RATE POLICY

In Slovenia's transition the relative prices of nontradable goods and services and the volume of net foreign capital inflows were probably the most important constraints on monetary and exchange rate policy's room to maneuver in its quest for sustainable internal and external equilibrium. Both constraints were not always binding simultaneously. However, basic changes in the orientation and implementation of policy were made whenever policymakers considered that trends in the constraining variables presented a serious threat to achieving sustainable internal or external equilibrium.

Relative Prices of Nontradables

In the early phase of the transition, the relative prices of nontradables (mainly services) increased considerably, reaching much higher levels than in other economies at a similar level of development. They also fluctuated considerably. These high and volatile relative prices of nontradables threatened to jeopardize the sustainability of price stabilization as well as long-run growth.

A traditional explanation for increasing relative prices of nontradables follows the arguments of Paul Samuelson and Bela Balassa.[1] This explanation of faster growth in the prices of nontradables and of currency appreciation assumes that the labor market efficiently equalizes wages in the nontradables sector with wages in the tradables sector; it also assumes a rapid increase in productivity in the restructured (or new) tradables industries. However, it is documented elsewhere that, in Slovenia during the period in question, market equalization of wages between the two sectors could not be detected. At the same time, empirical evidence rather strongly corroborates two other important causes of the increase in relative prices of nontradables: government intervention in regulated prices and the tax structure, as well as sectoral differences in the evolution of market structure, combined with a segmented, heavily unionized labor market, were crucial in bringing about the change in relative prices (Bole 2001).[2]

This mechanism underlying relative price increases undercuts the argument in favor of limiting the choice of an exchange rate regime to so-called corner options (for example, using a fixed exchange rate as a price anchor). Because relative prices were much higher (in comparison with other economies) than differences in development could explain, both types of corner exchange rate regime could jeopardize not only the sustainability of price stabilization but also long-term real convergence upon entering the European Union.[3]

Even in theory, differences in market structure have important implications for the specification of optimal stabilization and exchange rate policies. Certain theoretical results corroborate the idea that optimal monetary policy would target the prices of nontradables despite the impact of the resulting variability in the exchange rate on prices of tradables (Aoki 2001; Clarida, Galí, and Gertler 2001). Policymakers would therefore have to control domestic demand (by controlling the money supply or the real interest rate) and mitigate supply shocks,[4] in the short run, and stimulate development of the market structure in the nontradables sector, in the long run.

Net Foreign Capital Inflows

Slovenia also faced strong net foreign exchange inflows during the transition. These inflows accelerated after 1994. In the period 1995–98, net medium- and long-term capital inflows exceeded the average for developing countries, even attaining levels as high relative to GDP as those observed in East Asia in the 1990s (see, for example, Ishii and Dunaway 1995; Bole 1999). After 1999, net capital inflows further accelerated, even exceeding 8 percent of GDP.

Such a surge of foreign inflows mitigates the constraints on restructuring and investment imposed by insufficient domestic saving. However, such inflows also raise several well-known concerns (see, for example, Mishra, Mody, and Murshid 2001; McKinnon 1990; Corbo and De Melo 1985; Calvo, Leiderman, and Reinhart 1993a, 1993b; and Schadler and others 1993).

In Slovenia empirical evidence corroborates that capital inflows lowered the domestic real interest rate and the foreign exchange liquidity premium. Among the unfavorable macroeconomic effects were an appreciation of the tolar and an acceleration of real private consumption; these threatened and jeopardized control of the money supply. Considerable gross flows through the banking sector also destabilized Slovenia's banks (see, for example, Bole 1999; Oplotnik 2003). Probably the most important long-term harmful effect was the indirect impact of unmitigated financial inflows on already-distorted relative prices, making price stabilization unsustainable. Distortions on labor and product markets, combined with huge capital inflows in foreign exchange, boosted the relative prices of nontradables after 1992. The appreciation of the domestic currency held down the domestic prices of tradables, while prices of nontradables kept rising, as their strong market position (weaker competition) enabled enterprises in the nontradables sector to mark up their costs, especially wage costs, over marginal product. At the same time, with huge financial inflows loosening control of the money supply, monetary policy was unable to restrain demand. Unmitigated financial inflows could therefore have worsened the existing labor and product market distortions and made exchange rate–anchored price stabilization unsustainable.

The appropriate policy responses to huge financial inflows depend on the institutional characteristics and performance of the economy, primarily the fiscal stance, the foreign exchange rate regime, and possible microeconomic distortions. The most commonly recommended policies for neutralizing the effects of such inflows include trade policy measures, sterilized and unsterilized foreign exchange intervention, increased marginal reserve requirements, raising of interest rates on borrowing from the central bank, and reduced access to rediscount facilities. Tight fiscal policy, taxes and deposits on borrowing abroad (through asymmetric, Tobin-tax-like measures), and stricter banking regulation can be used to reduce future inflows of capital from abroad (see, for example, Schadler and others 1993; Calvo, Leiderman, and Reinhart 1993a, 1993b).

In Slovenia, measures to contain and neutralize financial flows were adopted after 1991. Of the policies just listed, only fiscal and trade policies were not especially adjusted to help contain and neutralize the effects of the inflows.[5] Indeed, the fiscal stance was relatively sound and foreign trade already liberalized almost from the beginning of the transition.[6] All the other policies were used at least to some extent during 1992–2000. However, their intensity changed over time and varied from policy to policy.

CHARACTERISTICS OF EXCHANGE RATE POLICY CHANGES

Revealed Preferences of Policymakers in Exchange Rate Intervention

During the "emergency" period, which lasted until the end of 1992, policymakers sought to regain control over the economy. Rebuilding the economy's robust external liquidity was a crucial objective in the choice of an exchange rate regime and corresponding policy measures during this period. After 1992, money was targeted and the exchange rate managed, at least de jure. But policymakers' objectives were disclosed only for money targeting. Interventions in currency markets were made without specifying any commitment or even a preannounced path for the exchange rate. The question, therefore, is how these interventions were decided upon.

To gain at least a heuristic impression of the reaction function for exchange rate intervention after 1993, it is worth looking at the intensity of central bank interventions directed toward foreign financial flows. In Figure 11.1 monetization on the retail foreign exchange market (net foreign exchange bought by the banking sector from the nonbanking sector) is used to indicate the timing and size of the monetary effects of foreign financial flows. Compared with the components of the balance of payments, monetization on the retail foreign exchange market enables much better insight into the preferences of monetary policymakers facing considerable swings in foreign financial flows. There are several reasons why these insights are especially valuable.

In Slovenia in the period under study, currency substitution was still substantial.[7] Therefore the size and dynamics of (net) monetization had more direct effects on the volume of broad money and banks' supply of credit than did the components of the balance of payments,

FIGURE 11.1 MONETIZATION ON THE RETAIL
FOREIGN EXCHANGE MARKET[a]

(percent of GDP)

a. Net foreign exchange bought from the nonbanking sector.
Source: Bole (2003).

because they directly affected items on bank balance sheets denominated in tolars. Because the exchange rate was not fixed and there was significant currency substitution, monetization on the retail foreign exchange market explicitly shows any imbalance in that market, and therefore the scale and timing of pressures on exchange rate dynamics. If microeconomic variables are important for these dynamics, monetization on the foreign exchange market must directly incorporate their effects.[8]

In Figure 11.1 monetization on the retail foreign exchange market is given in percentages of quarterly GDP. Asterisks indicate the dates when new instruments for containing and neutralizing foreign financial inflows were launched. These are periods when disequilibria on the retail foreign exchange market became dangerous in the perception of policymakers.

All such new instruments were obviously launched during periods when monetization on the retail foreign exchange market attained peak values (Bank of Slovenia Annual Report, various issues; Bole 1999), that is, when the central bank faced serious problems with money control and appreciation of the currency. In years of high monetization, net foreign exchange bought from the nonbank sector considerably exceeded 10 percent of broad money.

Heuristically speaking, policymakers in Slovenia target the money supply and seek to dampen the volatility of an otherwise floating exchange rate, especially during peaks. This basic "philosophy" of the exchange rate regime has not been changed as of 2003. The implementation of that regime was, however, changed several times. Starting conditions, external factors (capital flows), the relative prices of nontradables, and the performance of other sectors (especially the fiscal stance) largely determined the policy instruments through which the currency regime was implemented. The volatility of these determinants caused vigorous changes in the dynamics of the variables (for example, the exchange rate or the net foreign assets of the central bank) usually used as criteria for exchange rate regime classification. This is why more detailed technical classification of the de facto exchange rate regime used in Slovenia reveals several possible classification changes during the analyzed period (see, for example, Levy-Yeyati and Sturzenegger 2002), just as descriptive analysis can distinguish at least three significantly different phases in the implementation of Slovenia's managed floating regime.

Landmarks in Exchange Rate Policy since 1991

The revealed preferences of monetary and exchange rate policymakers and the known paths of certain basic constraining variables (the relative prices of nontradables, foreign capital inflows) make it possible to sketch the landmarks of exchange rate policy in Slovenia.

The external environment and the basic performance of the economy at the time the new currency was launched in 1991 were so different from those in the following, "normal" years of transition that the choice of exchange rate regime as well as the whole design of policy in that period cannot be compared with later periods. This "emergency" period lasted until the end of 1992, during which the exchange rate was freely floating.

Already in the middle of 1992, and especially after that year, foreign financial inflows increased considerably. Almost at the same time, regulated prices and prices of other nontradables also accelerated. Nevertheless, the structure of the central bank's balance sheet and the high risk premium on foreign exchange made the position of monetary policy still quite comfortable regarding capital inflows. The central bank started to manage the exchange rate.

By the middle of 1996, the foreign exchange risk premium had already fallen significantly. Capital inflows into the nongovernment sector increased, and, at the same time, the relative prices of nontradables increased considerably. Because of existing distortions on the labor market and the nontradable part of the product market, capital controls were enacted as a second-best solution to mitigate the harmful effects of increasing capital inflows.

As part of the government's commitments under the EU accession procedure after the second half of 1999, the capital controls had to be removed. Net capital inflows then accelerated considerably. This acceleration was again followed by a large increase in the prices of non-tradables, further driven by supply shocks generated by the restructuring of the tax system (the introduction of a value added tax and an increase in excise taxes) and some regulated prices.

POLICY IMPLEMENTATION IN THE EMERGENCY PERIOD, 1991–92

Gaining Control

At the time the new currency was launched in October 1991, galloping inflation, almost negligible foreign exchange reserves, and lack of access to foreign credits made standard stabilization measures, orthodox or heterodox, impossible.[9] It was necessary to proceed on two tracks—building foreign exchange liquidity and reducing inflation—at the same time. A pure float of the exchange rate and an exogenous money supply were therefore the only choice available to the central bank in the period immediately following the launching of the tolar.

This emergency period can be divided into two phases, as Figure 11.2 illustrates. In the first phase the excess liquidity of the banking system was wiped out: the money supply was cut in nominal terms. This phase of the emergency period lasted until February 1992, during which inflation fell and foreign exchange reserves started to accumulate. The exchange rate meanwhile skyrocketed, with the value of the tolar increasing by 90 percent, but after five months its path leveled off.

In the second phase monetary policy was able to more smoothly adjust the money supply toward targeted real demand. This phase lasted until the end of 1992. Reduction of inflation to a moderate level, an increase in foreign exchange reserves, very small changes in the exchange rate, and a strong acceleration of wages were the most outstanding accomplishments of the Slovenian economy during this period.

Policy Measures in the Emergency Period

In the first phase of the emergency period, the central bank reduced the money overhang, using only its lending instruments (Figure 11.2). In the second phase, after the second quarter of 1992, the central bank

FIGURE 11.2 BASE MONEY AND CENTRAL BANK CREDITS

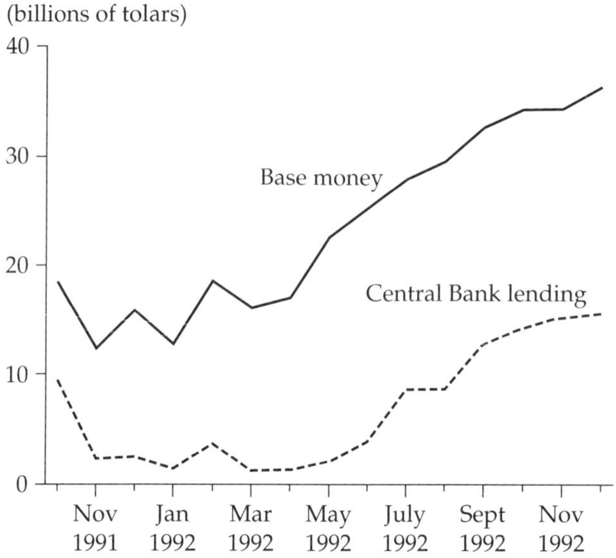

(billions of tolars)

Source: Bank of Slovenia, *Monthly Bulletin*, various issues; author's calculations.

started also to sterilize the increasing inflow of foreign exchange. It did this mainly by offering bills to be bought and redeemed in foreign currency, as well as bills bought in tolars and redeemed half in tolars and half in foreign currency. The central bank also limited access to the rediscount window to banks that were absorbing a greater-than-average excess of foreign exchange inflow (Bole 1997).

There was no special adjustment of fiscal or incomes policy toward supporting a deflation-oriented monetary policy. Fiscal policy supported the restrictive monetary policy by running a slight surplus in terms of the overall balance of the government in 1992, but badly needed incomes policy measures were completely absent. The relative prices of nontradables increased considerably, because price corrections for the output of public utilities (for example, gasoline, natural gas, and telecommunications) were made erratically and in large jumps.

At the launching of the new currency, it seemed that the standard monetary instruments and the existing institutional infrastructure of the foreign exchange market would not be enough to enable a rapid and safe reduction of the huge monetary overhang and close the imbalance on the spot retail foreign exchange market. Immediately after the switch to free floating and money targeting, the foreign exchange market was therefore reshaped and the instruments for management of the money supply correspondingly adjusted.

Reshaping the Foreign Exchange Market

To allow the robust and safe implementation of a foreign exchange regime based on a freely floating tolar, the institutional setting underlying the foreign exchange market was reshaped. The main reason for these changes was to boost the elasticity of the exchange rate with respect to demand on the retail foreign exchange market.

Had the exchange rate proved slow to adjust to increases in net quantities demanded, this, combined with Slovenia's negligible foreign exchange reserves and lack of access to foreign credit, could have endangered the economy's foreign liquidity. Moreover, inefficiencies caused by the highly monopolized retail foreign exchange market (at the end of 1991 one bank controlled over 60 percent of transactions) could have appeared, increasing uncertainty and endangering stabilization. By reshaping the institutional setting of the retail foreign exchange market, the authorities intended to make the spot market clear as quickly as possible. It was presumed that this acceleration of clearing would mitigate the danger of speculative attack and potential monopoly effects.

Banks, enterprises, and households could participate in the market for foreign exchange. Nonresidents, however, were excluded. Banks were completely free to trade in foreign exchange. Enterprises could sell foreign exchange to any economic unit (bank or other enterprise) operating on the market. However, they had to complete the transaction within 48 hours after the foreign exchange inflow. These basic characteristics of the foreign exchange market did not change until the beginning of 1995.

To increase the exchange rate's elasticity in response to considerable (speculative) jumps in quantity demanded, the central bank also adopted "time segmentation" of the foreign exchange market accessed by households. The central bank set the length of the time interval within which net cumulative purchases in foreign exchange offices had to be at least zero. (Initially this interval was set at one week.) With this requirement, the elasticity of the exchange rate to a shock to quantity demanded was drastically increased, and thus the possibility of speculative attack was reduced significantly. This was documented during the first three quasi-speculative attacks, in January 1992, March 1992, and February–March 1993, and in the last one in the second part of 1995. As the buildup of foreign exchange reserves diminished the likelihood of and the vulnerability to speculative attack, the time segmentation of the foreign exchange market was put on hold.

Adjustments of Monetary Instruments

Two special characteristics of the management of the money supply implemented during the emergency period are worth mentioning. First, central bank lending to banks was actually shrinking in nominal terms up to the beginning of February 1992. Credits to banks were stretched and smoothed, rather than cut in one move, to enable banks to lower their credit exposure to enterprises in a less harmful and more rational way (Figure 11.2).

Second, the central bank enforced the linear rescaling of nominal interest rates on old dinar bank credits to enterprises to a much lower level.[10] This rescaling mitigated any harmful effects from increasing real interest rates due to the expected fall in inflation. It was anticipated that, through such an operation, the expected capital gains of banks in the expected period of falling inflation would be neutralized in advance by immediate, mandatory capital losses of the same magnitude. For enterprises the effect would have to be just big enough to compensate for the increase in real interest rate costs (because of the lagged indexation) in the period of the targeted fall of inflation. This linear rescaling of interest rates was similar to the "tablita" used in stabilization episodes in Latin America (for example, in Brazil's Cruzado Plan), although there was no price freeze in Slovenia and it was not used for all contracts. Rather, it was applied only to existing bank credits denominated in old currency. The rescaling of interest rates also accelerated the conversion (done only on a contractual basis) of old credits denominated in dinars to the new currency. Therefore the rescaling further mitigated the harmful effects of the liquidity squeeze on economic activity and of the appreciation of the currency.

THREE PHASES OF POLICY IMPLEMENTATION DURING THE MANAGED FLOATING PERIOD, 1993–PRESENT

Regaining basic control over the economy and strengthening foreign exchange liquidity enabled Slovenia's policymakers to tackle the harmful effects of increasing net foreign financial inflows and of distortions in product and labor markets—effects transmitted and perpetuated by the free floating of the exchange rate. Therefore, after 1992, policymakers started to manage the exchange rate and to target the money supply.[11] However, the implementation of the floating exchange rate regime has changed considerably in that period.[12]

Implementation of the managed float depended on the path of foreign capital inflows and the relative prices of nontradables. This is illustrated in Figure 11.3, which traces central bank net foreign exchange

FIGURE 11.3 NET FOREIGN ASSETS OF THE CENTRAL BANK

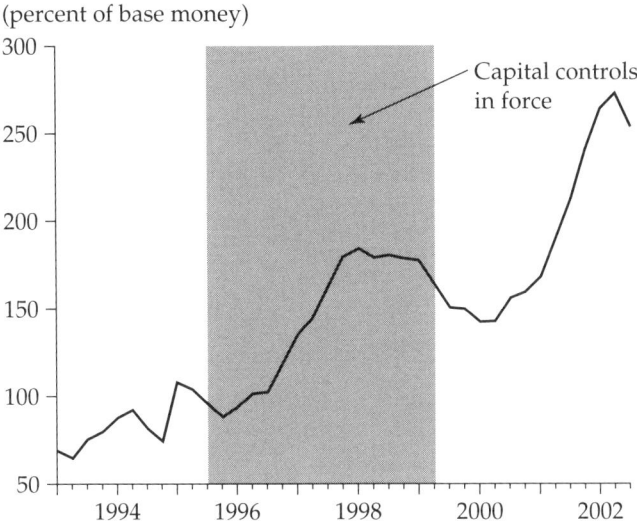

(percent of base money)

Source: Bole (2003).

assets since 1993, and Figure 11.4, which shows the difference in expected rates of return between short-term credits denominated in tolars and in German marks. Figure 11.3 reveals three phases in the implementation of the floating exchange rate regime. In every phase, money was controlled and the volatility of the exchange rate was dampened during peaks, but the explicit intermediate targets and the instruments used differed from phase to phase.

Independent Paths of Money and the Exchange Rate

The first phase coincides with the period in which the net foreign assets of the central bank were smaller than base money. During this phase, which lasted until the middle of 1995, the central bank targeted base money. Because base money exceeded net foreign assets, the central bank was able to influence the former very effectively by changing only the supply of its lending instruments. Fluctuations in the difference between expected rates of return could therefore be large and long-term, as Figure 11.4 documents. The central bank efficiently neutralized the potentially damaging offset effects of increased capital inflows simply by further shrinking its lending or increasing the supply of its borrowing instruments to banks. A high foreign exchange risk premium made the central bank's room for maneuver even greater.

FIGURE 11.4 DIFFERENCE IN EXPECTED RATES OF
                        RETURN ON DOMESTIC AND
                        FOREIGN CREDITS[a]

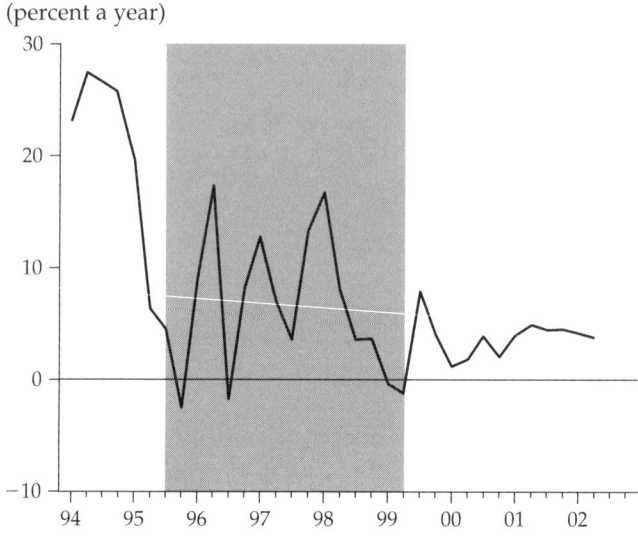

(percent a year)

a. Rate on domestic short-term credits denominated in tolars minus
rate on German short-term credits denominated in marks.
Source: Bole (2003).

The bulk of capital inflows came through the business and household sectors. Meanwhile the high foreign exchange risk premium
restrained nonresidents from buying foreign exchange bills of the
central bank through resident nonbank financial intermediaries used as
fronts. Thus the central bank could increase the returns on those bills
to a level high enough to absorb any excess supply of foreign exchange
in residents' portfolios. Warrants and foreign exchange bills of the central bank were the basic instruments used in this period. The central
bank also used credits collateralized by its foreign exchange bills and
repurchase operations using those bills (Bole 1999). To absorb excess
money created by monetization, the volume of tolar-denominated bills
also increased, but it was still less important. To increase the robust-
ness of the country's banks in the intermediation of volatile flows, their
minimum required capital was increased to 40 million marks. Sterilization costs in that period increased considerably.

Capital Controls

The second phase of the managed floating regime coincided with the
period of direct capital controls. This phase lasted from the second

half of 1995 until the middle of 1999, during which central bank net foreign assets systematically exceeded base money.

In this second phase, the central bank continued to target base money. Controlling money in that period became considerably more difficult and costly, however. Because the net foreign assets of the central bank significantly exceeded base money, the central bank had to neutralize the harmful capital inflow effects, which it did chiefly through borrowing (sterilization) instruments. In this phase controlling money became even more difficult because the foreign exchange risk premium dropped considerably at the beginning of that period.[13] However, capital controls, which were enacted in this phase, enabled the central bank to attain at least short-term independence of the exchange rate path from the interest rate path. As Figure 11.4 illustrates, the amplitudes of the swings in the difference in expected rates of return were still high, but the swings were much shorter in duration (on average, only about two quarters), and the average level of the difference in returns was lower, because the danger of interest-elastic capital inflows was much higher than in the first phase.

In addition to the instruments used already in the first phase, the central bank now offered its bills in domestic currency on a permanent basis. They soon became a crucial instrument in this phase of implementation of the managed floating regime. Capital controls were implemented as an asymmetric Tobin tax.[14] The central bank also used instruments, such as the so-called net foreign assets position of banks, to stimulate financial outflows. The volumes of foreign exchange- and tolar-denominated bills increased considerably, and so did sterilization costs; but even at the peak the costs did not exceed 0.5 percent of GDP (Bole 1999).

Closing the Gap in Expected Rates of Return

The final phase of the managed floating regime started after capital controls were removed in the middle of 1999. In that phase the control of money through short-term targeting of base money in periods shorter than one year became almost impossible. Because capital controls had been removed, any significant and even short-term change in the difference in expected rates of return could trigger a substantial flow of capital. The net foreign assets of the central bank already far exceeded base money, and it therefore could not appropriately increase the intensity of sterilization intervention to match the money target over shorter periods (two to three quarters).[15] Hitting the short-term money target was made especially difficult by the considerable increase in long-term capital inflows, which were less responsive to changes in interest rates; these inflows accelerated not only because of the lifting of capital controls but also because uncertainty about the successful end of the accession process had almost completely disappeared.

In the third phase, therefore, the central bank launched two changes in its intervention practices. In the short run it started to effectively target real interest rates, sticking to the base money volume target only over the longer horizon. To make effective real interest rate targeting possible (that is, to mitigate offsetting financial flows), the central bank has started to tightly manage exchange rate dynamics, through intervention, so as to prevent swings in the difference in expected rates of return. The exchange rate has therefore become a crucial tool for battling capital inflows, not through its unexpected volatility but through minimizing the volatility and size of expected-rate-of-return differences.

The central bank makes its commitment to the interest parity condition credible through a contract with the country's commercial banks. Through this contract the central bank offers foreign exchange swaps (on a permanent basis) as a crucial instrument for managing exchange rate dynamics. The credibility of the central bank's commitment to the interest parity was built up by pegging its interventions in exchange rate dynamics to the swap rate. In that period foreign exchange swaps and tolar bills became the crucial instruments. Swaps were used to steer the exchange rate and the swap rate (costs of bank financing) along a common path, while sterilization was implemented through longer-term tolar bills of the central bank.[16] Interest rates on these bills enabled the central bank also to control the lower bound of interest rates on bank short-term lending and thus further support interest rate targeting, implemented basically through swaps. The change in the implementation of monetary policy targeting is illustrated by the almost flat trend of the expected-rate-of-return difference shown in Figure 11.4.

CONCLUSIONS

This chapter's analysis of Slovenia's exchange rate regime and monetary policy has shown that the relative prices of nontradables and foreign financial flows were the most important constraints on the design of the exchange rate regime and the choice of monetary policy measures. Until 1999 the economy was stabilized by targeting the money supply; after capital controls were lifted, monetary policy switched from targeting money to targeting the real interest rate. Although the manner of implementation of the managed float has changed several times, depending on the central bank's ability to control the harmful effects of foreign financial flows, exchange rate intervention was used coherently to support the effectiveness of monetary control.

When Slovenia's monetary and exchange rate policy is compared with that in other transition economies, two important differences emerge. The first is the systematic interplay between monetary policy measures and exchange rate interventions, and the second is the way in which the microeconomic aspects of exchange rate dynamics were taken into account when designing foreign exchange interventions. The central bank's policy allowed price stabilization of the economy to be achieved without drastic deterioration in other important macroeconomic equilibriums. To accelerate disinflation and to increase overall policy efficiency, such a monetary and exchange rate policy needs support from fiscal policy to mitigate supply shocks, in the short run, and from structural policy to stimulate the development of appropriate market structures in the nontradables sector, in the long run. In the short period remaining until Slovenia becomes eligible for stabilization "landing" as a participant in European Monetary Union, the support of fiscal policy in mitigating supply shocks is absolutely crucial. Without such support, the microeconomic distortions still present in the economy, and especially the remaining differences in market structure, could considerably amplify and prolong any larger supply shock in prices, and thus endanger nominal convergence, because the Bank of Slovenia will lose control over interest rates upon entering Exchange Rate Mechanism II.

REFERENCES

Aoki, K. 2001. "Optimal Monetary Policy Responses to Relative-Price Changes." *Journal of Monetary Economics* 48: 55–80.

Begg, D., L. Halpern, and C. Wyplosz. 1999. "Equilibrium Exchange Rates." In L. Ambrus-Lakatos and M. E. Schaffer, eds., *Monetary and Exchange Rate Policies, EMU and Central and Eastern Europe*. London: Centre for Economic Policy Research and East West Institute.

Bhagwati, J. N. 1984. "Why Are Services Cheaper in the Poor Countries?" *Economic Journal* 94: 279–86.

Bole, V. 1997. "Stabilization in Slovenia: From High Inflation to Excessive Inflow of Foreign Capital." In M. I. Blejer and M. Skreb, eds., *Macroeconomic Stabilization in Transition Economies*. Cambridge, United Kingdom: Cambridge University Press.

————. 1999. "Financial Flows in a Small Open Economy; the Case of Slovenia." In J. Gacs, R. Holzmann, and M. Wyzan, eds., *The Mixed Blessing* of Financial Inflows—Transition Countries in Comparative Perspective. Cheltenham, United Kingdom: Edward Elgar.

————. 2001. "Disinflation and Labor Market Distortions: Lessons from Slovenia." Wiener Institut für Internationale Wirtschaftsvergleiche, Vienna (www.wiiw.ac.at/balkan/longterm.html).

————. 2003. "Managed Floating as a Second Best Option; Lessons from Slovenia." Ekonomski Institut Pravne Fakultete (Economic Institute of the Law School), Ljubljana (www.eipf.si).

Calvo, G. A., L. Leiderman, and C. M. Reinhart. 1993a. "The Capital Inflows Problem: Concepts and Issues." IMF Paper on Policy Analysis and Assessment. International Monetary Fund, Washington, D.C.

————. 1993b. "Capital Inflows and Real Exchange Rate Appreciation in Latin America." *Staff Papers* 40: 108–51. International Monetary Fund, Washington, D.C.

Clarida, R., J. Galí, and M. Gertler. 2001. "Exchange Rates and Choice of Monetary Policy Regimes." *American Economic Association Papers and Proceedings* 91: 248–52.

Corbo, V., and J. De Melo. 1985. "Overview and Summary." *World Development* 13: 863–66.

Frankel, J. A. 1999. "No Single Currency Regime Is Right for All Countries or at All Times." Working Paper 7338. National Bureau of Economic Research, Cambridge, Mass.

Ishii, S., and S. Dunaway. 1995. "Portfolio Flows to the Developing Country Members of APEC." In M. S. Khan and C. M. Reinhart, eds., "Capital Flows in the APEC Region." Occasional Paper 122. International Monetary Fund, Washington, D.C.

Levy-Yeyati, E., and F. Sturzenegger. 2002. "Classifying Exchange Rate Regimes: Deeds vs. Words." Universidad Torcuato di Tella, Buenos Aires (www.utdt.edu/~fsturzen/web.pdf).

MacDonald, R., and C. Wojcik. 2002. "Catching Up: The Role of Demand, Supply and Regulated Price Effects on the Real Exchange Rates of Four Accession Countries." *Focus on Transition* 2: 38–57.

McKinnon, R. I. 1990. "Financial Liberalization in Retrospect: Interest Rate Policies in LDC's." In G. Ranis and T. P. Schultz, eds., *The State of Development Economics: Progress and Perspectives*. Cambridge, United Kingdom: Basil Blackwell.

Mishra, D., A. Mody, and A. P. Murshid. 2001. "Private Capital Flows and Growth." *Finance & Development* 38(2): 2–5.

Oplotnik, Ž. 2003. "Capital Flows Adjustment Policy in Slovenia: Assessment of Design and Efficiency." *Post-Communist Economies* 15: 209–25.

Rose, A. K. 1994. "Are Exchange Rates Macroeconomic Phenomena?" *Federal Reserve Bank of San Francisco Economic Review* (1): 19–30.

Schadler, S., M. Carkovic, A. Bennett, and R. Kahn. 1993. "Recent Experiences with Surges in Capital Inflows." Occasional Paper 108. International Monetary Fund, Washington, D.C.

NOTES

1. See, for example, Begg, Halpern, and Wyplosz (1999). A more general explanation of the same phenomenon is given by Bhagwati (1984).

2. The importance of regulated prices has been documented for other transition economies as well (see, for example, MacDonald and Wojcik 2002).

3. In the second half of the 1990s, relative prices of services in Slovenia overshot those in Hungary by more than 60 percent and attained about 80 percent of the relative prices of services in Italy and Austria (Bole 2003).

4. This would include those shocks generated by the authorities themselves, by sharply increasing regulated prices and changing the tax structure in order to alleviate pressure on the general government balance.

5. Indirectly, fiscal policy also addressed the problem through limits on the possible yearly volume of new credits (raised by the government and enterprises in government ownership), which were part of the annual state budget law.

6. In 1992–2000 the average general government balance was –0.17 percent of GDP; in the same period the foreign trade ratio (exports plus imports, divided by GDP) was more than 1.15.

7. In 1999, on average, foreign exchange deposits still amounted to 28 percent of M3 (*Monthly Bulletin,* Bank of Slovenia).

8. On the possible importance of microeconomic variables for exchange rate dynamics, see Rose (1994).

9. Inflation was galloping ahead at more than 20 percent a month, while foreign exchange reserves were enough for only four days of imports. See, for example, Bole (1997).

10. The nominal component of interest rates was set to the targeted inflation rate of 2 percent a month, whereas the real component stayed approximately equal to the actual (contracted) level (see, for example, Bole 1997).

11. According to the International Monetary Fund, managed floating is an exchange rate regime in which the monetary authority influences exchange rate dynamics through active intervention in the foreign exchange market without specifying or precommitting to a preannounced exchange rate path. Under the IMF definition, Slovenia could be classified as a managed floater after 1992.

12. How intensive the changes were is documented, for example, in a cluster-based analysis of regimes, which classified Slovenia in that period in four different regime types at different times (Levy-Yeyati and Sturzenegger 2002).

13. In 1996 several events made Slovenia much more attractive to foreign investors. The restructuring of old debt inherited from SFR Yugoslavia was successfully completed; in the same year Slovenia launched its first bond issue on the euro market and got a single investment grade of A-minus.

14. A deposit (40 percent) on nontrade credit facilities was paid on all maturities of less than five years. The threshold maturity was later increased

to seven years, but nonbank economic entities also had to pay a deposit (10 percent) on credits with maturity longer than seven years.

15. At the end of 2001, for example, when the euro was launched, unexpected capital inflows through the household sector in one month alone attained almost 4 percent of GDP. It took the central bank more than three quarters to neutralize the corresponding increase in base money.

16. Normally, 270-day bills were used. During episodes of huge short-term inflows (such as the foreign acquisition of the Slovenian pharmaceutical firm Lek), special series of 360-day bills could also be offered to banks.

Chapter 12
Fiscal Policy and Public Finance Reforms

Milan M. Cvikl and Mitja Gaspari

This chapter discusses fiscal policy issues and public finance reforms in the first decade of Slovenia's independence. These reforms were key to stabilizing the economic situation and facilitating the transition of the Slovenian economy and were instrumental in preparation for EU membership. The main task of fiscal policy in the 1990s was to achieve stabilization. However, as part of the overall strategy of gradualism in economic reforms, fiscal policy had to ensure a smooth transition from a market socialist economic system to a full-fledged market system. Unfortunately, in this context and in line with EU practice, the role of the state in the Slovenian economy remained strong, with general government expenditure never falling below 40 percent of GDP. (Table 12.1 summarizes general government revenue, expenditure, and the fiscal balance in Slovenia since 1992.)

With general government spending at this level, a sophisticated tax system with high tax rates was required. This is still considered a normal state of affairs. Thanks mainly to low deficits, gradual privatization, and the ability of the Slovenian economy to expand its presence in external markets, the level of public debt was not problematic during this first decade.[1] Nevertheless, in the second half of the 1990s as the EU integration process got under way, Slovenia undertook major public finance reforms. These reforms were able to arrest a major increase in the deficit in 1997, resulting from changes in the structure of general government revenue and expenditure.

TABLE 12.1 CONSOLIDATED GENERAL GOVERNMENT REVENUE, EXPENDITURE, AND BALANCE

(thousands of tolars)

Year	Total revenue	Total expenditure	General government surplus or deficit	Primary surplus or deficit	Current surplus or deficit
1992	440,962	428,524	12,438	8,394	45,315
1993	640,895	628,363	12,532	22,300	61,006
1994	803,560	803,355	206	18,315	78,844
1995	958.186	957,273	913	21,161	91,820
1996	1,091,815	1,083,586	8,230	34,601	112,811
1997	1,222,587	1,256,668	−34,081	−4,289	81,536
1998	1,397,903	1,423,494	−25,591	9,804	107,852
1999	1,590,017	1,613,314	−23,297	20,709	133,711
2000	1,726,724	1,781,444	−54,720	−3,790	84,541
2001	1,967,785	2,030,978	−63,193	1144	105,334
2002	2,083,860	2,241,482	−157,622	−80,623	8,934

Source: Ministry of Finance, *Bulletin of Government Finance,* Year IV, No. 6, June 2003.

In 1999 Slovenia passed modern budget legislation, enabling a reform in the public expenditure management and in the tax system based on the value added tax (VAT) and excise taxes. Although major improvements in public expenditure management were undertaken in the second half of the 1990s, best practice in this area has yet to be implemented. In this context some public services will need to be reformed as part of the overall transition of the role of the state in a small, developed economy. This will present a major challenge for future public expenditure reform.

This chapter is organized as follows. First, we describe fiscal policy during the stabilization period and how it supported Slovenia's transition to a full-fledged market economy. Next, fiscal revenue trends during that period and developments in fiscal debt and debt management are presented. This is followed by a presentation of the status of public finance reforms in Slovenia and improvements in public expenditure management. Finally, we assess the current fiscal situation and present an agenda for further budget and tax reforms. These reforms are expected to ensure a sustainable budget in the long run, and especially in the upcoming period of EU membership and Slovenia's participation in Exchange Rate Mechanism II (ERM-II) and European Monetary Union.

FISCAL POLICY AND PUBLIC EXPENDITURE REFORM IN SUPPORT OF STABILIZATION AND TRANSITION

Slovenia's fiscal policies and public finance reforms have contributed to a successful transition in two ways. First, fiscal policy and public expenditure management reforms supported economic stabilization. Second, the achievement of stabilization in turn enabled the Slovenian economy to make a smooth transition from a market socialist economy to a full-fledged market economy during the first decade of independence. However, fiscal policies were not sufficient to ensure the development of an efficient and vibrant market economy.

One can identify two distinct periods in the 1990s. During the initial period, from 1990 to 1997, the country struggled to achieve economic stabilization while launching enterprise, banking, social security, and other reforms. For these reforms the abolition of enterprise self-control (i.e., self-management) and extremely decentralized budgetary systems were crucially important. The creation of an integral budget was linked to fiscal revenue reform and the introduction of a personal income tax in 1990. In the remainder of the 1990s, the economic reforms begun in the first period—especially banking, enterprise restructuring, and social security reforms—were continued as part of the transition. As a direct implication of these reforms, the national debt, and thus interest payments on that debt, rose as a percentage of GDP, contributing to an increase in the share of nondiscretionary spending within the central government budget.

Economic reforms were coupled with public finance reforms, providing the necessary adjustment in general government budgetary levels, structures, and new legislation and practice in revenue and expenditure control. On the expenditure side, new budgetary legislation as well as new, modern methodologies and techniques were prepared and developed. These included the transformation from input-output expenditure planning and provided the beginning of preparations for performance-oriented budgeting.

On the cash and debt management side, the treasury single account and improved public debt management were implemented. On the revenue side, VAT and excise taxes were introduced in mid-1999, thus providing a modern tax environment conducive to the support of exports and consistent with the EU tax environment.

These reforms were put in place to ensure that, upon Slovenia's entry into the European Union (planned for 2004), the core budgetary goals under the Maastricht rules would be met: Slovenia would have a balanced general government budget as measured over the business cycle. Unfortunately, these projections may not be realized. Currently, Slovenia's fiscal situation requires a new set of fiscal reforms, including changes in the rules and procedures of budgetary allocation. Since EU entry is itself fiscally costly, and a revenue shortfall is expected due to further economic opening and relatively high EU budget obligations for Slovenia, a fiscal crisis is not unlikely unless major expenditure cuts are made.

Supporting Economic Stabilization with a Restrictive Fiscal Policy Stance

Upon independence, the first essential task was macroeconomic stabilization. In the first few years after independence, Slovenia's fiscal policies and public expenditure management reforms supported stabilization and transformed a situation of hyperinflation into a normal, low inflation environment. A surplus in the fiscal accounts was achieved in those years, through actions on both the revenue and the expenditure side, supporting a restrictive monetary policy.

On the revenue side, a successful tax reform introduced a personal income tax. That tax and the existing sales tax and customs duties were key sources of revenue. Introduction of the personal income tax was an important change from the previous situation, as Slovenian residents became "taxpayers" overnight and for the first time had to fill out tax returns. Payroll taxes remained a key source of revenue throughout the 1990s. On the expenditure side, the transition had started with the abrupt abolition of fiscal "self-management" and the centralization of government functions. Before independence, Slovenian public expenditure had been fragmented into hundreds of programs at the local community level,[2] and some large social funds at the republican level. These programs were inflationary and formed the core of an economic environment based on soft budget constraints. Upon independence, the Slovenian government centralized the public expenditure management program, thus imposing hard budget constraints for the first time in many decades. Further substantial and methodological improvements in the program were implemented starting in 1998 and are discussed below.

Supporting the Transition to a Market Economy

In the mid-1990s fiscal policy and public expenditure management reforms supported the transition by creating room on the expenditure side for the costs associated with enterprise and bank restructuring and pension reform. In this context, fiscal policy enabled the full liberalization of the enterprise sector, the fostering of the private sector, and successful financial sector rehabilitation and reform.

For example, since 1993 the budget has supported bank rehabilitation by issuing government bonds to replace nonperforming assets held by the banks. The budget also provided support for the necessary technical assistance in financial sector institutional development and for the development of export insurance schemes, which were critically necessary for the promotion of exports. Given low budget deficits and thus low borrowing requirements, the potential for crowding out was avoided. Generous publicly financed programs of unemployment benefits, early retirement schemes, and social assistance provided an appropriate social safety net that enabled enterprise sector restructuring.[3]

Fiscal and Budgetary Trends During the Transition

The main feature of Slovenian general government expenditure throughout the period has been its similarity to the EU average: expenditure fluctuated in a narrow range between 42 and 45 percent of GDP. The structure of expenditure remained very much in line with the EU average as well (Bole 1999a). Spending on wages and salaries amounted, on average, to 18 percent of GDP, transfers to households and subsidies were 21 percent, debt servicing costs 1.5 percent, and capital expenditure 3.3 percent of GDP (Figure 12.1).

Despite this rather normal level and composition of general government expenditure, the worsening dynamics of some important variables in the expenditure structure created potential vulnerabilities.

FIGURE 12.1 COMPOSITION OF GENERAL GOVERNMENT EXPENDITURE

(percent of GDP)

Legend:
- □ Salaries, wages and other personnel expenditure
- ▣ Pensions
- ■ Transfers
- □ Expenditure on goods and services
- ▨ Interest payments
- □ Subsidies
- □ Other current transfers
- ▨ Capital expenditure
- ■ Capital transfers

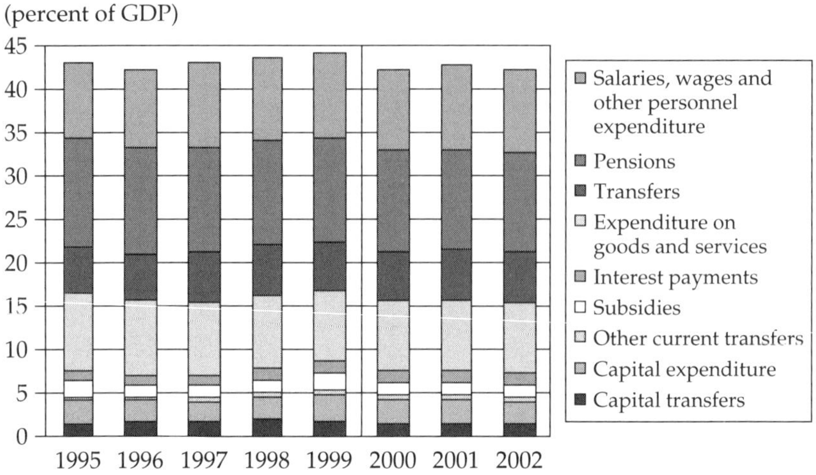

Source: Ministry of Finance, *Bulletin of Government Finance,* Year IV, No. 6, June 2003.

In the 1990s expenditure on wages and salaries increased its share of the budget by 1 percentage point of GDP, while the share of expenditure on goods and services fell proportionately. At the same time, transfers to households rose by at least 1.5 percentage points of GDP as the social safety net was adjusted and expanded. The most important single increase was in the area of pensions, largely due to early retirements. Transitional fiscal spending in the first part of the 1990s (unemployment benefits, early retirement, enterprise subsidies, and debt repayment costs) therefore rose by more than 1.7 percent of GDP, and expenditure on other budget items was held down so as to keep total expenditure roughly constant. This came to an end after 1996, allowing some structural adjustment in general government expenditure policy. Unfortunately, an emerging potential margin was used for an economically unviable increase in other transfers to households and weakly controlled expansion of wages and salaries in the public sector.

Although overall general government expenditure remained under control, the economic quality and sustainability of its structure worsened slowly but steadily. The main reason was that a diverse array of interest groups was lobbying either for new appropriations or the expansion of existing spending in the budget. One factor that contributed to a relatively stable budget balance throughout the period was the strong revenue position of the general government, a sign of solid efficiency in tax administration and a robust tax base (table 12.2). Over the whole period since 1991, one can observe systematic changes

TABLE 12.2 STRUCTURE OF FISCAL REVENUE IN THE EUROPEAN
UNION AND SLOVENIA

	European Union, 1995		Slovenia, 1998	
Revenue source	*Percent of GDP*	*Percent of total revenue*	*Percent of GDP*	*Percent of total revenue*
Indirect taxes	13.6	32.6	16.3	37.9
Wholesale	6.9	16.5	13.0	30.2
Excises	3.4	8.2	0.0	0.0
Other	3.3	7.9	3.3	7.7
Social contributions	15.0	36.0	16.8	39.1
Direct taxes	13.1	31.4	9.9	23.0
Households	9.7	23.2	6.5	15.1
Enterprises	2.4	5.8	1.2	2.8
Other	1.0	2.4	2.2	5.1
Total	41.7	100	43.0	100

Sources: Eurostat Statistics 1997; Ministry of Finance; Bole (1999b).

in tax collection on labor and consumption (Figure 12.2). A net decrease in tax returns on labor was affected mostly by shrinking tax returns on social contributions (by 5 percent of GDP) only partly offset by an increasing return on payroll taxation (by 1.4 percent of GDP). Increased returns on taxation for goods and services was the consequence of higher returns on taxation of domestic goods and services (by 5 percent of GDP) partly offset by lower returns on taxation of international trade (by 2 percent of GDP).

However, any further adjustment in the structure of Slovenia's tax system to meet EU-wide standards should take several considerations into account. First, what matters most is not the absolute level of tax rates, but whether the combination of tax rates and the tax base, tax exemptions, and tax incentives is appropriate. Second, only on the basis of those adjustments can correct judgments about actual tax burdens on labor, capital, and final consumption be made. Third, there are indications that, in Slovenia, the tax base will be broadened (mostly in the area of income taxation) and individual tax incentives and exemptions reduced, and thus that effective tax rates on labor can be reduced accordingly.

Based on previous analysis of general government expenditure and revenue dynamics and structure in the period 1991–2000, we can identify, by calculating Slovenia's cyclically adjusted budget balance, some structural rigidities in the fiscal and budget structure and trends. Some analyses (Žumer 2003, Ministry of Finance 2000) show that the cyclically adjusted balance deteriorated significantly after 1996 and that the cyclically adjusted deficit peaked in 2000 (table 12.3). This

Figure 12.2 Composition of General Government Revenue

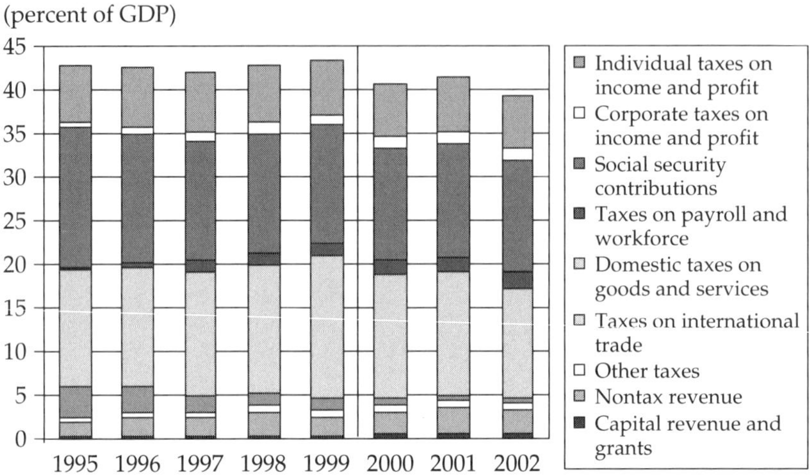
(percent of GDP)
45
40
35
30
25
20
15
10
5
0
1995 1996 1997 1998 1999 2000 2001 2002
Individual taxes on income and profit
Corporate taxes on income and profit
Social security contributions
Taxes on payroll and workforce
Domestic taxes on goods and services
Taxes on international trade
Other taxes
Nontax revenue
Capital revenue and grants

Source: Ministry of Finance, *Bulletin of Government Finance*, Year IV, No. 6, June 2003.

suggests that the budget balance as determined by permanent and structural factors deteriorated after the beginning of the transition process. The turnaround began in 2001, and the cyclically adjusted balance has improved since then, although in 2001–02 it was still negative. The fact that the cyclical component of the budget was not large confirms that the size and structure of general government show considerable lack of flexibility in adjusting to economic cycles. This is to be improved in the near future as Slovenia enters the European Union and European Monetary Union. That will be the key factor in determining fiscal developments in 2003–04 and the actual fiscal balance at the time of EU accession.

Public Debt and Borrowing in the Transition Period

The evolution of the public debt during the transition has to be evaluated by taking into account two different, but closely connected, factors: the consolidated general government budget position, and the restructuring measures undertaken in the financial sector and the negotiations with foreign creditors linked with succession issues. Most of the debt accumulated before 1996 was due to the restructuring of financial sector institutions (mainly banks) and some large enterprises (such as steel mills). In addition, the government started issuing state guarantees for private sector institutions to lower their excessive credit risk due to the continued unfavorable macroeconomic environment in that period. For

TABLE 12.3 FISCAL DEVELOPMENT, 1993–2002
(percent of GDP)

Item	1993	1994	1995	1996	1997	1998	1999	2000	2001	2002
Revenue	44.7	43.4	43.1	42.7	41.5	42.8	42.9	42.2	42.9	42.5
Expenditure	43.8	43.4	43.1	42.4	43.2	43.7	44.2	44.1	44.5	44.1
Primary expenditure	42.5	41.9	41.9	41.2	42.0	42.5	42.8	42.6	42.9	42.4
Interest expenditure	1.3	1.5	1.2	1.2	1.2	1.3	1.4	1.5	1.6	1.7
Budget balance	0.9	0.0	0.0	0.3	-1.7	-0.9	-1.3	-1.9	-1.6	-1.5
Cyclically adjusted balance	-0.1	-0.2	-0.7	0.2	-1.5	-0.5	-1.9	-1.9	-1.5	-1.3
Primary balance	2.1	1.5	1.2	1.5	-0.6	0.3	0.1	-0.4	0.0	0.1
Cyclically adjusted primary balance	1.2	1.3	0.4	1.4	-0.3	0.8	-0.6	-0.4	0.1	0.3
Central government debt	21.1	18.5	18.7	22.7	23.3	23.7	24.5	25.1	26.9	28.1

Source: Žumer (2003).

197

the same reason—high real interest rates on domestic markets and lack of domestic resources—most government borrowing had been in foreign currency or based on indexed instruments on the domestic market.

By the end of 1995, the total debt exposure of the public sector (direct government debt and government-issued guarantees) was less than 23 percent of GDP (Figures 12.3 and 12.4). As the government's primary budget was constantly in surplus, current transactions did not contribute to the further accumulation of public debt. Since 1996, however, the situation has deteriorated, as the budget situation worsened substantially and as Slovenia has had to take on part of SFR Yugoslavia's foreign debt under agreements with London and Paris Club creditors (see Chapter 7).

As the first stage of the transition was finalized, the government also switched its policies toward supporting public infrastructure development (in the energy sector, the highway and rail networks, local utilities, and elsewhere) with the issuance of additional guarantees. As a consequence, total public debt, outstanding and contingent liabilities (e.g., from guarantees or from restitution, etc.) started to grow, reaching an outstanding debt figure of 34 percent of GDP in 2002. The relatively larger public debt did not represent a severe fiscal burden, however, because the structure of the debt improved

FIGURE 12.3 GENERAL GOVERNMENT DEBT

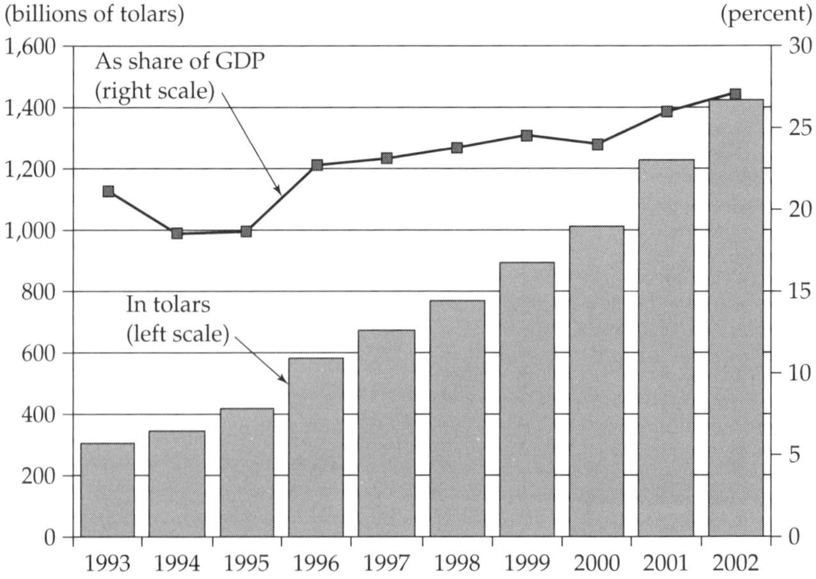

Source: Ministry of Finance, *Bulletin of Government Finance*, Year IV, No. 6, June 2003.

FIGURE 12.4 GUARANTEES FOR PUBLIC SECTOR ENTITIES

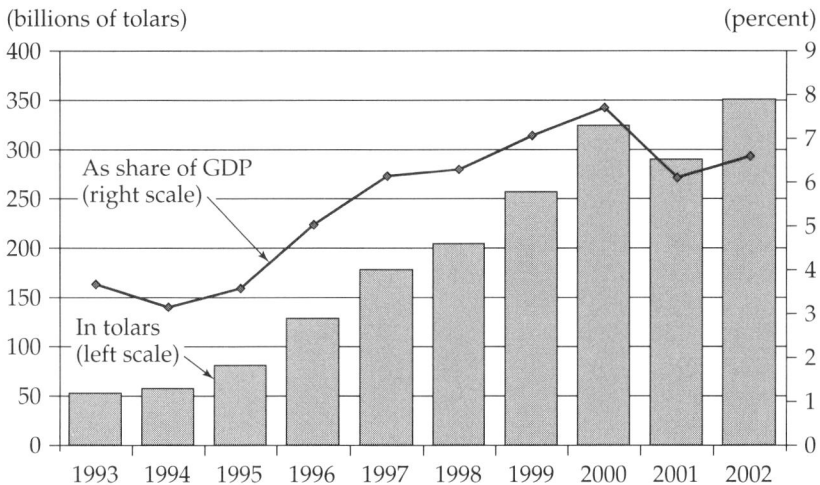

Source: Ministry of Finance, *Bulletin of Government Finance*, Year IV, No. 6, June 2003.

significantly (with more instruments at fixed nominal rates, more in domestic currency, and lower interest rates) and because large privatization receipts (from the banking sector and, in principle, other shareholding positions of the government) were, under the Public Finance Act, earmarked for repayment of the public debt.

Today, Slovenia is considered, by any international standard, to be a relatively modestly indebted country and in a position to fulfill the Maastricht debt criteria. Having said that, the validity of a very important proposition will be observed in the upcoming period. The debt situation will stay stable and sustainable only if the budget situation remains under control, that is, if the primary budget balance remains in constant surplus; if public sector investment is financed from private sources to a greater extent than before; and if macroeconomic stability in Slovenia prevails once the exchange rate regime has been adjusted to the conditions of ERM-II and European Monetary Union.

STATUS OF PUBLIC FINANCE REFORM AND THE ROLE OF PUBLIC EXPENDITURE MANAGEMENT IN ENFORCING HARD BUDGET CONSTRAINTS

The developments presented above depended and will clearly depend in the future on the ability of the Slovenian government to enforce efficient public expenditure management, that is, a hard fiscal budget constraint. We believe that Slovenia has developed the ability to manage public expenditure efficiently. Through appropriate budget legislation, the strengthened role of the budgetary authority in the substance of the state budget has been assured. Medium-term expenditure frameworks and budget preparation processes have been, from a methodological and technical point of view, well developed. Thus Slovenia possesses the capability for efficient budget execution, including accounting and reporting capabilities.[4]

Budget Legislation

Articles defining budget and public expenditure management rules were first integrated into the Slovenian constitution adopted in late 1991. The constitution contains fundamental articles on public finances, taxes, budgets, and state borrowing. These articles require that all revenue and expenditure be included in the budget and provide that debt may only be incurred on the basis of legal acts of the Slovenian National Assembly. The Standing Orders of the National Assembly, adopted in 1993, comprise many detailed procedural rules. These rules state that, when the National Assembly approves the state budget, it must also decide on an annual law containing provisions for its implementation. Most of the provisions of this law are unchanged from one year to the next, but some—mainly those including specific authorizations for the coming year (for example, limits on state borrowing and guarantees)— are changed from year to year. These annual budget implementation laws were used until the adoption of a Public Finance Act in 1999, the key legislative act defining detailed budgetary procedures.

   A new organic budget law, the Public Finance Act, was approved by the National Assembly in the autumn of 1999 and went into effect on January 1, 2000. The law includes many of the permanent provisions in the earlier budget implementation laws as well as a range of additional rules. The Public Finance Act clarifies the government's responsibilities and duties in preparing, implementing, and controlling the state budget. The National Assembly also adopted an Accounting Act for the Public Sector in March 1999. This law contains references to the general and the specific rules that are to be observed by the central government, local authorities, special funds, and other public institutions. Other pieces of budget-related legislation, such as the Public Procurement Act and the Law on Financing of Local Communities, were also approved in the 1990s.

Relationship Between the Legislative and Executive Branches

To ensure that the budget authority (that is, the National Assembly) plays its appropriate role, special rules and procedures have been developed over time. Thus, for example, the Standing Orders of the National Assembly mandate that when the government submits its draft budget, it must also submit certain other documents, including a budget memorandum in which the basic goals and tasks of budgetary policy are stated. The Public Finance Act defined detailed procedures for the preparation and presentation of the budget to be followed from 2000 onward.

An essential rule is that amendments proposed by members of the National Assembly and its standing committees should not change the balance between revenue and expenditure as proposed by the government. There are also rules concerning supplementary budgets and how to handle a situation where the state budget has not been approved before the start of the fiscal year.

Once members of the National Assembly have proposed amendments and the standing committees have reported their opinions, the government prepares a revised draft budget, which is then debated and voted on. Although this procedure may cause a delay in the budget procedure, it does ensure full parliamentary involvement and commitment to the budget that is finally approved.

Scope of the Budget

Central government budget expenditure (excluding transfers to the pension and health insurance funds) amounts on average to about 21 percent of GDP. The expenditures of the two extrabudgetary funds for pensions and health insurance are somewhat smaller. The proposed budgets for these two funds are presented to the National Assembly at the same time as the draft state budget but are voted on by the separate assemblies of the two funds.[5]

In addition to these two extrabudgetary funds, there are a large number of extrabudgetary operations with various legal status (funds, public institutions, and so on). Some of these are of a transitional nature, whereas others are permanent. Of special importance is the state highway company (known by its Slovenian abbreviation DARS), which receives earmarked funds and borrows extensively under a state guarantee. EU funds are channelled through the National Fund at the Ministry of Finance and fully integrated into the state budget.

A key feature of the Slovenian public sector is the relatively small size of local government operations and expenditures, which total about 5 percent of GDP. Services such as primary and secondary schools and, to a certain extent, other activities (such as hospitals and social care) are managed jointly by the central government, the local governments, and the health fund.

The state budget is structured mainly according to spending units, with expenditure in each unit subdivided into economic categories (salaries, goods and services, transfers, capital expenditures), which in turn are further subdivided. The total number of lines in the budget varies but can be up to 9,000. The situation was recently improved with a new program structure.

Medium-Term Expenditure Framework and Budget Process

The state budget for 2000 was prepared on the basis of a two-year (2000–01) framework. However, articles 14 and 15 of the Public Finance Act prescribe that the budget proposal shall include a three-year financial perspective and that, in April of each year, the government shall adopt a draft budget memorandum for the next three years. As mentioned above, this law took effect in 2000, and in that year a medium-term framework was worked out for use in the budget process. The budget memorandum contains the main macroeconomic assumptions, the fiscal policy targets (mainly the government deficit), and the measures planned for achieving them. Economic forecasting is carried out at present by the Institute of Macroeconomic Analysis and Development, which is now part of the prime minister's office and works closely in cooperation with the Ministry of Finance.

The budget preparation phase, based on the Public Finance Act, is clearly structured and planned. A detailed timetable for the preparation of the draft budget for 2000 (and 2001), covering the period February–September, was established in January 1999. In June 2000 the "Order on the Basis and Procedures for the Preparation of the Draft State Budget" (*Official Gazette,* No. 56/2000) was passed. This order regulates the preparation of strategic documents of the state and the preparation of the budget memorandum as a basis for a draft budget; the formulation and definition of state development priorities; and the procedures and documentation needed for preparation of the draft budget.

The budget memorandum, which is approved by the government in early April, also includes the expected allocation of expenditure by policy area and main program. On the basis of this memorandum, the minister of finance issues a budget circular specifying the priorities, economic indicators, ceilings for spending units, technical provisions, and forms to be used. Spending units are invited to submit their detailed budget proposals in June, at which time the Ministry of Finance starts technical consultations with them. In early September the final negotiations are carried out within the government, usually preceded by discussions between the coalition partners.

It is important to note that, through the new legislation, the budgetary procedure has been changed from a bottom-up to a top-down procedure. The budget is now also structured by policy areas and main programs, the latter based to a great extent on the international functional classification COFOG (Classifications of Functions of Government) of the OECD.

The government presents a number of documents (a total of up to 3,000 pages in various volumes) to the National Assembly containing detailed figures, descriptions, and justifications for the different proposals in the budget. To facilitate negotiation and final budget preparation, types of expenditure have been separately identified, coded, and grouped, applying both the economic classification and the program-functional structure of the budget enabling actual planning and execution of Government programs. From that position further reforms that will strengthen the role of the Ministry of Finance in the process and emphasize performance management techniques can be implemented.

Budget Execution and Monitoring

As of January 1, 1999, new accounting software (MFERAC) was introduced in the Ministry of Finance that allows for all new liabilities, payables, and outgoing and incoming payments to be accounted for and controlled within the accounting department, so that the budget department is no longer involved in these activities. The introduction of the treasury single account started in June 1999 for treasury bills, and the intent was to extend it to all budgetary expenditures by the beginning of 2000. It was actually implemented in the course of 2001–02 period.

Work on designing the various elements of reform needed for a modern treasury progressed well in 1999. These included the treasury single account, the treasury general ledger, and the creation of new treasury payments and receipts offices out of the former Agency for Payments.

The principal rules have been established for the execution of the budget. Public service salaries are legally defined according to a unified structure. Budget allocations, staffing ceilings, and the law on salaries provide for information to be published on personnel costs and on staff numbers.

The budgetary implementation law authorizes the various spending units, the minister of finance, and the government to reallocate certain expenditures between spending units and lines in the budget. The government is also authorized to block expenditures under certain conditions. Only under very specific conditions may unused funds be carried over from one year to the next. Together with legal limits on state borrowing, these discretionary powers contribute to a strengthening of budgetary discipline during the implementation phase.

The design and implementation of operational arrangements—covering budgeting, accounting, procurement, control, and audit procedures—for managing EU preaccession aid through the National Fund is covered by the adoption of special Rules on the Procedures of Implementation of the Budget.

Accounting and Reporting

In late March 1999 the National Assembly adopted the Public Sector Accounting Act. Under this legislation the central government, local authorities, social security funds, and a range of other public operations now use uniform rules for accounting and annual reporting. Accounting is on a cash basis for budget-financed operations. A uniform economic classification of expenditure and revenue complying with the IMF's Government Finance Statistics (GFS) and ESA95 (European Statistical Agency rules) requirements has recently been introduced. A functional classification of state expenditure according to the most recent COFOG (1999) has also been introduced.

The OECD recently reviewed the status of the Slovenian national accounts statistics (OECD 1999). In several areas the OECD's report suggests improvements of the existing national accounts. The report also proposes an extension of the accounts so as to complete the national accounts system in its essential respects. One of the proposals is to elaborate the accounts of individual subsectors of the general government and establish a consolidated account for the general government sector. The Ministry of Finance has produced data according to the IMF's Government Finance Statistics methodology (institutional, economic, and functional classification—the old COFOG) to be published in the IMF's *Government Finance Statistics Yearbook*.

The government is obliged to draw up a financial statement on the state budget for the previous year and submit it to the Court of Audit no later than March 31. The financial statement and the final report of the Court of Audit must be submitted to the National Assembly no later than June. The financial statement is examined in the standing committees, and, after a debate, the National Assembly votes on the financial statement.

ASSESSMENT OF THE CURRENT FISCAL SITUATION AND FURTHER BUDGET AND TAX REFORMS

We conclude with an assessment of the current fiscal situation and of the further budget and tax reforms needed to make the budget sustainable in the long run. In its first decade of independence, Slovenia achieved major improvements in its public expenditure management system, including the following:

- The organic budget law, the Public Finance Act approved by the legislature in 1999, constitutes, along with other important laws, a legal framework for the state budget and public finances comparable to that found in most EU member states.
- A medium-term fiscal framework has been worked out and is to be used in the budget process.
- In June 2000 the Order on the Basis and Procedures for the Preparation of the Draft State Budget was passed. This order calls for a radical overhaul of the budget process. This was established as a top-down process structured around 23 policy areas (increased to more than 25 in 2000) within the medium-term macroeconomic framework.
- A functional classification of state expenditure according to the most recent COFOG (1999) has been introduced for presenting information in relation to restructuring the budget for 2000 and onward around key policy-program areas.
- Implementation of a modern treasury has made good progress in the last several years. Advances included the treasury single account, the treasury general ledger, and the creation of new treasury payments and receipts offices out of the former Agency for Payments.
- There has been significant improvement in the design and implementation of operational arrangements—covering budgeting, accounting, procurement, control, and audit procedures—for managing EU preaccession aid through the National Fund.
- On the revenue side, progress has been made toward new tax legislation, but implementation has been postponed until after the 2004 elections.

Given the economic situation, the fiscal situation in 2003 remains critical. The deficit has been increasing. The public debt has also increased, especially through the issuance of government guarantees, and despite high proceeds from privatization of state assets. Further budget and tax reforms are needed to make the budget sustainable in the long run. In the short term they are connected with

- full implementation of technical capacity in the Ministry of Finance in such areas as implementing the treasury single account and general ledger systems; and
- establishing arrangements for managing EU preaccession aid through the National Fund for the implementation of the EU agriculture and structural funds programs.

In the medium term, reform will take three main directions, resulting in a changed role of the state in Slovenia:

- First, in order to implement ERM-II, a commitment by the authorities is needed to ensure that a restrictive fiscal stance remains a top priority. With elections scheduled in 2004, this can only be undertaken by the next government.
- Further progress needs to be made in the design and implementation of methods and procedures for full medium-term economic forecasting and budgetary planning. This should link government priorities with the main budgetary programs and allow for necessary adjustment within the budget.
- Last but not least, the design and implementation of performance-oriented budgeting will increase the efficiency of government services and change the role of the state in Slovenia. This will include reforms in many government services, from education, health, social assistance, and judicial systems to defense, security, and market regulatory services.

When the reforms described above are fully implemented, Slovenia will remain a competitive economy that will flourish within a united Europe.

REFERENCES

Bole, V. 1999a. "General Government Expenditures and Problems of Economic Policy." Gospodarska gibanja 6. Economics Institute of the Faculty of Law, Ljubljana.

———. 1999b. "Structure of Tax Systems and Membership in European Union." *Gospodarska gibanja* 9. Economics Institute of the Faculty of Law, Ljubljana.

Ministry of Finance. 2000. "Medium-Term Expenditures Framework 2001–2005." Republic of Slovenia, Ljubljana.

OECD. 1999. "National Accounts for the Republic of Slovenia—Sources, Methods and Estimates." Paris.

Žumer, T. 2003. "Calculating the Cyclical Adjusted Budget Balance for Slovenia." Analytical Research Centre, Bank of Slovenia, Ljubljana. Processed.

NOTES

1. Since 2000, however, fiscal deficits, public debt, and guarantees issued have increased sharply.

2. There were 60 local communities in Slovenia, each with up to 10 independent budgets organized in the form of self-management interest associations

(for education, social care, science and technological development, infrastructure, and so forth). Given that there were also budgets for these activities for the republic as a whole, more than 600 budgets with individual revenue programs existed.

3. The budget will appropriately play the same role for the forthcoming medium-term period. But first a sharp reduction of the general government fiscal deficit and a balanced budget will be required at the time of expected entry into ERM-II and European Monetary Union.

4. To present these details, we have utilized the assessment of the current status of public finance reforms by SIGMA (Support for Improvement in Governance and Management in Central and Eastern European Countries), a joint initiative of the Organisation for Economic Co-operation and Development and the European Union.

5. This is a legacy of the past, as the two social funds remained unreformed, despite major pressures on both pension and health expenditure in Slovenia.

Chapter 13
Building an Institutional Framework for a Full-Fledged Market Economy

Rasto Ovin and Boštjan Kramberger

The centrally planned economies of Central and Eastern Europe (CEE) differed from the Western market economies chiefly in terms of such features as property rights, free markets, the role of the state, and the financial system. Broadly speaking, the rules encompassing all of these constitute an institutional framework. Therefore it is natural that, when the CEE countries abandoned central planning and undertook the introduction of a market economy, one of the most important tasks for their governments was to build an institutional framework for that market economy. Their agenda was thus one of massive institutional change.

According to the European Commission (2003), Slovenia, like the other countries that are candidates for EU accession, is already a market economy, in which most of the institutions that are key to functioning within the EU common market have been established and are performing well. In comparison with the other transition economies scheduled to become EU members in 2004, Slovenia's advantages in institutional development lie especially in the field of taxation, where Slovenia's legislation is already almost fully aligned with the *acquis communautaire*; this task is still to be completed in the Czech Republic, Estonia, Hungary, Poland, and Slovakia. In addition, most of the other candidate countries are still struggling with some issues that in Slovenia have been brought under control. These include economic crime in the Czech Republic, money laundering in Slovakia, and corruption in both these countries and in Hungary and Poland as well. Slovenia cannot, however, boast outstanding performance in some other fields where there has been EU criticism of candidate countries, such as administrative capacity sufficient to ensure the effective implementation and enforcement of the *acquis* (only Hungary has escaped criticism on this score), reduction of the length of court proceedings, public procurement, and strengthening of intellectual property rights.

Slovenia also records a backlog in some essential areas. The first is in the implementation of its denationalization law. In addition, Slovenia's high inflation proves that the legal independence of the central bank is not yet being put fully into practice as had been promised in legislation (this is still to be improved in Poland as well). There has also been delay in removing restrictions on foreign investment in investment funds and management companies. Slovenia (together with Hungary and Slovakia) still needs to improve its regional policy and coordination as well as the structures supporting sound and efficient management of EU funds. Still other backlogs are in the privatization of state-owned banks and insurance companies as well as in telecommunications liberalization, where Slovenia lags behind most of the other candidate countries.

This chapter discusses the emerging institutional framework for a full-fledged market economy in Slovenia. The issue will be discussed from three perspectives: the role of the state, the environment for a market-based economy, and the development of public administration. For each of these an analysis of the legal setting, its development, Slovenia's EU accession, and the deficit in implementation as well as further steps to resolve the problems is presented.

THE IMPORTANCE OF INSTITUTION BUILDING
FOR THE TRANSITION PROCESS

By an institutional framework we mean a set of rules, norms, and institutions that constitute a legal structure within which economic agents can freely pursue their activities. Institutions are essential for the functioning of a market economy, because they reduce the transactions costs of these activities to market participants. Without adequate institutions in place, economic agents would have to monitor and supervise all contractual arrangements by themselves, which would impose unbearably high costs. Institutions are therefore considered a public good to be enforced and protected by the state (Brennan and Buchanan 1985).[1] This also means that, when institutions are deficient, it is the state that must reform them to ensure a functioning institutional framework.

The typical institutions of well-functioning market economies relate to key national economic functions (see Hare 2001): private property rights and contracts; banks and financial markets (their functioning and regulation, reliable access to credit, and provisions for bankruptcy); labor market institutions (social policy and a social safety net); a clear, predictable, and well-enforced fiscal environment; institutions dealing with competition policy, industrial policy, and trade policy; and trust between economic agents and in the honesty of public institutions.

As measured by income per capita, Slovenia was the most developed of the socialist countries, with quite developed social and economic structures. One could consider this an advantage, as a higher level of development presumably requires better-developed institutions. Slovenia's comparative performance on institutional development, however, proves that better-developed social and economic structures are not necessarily an asset when institutions must be reformed, as Table 13.1 illustrates.

The table compares results among eight transition economies, including Slovenia, after the first decade of transition. It allows us to draw several conclusions about the speed and scope of institutional reform in Slovenia:

- Compared with other transition economies that are candidates for the next EU enlargement, Slovenia recorded quite good initial conditions, with an initial conditions index of 3.2, exceeded by

TABLE 13.1 INDICATORS OF PROGRESS WITH INSTITUTIONAL
REFORM IN CURRENT EU ACCESSION COUNTRIES

Country	Initial conditions index[a]	Liberalization index[b] 1989	Liberalization index[b] 1997	Institutional quality index,[c] 1997–98	EBRD transition indicators[d] 1995	EBRD transition indicators[d] 1999
Czech Republic	3.5	0.00	0.93	6.8	3.5	3.4
Estonia	–0.4	0.07	0.93	6.1	3.2	3.5
Hungary	3.3	0.34	0.93	8.7	3.5	3.7
Latvia	–0.2	0.04	0.89	2.6	2.8	3.1
Lithuania	0.0	0.04	0.89	2.6	2.9	3.1
Poland	1.9	0.24	0.89	7.0	3.3	3.5
Slovakia	2.9	0.00	0.86	2.8	3.3	3.3
Slovenia	3.2	0.41	0.89	8.5	3.2	3.3

a. Weighted average of indicators of level of development, trade with other countries of the Council for Mutual Economic Assistance, macroeconomic disequilibria, distance from the European Union, natural resource endowments, market memory (measured by number of years of communist rule), and state capacity.
b. Weighted average of three components: domestic market liberalization (weight of 0.3), foreign trade liberalization (weight of 0.3), and enterprise privatization and banking reform (weight of 0.4). Each component (and the average in the table) is scored from 0 to 1.
c. Based on five components: extent of democracy, government effectiveness, extent of regulation, rule of law, and extent of graft and corruption. Each indicator (and the average) is scored from –25 to + 25. For Western industrialized market economies the average score is 12.6.
d. Simple average of eight indicators, each scored from 1 (no market reforms) to 4 (conditions as in a Western industrialized market economy).
Source: Hare (2001).

only the Czech Republic and Hungary. In 1989 Slovenia's liberalization index, at 0.41, was the highest among all the countries. The initial conditions index fell short of the highest mainly because of the hyperinflation Slovenia suffered in 1989; the high liberalization index reflects the relatively liberalized conditions in SFR Yugoslavia in general at the time.[2]

■ By 1997, however, Slovenia had fallen behind the Czech Republic, Estonia, and Hungary on the liberalization index and had reached only the same level as Poland, Latvia, and Lithuania. This is a consequence of the gradual approach to institutional reform taken in Slovenia, which is discussed below.

■ Slovenia's experience under the relatively liberal, tolerant system of SFR Yugoslavia contributed to the relatively high institutional quality index that Slovenia had achieved by 1997–98: at 8.5, Slovenia's score was second only to Hungary's.

■ As a consequence of its slower institutional development, as measured by the transition indicators of the European Bank for Reconstruction and Development (EBRD), by 1999 Slovenia had achieved the same result as Slovakia and outperformed only Latvia and Lithuania.

This comparison of Slovenia's good institutional performance, as reported in the European Commission 2003 Report, with its obviously worse institutional performance at the end of the 1990s, leads to the conclusion that, in Slovenia, two different patterns of institutional reforms were at work. It seems that a less efficient reform has been replaced recently by a more efficient one. With respect to institutional change in Slovenia, the more rapid changes can be described as efficient, whereas the more gradual changes have left Slovenia permanently in arrears with respect to the best reformers.

The gradual approach to institutional change was strongly promoted politically in Slovenia. It allowed the country to avoid a larger decline of GDP at the beginning of the transition than some other countries suffered, but at the same time it provided an excuse for a lack of political will for change. It is also consistent with the presence of well-developed arrangements among different structures in a small national community. In a country of only 2 million people, it is no wonder that personal contacts arise easily and spread both nation- and economy-wide. Furthermore, given the relation already described between the institutional environment and institutional arrangements, it is easy to understand that, with highly developed arrangements already in existence, it was not easy to carry out a fundamental reform of formal institutions.[3] It was not just the former socialist elite who opposed rapid change, but also the management of large enterprises.[4] Managers sought to maintain the environment of information asymmetry that had characterized the former system, so as to ensure their favored position in the transition process. It turned out that the existing institutional structures in Slovenia, which were relatively well developed because of the relatively tolerant environment of SFR Yugoslavia, used their experience so as to block institutional change rather than to support more rapid change and development.

The second impetus to rapid institutional change was imposed from outside: the requirements of the EU accession process seemed to compensate for the missing political will for change, as no political faction wanted to take responsibility for a failure of the integration efforts. In this way the Slovenian approach to institutional change emerged as a combination of the two principal strategies: gradual and rapid.

THE ROLE OF THE STATE

Normative and prescriptive discussions on how to reform the role of the state in a transition economy can typically be categorized into two contrasting positions. On the one hand, social democrats call for a state that intervenes in economic activity sufficiently to ensure a minimum of welfare and justice for all. On the other, neoliberals call for a state that does little more than guarantee property rights, enforce contracts, and support economic growth through a sound fiscal stance.

In Slovenia the prevailing position in this respect has tended to be the social democratic one. Such popular terms as "the social state" and "social cohesion" were, however, often used in political dialogue as cover for weak political will for change, as already noted. The consequence was that those sectors and procedures not yet endowed with new institutions remained under the control of the state, enabling it to intervene according to short-term political needs. Typical areas where this strategy was observed were the privatization of banks and denationalization and foreign investment. Under this strategy, the state maintained an important role, and the building of institutions necessary for a full-fledged market economy was neglected.

Under the Constitutional Act (adopted in 1991), which regulated the implementation of Slovenia's declaration of independence, all state bodies of SFR Yugoslavia functioning on Slovenian territory were transformed into state bodies of the Republic of Slovenia. The constitution of 1991 introduced new terms for the previous Executive Council (and later the government), which was responsible to the previous Peoples' Assembly (later the National Assembly). The functions and operations of the government are defined in the Government Act (1993, last amended in 2001).

The first law referring to the role of the state was the Bank of Slovenia Act, adopted on the eve of the declaration of independence in June 1991. This was followed by the Denationalization Act and acts regulating the fiscal system (the personal income tax and the turnover tax). In 1992 the Privatization Act and the Bank Rehabilitation Act were passed. The Government Act, as already noted, followed only in 1993. Since then, major changes in the legal position of the government have been defined through permanent changes and annexes to the Government Act, such as reducing the number of ministries or introducing additional central government bodies to support the prime minister.

Apart from its interventions to stabilize the economy, the Slovenian state has been present in the economy in many ways. The first of these worth mentioning is the restructuring campaign of 1992, where the state Development Fund of Slovenia managed the restructuring, sale, or closure of 98 enterprises. In 1997 the Development Fund was transformed into the Slovenian Development Corporation. It was responsible for the rehabilitation, restructuring, and privatization of enterprises as well as for assisting with their long-term investment financing (see Chapter 14).

Also very important was the role of the state in the campaign of bank rehabilitation starting in 1993. Depositors' claims toward the former National Bank of SFR Yugoslavia, mismanagement of loans, and excessive operational costs brought Slovenian banks into a situation where nonperforming assets exceeded 10 percent of the total. At the end of the rehabilitation, the two biggest banks (the Nova Ljubljanska Banka, NLB, and Nova Kreditna Banka Maribor, NKBM) became state-owned banks.

In 1996 Slovenia signed an Association Agreement with the European Union and, in 1999, a Europe Agreement. With its full accession to the European Union scheduled for May 1, 2004, Slovenia will have to acknowledge the supremacy of EU law, which will influence the role of the state in Slovenia. It is to be expected that the role of the legislature will be reduced, with the legislative function delegated mostly to the Council of Ministers and to the European Commission, whereas the role of the government (that is, the executive) will increase, as it will be responsible for carrying out EU membership obligations. In areas such as competition, the environment, regional policy, energy, consumer protection, and monetary issues, the sovereignty of member states has been to a greater or lesser extent transferred to the European Union. In other areas of economic policy, such as fiscal policy, social policy, health, science, and education, a subsidiarity principle will be followed, meaning that these will be the European Union's concern only if this would mean their better functioning at the supranational than the national level.

The implementation gap with respect to the role of the state in Slovenia reflects mainly the persistence of its considerable role in the economy. Here the privatization process serves as a good example, especially in the financial sector.[5] The privatization of banks started only in 2000. In 2002 the state reduced its share in the largest Slovenian bank, Nova Ljubljanska Banka, by selling part of its share to the Belgian firm KBC (34 percent) and to the EBRD (5 percent). Meanwhile the privatization of NKBM was halted and postponed. The Slovenian state still owns 85 percent of the largest insurance company, Triglav (which has a 42 percent market share), and through NKBM it controls the insurance company Zavarovalnica Maribor. Through the quasi-governmental pension fund (Kapitalska Družba, KAD) and the Restitution Fund (Slovenska Odškodninska Družba, SOD), the Slovenian state continues to directly control from one-fifth to one-fourth of the shares in already-privatized companies. If one also takes into account those companies in which the state maintains indirect control (through companies for the management of privatization investment funds, founded by both state banks in 1994), this share is even greater.

This kind of market-averse policy is inevitably reflected in Slovenia's international competitiveness, where the contribution of the state deserves special attention. According to the World Economic Forum's *Global Competitiveness Report 2002–2003*, Slovenia ranks second among transition economies (it ranked 28th worldwide in 2002), following Estonia (which was 26th worldwide). Slovenia ranks quite high on certain specific indicators, such as the technology index (25th), the public institutions index (23rd), the growth competitiveness index (28th), and the microeconomic competitiveness index (27th), and on most of these Slovenia's position has improved in recent years. However, Slovenia ranks much lower on the macroeconomic environment index, where it is in 50th place among 80 countries.[6]

The results of the *World Competitiveness Yearbook* (Institute of International Management Development 2003) are similar. Here, on the indicator "government efficiency," Slovenia ranked last in 2003 among countries with a population of less than 20 million. The same result was found on the index measuring the extent to which government policies are conducive to competitiveness: Slovenia dropped from 23rd to 29th place from 2002 to 2003. Slovenia's overall competitiveness deteriorated from 21st to 28th place in the same period.[7]

Slovenia shows a deficit in its reform of the role of the state in yet another area. A strong centralization of state and administrative functions after independence led to growing differences among the country's regions, with the central region (which includes Ljubljana) gaining mostly at the expense of the northeastern part of the country. This trend hinders the development of the already tiny Slovenian market: intolerable regional differences prevent markets from performing their integrating function, leading to a permanent demand for compensation in economic policy.

Given these shortfalls, Slovenia has no choice but to face the contemporary challenges of a modern state. Slovenia's economic policy must now consider how to promote factor mobility, increase the domestic and international transparency of its economic policy, and improve the sustainability of the social state (Ovin and Smeets 1999).[8] To a great extent these facts are incorporated in the government's Strategy for the Economic Development of Slovenia (Institute of Macroeconomic Analysis and Development 2001). They are:

■ *The state as a democratic actor:* Better-informed and increasingly mobile actors, enjoying ever-greater choices, require a transparent and fair economic policy, which is thus one of the most important factors in international competitiveness. Unlike under the former system, the state will have to act as a partner with other entities in pursuing the goals of economic development and growth.

- *Greater concern for legal order and security and for property rights:* Protecting human rights and ensuring private property rights reduce uncertainty and transactions costs.
- *Focus on structural and development policy:* On the one hand, Slovenia's room to maneuver in its traditional macroeconomic (monetary and fiscal) policies will be substantially reduced upon EU accession. On the other hand, participating in the European Union's structural policy (the structural and cohesion funds) and taking advantage of EU expansive economic policy measures will require a more coherent structural and development policy.
- *Decentralization of the role of the state in economic development:* Here a larger role for regional initiatives is planned, so as to exploit existing development potentials.
- *Reduction of the state's presence in the economy and in public services:* The Slovenian state is to become a regulator and supervisor in the field of public services rather than a supplier of these services. Here the state will be replaced by nonpublic suppliers on the basis of concession contracts. The state will also continue to reduce its presence in enterprises.

THE BUSINESS ENVIRONMENT

A functioning market economy requires that prices as well as trade be liberalized and that an enforceable legal system, including protection of property rights, be put in place. Macroeconomic stability and consensus on economic policy, plus a well-developed financial sector and the absence of any significant barriers to market entry and exit, define a well-developed business environment (European Commission 1998).

The following crucial laws shape the Slovenian business environment. Article 74 of the constitution stipulates that economic initiative is free. The Companies Act determines the procedure for establishing a company, and the termination of a company is regulated by the Compulsory Settlement, Bankruptcy, and Liquidation Act.

According to the constitution, the right to private property and inheritance is guaranteed. Foreigners may acquire the proprietary right to real estate and the proprietary right to land under the conditions provided by law. Intellectual property is regulated by the Copyright and Related Rights Act. Holders of copyrights and related rights who are citizens of or have headquarters in Slovenia enjoy protection under this act, as do foreigners if provided for under international contract, or by the act itself, or if actual reciprocity is achieved.

The labor market is regulated by the Labor Relations Act, which came into effect on January 1, 2003. This act provides protection to workers in accordance with the conventions of the International Labor Organization and the directives of the European Union.

The Employment and Work of Foreigners Act, in force since January 2001, covers all aspects of the work and employment of foreigners in Slovenia. Foreigners may be employed or work in Slovenia provided they have a work permit and that the person responsible has registered the foreigner as required by law.

The Space Management Act regulates all issues referring to the establishment of space or location conditions. The act clearly stipulates the division of competencies in the field of space management between the state and local communities.

The Building Construction Act came into force at the beginning of 2002 and sets the conditions for the construction of all buildings. It eliminates two major deficiencies of the previous system, namely, excessive delays in permit acquisition, and the two-stage procedure for obtaining location and building permits.

The adoption of the federal Foreign Investment Act and the federal Companies Act in 1988 (that is, while still within the framework of SFR Yugoslavia) and the establishment of the stock exchange in Ljubljana in 1989 marked the beginning of Slovenia's transformation from a socialistic economy into a market economy. The first step that the government of the Republic of Slovenia took in the transition was the elimination of hyperinflation by means of a stabilization policy and other measures of economic policy. In 1992 the Bank of Slovenia started pursuing a strict stabilization policy, supported by the government through sound fiscal policy, antimonopolistic measures, and the strengthening of personal and public consumption. In this period the Slovenian economy was marked, on the one hand, by great economic and social shifts and by a rapidly increasing rate of unemployment; on the other hand, it was hindered by the slowness of the privatization and denationalization process and by an aversion toward foreign investment. Since 1993 Slovenia's economic growth has accelerated. Inflation has slowed, partly as a result of the elimination of price controls. In 1997 and 1998 significant advances were made on the liberalization of administered prices, on the increase of cost recovery for utilities, and on the reduction of disparities between controlled prices of goods and world prices (European Commission 1998).

In 1999 much progress was made in a number of areas. In the financial sector, laws on banking and foreign exchange were adopted. A major reform of the tax system was implemented with the introduction of a value added tax on July 1 of that year. An agreement among the government, employers, and the trade unions on pension reform was reached in May. The Pensions Act, which represents a first step toward achieving long-term budgetary sustainability by modifying the country's pay-as-you-go public pension system, was also adopted in 1999 (European Commission 1999).

In April 2001 the Program of Measures to Promote Entrepreneurship and Competitiveness in 2002–2006 was adopted. This program focuses on measures and instruments of development policy to promote the entrepreneurial and small business sector.

Despite this progress, there are still some implementation deficits with respect to the business environment. In the period 1997–2001 the number of enterprises grew by only 0.9 percent annually on average; in 2001 the number actually fell by 1.3 percent. This is also the consequence of an inappropriate business environment. The transactions costs of setting up new businesses have been high relative to the size of the domestic market, and the labor market is rather rigid. The still relatively underdeveloped capital markets and low level of competition in the banking sector led to high costs of raising capital. Bureaucratic and lengthy procedures and difficulties in buying land for construction, obtaining site development approvals and work permits, and hiring and firing employees also deterred domestic and foreign investors (European Commission 2002). The deregulation of the labor market has not progressed, and the legal framework governing industrial relations has remained quite bureaucratic. Restrictions on layoffs prevent employers from hiring regular employees and lead them to prefer short-term employment contracts.

Although existing laws regulating the business environment in Slovenia are now largely in accordance with EU standards, nontransparent and inefficient procurement legislation still allows unfair business practices to persist. Considerable barriers to market entry remain through the award of contracts without an equitable procedure. Also, public procurement legislation sometimes suffers from inconsistency and nontransparency (Center for Strategic and International Studies 2003).

Another implementation gap in Slovenia is in the area of property rights in real estate markets. One problem is that the land register still cannot be completed; another is that a considerable share of the country's real estate is still subject to long-drawn-out denationalization procedures. Together with chronic arrears in court procedures, this of course hinders development of the real estate market and thus new investment.

To improve the business environment, Slovenian economic policy should ensure the proper functioning of the labor market; tax burdens should be reduced; and administrative procedures, especially for small companies, should be shortened. Meanwhile financing conditions and the availability of equity should be improved by making the financial market more attractive to investors (Pšeničny 2003). More should be done to prevent unfair competition, and the extent of the shadow economy should be reduced.[9] The state should protect small companies from having the knowledge and ideas they reveal in their business offers stolen by larger companies.

PUBLIC ADMINISTRATION

Under the socialist system, public administration in Slovenia had practically no power and only carried out orders issued by the political center. Accordingly, public administration was oriented only to implementing decisions and instructions and not to addressing and solving problems (Šmidovnik 1998). Public administration at the beginning of the transition in Slovenia was characterized by bureaucratic lethargy, dependence on orders, lack of creativity, and lack of professional knowledge (Bučar 1998). Public administration reform in Slovenia therefore had to deal with the following issues (Kovač 2000): the problem of political neutrality, a high degree of centralization, inconsistent interpretations of legal orders, and deficient human and financial management.

Upon independence in 1991, public administration reform began to develop, at first on a nonsystemic basis (Kovač 2002). As a result of independence, public administration began to expand increasingly in fields that had previously been under the control of the federal state. Consequently, the state structure was becoming a collage of old and new institutions, resulting in vaguely defined authority, overlap, and vacuums. Credible public administration reform started with the project called M.A.S.T.E.R (Managing Administrative Systems through Training, Education and Research), adopted with the assistance of the Swiss government. During 1995–96, when M.A.S.T.E.R took place, the state trained administrative workers in the fields of systemic development of public administration and training in administration. Implementation of the M.A.S.T.E.R project gave rise to the establishment of the Office for the Organization and Development of Public Administration within the Ministry of the Interior, which became responsible for public administration reform. The Academy of Administration was also founded to provide training in administration. The European Commission recognized the progress made by Slovenia in public administration reform starting in 1997 but was critical of the slowness of preparation, adoption, and implementation of the fundamental legal acts. Only in May and June 2002 did Slovenia adopt the acts required for reform.[10]

The implementation gap in the field of public administration in Slovenia refers to the shortcomings in implementation and enforcement of existing laws. The administration system as currently organized still does not supply officials with a precise definition of work procedures. Also, an absence of mission and objectives of public administration and its administrative management units are reducing the effectiveness of public administration. Questions of remuneration, promotion, employment, and training systems, which in practice are neither regulated nor satisfactorily solved, as well as an unclear distinction between politics and profession, give rise to a lack of motivation among employees (Kovač 2002).

With reference to the implementation deficit in general, the following classification of open issues in the field of public administration by the Institute of Macroeconomic Analysis and Development is useful: First, inappropriate public management is based predominantly on hierarchical rather than efficiency criteria, causing the suboptimal use of human resources. Second, the organization of government departments does not correspond to the required harmonization of economic policy measures, which is often an outcome of negotiations. Third, the high degree of centralization prevents synergistic effects, with large differences in regional development and a backlog in the development of local self-government.

In the area of the competence of public administration and organizational reform, Slovenia should speed up the reorganization of public administration and pay special attention to the preparation of legislation for the establishment and creation of regions. At the strategic level, preparation of public administrators is needed to qualify them to take an active part in social development.

In the area of enhancing the quality of public administration, the ultimate goals are to achieve the European model of quality assessment in public administration and to ensure the constant analysis of business procedures in administration with the aim of standardizing and optimizing those procedures. Further areas where improvement is necessary include computerization and human resource development, both of which are needed to enhance efficiency. Special emphasis should be given to the development of administrative management skills and to following up on efficiency and systemic training.

CONCLUSIONS

Slovenia has made great strides in the development of institutions suitable for a modern market economy. The transition in Slovenia has been accompanied by all manner of changes, which have strained the country's resources and the energy of policymakers and administrators. In the 12 years since independence, the country has achieved political and administrative consistency as a new state and has succeeded in complying with the requirements of membership in the European Union. However, many backlogs remain. These are in many cases connected with a weak political will for change, where Slovenia has failed to fully exploit its favorable starting position.

Obviously there is room for improvement in the building of institutions in Slovenia. Problems such as inflation, an inefficient financial sector, inefficient courts, and a need to improve the country's capability to use EU structural and cohesion funds all have their origins in deficient institutional settings. Therefore, if Slovenia is to contribute to the future development and growth of the European Union, it can do its best by mobilizing its sources of political will for change.

REFERENCES

Brennan, H. G., and J. M. Buchanan. 1985. *The Reason of Rules—Constitutional Political Economy*. Cambridge, Mass.: Cambridge University Press.

Bučar, F. 1998. *Demokracija in kriza naših ustavnih institucij*. Ljubljana: Nova Revija.

Center for Strategic and International Studies. 2003. "Report of April 29, 2003 Working Group: 'High-Technology Development and Manufacturing' Meeting." Washington, D.C.

European Commission. 1998. "Regular Report on Slovenia's Progress Towards Accession." Brussels.

————. 1999. "Regular Report on Slovenia's Progress Towards Accession." Brussels.

————. 2002. "Regular Report on Slovenia's Progress Towards Accession." Brussels.

————. 2003. "Strategy Paper and Report 2003." Brussels.

Hare, P. G. 2001. "Institutional Change and Economic Performance in the Transition States." Paper prepared for the UNECE Spring Seminar, Geneva.

Institute of International Management Development. 2003. *World Competitiveness Yearbook*. Lausanne, Switzerland.

Institute of Macroeconomic Analysis and Development. 2001. "Slovenija v Evropski uniji—Stategija gospodarskega razvoja Slovenije." Ljubljana.

Klun, M., M. Gostiša, V. Pšeničny, and P. Sedovnik. 2003. "Slovenska obrt in gospodarska politika Republike Slovenije." Obrtniški forum, Dnevi slovenske obrti. Portorož, Slovenia: Obrtna Zbornica Slovenije.

Kovač, P. 2000. "Javna uprava v znamenju ljudi." *Teorija in praksa* 37: 279–93.

————. 2002. "Podjetniška načela v upravljanju slovenske javne uprave." In V. B. Ferfila, ed, *Ekonomski vidiki javne uprave*. Ljubljana: Fakulteta za Družbene Vede.

Ovin, R. 1998. "Why Institutional Change Should Be Rapid—A Transaction Cost Perspective." *Communist Economies and Economic Transformation* 10(1): 63–79.

Ovin, R., and H.-D. Smeets. 1999. "The Role of the State and Economic Pol-
    icy Institution Building After Slovenia's Integration in the European
    Union." *IB Revija* 23: 87–107.
Pejovich, S. 1999. "Toward a Theory of the Effects of the Interaction of For-
    mal and Informal Institutions on Social Stability and Economic Develop-
    ment." *Journal of Markets and Morality*, Fall, no. 265.
Pšeničny, V. 2003. "Slovenija je dežela obrtništva, mikro in malih podjetij."
    Obrtnik 32: 9–12.
Šmidovnik, J. 1998. "Slovenska javna uprava v socializmu in tranzicijskem
    obdobju parlamentarne demokracije(strukturni problemi)." *Podjetje in delo*
    24: 1070–81.
World Economic Forum. 2003. *Global Competitiveness Report*. Oxford.
Županov, J. 1997. "Tranzicija i politički kapitalizam." *Hrvatska gospodarska
    revija* 46 (Prosinac): 1399–1407.

NOTES

1. We distinguish here between the institutional environment (formal institutions) established by the state, and institutional arrangements (informal institutions) arising from transactions among economic agents. According to Pejovich's interaction thesis (Pejovich 1999), the institutional environment must complement institutional arrangements, or else the costs of maintaining the institutional environment will be high.

2. "Tolerant" would be a better term than "liberalized," reflecting Tito's aim when trying to unite the very different nations that made up Yugoslavia. These nations indeed had quite different economic, cultural, and historical experiences, ranging from Slovenia (which had been part of the Austro-Hungarian Empire) to Serbia, Bosnia, and Macedonia (which had been part of the Ottoman Empire), and had indeed in some cases (Serbia and Croatia) fought on opposing sides in both world wars.

3. To lower transactions costs within institutional arrangements, economic agents carry out transaction-specific investments, which would of course be endangered by unexpected institutional change. These agents can then represent a qualified opposition to institutional change. This situation stresses the importance of rapid and credible institutional change (Ovin 1998).

4. Noting the economic power of the management of the larger Yugoslav companies, Županov (1997) claims that capitalism had started developing already under SFR Yugoslavia in the form of "managerial capitalism."

5. On the consequences of the persisting role of the state in the enterprise sector, see Chapter 14.

6. The macroeconomic environment index consists of three subindexes measuring macroeconomic stability (including inflation, national saving, and exchange rate developments), the country's credit rating, and general government expenditure. There is no doubt that, within this constellation, high

inflation rates have contributed to poor results for Slovenia. This is again the consequence of the large role of the state, as most inflationary pressure in recent years has occurred in the field of controlled prices.

7. Areas where Slovenia performed better were (ranked by efficiency) human resources (costs, relations, and availability of skills), infrastructure (basic infrastructure, technological infrastructure, scientific infrastructure, health and environment, and the value system), and the domestic economy (size, growth, wealth, and forecasts). The backlog was mainly in the areas of (ranked by inefficiency) government (public finance, fiscal policy, the institutional framework, business legislation, and education), internationalization (openness to international trade and investment), and finance (bank efficiency, stock market efficiency, and self-financing).

8. Elements of internationalization are progressively changing Slovenia's attitude toward economic policy from what prevailed under the previous system. The former eligibility criteria were focused on the economic policy supply side (measures had to comply with the vision of a politically unified government). Globalization, however, moves the economic policy focus toward the demand side: toward national and international economic agents, who are constantly reconsidering the competitiveness of their resident locations.

9. The shadow economy in Slovenia has been growing since 1990 and amounts at present, according to domestic and foreign experts, to approximately 25 percent of recorded GDP (Klun and others 2003).

10. These laws were the Public Administration Act, which introduced the distinction between the political and the administrative parts of governmental agencies; the Public Agencies Act, which enabled the development of the quality of services; the Inspection Act; the Public Servants Act, which introduced a unified public staff system, decentralization, and greater transparency of professional functions; and legislation on elections, as a condition for the integration of Slovenia into the European Union.

Chapter 14
Privatization, Restructuring, and Corporate Governance of the Enterprise Sector

Marko Simoneti, Matija Rojec, and Aleksandra Gregorič

Slovenia ranked among the most developed economies in the socialist world, with an economic system based on enterprise self-management that was for many years quite decentralized, market oriented, and open to foreign competition. The Slovenian manufacturing sector was comparatively efficient, with exports of goods and services in 1990 amounting to almost 50 percent of GDP, and about 70 percent of merchandise exports directed to the European Community.

However, the enterprise sector suffered a number of severe blows during the transition (Korže and Simoneti 1993). First, it lost a substantial part of its traditional markets in the countries of the former Council for Mutual Economic Assistance, in the Middle East, and later in the rest of former SFR Yugoslavia. A large number of enterprises became overindebted as a result of past losses and acute overstaffing. The restrictive monetary policy imposed by the Bank of Slovenia to curb inflation caused a liquidity crisis and contributed to a sharp increase in real interest rates. In the absence of any governmental bank restructuring, the banks reacted by increasing the interest rate on loans to companies in order to cover the losses and write-offs in their "contaminated" portfolios. Not only did new investment stop, but this policy badly hurt sound and healthy exporting companies. After banks closed their doors to additional borrowing, firms went out and raised money on the interenterprise short-term money market, characterized by sky-high interest rates.

As a consequence, about 800 Slovenian socially owned enterprises found themselves insolvent and on the verge of bankruptcy in 1992. Owing to an underdeveloped judicial system as well as social and political factors (including the fear of instantaneous layoff of thousands of workers), the government adopted a moratorium on bankruptcies while it searched for a better solution for enterprises. At the same time, banks had accumulated a large volume of nonperforming assets, and how to resolve the financial problems of the enterprises became one of the main questions in the banks' restructuring. Although the economic program at the beginning of 1991 focused primarily on economic and monetary sovereignty and macroeconomic stabilization, structural reform in the financial and enterprise sector assumed the highest priority after 1992. The Bank Rehabilitation Act of November 1992 should in fact allow the "spontaneous" rehabilitation of banks at the expense of the enterprise sector to be replaced by an organized effort to protect bank depositors, take into account losses from the previous system, and set up a financial sector that can support viable enterprises in the transition to a market economy.

At first, the government endorsed the idea that government subsidies to unprofitable companies should be stopped and privatization speeded up. Indirectly, as their owner and major creditor, the government was in a position to propose financial restructuring and privatization plans as an alternative to bankruptcy for troubled enterprises. It was intended that restructuring should be limited to the short-term financial and organizational changes necessary to make the company salable. The Development Fund of Slovenia assumed the responsibility of ownership of firms and of coordinating this prepriva-tization restructuring effort of large unprofitable companies. Reduction of employment was an integral and key element of this strategy. Banks and other creditors were expected to face reality and at least partially reduce their claims or convert them into equity, as they would be forced to do in the case of bankruptcy (Korže and Simoneti 1993).

With the improvement in Slovenia's economic situation and the availability of additional financial resources, this "big bang" approach to restructuring was gradually replaced by a less radical approach, and alternative strategies were developed for smaller groups of companies in various industries. In the end Slovenia implemented a gradual and multitrack approach to enterprise restructuring and privatization, which should ensure a consensus among the main stakeholders and a distribution of the burden among governmental, semi-governmental, and private entities. By dividing this large task into smaller and more controllable projects and partially privatizing the process,[1] the government hoped to attract sufficient domestic human and financial resources while limiting foreign participation. Enterprises were essentially divided into three groups: The first consisted of large unprofitable enterprises owned and under the responsibility of the Development Fund. The restructuring of these enterprises was closely related to privatization and was indeed intended to prepare them for sale to the private sector. The second group consisted of enterprises in social ownership, to be privatized under the provisions of the Ownership Transformation Act. The third group included enterprises under the direct supervision of the government, such as public utility companies and steel works, which were to remain in the government domain.

This chapter outlines the main components of postindependence enterprise sector reform in Slovenia and identifies the most critical issues for the future. It begins in the next section with a description of efforts at financial restructuring for the country's largest unprofitable enterprises. The next two sections are devoted to the politics and results of mass privatization. This is followed by an analysis of the evolution of ownership and control in firms after privatization, and a discussion of the problems of residual state ownership and transformation of privatization investment funds (PIFs). The role of foreign direct investment (FDI) in privatization and restructuring is then discussed. The final section reviews the effects of various government programs on the performance of companies, identifies some related issues for the future, and concludes.

RESTRUCTURING OF UNPROFITABLE ENTERPRISES

The government defined the following strategy for the implementation of financial restructuring of unprofitable enterprises taken over by the Development Fund in 1992 (Korže 1994). First, it would install a system of corporate governance, with boards of (nonexecutive) directors responsible for monitoring the performance of management. Second, it would reduce overstaffing, streamline management and the organizational structure, and set up incentive schemes for management and employees. Third, it would negotiate workouts of the enterprises' old debt with creditors, while supporting the enterprises by providing access to the necessary liquidity. Finally, it would divest and privatize the enterprises. It was intended that, within a two-year period at the latest, the Development Fund should cease to hold a controlling stake in any of the acquired enterprises.

Since all of the unprofitable enterprises were socially owned, formally controlled by the workers' council but actually run by the enterprise managers, bankers, and (behind the scenes) politicians, no active restructuring or privatization was possible without establishing a clear owner. The diffuse ownership situation was one of the most important reasons why management teams hesitated to apply decisive restructuring measures. Hence the first condition for participation in the program was that the enterprise be corporatized, its shares transferred to the Development Fund, and its workers' council dissolved. The only concession offered was a promise that 20 percent of the shares would be reserved for sale or free distribution to employees.

About 217 companies applied, 98 of which, consisting of more than 250 separate legal entities, were ultimately included in the program. This number was far beyond the government's expectations and its administrative and financial capacity. These companies employed 56,000 people, approximately 10 percent of the total workforce in the enterprise sector, and accounted for 40 percent of total enterprise losses outside the public utilities.

One of the most important prerequisites for increasing the operational efficiency of these companies was to bring the number of employees down to a level that could be economically justified. According to independent appraisers, 25 percent of the total workforce was redundant. In the framework of the prevailing Slovenian labor legislation, however, dismissing employees was expensive. Needless to say, companies in financial distress could not afford the generous severance packages required under the law, and therefore most of the costs connected with reductions in overstaffing had to be absorbed by the government.

Simultaneously with the program for reducing surplus employment, debt workout plans were developed. Settlements had to be negotiated with creditors practically without any government funds. They were generally based on appraisal, determining what portion of existing and new debt could be regularly serviced from the company's operating cash flow, and what portion should wait to be paid out of the proceeds of divestiture and privatization.

The general problem that arose was that the pace of the project was not well coordinated with the process of bank rehabilitation. Some banks simply waited for a government-sponsored bailout and were not prepared to negotiate with the Development Fund. They feared that any action that accelerated the restructuring of their portfolios would worsen their position as regards a final solution to their problem loan portfolios through the bank rehabilitation program. Many problem loans were taken over by the Bank Rehabilitation Agency (BRA). Although the Development Fund as the owner of the enterprises and the BRA as their creditor are both government agencies, their objectives, operational techniques, and timing priority often proved to be in conflict. The focus of the Development Fund, as the owner, was on the long-term survival of the company, whereas the BRA was legally bound to maximize the proceeds from collection on old debts so as to minimize the public debt.

As the financial condition of these companies had been deteriorating over a long period, capable managers and other professionals had gradually left. The issue was therefore not only how to recruit senior managers but also how to rebuild middle management, whose commitment and skills are usually essential for any successful turnaround. Many experienced managers as well as younger executives offered their help under different arrangements, ranging from straight full-time employment to management contracts with some equity participation.

The goal of the program was to liquidate or sell companies through trade sales, debt-for-equity swaps, and joint ventures over a period of two years. There were, however, several constraints on the speedy execution of the privatization process: One was the fear of managers and employees that the new owners would lay off more employees or even close the company. A second was a lack of financing for domestic investors. A third was a lack of foreign investor interest given the economic and legal uncertainties facing these troubled companies. Yet another constraint was the restitution procedure, in which former owners could easily get court injunctions against any ownership change in the company until restitution was completed. There were also difficulties with secured creditors, particularly in asset deals, and skilled professionals able to prepare companies for sale were in short supply (Korže 1994).

Initially, the program was clearly defined as a temporary alternative to economy-wide bankruptcy, and the results in the first two years of the project were impressive: settlements with creditors were reached for 50 percent of the companies; annual losses were reduced from DM 630 million to DM 130 million; the labor force was reduced by almost 20 percent; and 30 companies (out of the original 98) were privatized in short order. Most of the problems with the program were related to unrealistic expectations on the part of the participating companies, poor coordination on the part of the participating government institutions, and diminishing political will to confront the difficult economic reality of these troubled companies.

Gradually the program became more tractable, and the Development Fund (by now transformed into the Development Corporation of Slovenia) evolved into a permanent institution for providing various forms of nontransparent and often politically motivated state assistance to troubled companies, with no clear mandate in the companies and with limited budgetary supervision of its operations. The Development Corporation was liquidated only in 2002, when government support for companies in Slovenia had to adjust to EU rules on state aid. Most of the remaining companies in its portfolio were transferred to PIFs in exchange for unused privatization vouchers. Several studies (for example, Mrak, Potočnik, and Rojec 1998, chapter 3; Simoneti, Rojec, and Rems 2001b; Simoneti and others 2003b) have concluded that it would have been much better for these companies, for the state budget, and for the small shareholders of the PIFs had the government done this many years earlier.

POLITICS OF PRIVATIZATION

Slovenia's socially owned enterprises were endowed with social capital and controlled by workers' councils;[2] the workers in principle selected the management team and were relatively independent in governing the firm as long as the social capital entrusted to them was not at risk. Although their market orientation and decentralization constituted an important advantage for firm performance, it made it very difficult to find a consensus on an appropriate privatization program, since many workers and managers expected to gain control of the enterprises free of charge. After two years of public debate,[3] the resignation of several ministers, and, ultimately, the fall of the government over the issue, the Ownership Transformation Act (OTA) was finally passed by the legislature in November 1992.

The first, "Korže-Mencinger-Simoneti" concept of the OTA (see Mencinger 1992, 2000), submitted to the legislature in June 1990, opted for decentralized privatization, with most of the initiatives coming from enterprises, creditors, employees, and foreign partners; a multi-track and diversified approach, with various privatization techniques allowed; limited free distribution of property; preferential terms for insiders; and the possibility for partially privatized enterprises to raise additional private equity to finance their development needs. The process would not be administered by the government but only supervised by special governmental agencies. The proposed approach was gradual and, being decentralized, should have captured the advantages of the decentralized nature of the Slovenian economy, its established commercial ties with foreign partners, and the financial resources of the population. However, from an economic point of view, the concept failed to provide a good solution for the large unprofitable enterprises, whereas from a political point of view it was unacceptable since it did not provide for any free distribution of shares to citizens, and special privileges in buying shares were granted only to insiders.

Later, an alternative "Sachs-Peterle-Umek" concept was presented to the legislature, emphasizing massive and speedy privatization based on free distribution of shares and centrally administered by the government. As in the Polish privatization program, all large companies would be privatized through the free distribution of shares to citizens through PIFs. Economically, the concept proposed only a "quasi-privatization," with very limited effects on corporate governance and firms' efficiency (see Simoneti 1992). Politically, this "top-down" approach, with a central role for the government in setting up and managing PIFs, was not acceptable given the strongly decentralized nature of the Slovenian economy. Finally, a compromise approach was embedded in the new OTA, which mandated the initiation of the privatization process as a combination of free distribution of shares to both insiders and citizens through privately managed PIFs and standard privatization techniques.[4]

RESULTS OF PRIVATIZATION

Companies implemented their programs of ownership transformation under the supervision of and upon two compulsory approvals by the Agency for Restructuring and Privatization. The process of ownership change lasted more than six years, during which 1,381 enterprises (96.2 percent of the total) obtained approval for privatization and inscription in the Court Register.[5] The remaining 55 companies did not complete the privatization program but instead were either transferred to the Development Fund or liquidated. The social capital subject to ownership transformation represented only 68 percent of existing social capital. Most of the remaining 32 percent stayed under the ownership of the state (Agency for Restructuring and Privatization 1999).

Most companies were privatized through the free distribution of vouchers that citizens could exchange for shares in the privatizing company either directly or indirectly through PIFs. In addition, 20 percent of the shares of each company were transferred to the quasi-governmental pension fund (Kapitalska družba, or KAD) and the Restitution Fund (Slovenska odškodninska družba, or SOD) with the objective of covering future state liabilities toward the underfunded social pension system and the former owners of nationalized property. These artificially created, privately managed and state-managed funds, in fact, became the new majority owners of the entire Slovenian enterprise sector, while the rest of the privatizing shares were mostly taken up by employees, former employees, and managers (Figure 14.1). Although internal ownership prevailed in smaller, labor-intensive companies, these insiders ended up holding only about 40 percent of capital subject to ownership transformation. On the one hand, workers and management obtained more than 50 percent of shares in 802 companies (61.3 percent), but these accounted for only 22.9 percent of total capital. On the other hand, in 150 companies (11.5 percent), accounting for nearly 45 percent of total capital, insiders did not acquire more than 20 percent of shares (Table 14.1).

Companies that were owned by funds and a large number of small investors (mostly insiders) ended up with no one really interested in supervising management. Hence, in order to improve their performance, the postprivatization period should have brought about appropriate

FIGURE 14.1 OWNERSHIP STRUCTURE OF PRIVATIZED COMPANIES
AT THE TIME OF COMPLETED PRIVATIZATION AND
AT END 2002

(in percent by types of owners)

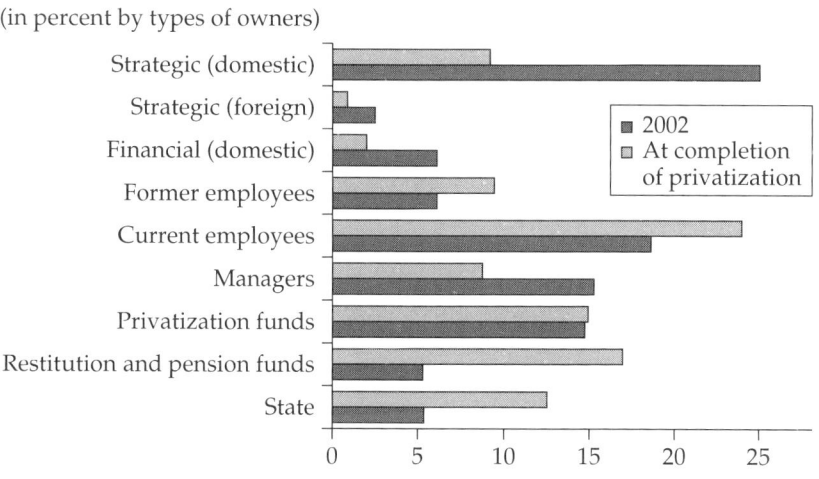

Source: Database of Central and Eastern European Privatization Network; based on survey of companies conducted in 2002.

TABLE 14.1 TOTAL CAPITAL, NUMBER OF COMPANIES, AND
EMPLOYMENT BY SHARE OF INSIDER OWNERSHIP
IN PRIVATIZED COMPANIES

Insider ownership (percent of total)	Total capital		Companies		Employment	
	Thousands of tolars	Percent of total	Number	Percent of total	Number	Percent of total
0 to 10	238,909,289	29.0	82	6.3	20,912	7.8
10 to 20	128,067,033	15.5	68	5.2	18,570	6.9
20 to 30	92,248,314	11.2	81	6.2	27,714	10.3
30 to 40	93,379,520	11.3	122	9.3	31,700	11.8
40 to 50	82,526,405	10.0	155	11.8	47,302	17.6
50 to 60	122,317,335	14.8	483	36.9	78,990	29.3
More than 60	66,778,045	8.1	319	24.4	44,083	16.4
Total	824,225,941	100.0	1,310	100.0	269,271	100.0

Source: Agency for Restructuring and Privatization (1999, 145).

changes in the companies' initial ownership structure and provided
the institutional conditions for finding solutions to several problems
(Simoneti and others 2003a). These included conflicts of interest
between inside and outside owners resulting from the distribution of
ownership between two large groups with very different and often
opposing objectives;[6] the entry of domestic and foreign strategic
investors, who were practically excluded from mass privatization in
Slovenia and were, at least until recently, deterred by the high costs
of takeovers (in the case of public companies) and the opposition of
insiders (in the case of nonlisted firms); the transformation of PIFs and
quasi-governmental funds into normal financial institutions more
interested in managing their portfolio of shares than in managing the
companies in their portfolio;[7] and ensuring the exit of small shareholders transparently and at fair market prices, especially in firms not
listed on the stock exchange.

EVOLUTION OF OWNERSHIP AND CONTROL
AFTER PRIVATIZATION

Mass privatization in Slovenia initially set up relatively concentrated
ownership structures in companies. At the end of 1999, the five largest
shareholders controlled close to 50 percent of capital in the average
privatized company. By the end of 2001 the five largest owners on
average held 73 percent of votes (Rojec, Simoneti, and Rems 2003).
This trend toward ownership consolidation is also observed when

looking at the number of shareholders. Initially, the number of shareholders in the average listed (public) company was 6,898, whereas in nonlisted companies the average did not exceed 500. By the end of 2001 the number of shareholders had fallen by almost 50 percent, and it fell faster in listed than in nonlisted companies (Rojec, Simoneti, and Rems 2003).

The observed concentration of ownership should in principle provide for active outside control and hence the establishment of good corporate governance. However, three major factors have prevented outside ownership from efficiently translating into control. First, the largest shareholder in listed companies typically does not hold majority control. For instance, at the end of May 2001 the largest shareholder held only about 32 percent of the average firm's voting rights, and in half of the companies, the size of the largest voting block did not exceed 25 percent (Gregorič 2003).[8] Second, the largest shareholders in Slovenian firms are in most cases quasi-governmental funds and PIFs rather than strategic investors. Although the share of firms owned by quasi-governmental funds has been decreasing, mostly out of the need to cover their liabilities, PIFs have mostly maintained their ownership stakes; in fact, at the end of May 2001 they still held the largest blocks in more than 42 percent of listed companies.[9] The new strategic owners are almost entirely of domestic origin and, on average, hold fewer but larger blocks (the average size is 24.9 percent) compared with PIFs. By contrast, nonfinancial companies are most frequently found among the largest owners of nonlisted firms. Third, although in the listed firms one observes a decrease in insider ownership, in nonlisted firms the role of managers is strengthened within the group of insider owners. Moreover, shares are transferred between insiders at low prices and in a nontransparent way. Given that insider shareholders might actually behave as a homogeneous group and oppose outsiders, they represent a further obstacle to effective outside control. For instance, the tying up of insiders' shares in the so-called workers' associations is in fact nothing else than a defensive strategy on the part of the target nonlisted companies, initiated by their managers to prevent institutional investors from acting in their own interest.[10]

The main corporate governance problem in Slovenia seems not to be the typical agency problem arising out of separation of ownership and control in large corporations with dispersed ownership, but rather the limited contestability of management control. Hidden support by insider owners (with managers collecting votes from employees through the organized gathering of proxies), anti-takeover provisions, limitations on share transfers, and the tying up of shares in workers' associations are examples of the devices that Slovenian managers can use to limit the control of external owners; as a consequence,

Slovenian firms are often run by managers who are in effect unaccountable, able to protect themselves against any kind of external investor (or market) interference (Gregorič 2003). Hence corporate governance in Slovenia is more likely to have "management control bias" than "private control bias."[11]

THE PRIVATIZATION GAP, TRANSFORMATION OF FUNDS, AND RESIDUAL STATE OWNERSHIP

As already stated, the largest stakes in privatized firms were given to the quasi-governmental funds and PIFs. The former have decreased the number of companies in their portfolio from an initial 1,200 to 347 (in the case of KAD) and 311 (in the case of SOD) at the end of 2002; they are expected to further decrease their stakes, especially in smaller companies, and to concentrate their investments in the large, listed "blue chip" companies. As they are controlled by the state, the quasi-governmental funds' involvement in firms provides plenty of opportunities for political interference in firms' decision-making, and the fact that they consider their investments "strategic" and are therefore reluctant to sell their stakes further reduces the liquidity of the Slovenian capital market. However, in the long run the importance of these funds should be reduced, and they might even be liquidated, since the property they have received through privatization is not enough to cover future state liabilities toward restitution claimants (in the case of SOD) and the social pension system (in the case of KAD).

As in the Czech Republic, small blocks of nontradable shares were distributed through closed-end funds (PIFs) to a large number of small Slovenian investors. However, although privatization had already started in 1994, it took eight years for the PIFs to exchange all their vouchers for privatized shares; the delay was due to the so-called privatization gap: the fact that the PIFs collected many more vouchers than there was property available for privatization. The long-drawn-out negotiations between the government and the funds on how to close this gap went mostly at the expense of small investors and, along with the long debate over the privatization concept, followed by its complex and gradual implementation,[12] prevented the main potential advantage of mass privatization—the greater speed of the process—from materializing. Moreover, upon the postponement of the formal transformation of PIFs into normal institutional investors or holding companies,[13] the PIFs' management companies have taken advantage of the situation, charging relatively high fees for managing the funds, doing little to restructure their portfolios, and gradually becoming the main owners of the funds at a very low price.[14] As a result, much more property from privatization ends up in holding companies controlled by the management companies.[15] In addition, many initial small investors in PIFs have sold shares at huge discounts to book value and will have no confidence in institutional investors for many years in the future.[16]

ROLE OF FDI IN PRIVATIZATION AND RESTRUCTURING

The present stock of inward FDI in Slovenia stands at just over $4 billion. FDI inflows increased significantly in 2001 and especially in 2002, rising from $136 million in 2000 to $503 million in 2001 and $1.9 billion in 2002. This surge was predominantly the consequence of several relatively large foreign acquisitions.[17] In 2001 the inward FDI stock was equivalent to 13.6 percent of GDP; by the end of 2002 that proportion had increased to 18.2 percent. Foreign investment enterprises (FIEs, defined as enterprises with a 10 percent or higher foreign equity share) make up an important segment of the Slovenian economy. In 2001 FIEs accounted for only 14.2 percent of total assets and 11.6 percent of all employees in the Slovenian nonfinancial corporate sector, but they realized 18.6 percent of total sales, 21.9 percent of total operating profits, and 31.3 percent of total exports. In the manufacturing sector, FIEs accounted for 29.3 percent of total sales and 36.8 percent of total exports (authors' database, based on Bank of Slovenia and Agency for Payments data).

By tending to locate in manufacturing industries with above-average profitability, value added per employee, and export propensity, FDI fosters the restructuring of the Slovenian manufacturing sector in a way that promotes allocative efficiency (Rojec and Šušteršič 2002). FIEs in general perform better than domestically owned enterprises. The reasons for this lie not only in the integration of FIEs in the foreign parent companies' network and in their superior sectoral allocation, but also in the fact that, compared with domestically owned enterprises, FIEs are much larger and more capital intensive, have a more favorable asset structure (with relatively more machinery and equipment and less land and buildings), and are much more export oriented.[18] Except for company size and export propensity, most of these differences between FIEs and domestically owned enterprises seem to have narrowed over time. FDI is an important source of technology transfer in the Slovenian manufacturing industry (Damijan and Majcen 2001). Besides technology, foreign investors usually bring resources for investment and access to foreign markets. FIEs in the Slovenian manufacturing sector also exhibit positive vertical spillover effects on domestic suppliers, although horizontal spillovers have proved to be neutral (Damijan and others 2003).

The level of FDI penetration in Slovenia is relatively low compared with that in the existing EU countries and other EU accession candidates.[19] Almost 70 percent of the existing FDI stock and most of the relevant FDI projects in Slovenia have been realized as foreign acquisitions of companies that were not directly subject to the OTA.[20] Privatization has contributed little to FDI inflows for several reasons. The first is that the form of mass privatization used in Slovenia implicitly favored internal buyouts. A second is the slow restructuring process in the privatized enterprises, which gives them little encouragement to search for strategic foreign partners. A third is the hesitant privatization of enterprises in the financial and public utilities sectors, where initiatives have been undertaken only recently. Another reason for the relatively low level of FDI penetration is the small local market, and yet another is monetary considerations, which for a long time have been one of the major scruples of the Bank of Slovenia regarding foreign capital inflow. Although the central bank's measures have served a valid monetary purpose, and although they were not aimed specifically at FDI, they have also tended to discourage FDI. Still other reasons include administrative barriers, which increase the costs of a company seeking to establish itself and operate in Slovenia; problems in acquiring industrial locations; relatively protective labor legislation; and a relatively rigid labor market. Slovenia has a relatively well-educated and productive labor force, but labor costs are high compared with those in alternative investment locations, and the mobility of the labor force is relatively low.[21]

The other dimension of the role of FDI in manufacturing sector restructuring is outward FDI. Slovenian investors believe that their FDI abroad improves the competitiveness and speeds up the restructuring of the investing firms and of the Slovenian economy in general (Jaklič and Svetličič 2003). Most of this outward FDI goes to the other successor countries of SFR Yugoslavia. Slovenian investors obviously see these countries, which they know better than other investors, as their distinctive investment opportunity—and one that needs to be acted upon before major multinational players decide to come in (see Chapter 20).

CONCLUSIONS, POSTPRIVATIZATION PERFORMANCE, AND FUTURE AGENDA

The Slovenian economy already shared many features of the Western market economies before its transition. However, the loss of traditional markets, a restrictive monetary policy, the banks' contaminated portfolios, and, consequently, the hardening of budget constraints pushed a large number of Slovenian firms to the verge of bankruptcy just as the transition was getting under way. Moreover, the reluctance of those actually in control of firms—the managers, trade unions' representatives, bankers, and politicians—to accept the proposed changes made it clear that no active restructuring of enterprises and no real transition to the market economy were possible unless firms were given a clear owner. After much discussion, Slovenia in the end implemented a gradual and multitrack approach to firms' restructuring and privatization, mostly driven by the aim to reach a consensus among the main stakeholders and to distribute the burden among governmental, quasi-governmental, and private entities.

The resulting gradual and complex implementation of the enterprise reform program, the long-drawn-out negotiations on the approach to privatization, problems related to the role of the quasi-governmental investment funds and PIFs, and obstacles to the participation of foreigners, as well as the lack of transparency and insufficient minority investor protection, prevented much of the potential for improved performance under the chosen privatization program from being realized. Even so, the program proved appropriate for several hundred relatively small and labor-intensive companies and for about 100 well-performing, large, capital-intensive and export-oriented companies. In the former group, the majority of shares were acquired by the employees, whereas the latter were listed on the stock exchange through public offerings. However, the privatization program proved inappropriate for those relatively large and capital-intensive companies that required substantial corporate restructuring and hence substantial outside strategic financing.[22] Except for some unprofitable companies that were subject to the governmental restructuring program, the insider-outsider conflict slowed restructuring in the remaining firms.

The problem of "employeeism"—the tendency for worker-owners to use their decisionmaking power to influence decisions in the direction of excessive wages and employment—seems to have presented a significant obstacle to restructuring in these firms. For instance, firms in which the share of workers' representatives on the supervisory board is below 50 percent have been found to be more successful in defensive restructuring (defined as adjusting the number of employees and the financial rehabilitation of a company, which includes also profitability indicators) than firms where that share is 50 percent or more (Prašnikar 1999). Workers' representatives on firms' supervisory boards can weaken managers' power in implementing strategic plans and in adopting the measures necessary to succeed in international competition (Prašnikar and Gregorič 2002). At any rate, although empirical studies for the period 1995–99 reveal no significant effect of ownership consolidation on firms' performance, the nonlisted privatized firms in general seem to have performed worse than the listed firms. Hence, because the current consolidation of control does not seem to have yielded the expected results, the current institutional framework for ownership consolidation and corporate governance should be improved, in particular in nonlisted firms (Simoneti and others 2003a).

Empirical analyses, moreover, provide evidence that consolidation of control and the corporate governance system, the necessary preconditions for large-scale basic restructuring, are still in the initial stages in many privatized companies. Although, in the 1994–98 period, private companies that were not part of the privatization process expanded their activities through offensive restructuring (that is, through new investment and employment), the privatized firms did not expand but rather improved their productivity very slowly, mostly through defensive restructuring. Nonprivatized firms remain unprofitable, although they have managed to cut their operating losses and increase their labor productivity, mostly through defensive restructuring and downsizing, reduced employment, and disinvestment (Simoneti, Rojec, and Rems 2001a, 2001b).

Existing analyses and empirical data leave little doubt about, on the one hand, the positive and relevant contribution of FDI to the restructuring of Slovenia's enterprise sector and, on the other hand, the modest role of FDI in the Slovenian privatization process and postprivatization consolidation of ownership. The reasons behind this are partly related to the small scale of the Slovenian market, but even more to the lack of an active FDI policy and to the gradualist approach taken in Slovenia to transition in the enterprise sector. That approach has favored long-lasting government support for unprofitable firms, active exchange rate policy support to exporters, slow liberalization and privatization of the public utility sector, free distribution of shares, internal buyouts, and domestic postprivatization ownership consolidation. Given the comprehensive restructuring process that is taking place in the Slovenian enterprise sector, which will indeed intensify with EU accession, more foreign acquisitions of already privatized Slovenian companies are expected to follow the domestic nontransparent ownership consolidation that has characterized ownership changes in the past. Companies are increasingly aware of the potential for FDI to speed their restructuring. The entry of a strategic foreign investor in a company clearly challenges the position of the existing management, which still de facto controls most of the privatized companies, in particular the nonlisted firms that represent an important segment of the Slovenian economy.

Although it seems clear, from the point of view of performance, that it was better to privatize and consolidate ownership and control the "Slovenian way" than to postpone privatization even further, there is still a long way to go. Given that firms with well-defined domestic and foreign ownership seem to perform better than other firms in the same institutional environment, the following steps should be taken to further improve the performance of the Slovenian enterprise sector: complete the privatization of poorly performing enterprises still under state ownership, speed up ownership consolidation and improve corporate governance in the privatized companies, eliminate barriers to FDI, and, finally, promote the establishment and growth of new private companies.

REFERENCES

Agency for Restructuring and Privatization. 1999. "Lastninsko preoblikovanje podjetij." Poročilo o delu Agencije RS za prestrukturiranje in privatizacijo 1999. Ljubljana.

Barca, F., and M. Becht, eds. 2001. *The Control of Corporate Europe.* Oxford: Oxford University Press.

Borak, N., ed. 1995. *Ekonomski vidiki upravljanja.* Zbornik 3. letnega srečanja Zveze ekonomistov Slovenije. Ljubljana: Zveza ekonomistov Slovenije.

————, ed. 1998. *Korpoaracijsko prestrukturiranje.* Zbornik referatov 6. letnega srečanja zveze ekonomistov Slovenije. Ljubljana: Zveza ekonomistov Slovenije.

Damijan, J. P., and B. Majcen. 2001. "Transfer of Technology through FDI and Trade, Spillover Effects, and Recovery of Slovenian Manufacturing Firms." Institute for Economic Research, Ljubljana. Processed.

Damijan, J. P., M. Knell, B. Majcen, and M. Rojec. 2003. "Technology Transfer through FDI in Top-10 Transition Countries: How Important Are Direct Effects, Horizontal and Vertical Spillovers?" William Davidson Working Paper 549 (February). William Davidson Institute, Ann Arbor, Mich.

Foreign Investment Advisory Service. 2000. "Administrative Barriers to Foreign Investment in Slovenia." Washington, D.C.

Gregorič, A. 2003. "Corporate Governance in Slovenia: An International Perspective." Ph.D. dissertation. Faculty of Economics, University of Ljubljana, Ljubljana.

Gregorič, A., J. Prašnikar, and I. Ribnikar. 2000. "Corporate Governance in Transitional Economies: The Case of Slovenia." *Economic and Business Review for Central and South-Eastern Europe* 2(3): 183–207.

Jaklič, A., and M. Svetličič. 2003. *Enhanced Transition through Outward Internationalization: Outward FDI by Slovenian Firms.* Aldershot, U.K.: Ashgate Publishing.

Jaklin, J., and B. Herič. 1997. "Economic Transition in Slovenia—1996." In A. Böhm, ed., *Economic Transition Report—1996.* CEEPN Annual Conference Series 7. Ljubljana: Central and Eastern European Privatization Network.

Jašovič, B., J. Lukovac, G. Sluga, and B. Herič. 2001. "Trg kapitala." In M. Simoneti, ed., *Razvoj trga kapitala v Sloveniji: Razvojno poročilo o finančnem sektorju v Sloveniji 2000.* Ljubljana: Central and Eastern European Privatization Network.

Korže, U. 1994. "Restructuring of the Loss-Making enterprises in Slovenia." In A. Böhm and U. Korže, eds., *Privatization through Restructuring.* CEEPN Workshop Series 4. Ljubljana: Central and Eastern European Privatization Network.

Korže, U., and M. Simoneti. 1993. "Privatization in Slovenia—1992." In A. Böhm and M. Simoneti, eds., *Privatization in Central and Eastern Europe 1992.* CEEPN Annual Conference Series 3. Ljubljana: Central and Eastern European Privatization Network.

Mencinger, J. 1992. "Decentralized versus Centralized Privatization—The Case of Slovenia." In *Privatization.* International Symposium on Privatization. London: Centre for Research on Communist Economies.

———. 2000. "Deset let pozneje. Tranzicija—uspeh, polom ali nekaj vmes." *Gospodarska gibanja.* Economics Institute of the Faculty of Law, Ljubljana.

Ministry of Finance. 2003. *Bilten Finančni trgi v Sloveniji* 6 (19). Ljubljana.

Mrak, M., J. Potočnik, and M. Rojec, eds. 1998. *Strategy of the Republic of Slovenia for Accession to the European Union: Economic and Social Part.* Ljubljana: Institute of Macroeconomic Analysis and Development.

Prašnikar, J., ed. 1999. *Poprivatizacijsko obnašanje slovenskih podjetij.* Ljubljana: Gospodarski vestnik.

———, ed. 2000. *Internacionalizacija slovenskih podjetij.* Ljubljana: Finance.

Prašnikar, J., and A. Gregorič. 2002. "The Influence of Workers' Participation on the Power of Management in Transitional Countries. The Case of Slovenia" *Annals of Public and Cooperative Economics* 73(2): 269–97.

Rojec, M., J. P. Damijan, and B. Majcen. 2002. "Foreign Ownership and Export Propensity: The Slovenian Experience." *Prague Economic Papers* 11(4): 339–55.

Rojec, M., M. Simoneti, and M. Rems. 2003. "Koncentracija lastništva v podjetjih." *Ekonomsko ogledalo* 9(1): 15.

Rojec, M., and J. Šusteršiš. 2002. "Razvojna vloga in politika do neposrednih tujih investicij v Sloveniji." *IB Revija* 36(1): 78–94.

Rop, A., D. Mramor, and I. Kušar. 1995. "Privatization in Slovenia—1994." In A. Böhm, ed., *Privatization in Central and Eastern Europe 1994.* CEEPN Annual Conference Series 5. Ljubljana: Central and Eastern European Privatization Network.

Simoneti, M. 1992. Comment on "Accelerating Privatization in Eastern Europe," by J. Sachs. In *Proceedings of the World Bank Annual Conference 1991 on Development Economics.* Washington, D.C.: World Bank.

Simoneti, M., I. Erker, and J. Lukovac. 2003. "Institutional Investors in Slovenia: Current State of Development and Prospects for the Future." *Journal for Money and Banking* 52(7–8): 113–23.

Simoneti, M., S. Estrin, and A. Böhm, eds. 1999. *The Governance of Privatization Funds: Experiences of the Czech Republic, Poland and Slovenia.* Cheltenham, U.K.: Edward Elgar.

Simoneti, M., M. Rojec, and M. Rems. 2001a. "Restructuring in a Small Economy. The Case of Slovenia." In M. Svetličič, D. Salvatore, and J.P. Damijan, eds., *Small Countries in a Global Economy: New Challenges and Opportunities.* London: Palgrave MacMillan.

————. 2001b. "Ownership Structure and Post-Privatization Performance and Restructuring of the Slovenian Non-Financial Corporate Sector." *Journal of East-West Business* 7(2): 7–36.

Simoneti, M., A. Böhm, M. Rems, M. Rojec, J. P. Damijan, and B. Majcen. 2003a. "Firms in Slovenia Following Mass Privatization." In B. Blaszczyk, I. Hoshi, and R. Woodward, eds., *Secondary Privatization in Transition Economies: The Evolution of Enterprise Ownership in the Czech Republic, Poland and Slovenia.* Basingstoke, U.K.: Palgrave-MacMillan.

Simoneti, M., J. P. Damijan, M. Rojec, and B. Majcen. 2003b. "Efficiency of Mass Privatization vs. Gradual Privatization: Owner and Seller Effects on Performance of Companies in Slovenia." GDN Research Medal Paper, presented at the 4th Global Development Network Annual Global Conference on Globalization and Equity (January), Cairo.

United Nations Conference on Trade and Development. 2002. *World Investment Report 2002.* New York: United Nations.

NOTES

1. All projects were supported by a social safety net program and, later in the 1990s, by programs that help profitable companies preserve and improve their competitive edge, as well as programs for the development of small and medium-size enterprises.

2. Social capital was in fact the cornerstone of the system. It was considered to belong not to the state but to everyone (see Chapter 2).

3. The final discussions were more or less political in nature, with issues of justice and fairness taking priority over economic efficiency.

4. The compromise was proposed by three members of the National Assembly: Janko Deželak, Emil Milan Pintar, and Mile Šetinc.

5. The agency gave its first approval of a program of ownership transformation on July 29, 1993, and its last approval on October 30, 1998.

6. Insiders have a strong interest in job security and the company's long-term survival, whereas outside owners seek profits and opportunities to exit profitably from their investments by selling their shares.

7. The role of privatization funds and quasi-governmental funds in the corporate governance of companies remains a very controversial issue, as there is no good answer to the simple question: Who will "govern the governors"? More on the issue of the governance of privatization funds in Poland, Slovenia, and the Czech Republic can be found in a comparative study by Simoneti, Estrin, and Böhm (1999).

8. Voting power in nonlisted companies was slightly more concentrated. For instance, at the end of July 2000, the largest shareholder in 579 nonlisted firms in the Shareholder Register held, on average, 38.8 percent of voting rights. In half of the companies the voting stake of the largest shareholder exceeded 31.6 percent (Gregorič, Prašnikar, and Ribnikar 2000).

9. The concentration of voting power in their hands is supported by the friendly legal environment, starting with the Takeovers Act (1997), which allows PIFs to increase their voting blocks by up to 40 percent without any obligation to make a public bid.

10. Employees could constitute an authorized workers' association for the implementation of the internal buyout in order to provide a common representative to inside owners in nonlisted companies.

11. For more on private, management, and market control bias, see Barca and Becht (2001).

12. The need for speedy legalization of a chosen privatization concept was mainly urged by the phenomenon called "wild" privatization. Socially owned companies would establish many new companies with their assets and privatize them later without strict supervision, or simply transfer the business activities to private "bypass" companies without proper compensation. However, instead of amending the legislation immediately, Slovenia chose to debate a new comprehensive privatization law for two years. In the meantime, the process earned a bad reputation, to the point that it became almost impossible to undertake any reorganization of a company without running the risk of being accused of wild privatization. More on the problems of implementation of the privatization process in Slovenia can be found in Korže and Simoneti (1993), Rop, Mramor, and Kušar (1995), and Jaklin and Herič (1997), and in the final report of the privatization agency (Agency for Restructuring and Privatization 1999).

13. The uniform Czech solution of mandatory transformation of funds into open-ended funds was not acceptable at the time, as this would have required a massive sell-off of shares at very low prices in the isolated Slovenian economy. However, funds' management companies were allowed to split funds' portfolios into tradable and nontradable, but in a transparent way so as to protect small investors. For more on the issue of PIF transformation, see Simoneti and others (1999) and Jašovič and others (2001).

14. For instance, the annual operating costs of KAD and SOD are only about 0.5 percent of the value of their assets, much less than the management fees charged by privately managed privatization funds (Jašovič and others 2001).

15. The recent estimate by the Ministry of Finance is that out of the total assets given initially to PIFs, currently about 55 percent is still with privatization funds, 23 percent with funds transformed into investment funds, and 22 percent with funds transformed into holding companies (Ministry of Finance 2003, p. 116).

16. The market appreciates the transformation toward open-end funds, as the average discount to net asset value was about 60 percent in nontransformed funds and 30 percent in transformed funds at the end of 2002, whereas the only fund that has declared its intention to become an open-end fund

traded at only a 10 percent discount in 2003. For more on the development of institutional investors in Slovenia, see Simoneti, Erker, and Lukcvac (2003).

17. These included the acquisition of the pharmaceutical firm Lek by the Swiss firm Novartis, of Nova Ljubljanska Banka by the Belgian company KBC, of Simobil by the Austrian firm Mobilkom, of the bank SKB by the French Société Générale (which also invested additional funds), and of Banka Koper by the Italian company San Paolo IMI.

18. FIEs also show a higher import propensity than domestically owned enterprises. In 1997 the imports-to-sales ratios in the manufacturing sector averaged 54.4 percent in FIEs and 27.7 percent in their domestically owned counterparts (Rojec, Damijan, and Majcen 2002).

19. In 2000 the only EU members with a smaller inward FDI stock as a percentage of GDP were Italy and Greece; Austria's was about the same as Slovenia's. Among accession countries, Slovenia had the smallest stock of inward FDI relative to GDP. Despite the significant increase in the FDI stock in 2002 (to 18.2 percent of GDP), Slovenia remained among those countries with a small FDI stock relative to GDP (United Nations Conference on Trade and Development 2002).

20. This was effected through various modalities: some were already in place before the adoption of the OTA, on the basis of legislation under SFR Yugoslavia, others before or after adoption of the OTA, as Slovenian parent companies for various reasons sold off some of their subsidiaries. There have also been some foreign acquisitions of companies as a result of court-led reha-bilitation or liquidation procedures. Some foreign investors formed joint ventures with existing Slovenian companies. One specific case of foreign pri-vatization was the transformation of an existing contractual joint venture with foreign partners, formed in the 1970s and 1980s, into equity joint ventures. Finally, there have also been foreign acquisitions of already privatized Slovenian companies.

21. On the various barriers to FDI in Slovenia, see especially Foreign Investment Advisory Service (2000).

22. Some basic findings of Slovenian researchers on the different aspects of postprivatization management, restructuring, and performance of the Slovenian corporate sector can be found in the volumes edited by Borak (1995, 1998) and Prašnikar (1999, 2000).

Chapter 15
Enterprise Restructuring in the First Decade of Independence

Polona Domadenik and Janez Prašnikar

Endogenous growth models stress efficiency gains, whatever their source, as the crucial factor that provides a lasting boost to economic growth. Such permanent effects are especially important for transition economies. The efficiency gains that originate from either reductions in slack (moving toward the efficiency frontier), greater allocative efficiency (moving from less efficient to more efficient use of inputs), or greater organizational efficiency (an outward shift of the production frontier as a result of reorganization) lift the level of output that can be produced with given inputs (Filer and others 2001). Svejnar (2002) notes that virtually all the transition economies, both in Central and Eastern Europe (CEE) and in the former Soviet Union, implemented so-called type I reforms (macroeconomic stabilization, price liberalization, breakups of state-owned enterprises and the monobank system, small-scale privatization, reduction of direct state subsidies, and so on), but that several countries—those of the former Soviet Union, Bulgaria, and Romania, among others—were less successful in carrying out type II reforms (large-scale privatization, establishment and enforcement of a market-oriented legal system and its accompanying institutions, further development of the commercial banking and financial system). They also performed worse than did those CEE countries that carried out both types of reforms in the 1990s. Type II reforms are crucial for realizing efficiency gains through different types of restructuring at the firm level, and countries that are less successful at implementing those reforms have lagged behind in economic growth.

The reform path chosen by a transition economy is subject to a high degree of hysteresis and depends crucially on when reforms are implemented. The windows of opportunity that were present in the initial, heady days of reform can close, as the political will to bear the necessary pain decreases. Countries can thus find themselves heading toward either a good (growth-promoting) or a bad (growth-depressing) equilibrium.

The mix of macroeconomic policies that Slovenia chose after independence introduced export demand as the most important factor in accelerating growth, resulting in higher investment demand. Given the hard budget constraints introduced at the beginning of the transition, and given Slovenia's underdeveloped capital markets, internal funds represented the most important source of investment by firms. Slovenian firms did react to the incentives they faced. But although this strategy was quite successful in the past, it is not so any longer. Microeconomic reforms have been proceeding slowly, impeding corporate restructuring—some (such as reform of the labor market) have not yet started even today. The further development of markets and institutional structures represents one of the most important factors that will determine the future growth of the Slovenian economy.

The first section of this chapter describes the issues relating to privatization and restructuring in the CEE economies and the countries of the former Soviet Union. The second section highlights the initial conditions during the first (1991–95) and second (1996–2002) phases of the microeconomic transition in Slovenia. The final section offers some conclusions.

PRIVATIZATION AND RESTRUCTURING
OF FIRMS IN TRANSITION

Privatization and restructuring were usually perceived as among the most important processes in the transition to a market economy. Yet the performance of most transition economies has fallen short of expectations: studies based on early transition data provide only tentative answers, and there is a major debate about the actual performance of firms in transition economies and what policies ought to be pursued to enhance restructuring and growth of the economy. The generally perceived assumption behind privatization at the beginning of the 1990s was that private ownership improves corporate performance, through depoliticization and greater efficiency. The fact of privatization itself was regarded as more important than the particular way in which firms are privatized (Djankov and Pohl 1997). The results of surveys of the effects of privatization on performance in transition economies after a decade vary from finding no systematic effect (Angelucci and others 2002), to finding that a weak positive effect probably dominates (Megginson and Netter 2001), to concluding that the overall effect is probably positive (Djankov and Murrell 2002; Carlin and others 2000; Shirley and Walsh 2000). Combined with the finding that the better-performing firms tend to be privatized first and that many studies are hence likely to overestimate the positive effect of privatization (Gupta, Ham, and Svejnar 2000), one can conclude that any such positive effect is smaller and less definitive than was originally expected. Stiglitz (1999) argues that the main reason for this shortcoming lies in the fact that successful privatization requires an institutional infrastructure that supports markets; he also stresses the role of effective corporate governance.

The issue of privatization, efficiency, and the ownership structure of firms in the postprivatization period is significantly linked to the question of restructuring. Firms that achieved higher profitability in the period under study are considered to have undergone deep restructuring. On the other hand, unprofitable firms tend to be grouped among firms that did not adjust sufficiently (see Pinto, Belka, and Krajewski 1993, for example). Carlin, Van Reenen, and Wolfe (1995) show that this is not necessarily the case, as a firm might be more productive than other firms for various reasons; for example, it might enjoy a monopoly position in the period under study or have better starting conditions. Hence the empirical evidence based only on studies of efficiency is vastly inadequate.

Evaluating both the extent to which restructuring has been successful and the determinants of the desire and ability to restructure is crucial in the CEE economies. Carlin, Van Reenen, and Wolfe (1995) catalogue restructuring actions along four dimensions: changes in internal organization, such as the separation of noncore from core activities, the closure of unviable units, and the spinning off of social assets; finding markets and adapting product ranges; labor shedding and the reform of incentives for managers and employees; and the modernization of equipment. Recent theoretical and empirical studies highlight firm managers as the key agents in restructuring. Indeed, managerial incentives may be the dominant influence on whether or not restructuring occurs. Aghion, Blanchard, and Burgess (1996) provide one way of conceptualizing the incentives for and constraints on restructuring by managers. Managers face two choices: they can either restructure, thus incurring a cost to the enterprise in the current period and an uncertain payoff in the future; or they can maintain the status quo, incurring no cost in the present but certainly incurring costs in the future. A manager's incentive to restructure can be increased by imposing the principles of a market economy: introducing hard budget constraints, ending direct subsidies, enforcing bankruptcy procedures, and so on. Improved functioning of the managerial labor market might prove to be the most important part of improving incentives to restructure, because it allows those managers who are successful at restructuring to be identified and rewarded. Conversely, the signaling of the quality of their work would be much less effective. If outside opportunities for managers are few, the manager will have to balance the risk of job loss from closure of the firm if restructuring is not undertaken, on the one hand, with the threat of being opposed and possibly replaced by the firm's workers if it is undertaken, on the other.

The issue of competition and its impact on restructuring as the accession countries approach the condition of EU internal markets has received much attention in recent years. Theory provides good reasons to expect that a monopolist will be less efficient and innovative than rivalrous oligopolists. Empirical evidence tends to confirm this view, although the results for transition economies are mixed. Some studies report a positive effect of competition on firms' performance: see, for example, Grosfeld and Tressel (2002) for Poland; Jones, Klinedienst, and Rock (1998) for Bulgaria; and Brown and Earle (2000) for Russia. Others report that the effect is either insignificant (Konings 1998 for Estonia) or negative (Djankov and Kreacic 1998 for Georgia). Carlin and others (2003) report that the relationship is probably not monotonic but rather takes an inverted U-shape, with competition among a few rivals, rather than none or many, having the most positive effect. Although increased competition has a direct effect on sales and productivity growth (used as proxies for strategic restructuring), market power works primarily through providing an incentive for developing new products and finding new markets. In the latter context, the relaxing of financial constraints resulting in retained earnings appears crucial for firms to succeed. Whether there is an overall effect is ambiguous and depends on which effect, the direct or the indirect, prevails. The crucial role in the whole process is played by managers who react proactively to increased competition while, in the case of some degree of market power, their firms are also able to generate and retain earnings that enable investment. Moreover, the threat of actual or potential competition prevents rent-seeking behavior on the part of firms' stakeholders.

EVIDENCE FROM SLOVENIA

Slovenian Firms at the Beginning of the Transition

Slovenia embarked on its transition to a market economy in a relatively favorable position, thanks to the Yugoslav enterprise self-management system, which gave enterprises greater autonomy than they enjoyed in other centrally planned economies. A relatively well functioning product market had a significant impact on the performance of Slovenian companies. Enterprise decisionmaking, formally under the jurisdiction of the self-managed companies, was actually the result of bargaining among workers, management, and the state (Prašnikar and Svejnar 1988).

The literature on labor-managed firms has for a long time debated the existence and seriousness of the so-called underinvestment problem, which originated from the assumption that employees in these firms had a short time horizon. The first contributors to this literature (for example, Furubotn and Pejovich 1970; Vanek 1970) argued that insiders, unlike external owners, would prefer to distribute a firm's surplus in the form of additional wages and fringe benefits rather than reinvest it in the firm for future growth. Several empirical studies report that extremely large interfirm and interindustry wage differentials in Yugoslav enterprises emerged after they were allowed to operate in a relatively free market environment in the 1960s (see, for example, Estrin and Svejnar 1993). These differentials were evident even after controlling for skill, region, and job characteristics (see, for example, Estrin 1983). The huge variation in wages, which could not have emerged in other centrally planned economies, naturally raised the question of whether employees were able to capture part of the cash flow that would otherwise be invested in production. This question received extreme attention when the transition process was launched and employees regained decisionmaking power within the newly privatized firms, depending on the privatization method adopted (internal privatization in Slovenia and Russia) or the institutional setting (for example, the Codetermination Act in Slovenia and Croatia).

Prašnikar and others (1994) generalize the model of labor-managed firms by assuming that parties other than workers also influence firms' decisionmaking. Institutional as well as empirical evidence suggests that, in practice, three main parties jointly determined the policies of labor-managed firms in the Yugoslav institutional setting: workers, managers, and government authorities. It is reasonable to assume that each of these three parties follows different objectives and hence that the outcome is the result of bargaining among them. Although this model was derived on the basis of the Yugoslav experience, one can draw many parallels to the decisionmaking process within other firms in transition economies.

From a policy standpoint, these findings demonstrate that Yugoslav firms misallocated resources compared with their allocation by an "ideal" or capitalist firm that equates labor's marginal product to the shadow or reservation wage. They also demonstrate that this misallocation of resources continued after the transition was launched.

The Early Period of Transition: 1991–95

After the process of transition officially started, debates about the role of insiders (workers and managers) in the privatization process became intense. Moreover, policymakers and analysts saw the early period of transition as one in which insiders seized power and economies took on labor-management features in many transition economies (Prašnikar and Svejnar 1991; Commander and Coricelli 1995), resulting in problems of underinvestment brought about by the relatively short time horizon of individual workers. Indeed, in most economies in CEE and the former Soviet Union, investment did fall significantly, led by a decline in enterprise saving.[1] On the other side, real wages fell together with output in the early 1990s but started to rise from about 1992–93 onward in most CEE countries (European Bank for Reconstruction and Development 1996).

Prašnikar and Svejnar (2000) analyzed the investment and wage (or labor cost per worker) behavior of 458 Slovenian firms in 1991–95, a period when firms still had not been privatized but the relevant decisionmakers already knew how they would eventually be privatized. The average firm in their sample employed 301 workers and generated SIT 51 million ($4.7 million) in value added. Interestingly, during the study period, the mean value of gross investment fell short of the legally prescribed mean level of depreciation investment, indicating that unprofitable firms were paying wages and fringe benefits out of funds earmarked for depreciation. The majority of firms in their sample (303) were subsequently privatized to insiders, whereas the remaining 155 firms ended up in external ownership. Firms that were subsequently privatized by the internal buyout method had been on average smaller and less capital intensive than firms that ended up externally privatized. Internal buyout firms were also more profitable, suggesting that insiders had been able to cherry-pick the firms that they subsequently privatized.

In almost 20 percent of firms, the general manager established their own private (so-called bypass) firms before this was limited by the introduction of the so-called competition clause in the statutes of enterprises in 1993. These firms were relatively capital intensive, with high value added. They reported high profits and relatively high rates of investment compared with other types of firms. Although it was widely perceived that managers were primarily selfishly motivated in establishing bypass firms (which allowed them to siphon off profits and strip assets), Prašnikar and Svejnar (2000) did not find any evidence of such behavior in the period under study.

To assess the process of early restructuring in Slovenian enterprises, Prašnikar and Svejnar (2000) carried out the analysis in a way that permitted them to examine the wage-investment tradeoff, as well as to compare the investment and wage behavior of firms in transition economies with that observed in firms operating in market economies. That study reported that enterprise investment is positively linked to cash flow (supporting the credit rationing hypothesis) and negatively linked to labor costs, suggesting a strong tradeoff between investment and wages in Slovenian firms during the early transition before they were privatized. The estimated earnings equation confirms that firms in the 1991–95 period were still behaving much as they did before, and that employees were still able to appropriate part of the firms' surplus in the form of additional wages. Workers were also able to appropriate some of the funds that firms were legally obliged to use for depreciation investment. Prašnikar and Svejnar (2000) proved that, early in the transition before firms were privatized, the reduction of government influence over firms, in the absence of developed factor markets when firms still held market power resulted in rent sharing by workers and higher wages at the expense of net and gross investment.

The Postprivatization Period: 1996–2002

The behavior of enterprises in the postprivatization period was heavily influenced by which method of privatization was used.[2]

Domadenik, Prašnikar, and Svejnar (2003) and Domadenik (2003) analyzed ownership structure in 130 and 157 large and medium-size privatized firms in the periods 1996–98 and 1996–2000, respectively. They divided owners into several ownership groups, which were assumed to pursue the same strategy. Analysis of the firms' ownership structure reveals that internal owners owned the largest share on average, with almost 35 percent in 1996, although their share fell sharply, to 25 percent, in 2000 because of the decreasing ownership share of non-managerial employees (Figure 15.1). On the other hand, managers slightly increased their share. The most striking trend was the growing ownership share held by other nonfinancial firms, especially in 1999 and 2000. The state funds, as expected, decreased their share, although many studies argue that the withdrawal of the state (indirectly through the state funds) has been slow (see, for example, Gregorič, Prašnikar, and Ribnikar 2000). On the other hand, the privatized investment funds obviously did not play their assigned role as efficient intermediaries to strategic investors but rather kept their shares within firms and played the role of active owner.

In the above sample, 49 percent of firms chose the external privatization method, and the remaining 51 percent opted for internal privatization. Although internal privatization was the preferred strategy of firms, especially among those that had enjoyed sound economic

FIGURE 15.1 OWNERSHIP STRUCTURE IN A SAMPLE OF
LARGE AND MEDIUM-SIZE PRIVATIZED
FIRMS, 1996–2000

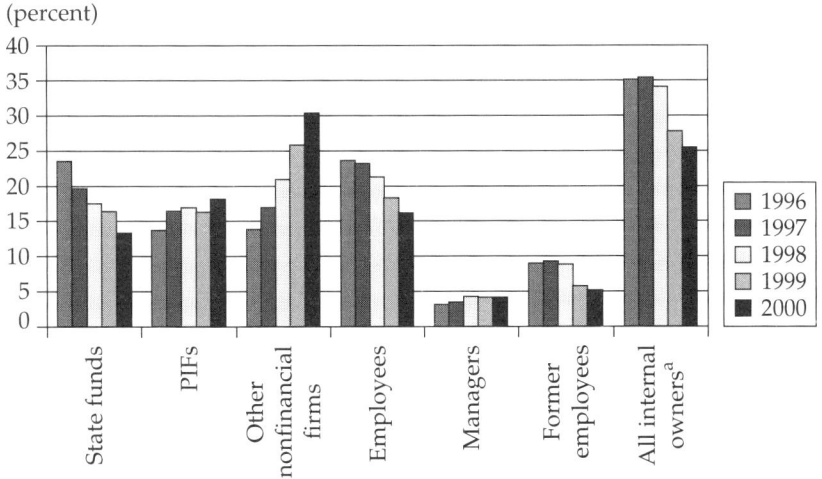

a. Employees, former employees, and managers.
Source: Domadenik (2003).

performance, the largest firms were too big and owned too much valuable capital for this to be done. Many studies report that there were no differences in economic efficiency between internally and externally privatized firms (see, for example, Prašnikar and others 2002). But the interesting trends in ownership structure were observed in the second half of the 1990s. The share of internal owners decreased dramatically in the case of internally privatized firms, but in those same firms, managers increased their share by more than half, from 4.3 percent to 6.6 percent. On the other hand, externally privatized firms were more interesting targets for takeovers, probably because of the power of insiders in decisionmaking in insider-owned firms.

In Slovenian firms, employees have a significant role in decision-making within the firm because they are represented on the firm's supervisory board, as entitled through their part ownership and through the Codetermination Act. The structure of supervisory boards in the sample of firms discussed above (see Domadenik, Prašnikar, and Svejnar 2003 for a detailed description) reveals that, on average, insiders and their representatives held half or more of the seats on the board in the first three years under study. For firms with more than 1,000 employees, it was even required by law (under the Codetermination Act, starting in 1993) that more than 50 percent of supervisory board members be chosen by insiders.[3] In 1999 and 2000, when the largest increase in the share of other nonfinancial firms was detected, the supervisory board structure also changed in favor of members appointed by external owners.

Many contributors to the literature on transition (see, for example, Carlin and others 1995; Claessens and Djankov 1999; and Djankov and Murrell 2002, for reviews) argue that the success of the restructuring process depends crucially on removing old managers who had been appointed under the old system, usually for political rather than economic reasons, and replacing them with new, younger managers who know how to run a firm in a market environment. Slovenia is the classic counterexample to this argument. Summary statistics on management turnover show very low variability in the period 1996–2000. The firms in the sample, on average, employed 8.94 top managers, increasing from 8.6 in 1996 to 9.6 in 2000. In the same period an average of 0.8 top managers (less than 10 percent of the total) were replaced. More than 60 percent of top managers in the sampled firms had a university degree, rising to almost 70 percent in 2000 (Figure 15.2). The percentage of young (less than 45 years old) and new managers (with the firm for less than five years) was found to be slightly increasing, to 52 percent and almost 20 percent, respectively, in 2000. Correspondingly, the percentage of managers with more than 16 years of service in the firm decreased slightly, to 44.5 percent.

Domadenik and others (2003) and Domadenik (2003) discuss the postprivatization restructuring of Slovenian firms using a framework

FIGURE 15.2 CHARACTERISTICS OF TOP MANAGEMENT IN A
SAMPLE OF LARGE AND MEDIUM-SIZE
PRIVATIZED FIRMS, 1996–2000

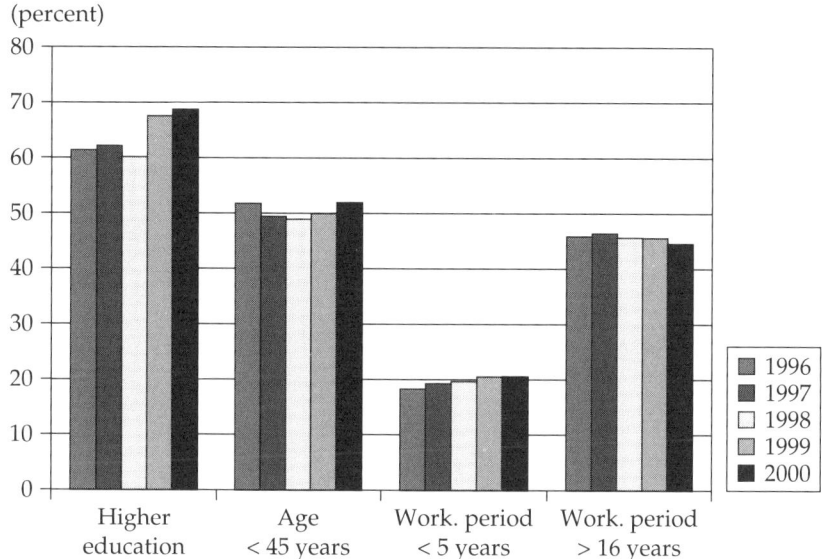

Source: Domadenik (2003).

that follows the original contribution of Roland (1996, 2000) and
Grosfeld and Roland (1997). He divided the restructuring process of
transition firms into two types: defensive (cost-related) restructuring
and strategic (revenue-focused) restructuring. Whereas defensive
restructuring deals with rehabilitating or eliminating unprofitable
activities, strategic restructuring includes investment in developing
firms' primary capabilities to gain comparative advantage. Domadenik
and others (2003) and Domadenik (2003) studied defensive restructuring by applying a labor demand model to estimate how quickly
firms were adjusting their payrolls in response to changes in wages
and in sales. Strategic restructuring crucially depends on firms' investment in fixed capital (buildings and equipment) and in "soft" capital
(research and development, marketing, management, human resources).
Soft investment can play just as important a role as fixed capital
investment, as was clearly shown when Slovenian firms lost a substantial part of their markets in SFR Yugoslavia almost overnight at
the beginning of the transition (Prašnikar, Svejnar, and Domadenik
2000). In 1996 the large privatized Slovenian firms on average invested
about 10 percent of their sales revenue in fixed and soft capital.

The estimated model of labor adjustment and the calculated elasticities for the period 1996–98 (Domadenik and others 2003) indicate that although firms' defensive (immediate) adjustment in employment was sizable, it was not complete, and that their gradual adjustment over time, associated with strategic restructuring, was both sizable and statistically significant. The impact of the number of employees in the previous period was large, and the estimated elasticities of labor demand with respect to sales and wages were lower than in other CEE economies where such analyses have been conducted (Czech Republic, Hungary, and Poland). The analysis also points to slower defensive restructuring in cases where employees have a higher percentage of their representatives on the supervisory board; this indicates the effect of rigid labor market regulations, including provisions on obligatory membership of workers on the board. Ownership structure did not have any significant effect on the level of employment in the period under study. Also, the later study (Domadenik 2003) confirmed the findings of slow labor adjustment but did not find any statistically significant effect of employee participation on supervisory boards.

Concerning strategic restructuring, firm-level data from 157 large and medium-size enterprises reveal that fixed and soft capital investments tended to increase over the period 1996–2000 (Table 15.1). On average, firms spent almost 6 percent of their revenue on fixed capital investment in 1996 and 8 percent in 2000. Fixed capital investment as a percentage of sales revenue declined in relative terms in 2000 from its level in 1999, but in absolute figures it increased by almost 4 percent in real terms and 10 percent in nominal terms, compared with the 1996 figure. Research and development (R&D) and marketing expenses were rising and amounted to about 3 percent and 6 percent of net sales in 2000, respectively. Compared with figures from 1996, this contributed to an 81 percent increase in real R&D expenditure and a 232 percent increase in real marketing expenditure.[4] Firms, on average,

TABLE 15.1 EXPENDITURE ON FIXED AND SOFT CAPITAL
INVESTMENT

(percent of net sales)

Year	Fixed capital	R&D	Marketing	Training
1996	5.81	1.94	4.40	0.34
1997	6.54	2.06	4.54	0.28
1998	6.92	2.18	4.82	0.33
1999	8.55	2.47	5.88	0.24
2000	7.89	2.83	6.01	0.26

Note: Data are for 157 large and medium-size Slovenian enterprises.
Source: Domadenik (2003).

invested less than 0.5 percent of net sales in training in the period under study, but in absolute terms, expenses for external training increased by 72 percent in 2000 compared with 1996.[5]

The firms in the sample financed almost 75 percent of their fixed capital investment in 2000 with internal funds (retained profits, depreciation, and disinvestment). The share of loans in their total financing increased slightly in the period under study, from almost 19 percent in 1996 to more than 21 percent in 2000. Similarly, aggregate data for 1996 show that 75 percent of total investment was financed by the enterprise's own funds, 16.5 percent by loans, and 7 percent from funds provided by government institutions. In 1999 the proportion financed by the enterprise's own funds decreased to 66 percent of the total investment bill, while the proportion of loans increased to 19 percent and funds provided by government institutions to 11 percent (Statistical Office of the Republic of Slovenia 2001).

An even more profound shift in favor of internal financing is seen in the case of R&D investment. Firms in the sample covered more than 90 percent of their total R&D expenses from internal funds, whereas the percentage of loans slightly decreased, and funds provided by governmental institutions are now showing a weak but positive upward trend. In the aggregate, among firms in manufacturing that reported R&D activities in 1998, on average 92.7 percent of total R&D expense was covered by internal funds; the state contribution was a mere 1.7 percent. The state contribution almost doubled, however, from 1996 until 1998, to SIT 835 million (Statistical Office of the Republic of Slovenia 2001).

The greater part of funds for R&D in the sampled firms was spent either on the improvement of existing products and technologies (35.5 percent in 2000 and 34.3 percent in 1996) or on the introduction of new products (30.5 percent in 2000 and 32.6 percent in 1996). The share of R&D devoted to basic research into new products and technologies exhibits a downward trend, indicating that firms are risk averse and prefer to spend their R&D funds on less risky projects.

The investment activity of firms in an economy in transition might depend on the institutional framework. With the financial system still underdeveloped and capital markets unable to provide sufficient funds for successful restructuring, firms should rely more on internally generated funds. However, the important role of employees in the decisionmaking process in Slovenia and other transition economies might introduce bargaining for funds that can be used either to pay higher wages or to finance necessary investment. The estimation framework of the investment equation corresponds to those tested in Western industrial economies, but it also enables one to draw parallels with the empirical study of Prašnikar and Svejnar (2000), which tackles the problem of preprivatization restructuring of Slovenian firms.

As already mentioned, empirical study of the investment behavior of Slovenian firms during the early years of transition (1991–95), before privatization, confirmed the cash flow and bargaining hypotheses (Prašnikar and Svejnar 2000). In a context of underdeveloped financial markets, investment in fixed capital depended on internally generated funds and on bargaining between workers and managers over the allocation of value added to wages and fringe benefits or to investment. However, the study of Domadenik and others (2003), which analyzed postprivatization investment behavior in the period 1996–98, led to somewhat different conclusions. Among its findings were the following: First, the data give considerable but not complete support to the notion that firms' restructuring through investment is consistent with profit-maximizing behavior. This is reflected in investment being positively related to the demand for a firm's products in the domestic or the foreign market. Although firms rely primarily on internal financing to fund most of their investment, the evidence that restructuring through investment depends positively on the firm's level of internal funds is strong but not conclusive. Slovenian capital markets hence appear to have suffered from imperfections in the second half of the 1990s, and firms may have suffered from credit rationing that impeded the restructuring of the less successful firms.

Second, the ability of a firm's workers to appropriate its internal funds in the form of above-market wages does not appear to adversely affect restructuring through investment in fixed capital or training, but a tradeoff between wages and investment is detected with respect to investment in R&D and, less robustly, with respect to investment in marketing. Third, investment in employee training was small and virtually unrelated to any of the explanatory variables, suggesting that, in the period 1996–98, firms still did not treat employee training as an investment. Fourth, the firm's market orientation (export or domestic), a variable that served as a proxy for the level of competition, was found to be unrelated to investment activity. This evidence may suggest that the corresponding relationship between restructuring and competition is not monotonic but rather inverse U-shaped, as suggested by Carlin and others (2003). In this case the linear regression yields insignificant results. It may also be that Slovenian firms that are internationally oriented and sell a significant proportion of their production on the domestic market are the leaders in restructuring, whereas firms in a monopolistic position (selling only on the domestic market) lack sufficient motivation to engage in restructuring. On the other hand, there is a group of firms that face severe international competition yet have low market power (cost competitiveness), resulting in low profit margins and retained earnings. This group of firms is indeed the victim of underdeveloped capital markets, with low investment in R&D, marketing, and training (Prašnikar and others 2003).

The study by Domadenik (2003) on a sample of 157 firms in 1996–2000 confirms the findings from the 1996–98 period. By estimating an augmented error correction model that proxies a long-term relationship, and a neoclassical model that is short term, the credit rationing hypothesis in the case of fixed capital investment received full support in the case of short-term but not in the case of long-term impact. The bargaining hypothesis did not receive support in any model, whereas current and past sales contributed significantly to the level of investment. In the case of R&D investment, the picture is more complex, suggesting that firms plan their R&D activities on the basis of the portion of their sales and cash flow that is considered permanent. Although one can find support for credit rationing and bargaining hypotheses in the case of an error correction model (but a zero elasticity of R&D investment with respect to sales), the neoclassical model indicates that lagged sales and current cash flow have a significant positive impact on current R&D, and lagged wages a negative impact. Both hypotheses, credit rationing and bargaining, as well as sales as a significant regressor in the case of the investment equation, were supported in the case of marketing, whereas in the case of training, the variables have the predicted signs but are not statistically significant.

Interestingly, in none of the studies did ownership structure have a significant impact on investment activities or labor adjustment. In the early period after privatization, we were able to detect a small but significant effect of supervisory board structure (the proportion of insiders versus outsiders) on labor adjustment. But this effect obviously vanished in the following years (1999 and 2000). The major determinants that matter in the case of restructuring are linked to institutional structure: underdeveloped capital markets resulting in underprovision of loans (especially for more risky projects such as R&D), and a labor market with centrally set minimum wages and restrictive employment legislation.

One explanation for these findings is, as Prašnikar and Gregorič (2002) have shown, that there exists a "leading" group of internationally oriented firms in Slovenia that accumulate internal resources and are no longer limited by external constraints in obtaining funds for their investment activity. Those firms carried out the largest share of the burden of the Slovenian transition. Many successful and internationally accepted firms in fact took advantage of internal buyouts. Any excessive "employeeistic" behavior would have damaged the international position of these firms. This could be the main reason why their workers behave more like a firm's shareholders than like other stakeholders. In doing so they do not prevent managers from making correct and timely decisions. Moreover, firms with stronger management are more successful at carrying out growth strategies.

CONCLUSIONS

In Slovenia, the restructuring of formerly socially owned firms has been one of the most important stimuli to economic growth in recent decades. The restructuring of firms before their privatization was largely influenced by the previous enterprise self-management system, signaling a steep trade-off between investment and wages. In the period after privatization, empirical evidence suggests that privatized Slovenian firms faced limited defensive restructuring and relatively successful strategic restructuring compared with other transition economies. A group of leading, internationally distinguished Slovenian firms carried a large share of the burden of the Slovenian transition. The adjustment of other firms lagged behind.

In this respect, it is important to note that the restructuring of Slovenian firms in the postprivatization period is taking place under circumstances of underdeveloped markets. Underdeveloped capital markets have resulted especially in the underprovision of financing to more risky projects, whereas the lack of labor market reform (with minimum wages still set in collective bargaining, and with restrictive employment legislation) has resulted in a trade-off between wages and investment, slow labor adjustment, and increasing discrepancies between tradable industries (which are more competitive and mainly outward-oriented) and nontradable industries (which are less competitive and mainly inward-oriented). The state should withdraw from the productive sector more quickly than it is doing and should abandon its paternalistic role, as manifested in slow institutional changes on capital and labor markets. The window of opportunity is getting smaller, and the political will for necessary reforms is diminishing. However, further microeconomic reforms not only will induce faster economic growth, but are also important in the context of approaching EU membership.

REFERENCES

Aghion, P., O. Blanchard, and R. Burgess. 1996. "The Behaviour of State Firms in Eastern Europe Pre-Privatisation." *European Economic Review* 38(6): 132–49.

Angelucci, M., A. A. Bevan, S. Estrin, J. A. Fennema, B. Kuznetsov, G. Mangiarotti, and M. Schaffer. 2002. "The Determinants of Privatized Enterprise Performance in Russia." CEPR Discussion Paper 3193. Centre for Economic Policy Research, London.

Brown, D., and J. Earle. 2000. "Privatisation and Restructuring in Russia: New Evidence from Panel Data on Industrial Enterprises." RECEP Working Papers 1. RECEP, Moscow.

Carlin, W., J. Van Reenen, and T. Wolfe. 1995. "Enterprise Restructuring in Early Transition: The Case Study Evidence." *Economics of Transition* 3(4): 427–58.

Carlin, W., S. Frier, M. Schaffer, and P. Seabright. 2000. "Competition and Enterprise Performance in Transition Economies: Evidence from a Cross-Country Survey." Paper presented at the CEPR/WDI Annual International Conference on Transition Economies, Moscow, July 2–5.

————. 2003. "Competition, Restructuring and Firm Performance: Evidence of an Inverted U-Relationship from a Cross-Country Survey of Firms in Transition Economies." Draft version available at www.ucl.ac.uk/~uctpa36/progress.htm.

Claessens, S., and S. Djankov. 1999. "Enterprise Performance and Management Turnover in the Czech Republic." *European Economic Review* 43: 1115–24.

Commander, S., and F. Coricelli. 1995. *Unemployment, Restructuring, and the Labor Market in Eastern Europe and Russia.* Washington, D.C.: World Bank.

Djankov, S., and V. G. Kreacic. 1998. "Restructuring of Manufacturing Firms in Georgia: Four Case Studies and a Survey." World Bank Occasional Paper. Washington, D.C.

Djankov, S., and P. Murrell. 2002. "Enterprise Restructuring in Transition: Quantitative Survey." Working Paper. World Bank, Washington, D.C.

Djankov, S., and G. Pohl. 1997. "Restructuring of Large Firms in Slovakia." World Bank Occasional Paper. Washington, D.C.

Domadenik, P. 2003. "Defensive and Strategic Restructuring of Firms in Transition Economies: The Case of Slovenia." Ph.D. dissertation, University of Ljubljana.

Domadenik, P., J. Prašnikar, and J. Svejnar. 2003. "Defensive and Strategic Restructuring of Firms During the Transition to a Market Economy." William Davidson Institute Working Paper 541. William Davidson Institute at the University of Michigan Business School, Ann Arbor.

Estrin, S. 1983. *Self Management: Economic Theory and Yugoslav Practice.* New York: Cambridge University Press.

Estrin, S., and J. Svejnar. 1993. "Wage Determination in Labor-Managed Firms under Market-Oriented Reforms: Estimates of Static and Dynamic Models." *Journal of Comparative Economics* 17(3): 687–700.

European Bank for Reconstruction and Development. 1995. *Transition Report 1995.* London.

————. 1996. *Transition Report 1996.* London.

Filer, R., T. Gylfason, S. Jurajda, and J. Mitchell. 2001. "Markets and Growth in the Post-Communist World." GDN Study. Global Development Network, Prague.

Furubotn, E., and S. Pejovich. 1970. "Property Rights and the Behaviour of the Firm in a Socialist State: The Example of Yugoslavia." *Zeitschrift für Nationalökonomie* 30: 430–54.

Gregorič, A., J. Prašnikar, and I. Ribnikar. 2000. "Corporate Governance in Transitional Economies: The Case of Slovenia." *Economic and Business Review* 2(3): 183–207.

Grosfeld, I., and G. Roland. 1997. "Defensive and Strategic Restructuring in Central European Enterprises." *Journal of Transforming Economies and Societies* 3: 21–46.

Grosfeld, I., and T. Tressel. 2002. "Competition, Corporate Governance: Substitutes or Complements? Evidence from Warsaw Stock Exchange." *Economics of Transition* 10(3): 525–51.

Gupta, N., J. Ham, and J. Svejnar. 2000. "Priorities and Sequencing in Privatization: Theory and Evidence from the Czech Republic." William Davidson Institute Working Paper 323. William Davidson Institute at the University of Michigan Business School, Ann Arbor.

Jones, D., M. Klinedienst, and C. Rock. 1998. "Productive Efficiency During Transition: Evidence from Bulgarian Panel Data." *Journal of Comparative Economics* 26(3): 446–64.

Konings, J. 1998. "Firm Performance in Bulgaria and Estonia: The Effects of Competitive Pressure, Financial Pressure and Disorganisation." William Davidson Institute Working Paper Series 185. William Davidson Institute at the University of Michigan Business School, Ann Arbor.

Megginson, W., and J. Netter. 2001. "From State to Market: A Survey of Empirical Studies on Privatization." *Journal of Economic Literature* 39: 321–89.

Pinto, B., M. Belka, and S. Krajewski. 1993. "Transforming State Enterprises in Poland: Evidence on Adjustment by Manufacturing Firms." *Brookings Papers on Economic Activity: Macroeconomics*, 213–69.

Prašnikar, J., and A. Gregorič. 2002. "The Influence of Workers' Participation on the Power of Management in Transitional Countries: The Case of Slovenia." *Annals of Public and Cooperative Economics* 73(2): 269–97.

Prašnikar, J., and J. Svejnar. 1988. "Enterprise Behavior in Yugoslavia." *Advances in the Economic Analysis of Participatory and Labor Managed Firms* 3: 237–311.

————. 1991. "Workers' Participation in Management vs. Social Ownership and Government Policies: Lessons for Transforming Socialist Economies." *Comparative Economic Studies* 4: 27–45.

————. 2000. "Investment, Wages and Ownership During the Transition to a Market Economy: Evidence from Slovenian Firms." RCEF Working Paper 79. University of Ljubljana, Faculty of Economics.

Prašnikar, J., J. Svejnar, and P. Domadenik. 2000. "Enterprise in Post-Privatisation Period: Firm-Level Evidence for Slovenia." *East European Economics* 38(5): 60–92.

Prašnikar, J., J. Svejnar, D. Mihajlek, and V. Prašnikar. 1994. "A Test of Enterprise Behavior under Yugoslav Labor-Management." *Review of Economics and Statistics* 4: 728–41.

Prašnikar, J., W. Bartlett, P. Domadenik, and V. Markovska. 2002. "The Productivity Analyses of Slovenian and Macedonian Firms." RCEF Working Paper 130. University of Ljubljana, Faculty of Economics.

Prašnikar, J., V. Bole, A. Ahcan, and M. Koman. 2003. "Sensitivity of the Exporting Economy on the External Shocks: Evidence from Slovene Firms." Paper presented at the 8th Conference on Economics in Transition, Budapest, July.

Roland, G. 1996. "Economic Efficiency and Political Constraints in Privatisation and Restructuring." Paper presented at the Policy Studies to Promote Private Sector Development workshop, European Bank for Reconstruction and Development, London.

————. 2000. *Transition and Economics: Politics, Firms, Markets.* Cambridge, Mass.: MIT Press.

Shirley, M., and P. Walsh. 2000. "Public versus Private Ownership: The Current State of the Debate." Policy Research Working Paper 2420. World Bank, Washington, D.C.

Statistical Office of the Republic of Slovenia. 2001. *Statistical Yearbook of the Republic of Slovenia.* Ljubljana.

Stiglitz, J. 1999. "Whither Reform? Ten Years of Transition." Paper presented at the Annual World Bank Conference on Development Economics, World Bank, Washington.

Svejnar, J. 2002. "Transition Economies: Performance and Challenges." *The Journal of Economic Perspectives* 16(2): 3–28.

Vanek, J. 1970. *The General Theory of Labor-Managed Market Economies.* Ithaca, N.Y.: Cornell University Press.

NOTES

1. The European Bank for Reconstruction and Development, for instance, estimates that between 1985 and 1993 gross fixed investment declined from 29.5 percent to 19 percent in the former Soviet Union, and from 24 percent to 18 percent in Eastern Europe (European Bank for Reconstruction and Development 1995).

2. See Chapter 14 for a detailed description of the privatization process in Slovenia.

3. According to the Codetermination Act, in firms with between 500 and 1,000 employees, at least one-third of supervisory board members had to be workers' representatives, whereas in companies with more than 1,000 employees the requirement was at least one-half; see Prašnikar and Gregorič (2002) for an analysis of the influence of worker participation on the power of management in Slovenian firms. According to new legislation passed in 2001, the number of workers' representatives on a supervisory board can neither be less than one-third nor more than one-half.

4. Aggregate data for all Slovenian firms, collected by the Statistical Office of the Republic of Slovenia, reveal that expenses for fixed capital investment and intangibles rose, on average, by 19 percent yearly. Investment in the manufacturing sector contributed 65.1 percent to total investment and rose by 11 percent on average on a yearly basis. Moreover, data show a substantial

increase in R&D and marketing expenses. (See Domadenik 2003 for an analysis of data taken from the *Statistical Yearbook of the Republic of Slovenia* 2001).

5. In the same period, cash flow in the representative firm increased by 83 percent and wages per employee by 8 percent in real terms. Interestingly, the difference between paid wages and employees' reservation wage increased by 7.5 percent by 1998 but decreased in the subsequent year. Compared with 1996, the difference in 2000 was lower by almost 7 percent. Obviously, firms on average increased their expenditure on marketing, whereas investment in R&D and training increased almost proportionally to the increase in augmented cash flow.

Chapter 16
The Banking Sector

Franjo Štiblar and Marko Voljč

Slovenia, alone among the transition economies, did not suffer a crisis in its banking sector in the 1990s. Rehabilitation of the sector after independence was undertaken according to the Western model for rich countries, using government budget resources and government intervention. Rehabilitation was succesfully completed in 1997, so that banking became one of the three pillars of the successful financial transformation of the Slovenian economy, the other two being an independent central bank with a prudent monetary policy, and a prudent fiscal policy with a budget close to balance.

Slovenia opted for a universal banking system with indirect financing to play the predominant role in the financial sector. The stock exchange, although technically well developed, plays a minor role, and the insurance sector lags behind banking in its transformation. Banking accounts for approximately 65 percent of the total financial sector assets, insurance 10 percent, and the capital market (the stock exchange) 25 percent. In 2001 banking assets were equivalent to 85 percent of GDP, the gross insurance premium per capita was €530, and total gross insurance premiums were equivalent to 5.1 percent of GDP. The average volume of premiums per insurer was €67 million. Market capitalization of the stock exchange equaled 28 percent of GDP, and annual turnover was 20 percent of market capitalization.

This chapter discusses the transition of the Slovenian banking sector since independence and the challenges it is expected to face in the future. The chapter consists of four parts. The first presents a historical perspective on banking in Slovenia. The second describes the rehabilitation and privatization of the sector, and the third its development since independence. The chapter ends with some perspectives on the future of the banking sector upon Slovenia's accession to the European Union.

HISTORICAL PERSPECTIVE

Slovenia has a long tradition of sound banking. The first incorporated domestic bank, Ljubljanska Banka, was established in 1900, when the Slovenian territory was still part of the Austro-Hungarian Empire. Slovenian banks were strongholds in the economic boom of the region in the early 1920s, survived the crisis of the early 1930s, and continued to operate during World War II. They were abolished as independent commercial banks during the early socialist period from 1945 to 1960. During the period of economic reform that began in 1965, they reemerged as profit-oriented financial institutions, but later they were converted into captive financial service providers to self-managed enterprises. Only later, in the 1980s, did banks increasingly regain the role of for-profit financial institutions.

Since the early 1990s the economy of Slovenia has been experiencing major changes due to the dissolution of SFR Yugoslavia and the transformation from a socialist economy based on labor self-management to a capitalist market economy. These changes have had a profound effect on the large "old banks" that had been formally owned by enterprises. Smaller "new banks" started to emerge shortly before Slovenia proclaimed its independence in June 1991. The "old banks" in Slovenia suffered enormously from the dissolution of SFR Yugoslavia. Even as they were losing assets in other parts of the former federation, they remained saddled with joint and several liability for obligations to SFR Yugoslavia's foreign creditors. They also suffered from an increasing share of nonperforming loans to enterprises hit hard by the dissolution of the country and by the transformation depression.

Certain salient features of Slovenian banking—including the early introduction of a two-tier banking system in the late 1950s, the ownership of banks by enterprises, and openness to the world—led to a unique starting point for the country's banks at the beginning of transition in the 1990s. Later they also paved the way for specific solutions in the area of bank restructuring.

REHABILITATION AND PRIVATIZATION

The rehabilitation of the major Slovenian banks was a central element in the restructuring of the financial sector. Rehabilitation was needed because of the banks' heavy losses and their liquidity and solvency problems. Most of the costs of Slovenia's independence and transition ended up being concentrated as a "black hole" in the banking sector. The two largest "old banks" were placed in formal rehabilitation status at the beginning of 1993, and a third, smaller bank followed at the beginning of 1994. These three banks accounted for more than half of the entire banking sector, making bank restructuring in Slovenia a venture of unprecedented scope. The main objectives of the rehabilitation were the following: to achieve capital adequacy according to international standards, to achieve positive cash flow and current operating income, to reduce banking interest rates, to regain credibility in international financial markets, and to introduce the basic principles of prudential behavior.

Slovenia's unique initial conditions, both macroeconomically (a newly established open market economy with a small monetary area) and microeconomically within the banking sector, led to the choice of a mixed centralized-decentralized approach to bank rehabilitation. The bad assets of the banks were swapped for government bonds through the state Bank Rehabilitation Agency (BRA), which became the owner of banks, but not full owner, thus forcing the banks to engage in intensive internal rehabilitation as well. The BRA, established in 1991, played a major role in the supervision of banks in rehabilitation, in the management of bad assets, and in the management of part of the public debt, through its servicing of government bonds swapped for bad bank assets.

By the end of 1996 these banks had been successfully rehabilitated, and their rehabilitation status was ended in mid-1997. Slovenia succeeded in stabilizing the economy and rehabilitating the banks (and later the insurance sector) without major formal involvement of the international financial institutions. The only exception was the 1993 EFSAL (Enterprise and Financial Sector Adjustment Loan) arrangement with the World Bank, which had a bank rehabilitation and restructuring component. Thus, strict external conditionalities did not play an important role in the restructuring of the banking sector or later in bank privatization, the second phase of which was delayed several times by the government.

The procedure adopted for the banks put into rehabilitation included the following four steps: a write-off of current losses, a swap of bad assets for BRA or state bonds, the transfer of bad assets to the BRA, and the engagement of the BRA as temporary owner (supervisor) as delegated by government decree. Five interventions by the state were of particular importance. The first was a swap of bad assets for rehabilitation bonds in January 1993. The second was the establishment of Nova Ljubljanska Banka (NLB) and Nova Kreditna Banka Maribor (NKBM) in July 1994, whereby the old banks retained claims and liabilities associated with Slovenia's succession to the former SFR Yugoslavia. The third was the exchange, in October 1995, of rehabilitation bonds denominated in foreign currency for bonds denominated in tolars. The fourth was the resolution of the issue of unconfirmed debt swaps under the New Financing Agreement with the London Club of international commercial banks in February 1996. The final intervention was the ending of the banks' rehabilitation status in June 1997.

Bank rehabilitation in Slovenia was slow in getting started but well thought through, with much learning by doing. The partial carving out of bad assets had a net positive effect, and cooperation among the key players (the Bank of Slovenia, the BRA, the Ministry of Finance, and the banks themselves) was satisfactory. Banks in rehabilitation achieved improvements in their corporate governance, organization, lending procedures, loan monitoring and recovery, and risk assessment. The Bank of Slovenia's liquidity support was not always adequate, leading to overly high interest rates in the market. External advice and experience were helpful in designing and implementing the rehabilitation program, although that advice was taken selectively, and specific domestic solutions were implemented as well.

The cost of bank rehabilitation can be measured by the amount of public debt attributable to the operation. Slovenia issued approximately DM 1.9 billion in bonds, less than 10 percent of GDP at that time, for bank rehabilitation. This is estimated to be an acceptable price for the rehabilitation of more than half the country's banking sector, especially when compared with the costs of similar operations in Western industrial economies. Of this amount, the rehabilitation of the largest bank, NLB, accounted for roughly half. For comparison, the sale of 34 percent of NLB to the Belgian company KBC in 2002 brought the state €435 million. This implies that the total market value of NLB in that year was more than twice the cost of its rehabilitation. This was the result of well-designed and well-implemented bank rehabilitation at the macroeconomic level (by the Ministry of Finance, the BRA, and the central bank) as well as the successful self-rehabilitation of the NLB at the microeconomic level.

The major results of Slovenia's bank rehabilitation, as observed at the end of the process in 1997, can be summarized as follows. First, as already noted, the public debt of the country increased by DM 1.9 billion, although later this debt was reduced through partial recoveries on bad loans by the BRA. Second, the share of bad assets in the entire banking sector portfolio was reduced from 10 percent to less than 4 percent, while at the same time the share of loans of the highest classification increased from less than 80 percent to 89 percent. As a consequence, the banking sector started to report profits instead of losses and achieved a much more normal structure of its balance sheet than in the past. Third, the banks in rehabilitation registered a positive capital of DM 850 million in 1997, compared with negative capital of DM 1,500 million in 1992. Their combined capital adequacy ratio increased to more than 12 percent, and their returns on equity and on assets were above the average for the banking sector as a whole. The rehabilitated banks have also introduced significant institutional and organizational improvements and better management of human resources.

After the rehabilitation process was completed, preparations were made for the privatization of the two large rehabilitated banks. This included the transfer of their ownership from the BRA back to the state, the appointment of an interim professional supervisory board, and clarification of the legal framework through legislation and decrees for privatization.

The major objectives of privatization were to find active owners and to generate cash in order to retire public debt. The process was also expected to be quick and transparent. The privatization process was carried out through a tender. However, only one of the two tenders—that for privatization of the NLB—was successful, and that only in part. After completion of this stage of NLB's privatization, its ownership structure was as follows: KBC obtained 34 percent, the European Bank for Reconstruction and Development 5 percent, and other private owners 17 percent; the remainder is still in state or quasi-state ownership. Tender for the second-largest bank, NKBM, was not successful in 2002; thus, for the time being, it remains in 100 percent state ownership.

Slovenia decided that the privatization of state banks was necessary but should be done gradually, in keeping with all the other institutional reforms in the country's transition. Because the country's budget is not in urgent need of receipts from privatization, banks will be privatized only if and when a suitable offer from suitable foreign institutions is made.

BANK PERFORMANCE DURING THE TRANSITION

All of Slovenia's basic laws on banking were enacted in the package of constitutional laws on the day of independence, June 25, 1991. The new legislation brought the country's system of bank regulation closer to modern standards. The new banking law adopted in February 1999 took a step further toward the requirements of the EU *acquis communautaire*. The provisions of the EU Second Banking Directive will enter into force when Slovenia formally becomes a member of the European Union in May 2004.

The regulatory framework for the banking sector was liberalized gradually. Throughout the transition, the sector has been open to entry by foreign banks. Initially, foreign banks were only allowed to establish subsidiaries, but starting in 1999 they were permitted to operate branches as well. To date only one (Austrian) bank has opened a branch in Slovenia. There are four banks with majority foreign capital, and over half of Slovenia's banks have some foreign ownership participation. Until May 2004 the licensing of foreign banks remains at the discretion of the Bank of Slovenia, which relies in making its decision on reciprocal treatment with the foreign country and a positive report on the investor by the home country regulator. At present, foreigners control about one-third of assets in the banking sector, making Slovenia the only transition economy in which banking is not yet majority foreign-owned.

Over the first 12 years of independence, the Slovenian banking sector has experienced slow but continuous growth and deepening. Table 16.1 presents some basic statistics. Before independence Slovenia had 16 banks. This figure had more than doubled at the peak in mid-1994 and later declined steadily to 19 at the end of 2002. Four of these banks are part of the NLB Group, so that the number of independent banks is only 15—close to the number planned by the Bank of Slovenia at the beginning of the 1990s.

TABLE 16.1 BASIC STATISTICS FOR THE BANKING SECTOR, 1991–2002[a]

| Year | No. of banks | No. of employees | Billions of tolars | | | | Exchange rate (tolars per euro) |
			Capital	Assets	Costs	Profit	
1991	26	—	63	327	—	—	—
1992	30	—	103	628	16.26	–15.52	105.07
1993	32	—	142	937	22.18	0.34	132.28
1994	33	—	220	1,174	36.83	4.67	152.36
1995	31	—	263	1,493	44.69	15.17	153.12
1996	30	10,317	285	1,799	52.03	15.75	169.51
1997	29	10,417	320	2,094	60.22	19.60	180.40
1998	24	10,386	355	2,412	73.71	21.91	186.27
1999	24	10,455	392	2,763	84.79	17.66	193.63
2000	24	10,929	444	3,270	98.85	31.05	205.03
2001	20	11,258	481	4,041	110.51	9.91	217.19
2002	19	—	530	4,586	132.39	47.22	226.22

— Not available.

a. All data are as of the end of the year.

Source: Bank of Slovenia data.

Surprisingly, and contrary to general trends in Western industrial economies, employment in the Slovenian banking sector increased at the beginning of the current decade, after stagnating at 10,000 employees (1.3 percent of total employment in Slovenia) throughout the 1990s. This increase is probably transitory. Modern e-banking is apparently only in its early stages.

Between 1991 and 2002, bank capital increased 8.4 times, and the assets of the banking sector 14 times, both in nominal terms. Between 1992 and 2002 the operating costs of the banking sector increased 8.2 times, and profits improved from SIT –15 billion to +47 billion. In euro terms, capital increased from €1 billion in 1992 to €2.34 billion in 2002, while assets increased from €6 billion to €20 billion; operating costs rose meanwhile from €150 million to €580 million; and a loss of €140 million in 1992 became a profit of €208 million in 2002. Table 16.2 provides an overview of basic financial indicators for the Slovenian banking sector during 1992–2002.

The income efficiency of banks was almost continuously on the rise during the 1992–2002 period; exceptions were in 1999 and especially in 2001 with losses in the SKB bank, the third-largest bank in Slovenia at that time. The return on equity exceeded 10 percent in 2002 and the return on assets was close to 1 percent in most recent years. Cost efficiency deteriorated in the first half of the observation period but improved toward its initial levels in the second half. The

TABLE 16.2 BASIC FINANCIAL RATIOS FOR THE BANKING SECTOR, 1992–2002
(percent)

Year	Return on equity	Return on assets	Assets-to-capital ratio	Capital adequacy ratio	Costs-to-assets ratio	Assets-to-GDP ratio	Concentration[a]
1992	−15.1	−2.5	6.1	—	2.59	—	69.1
1993	0.2	0.0	6.6	—	2.37	—	66.9
1994	2.7	0.4	6.9	17.8	3.14	—	56.9
1995	7.2	1.0	7.0	19.5	2.99	67	59.1
1996	6.3	0.9	7.3	18.2	2.89	70	59.9
1997	7.1	1.0	7.6	17.6	2.11	72	60.0
1998	7.5	1.0	6.8	15.6	3.06	74	61.4
1999	5.5	0.7	7.0	14.0	3.07	75	61.3
2000	8.8	1.1	7.4	12.6	3.02	75	60.8
2001	2.5	0.3	8.4	12.8	2.74	85	67.4
2002	11.5	1.1	8.7	—	2.89	87	68.4

— Not available.

a. Share of the five largest banks in total assets.

Sources: Bank of Slovenia internal documents; authors' calculations.

cost-to-assets ratio is now below 3 percent (but not all costs are included, so that the true ratio is higher). World benchmark figures (before the recent consolidation under increased competitive pressure), for comparison, were as follows: return on equity above 10 percent, return on assets about 1 percent, and cost-to-assets about 3 percent. International comparisons for 2000 also show that Slovenian banking was relatively efficient compared with the banking sectors of seven EU members and six other transition economies. It was more efficient than in the latter group and somewhat less efficient than in the former (Štiblar 2001).

The assets-to-capital multiplier increased moderately, from 6.1 to 8.7, between 1992 and 2002, and the capital-to-assets ratio declined accordingly, from 17.8 percent to 12.8 percent between 1994 and 2001—the reason being the fulfillment of the high founding capital requirement imposed by the Bank of Slovenia in the first half of the 1990s. The total assets of banks in Slovenia increased by close to 15 percent in 2002, significantly more than the growth of nominal GDP, indicating further deepening. Nevertheless, the present bank assets-to-GDP ratio of 90 percent still indicates a very shallow banking structure in which further financial deepening can be expected, if the 250 percent average ratio in the EU countries is taken as a benchmark.

The concentration of banks in Slovenia, as measured by the share of the five largest banks in total banking assets, is not extremely high for a small, open economy. That ratio declined substantially, from 69.1 percent to 56.9 percent, during the first half of the 1990s because of disinvestment connected with the rehabilitation of the largest bank, NLB, and two other banks. From 1994 on, concentration again increased continuously, as part of the second phase of bank consolidation, where economies of scale and scope were major driving forces. In 2002 the asset share of the five largest banks reached 68.4 percent, still below the 70 percent observed in some of the larger EU economies, such as the Netherlands.

If €10 billion in assets is taken provisionally as the minimum required size for a bank to engage in international competition (because of economies of scale), total bank assets in Slovenia (€20 billion) provide room for two such large banking groups in the country. Therefore expansion abroad is necessary for Slovenian banks to achieve the required economies of scale. The same is true for other financial institutions as well as for the leading firms in the real sector, if they want to survive as independent legal entities with their final business decisions made in Slovenia. The most appropriate direction for the geographical expansion of Slovenia's banks is southeastward, because of their comparative advantages in the region (existing links, language, common history and culture). Another solution is diversification of financial services in search of economies of scope, including development of bank assurance, investment and private banking, and para-banking services.

What type of ownership structure is most appropriate for banks in Slovenia seeking to be efficient and internationally competitive? Comparative data for 24 banks in Slovenia (divided into three groups: 4 majority foreign-owned banks, 4 state-owned banks, and 16 others) show that, in 2000, the majority foreign-owned banks were less income efficient, paid less in taxes, and were a little better at cost efficiency than the other two groups. These banks had smaller loan-loss provisions and higher commercial bank multiplication. On the other hand, the state-owned banks lacked capital and, together with the majority foreign-owned banks, had higher ownership concentration. Other banks had much more dispersed ownership and were more profitable, despite their lower interest rate margins.

In 2000 the ownership concentration of banks in Slovenia was higher than in companies in the country's real sector; this was expected and is being experienced in other countries as well. In all EU member states, at least 80 percent of leading banks are in domestic ownership, whereas in transition economies, excepting only Slovenia, this share is much lower and in some cases close to zero. In the process of restructuring its banking sector, Slovenia has tried to follow the strategy of the less developed EU countries: it has first consolidated and sought to retain the international competitiveness of the banking sector, and to privatize gradually later, when domestic capital would be sufficient to keep at least some of the larger banks majority owned by domestic institutions capable of contributing efficiently toward the execution of the country's business development strategy.

FUTURE TRENDS

Banking in Slovenia is expected to follow general world trends. That means increasing prudence and supervision to improve confidence, together with the introduction of new banking standards (those of the Bank for International Settlements as well as EU banking directives). Banks will thus become centers of financial advice for customers.

Banking assets are expected to grow in Slovenia at an average annual rate of 12 percent until 2006—slower than the expected 15 percent annual growth of the insurance sector. But since the insurance sector is less than half the size of the banking sector, their relative positions in Slovenia's financial market will not change substantially (Štiblar 2002).

Universal banking is expected to remain the prevailing form of financing in the Slovenian economy in the medium term. The adjustment of the term structure from shorter-term deposits to longer-term loans will be accomplished through foreign banks and the international financial institutions. Slovenian banks will be net receivers of foreign equity investments from Western countries and will be net investors in the less developed countries of southeastern Europe.

The retail business will remain the core of Slovenian banking; therefore, cost efficiency will be lower than in the banking sectors of the large industrial countries of the West. Simple savings and loan institutions, already minor players, will either disappear, be acquired by existing banks, or be transformed into banks. Some will be able to remain independent if they are highly specialized and can find niche positions. Electronic banking will develop in parallel with classic relationship banking, but not replace it entirely, especially if private banking thrives.

Household financing will be developed through securitization. The tax burden for banks will be changed from the taxing of assets to taxing the interest rate earnings of customers, as is usual in Western industrial countries. Nominal interest rates will fully replace the indexation system.

Financial institutions have proved to be the most stable active owners of other financial institutions in banking systems elsewhere in Europe, because of their good understanding of the banking business. Domestic institutions and, later, foreign financial institutions should become important owners of banks in Slovenia. That will put Slovenia in a stronger position as a new member of the European Union and provide a financial foundation for executing the country's strategy regarding development of its social and ecological environment and economic infrastructure within the enlarged European Union.

Slovenia is already fulfilling the requirements of EU membership as they relate to banking legislation (Table 16.3). The Banking Act of 1999 together with the Securities Act (2000), the Insurance Companies Act (2000), and the Central Bank Act (2000) incorporate the *acquis* as determined by EU banking directives. The only exceptions are in the regulation of savings and loan institutions and the development of a deposit insurance scheme; for these the new regime will be delayed for two to three years.

EU membership will affect the Slovenian banking sector, although major shocks are not expected, as adaptation to the competitive environment has already been happening gradually. Further consolidation of the banking sector is expected, with the number of existing banks and banking groups projected to fall from 12 to 15. Foreign ownership will increase toward 50 percent, but not much more, as domestic financial conglomerates are expected to emerge.

In the future the development of Slovenia's new banking services will become increasingly important. Investment banking will grow slowly in the larger banks. Private banking has a long way to go. Bank

TABLE 16.3 HARMONIZATION OF SLOVENIAN LEGISLATION WITH
        EU BANKING DIRECTIVES

Item	EU directive	Slovenia
Minimum starting capital	€5 million	Yes
Capital adequacy	>8 percent of risk-weighted assets	Yes
Nonfinancial investments	<15 percent of capital in one enterprise; <60 percent of own assets in all enterprises	Yes
Large exposure	<10 percent of bank capital	Yes
Connected exposure	<25 percent of bank capital	Yes
Aggregate large exposure	<800 percent of bank capital	Yes
Deposit insurance	€20,000 per account	Yes
Bank supervision	Independent agency	Yes
Licensing	Open entry	Open

Source: Benčina (2003).

activity in insurance markets will grow, especially in the area of life insurance. Financing of small and medium-size enterprises will become an area of fierce competition among banks, as domestic banks will lose the opportunity to serve large international corporations, either to competition from banks abroad or to direct financing through the capital market (Voljč and Šega 2001).

Increased international competition in the banking market at home and abroad will require Slovenia's banks to achieve greater cost and income efficiency. The average return on equity before taxes should increase toward 20 percent, and the return on assets should rise above 1 percent, as measured by international accounting standards. The cost-to-income ratio should decrease to below 60 percent, and the ratio of operating costs to assets below 3 percent. Capital adequacy will be adjusted to the requirements of the new Bank for International Settlements standard, still in preparation. It is safe to say, however, that only the largest banks and affiliates of foreign banks in Slovenia will be able to introduce a more advanced approach in calculating capital; most domestic banks will stick to the standardized approach. After a decade of stagnation in bank employment, at about 10,000 up to 2001 and 11,000 in 2002, the introduction of new technology will cause this number to decline moderately.

Within the financial sector, banks will retain a dominant position, only slightly losing share to insurance companies and to institutions of the capital market. Insurance companies will be strong in life insurance and in health insurance and pensions. Brokers and investment companies will compete with banks in providing various other financial services, including advice to customers.

It is expected that Slovenia will eventually have two or three financial groups with a substantial (but still a minority) share of foreign ownership in the period until entry into Exchange Rate Mechanism II. Several ideas for financial pillars are floating around, but their creation depends on future developments. Until then, inflation and long-term interest rates will decline toward the levels required by the Maastricht criteria, and the tolar-euro exchange rate will be adjusted accordingly, with nominal depreciation decreasing toward the fixed rate (within a 2.25 percent band).

Declining interest rates and, even more, declining interest margins due to increased competition and sometimes even dumping by foreign newcomers on the Slovenian banking market (as a strategy to increase market share) will increasingly force banks to seek increased income from fees and services as opposed to interest on loans. The payments system will not be adequate to future needs—the development of new banking services and modern banking techniques will be necessary. Information technology will become increasingly important.

Slovenia's membership in European Monetary Union will decrease banks' earnings from the foreign exchange business but will also lower transaction costs and the risks of the banking sector—country risk as well as market (interest, liquidity) and operational risk. Credit risk could even increase as banks are forced to expand their credit activity in order to survive in an increasingly competitive environment. On balance, however, the banking sector in Slovenia has good prospects to continue its successful development.

REFERENCES

Benčina, D. 2003. "Bančništvo Slovenije v EU." Nova Ljubljanska Banka, Ljubljana. Processed.

Štiblar, F. 2001. "Vpliv lastništva na corporate governance bank." *Gospodarska gibanja* 10. Economic Institute of the Faculty of Law, Ljubljana.

———. 2002. "Bančništvo Slovenije v mednarodni primerjavi in napoved za 2005." *Gospodarska gibanja* 11. Economic Institute of Faculty of Law, Ljubljana.

Voljč, M., and P. Šega. 2001. "Future Development of Slovenian Banks." *Bančni Vestnik* (May): 111–19.

Chapter 17
Capital Market Development

Dušan Mramor and Božo Jašovič

The main purpose of the capital market is to stimulate savings and channel those savings into optimal investments. From this point of view, the capital market (defined here as the primary and secondary markets for publicly offered long-term securities) is part of the much broader financial system. On the one hand, capital market institutions compete for savings with other institutions in the financial system, such as commercial banks; on the other hand, they complement those institutions by performing functions that the other institutions cannot.

It is very likely that the opportunity for the capital market to play a central role in the Slovenian financial system has been lost. The potential competitive advantage of the capital market was not fully exploited and in fact was largely unexplored during the initial restructuring of the banking system at the end of the 1980s and the beginning of the 1990s. Banks were very inefficient, with interest margins exceeding 10 percent, and little trust was placed in them. Now that the restructuring of the banking system has been completed, interest margins are falling and public opinion polls have been showing that banks are enjoying increasing trust. At the same time, the extreme short-term orientation of key players in the capital market is viewed very negatively by the general public. At the moment, therefore, it appears that the capital market in Slovenia will not play the central role in its financial system that it does in the United States or the United Kingdom. If so, further development of the capital market will mean targeting a complementary role for it, emphasizing its comparative advantages in such fields as the management of pension and life insurance savings. Thus the Slovenian capital market will most likely come to resemble those in Germany, Austria, and Switzerland.

This chapter is organized as follows. The first section depicts the development of Slovenia's capital market in the context of the mass privatization process, which provides important momentum for the further development of capital market institutions. The next section links pension system reform with capital market development through the beneficial effects of accumulating long-term pension savings. A similar approach is used in the third section with regard to the insurance sector. The fourth section gives some perspectives on the further development of the capital market, and the fifth section concludes.

PRIVATIZATION AND CAPITAL MARKET DEVELOPMENT

The development of the capital market in Slovenia began while the country was still part of SFR Yugoslavia, after the reforms of the economic system in 1988–89. Initially, the main purpose of capital market development was not to enable the issuance of shares in the first phase of privatization, or their redistribution in the second phase. Rather, a well-organized, safe, transparent, low-cost, and liquid capital market was viewed as necessary to provide new financial services and facilitate the flow of a growing amount of savings into productive investments, both before and after privatization. Public issuance of stocks and bonds, the commencement of stock exchange operations, and the creation of mutual funds all preceded the mass privatization schemes, which became operational in 1994. Therefore, although it was not the initial stimulus, privatization still provided important momentum for the development of the Slovenian capital market. However, the privatization process also caused extensive instability in the capital market in the postprivatization period, reducing the general trust in it and thus delaying its development as a normal part of the Slovenian financial system (Mramor 2000).

Regulatory Framework

The old Yugoslav legislation from the late 1980s proved inappropriate for regulating the capital market in an independent Slovenia. New legislation, the Slovenian Securities Markets Act and the Investment Funds Act, was therefore enacted at the beginning of 1994, and the Takeovers Act followed in 1997. The logic behind all these laws was that privatization was to be regarded only as a transition process; therefore the core of these laws was devoted to capital market regulation in normal (postprivatization) circumstances; privatization issues were dealt with in "transitory" articles. These special articles had a limited period of validity, forcing market participants to adjust within this period of time to normal operation. In the second half of the 1990s, a group of economists and lawyers prepared extensive changes to the Securities Market Act, and a new law passed the legislature in 1999. It followed all the relevant EU directives and enhanced the role of the supervisory and regulatory body in investor protection. Also, following a case of extensive market manipulation by mutual funds, some amendments to the Investment Funds Act were prepared and enacted at the beginning of 1997. Other changes, including those following the remainder of the EU directives, were adopted in the new Investment Funds Act, which was passed in late 2002.

Along with these laws, the independent Securities Market Agency (SMA) was established in March 1994, with full authority to make rules, grant licenses, approve public offers, oversee securities markets, and investigate possible wrongdoing and initiate prosecution (or even prosecute on its own in certain cases) for violation of securities laws and regulations. The Takeovers Act gives the SMA the authority to regulate the corporate takeover process, with an emphasis on the protection of small shareholders. The SMA shares its powers only with the Bank of Slovenia and the Insurance Supervisory Agency concerning the securities activities of banks and insurance companies, respectively, although it is allowed to transfer some of its powers to self-regulatory organizations, such as the stock exchange, the association of brokers, and others.

Policy Issues

The year 1994 and the first quarter of 1995 was a critical period for finalizing the broad concept of development of the capital market in Slovenia, and the period during which that concept began to be realized. Along with the beginnings of an appropriate information base for public securities, to satisfy disclosure requirements, and of other activities concerning market safety such as licensing, trading rules, and surveillance, some important policy measures were taken to increase the cost efficiency and liquidity of the capital market.

To achieve better cost efficiency, increased emphasis was placed on the competitiveness and computerization of the securities industry. To promote the greatest possible competition among brokerage houses, the SMA tailored licensing, reporting, and other requirements for brokerage houses in such a way that a sufficient number were licensed while still meeting minimum safety requirements. Brokerage houses, which are members of the stock exchange on an equal share basis, were expected to apply constant pressure to reduce the costs of operating the stock exchange. Toward this end, the Ljubljana Stock Exchange (LSE) introduced electronic trading, which resulted in a considerable decrease in the cost of transactions as their number increased with privatization. The LSE has also obtained (in competitive bidding) from the SMA a license to organize an over-the-counter (OTC) or "free" market using the same electronic system; it organizes a part of the money market on this system as well.

To achieve greater safety, speed, and efficiency, it was decided that complete dematerialization of publicly offered securities would be implemented starting in 1995: paper receipts of transactions would no longer be issued. To manage the automated process, a new central clearing and depository institution compatible with the electronic trading system at the LSE was founded in 1994 and became operational in December 1995.

The SMA has put considerable effort into achieving competitiveness among the country's "privatization" investment funds. The law on investment funds already limited the size of a single privatization fund to approximately €80 million, and it gave the SMA the authority to limit the total market share of all privatization funds under the control of any single management company.[1] In addition to these private funds, two large government funds, the Pension Capital Fund (Kapitalska družba, or KAD) and the Restitution Fund (Slovenska odškodninska družba, or SOD) were established, which under the privatization law received part of the capital of privatized companies. Although these funds might be considered a threat to competitiveness within the investment industry, in fact their influence is limited, since neither of them can acquire new capital in the future, and the Restitution Fund will slowly decrease in size as the restitution bonds are paid off. Since both funds are for now important institutional players out of the reach of systemic regulation, the most important challenge is how to subject them to the same regulation that applies to all other investment funds (Deželan and others 2001).

Special efforts were undertaken to increase the liquidity of the capital market, which had been growing quickly but as a whole can still be considered thin. A more appropriate system of capital market segmentation was designed in 1994 and introduced on January 1, 1995. It imposed more rigorous requirements on the largest and most widely distributed issues of the A listing of the LSE and tightened the requirements for the smaller and more concentrated B listings. The aim of these changes was to direct more financial investors to a smaller number of the largest and most thoroughly analyzed issues and in this way establish a satisfactory level of liquidity, at least for a certain market segment. At the same time, the new OTC segment of the market was introduced, for which there are practically no listing requirements beyond the legal requirements applicable to all publicly offered securities. The growing number of securities traded increased public interest in the capital market, and 1998 witnessed the first signs of substantially increased liquidity in the market as a whole.

Unfortunately, the liquidity of the capital market was reduced to a certain extent in 1994, in the first half of 1995, and in the first half of 1997 by interventions of the Bank of Slovenia on the money market, intended to neutralize the huge effect of a foreign exchange surplus on the money supply. In 1997 the Bank of Slovenia also introduced obligatory custodial accounts for foreign investors, and the high fees that foreign investors had to pay on these accounts reduced their speculative demand. Not surprisingly, along with turnover, security prices on the capital market also fell as a result of these activities.

Effect of Mass Privatization on the Primary Market

The dominant feature of the mass privatization program was that many new shareholders were created through the primary distribution of shares, many of whom wished to sell their shares at the first good opportunity. The situation of many sellers and few buyers lasted for a long time, and the resulting excess supply of securities on the secondary market had a strong negative impact on the primary market. Opportunities for issuing new shares after the mass privatization were therefore limited, and the capital market could not yet be considered as an alternative source of financing to the banking system. Cash public offerings were negligible in comparison with total market capitalization in the period 1995–2002 and were declining in real terms (Table 17.1). Moreover, the fact that during this period it was mostly institutions from the financial sector (banks) that were raising financing by means of public offerings proved the conjecture that the role of the capital market as a potential source of corporate finance would be negligible.

In the process of ownership consolidation, shares were traded with the final aim of concentrating corporate control in the hands of interested owners (Pohl, Jedrzejczak, and Andersen 1995). It seemed as though sustainable active trading were taking place, but in reality some investors were accumulating shares in order to obtain control. Postponement of the ownership consolidation process would mean that the mass privatization would amount to a mere administrative distribution of shares, with negligible effects on improving corporate governance and thus the efficiency of the privatized enterprises.

The main dilemma concerning the development of the capital market in Slovenia was how to deal with such undesirable consequences of privatization. On the one hand, voucher privatization had suddenly introduced corporations, shares, and investment funds into the financial system, and active trading among interested shareholders was necessary to achieve the desired benefits of effective corporate governance. But, on the other hand, active trading had a downside. Much discussion among economists and regulators had more or less reached a consensus that the immediate effect had been more securities and lower security prices, which had depressed the market for new issues (Ribnikar 1997). There was, however, marked disagreement concerning future directions. One group envisioned the capital market as an unfettered tool for a rapid redistribution of shares after privatization, and likely concentration of ownership, which should have led to greater corporate efficiency under the watchful eyes of shareholders. The second group, on the other hand, argued that the capital market should be managed so as to preserve economic and social stability, with prices kept at levels consistent with an active market for primary issues and acceptable redistribution of ownership.

TABLE 17.1 SELECTED INDICATORS OF CAPITAL MARKET ACTIVITY, 1995–2002

Indicator	1995	1996	1997	1998	1999	2000	2001	2002
New public offerings[a] (millions of euros)	40.5	57.2	52.7	27.4	35.1	57.6	10.1	13.3
Market capitalization[b]								
Billions of euros	0.7	1.0	2.2	3.8	4.7	5.6	6.4	9.6
Percent of GDP	5.0	6.9	13.7	21.8	25.2	27.0	29.1	41.1
SBI[b,c]	1,390	1,183	1,405	1,706	1,806	1,808	2,152	3,340
No. of securities traded[b]	48	82	129	173	236	266	270	264
Turnover								
Billions of euros	0.6	0.5	0.6	0.9	1.4	1.3	1.6	2.1
Percent of GDP	4.0	3.4	3.7	5.3	7.3	6.4	7.4	9.1
Percent of market capitalization[d]								
Shares	1.12	0.54	0.28	0.28	0.30	0.21	0.28	0.23
Bonds	0.38	0.25	0.14	0.15	0.16	0.22	0.14	0.16

a. Public offerings due to the privatization process are excluded, as are issues of government and central bank securities. The figures consist of new issues of stocks and bonds.

b. At end of year.

c. An index of prices on the Slovenian stock exchange.

d. Calculated as the ratio of trading volume to market capitalization.

Sources: Ljubljana Stock Exchange (2003); Securities Market Agency of Slovenia (2003); Bank of Slovenia *Monthly Bulletin* (May 2003).

PENSION REFORM AND CAPITAL MARKET DEVELOPMENT

Having concluded that secondary securities trading was mostly motivated by ownership consolidation, one could infer that the liquidity of the market should decline once this process is over. From a more optimistic point of view, however, additional demand for securities induced by the introduction of funded pension schemes would undoubtedly have a beneficial effect on securities market development.

To reinforce the current role of the capital market in the financial system and the overall economy, its further development should be made congruent with the recent pension system reform. The promised benefits of the newly introduced funded pillar in the pension system are crucially dependent on the absorption capacity and stability of the capital market; conversely, the stability and enhancement of the latter will inevitably be a function of the additional savings created by the reformed pension system and channeled through the financial system to productive uses. In other words, the process is a mutually reinforcing one that will undoubtedly lead to greater integration of the domestic financial market into global markets.

The initial preconditions for a well-functioning funded pension scheme are, first, reasonably well developed, regulated, and supervised financial markets and financial institutions, and, second, full integration of the funded pension scheme into the existing financial system. The second precondition seems not to have been completely met, as the management of the funded pension schemes in Slovenia is entrusted only to the existing insurance companies and newly established pension companies (specialized insurance companies) and pension funds. Managers of privatization funds and mutual funds are thus not allowed to set up and manage pension schemes directly, but they may act as subcontracting asset managers of pension savings.

Regulatory Framework

After long discussion, Slovenia enacted changes to the pension system by the end of 1999, when the legislature passed the Pension and Disability Insurance Act. This act introduced, besides the reform of the existing pay-as-you-go pillar, an additional, voluntary, funded pillar. It was envisaged that the funded pillar would partly substitute for the existing old-age savings and insurance schemes provided by insurance companies and complement the reformed pay-as-you-go system. The general objectives of the funded pillar are to insure against poverty in old age, to promote saving, and to promote economic growth. To meet those objectives, the main characteristics of the voluntary pillar are the following (Jašovič and Simoneti 1997). First, the schemes are fully funded with individualized accounts so that, in the case of early death or disability of the participant, the accumulated balance can be returned to the participant or his or her heirs. Second, the schemes are defined contribution schemes whereby the pension (in the form of a lifetime annuity) depends on the accumulated savings plus returns on investments, although the sponsors of the scheme will guarantee a minimum return. Third, the schemes have standardized disclosure rules concerning realized returns on the investment portfolio. Fourth, there are limited tax incentives (deferral of personal income taxes on funds held within the schemes) for individuals and employers in the case of occupational schemes. Fifth, the schemes are privately managed.

Shortly after the law was adopted, financial institutions began preparatory activities to set up either pension funds or specialized pension corporations. At the end of 2002 there were 12 providers of voluntary funded pension schemes: 4 specialized pension companies, 5 pension funds, and 3 insurance companies that offer other insurance services as well. By the end of 2002 more than 200,000 people had enrolled in voluntary schemes either individually or collectively through occupational arrangements, and total paid-in premiums amounted to SIT 28 billion (€122 million). A major part of the accumulated pension savings is being invested in long-term government and other bonds (because the minimum guaranteed return is linked to 40 percent of the yield to maturity on certain issues of government bonds) and only a minor part in domestic or foreign equity shares.

Policy Issues

The beneficial effects of increased long-term pension savings on the development of the capital market would be strengthened with the increased scope provided as a consequence of the introduction of an obligatory funded pillar. As the objectives of the voluntary and obligatory funded pension schemes are the same, there is no good reason why they should be organized any differently. The tax treatment and the extent of guarantees for the schemes could vary, but the basic structure and operating principles could be the same, and the existing pension scheme providers who have become sufficiently professionally experienced could be entrusted with the management of the obligatory schemes.

The introduction of fully funded pension schemes is claimed to have a positive impact on long-term saving. However, once mandatory pension saving has been imposed, it is very likely that voluntary individual saving in other financial institutions will be partly cut back (World Bank 1994). To what extent this crowding-out effect will occur, or, put differently, by how much net saving will increase, will depend primarily on the mandatory contribution rate for pension savings, the impact of tax incentives for voluntary saving, and the possibilities available to individuals to offset their mandatory saving (for example, by borrowing). No matter what the net increase in saving, it is more important, in terms of the broader implications for the economy, that the composition of that saving change substantially in favor of long-term instruments, to enhance the resources available for long-term investment via the capital market.

Expanding the scope of pension saving will contribute to the further development of institutional investors and, as a consequence, to more efficient corporate governance. Institutional investors are better able than individuals to get the information needed to make prudent investments and are more motivated to enforce higher reporting and information disclosure standards and to exert supervisory pressure on managers. On the other hand, some doubts surround the efficiency of a mere market mechanism of early exit (that is, divesting poorly performing shares) in enhancing portfolio value, and the question could be especially relevant for a nascent capital market environment. If institutional investors have substantial holdings, they may find it impossible to sell certain parts of their portfolio without influencing prices. Therefore reliance on enhanced corporate governance would avoid potential disruptions in a shallow capital market and would ultimately contribute to better corporate performance.

THE INSURANCE INDUSTRY AND CAPITAL MARKET DEVELOPMENT

Before 1990 the Slovenian insurance industry was dominated by a single company with a 95 percent market share and one reinsurance company. In that year the single insurance company was broken up into five companies, all of which have been organized as joint-stock companies with mixed private and social (state) ownership. The state-owned shares, which exceed 50 percent of total capital in two cases and minority shares in another four cases, were transferred in a trusteeship to the state-owned SOD and KAD, as mandated by the Insurance Companies Ownership Transformation Act, which passed the national legislature in 2002. Both funds act as trustees and will ultimately have to sell the shares to individuals or other entities, who are entitled to buy shares in proportion to past paid-in insurance premiums. In addition to these companies, another eight insurance companies were operating in the country at the end of 2001. Three insurance companies are partly foreign owned.

The insurance market in Slovenia is underdeveloped by Western standards in terms of its concentration and depth. The largest company accounted for 40 percent of total nonlife insurance and 50 percent of total life insurance premiums in 2001. The five largest companies accounted for 94 percent and 93 percent of these premiums, respectively. In 2001 this highly concentrated industry generated gross premiums equivalent to about 4.7 percent of GDP, well below the corresponding ratios in OECD countries. Also, the range of products offered is rather narrow. In most other European countries about one-half of all insurance premiums are for life insurance. In Slovenia the share of life insurance premiums is growing but was still only about 19 percent in 2001. Voluntary health insurance, with almost a 26 percent share, accounts for the largest proportion of collected premiums, followed by compulsory automobile third-party liability insurance and life insurance, which are tied for second place with a 19 percent share each.

Regulatory Framework

The first contemporary legal framework for the insurance industry was set out in the 1994 Insurance Companies Act, which laid out the basic principles for establishing, operating, and supervising the industry. This law stipulated that insurance activity should be conducted by joint-stock companies or mutual insurance companies. There was no branch separation required between life and nonlife insurance activities, although separate accounting was required. Reinsurance abroad was permitted once domestic capacities were exhausted. The supervisory function was entrusted to the Insurance Supervisory Authority (ISA), incorporated within the Ministry of Finance. The ISA was empowered to grant licenses subject to approval of the company's business plan; it could also suspend and revoke licenses. It was authorized to make off-site and on-site inspections, although because of institutional constraints, in particular an insufficient number of competent staff, there is still much room for improvement in this area.

The accumulated reserves from life insurance programs were separated from other assets of the insurance company and could not be used to cover other liabilities. The Insurance Companies Act provided this basic safeguard, but in practice there were still no generally acceptable standards on the level of reserves that had to be set aside or on how they should be invested. Such standards would protect consumers and restrict the start-up costs of life insurance contracts in the first few years. This was one of the main reasons for improving the regulatory framework, which was actually realized with the adoption of the 2000 Insurance Act. In addition, the new insurance law eliminated some other regulatory inadequacies and addressed more effectively the problem of how to deal with financially troubled insurance companies. In this regard, the ISA (which was constituted as an independent agency in 2000) was vested with the clear-cut power to initiate necessary remedial measures. Current insurance laws and bylaws are completely in line with EU regulations. Moreover, Slovenia did not take advantage of the transition period with regard to the entrance of foreign insurance providers, but instead fully opened up the market to foreign competition.

Policy Directions

Insurance companies will have to adjust to the increased competitive pressures they will face with Slovenia's accession to the European Union. As a consequence they will have to intensify their restructuring efforts. The most serious problem of the insurance sector is its rather poor financial health and the low efficiency of the smaller and medium-size companies. To address this problem, a major restructuring and eventual reorganization process has to be undertaken. Those activities could even be reinforced through the accomplishment of ownership transformation procedures, which are well behind the original schedule.

Slovenia's insurance legislation has already become fully harmonized with EU legislation, and in some areas even more rigorous rules are being applied to ensure the satisfactory financial health of companies. But proper regulation alone would not be enough to ensure that insurance companies become important and efficient participants in the capital market. Insurance companies will have to focus on restructuring and necessary reorganization in order to respond to increased competition and take advantage of the market potential in life insurance.

LEGAL AND INSTITUTIONAL ISSUES FOR FUTURE CAPITAL MARKET DEVELOPMENT

A major consequence of voucher privatization was that, in a short period of time, a large volume of shares flooded a relatively undeveloped capital market dominated by the special privatization shares. Under such conditions, the safety of the market could not be adequately guaranteed. There were simply too few supervisors with appropriate knowledge and skills to monitor trading. The transparency of trading for most of the privatization shares was extremely low, market prices and quantities traded (enforced with regard to foreign portfolio investments) were enormously unstable, and all of this was accompanied by low and variable liquidity. As a result, it was almost inevitable that numerous opportunities for manipulation would arise, including insider trading. Because different parts of the capital market are strongly interrelated, the "privatized" capital market affected the "nonprivatized" capital market, lowering trust in both. Thus it is no surprise that overall trust in the capital market is rather low, and it probably would not be much higher even if there were no manipulation occurring on the nonprivatized market.

In light of this situation, the SMA faces a difficult decision. Should it care only for small investors by ensuring that they receive sufficient information (transparency) and monitoring of trading (security) and otherwise allow the market to operate on its own? Or should it also intervene in the market with special measures aimed to increase its stability, liquidity, and cost efficiency? One school of thought asserts that the SMA should take an especially aggressive role in the development of the capital market. Given the special (transitional) circumstances of the Slovenian economy compared with those of more developed market economies, in this view, the SMA should more actively intervene in the capital market to provide not only security and transparency but also stability, liquidity, and even cost efficiency.

As presented in Mramor (1996), one of the main problems of voucher privatization from the perspective of capital market development has been the lack of efficient corporate governance and the need to establish such governance as quickly as possible after privatization. But if the major role of the SMA is to be development of the capital market, it cannot at the same time promote the postprivatization process. The SMA cannot bear the additional burden and responsibility for the completion of that phase of privatization in which an appropriate ownership structure and corporate governance are established, regardless of how crucial this is for the chosen model of privatization. If the SMA should undertake this task, not only would the long-term development of the capital market be endangered, but its very existence as well.

One result of emphasizing privatization at the expense of capital market development has been an excessive focus on short-term profits on the part of brokers and mutual funds, stimulated by "postprivatization opportunities." Thus brokers' professional codes had still not been created even after many years of capital market activities, and, when finally created, they were not enforced. Many stockbrokers even publicly defended those who manipulated prices. Therefore the recent efforts of the SMA to prosecute professional malpractice and manipulation were more than welcome. Amendments to the existing legislation are in preparation, to empower the SMA to directly impose sanctions on those participants who violate its regulations and the professional practices of the industry.

A second example concerns the privatization investment funds. With the lack of control by shareholders, and given the uncertainty concerning the exchange of vouchers, some management companies, instead of transforming the privatization funds into open-end mutual funds or pension funds, began stripping them of assets and transforming them into holding companies, out of the reach of SMA supervision. There were indications that, in this process, management companies were also directly or indirectly buying shares of the privatization funds or transformed holding companies at depressed prices.[2] Because of the huge investment portfolios they are managing, the management companies have by now gained such political importance that the final outcome of this process might be completely in their favor and against the interests of shareholders and the development of the capital market. Therefore a draft bill concerning the reorganization of privatization funds into holding companies is being discussed, with the final aim of discouraging conversions into holding companies, through the enactment of more stringent disclosure requirements and the introduction of additional measures for small shareholder protection. As far as closed-end investment funds—which emerged from the privatization funds—are concerned, their future institutional development is well defined in current law: they will have to be transformed into open-end mutual funds within a maximum of eight years.

So far, the privatization funds and their later successors (investment funds) have contributed little to the development of institutional investors in the capital market. They are mainly concerned with how to concentrate ownership stakes in a few blue-chip companies and then, as portfolio investors, to hold their positions indefinitely. Instead of being active portfolio managers, these fund managers resort to internal corporate governance activities, thus decreasing trading and impairing market liquidity. With compulsory conversion into mutual funds, they will have to change their current focus and become more active portfolio managers and less directly involved in corporate governance (Jašovič 1999).

Such an activist role for the SMA in capital market development also requires constant and thorough analysis of the capital market and the financial system as a whole from a tax perspective. Obviously, fiscal policy can be either advantageous, neutral, or disadvantageous to the securities market and the prospects for its further development. Unfortunately, Slovenian tax regulations do not provide for coherent tax relief for financial investments and are somewhat discriminatory toward certain parts of the financial system.

Another problem that needs some consideration relates to the liquidity and financial deepening of the capital market. A situation of already poor liquidity is being aggravated with the trend toward delisting of public companies from the stock exchange. Newly emerging institutional investors (for example, pension funds) will thus inevitably face a problem of where to invest accumulated savings. Moreover, they will even require new instruments tailored according to their preferences. As a consequence, capital market deepening and financial innovations, initiated by an adequate regulatory framework (for example, mortgage banking law) will ultimately provide a sufficient supply of securities designed to meet the specific requirements of institutional investors. Thus, not only would government and bank bonds dominate the market, but more and more low-risk instruments would become available, such as mortgage-backed securities, collateralized bonds, and guaranteed income bonds. If the efforts toward financial innovation and market deepening described above end in failure, it is inevitable that a major part of accumulated domestic long-term savings would have to be redirected to international capital markets.

CONCLUSIONS

The status and development of a country's capital market are usually measured by data such as those presented in Table 17.1 for Slovenia. The table shows that Slovenia has made considerable progress, and if one also considers the status of the legal environment, the enforcement of the laws, and other elements of well-organized capital markets, the picture is even brighter. Slovenia is still an economy in transition, however, and during the transition some other questions have become even more important when assessing the capital market's prospects for further development. The major question is the role of the capital market in the privatization process, especially given that voucher privatization has been chosen as the principal method. As this chapter has shown, it is important for the development of the capital market that its role in privatization be as narrow as possible and that the essential rules of a safe, transparent, low-cost, liquid, stable, and well-organized capital market be strictly followed. In our opinion, in such an environment, this cannot be achieved using only the usual regulatory and supervisory tools found in developed market economies, especially when a satisfactory level of stability is in question. These two conclusions—no direct role in privatization for the capital market, and the need for additional powers for the regulatory and supervisory body during the transition—are hotly debated, and often such a position is labeled "antimarket." However, we believe that the prospects for the development of the Slovenian capital market will be better if these issues are debated and recognized as important.

ACKNOWLEDGMENT

Parts of this chapter draw from articles written by Mramor and McGoun (2002) and Mrak, Jašovič, and Simoneti (1999).

REFERENCES

Deželan, S., P. Groznik, B. Jašovič, D. Mramor, and G. Sluga. 2001. "Strategija razvoja trga kapitala v Sloveniji." Ministry of Finance, Ljubljana.

Jašovič, B. 1999. "Management Companies and Issues of Governance of Privatization Funds." In M. Simoneti, S. Estrin, and A. Bohm, eds., *The Governance of Privatization Funds—Experiences of the Czech Republic, Poland and Slovenia*. Cheltenham, U.K.: Edward Elgar.

Jašovič, B., and M. Simoneti. 1997. "Financial Sector Conditions for the Development of Funded Pension Schemes in Slovenia." Central and Eastern European Privatization Network, Ljubljana.

Ljubljana Stock Exchange. 2003. *Annual Report 2002*. Ljubljana.

Mrak, M., B. Jašovič, and M. Simoneti. 1999. "Financial Sector." In *Slovenia: Economic Transformation and EU Accession*. World Bank Country Study. Washington, D.C.: World Bank.

Mramor, D. 1996. "Primary Privatization Goal in Economies in Transition." *International Review of Financial Analysis* 5(2): 131–43.

―――――. 2000. "Vloga in pomen trga kapitala." In D. Mramor, ed., *Trg kapitala v Sloveniji—prikazi, analize, mnenja*. Ljubljana: Gospodarski vestnik.

Mramor, D., and E. G. McGoun. 2002. "Privatization and the Capital Market in Slovenia." In A. E. Young, I. Teodorović, and P. Koveos, eds., *Economies in Transition: Conception, Status and Prospects*. River Edge, N.J.: World Scientific.

Pohl, G., G. T. Jedrzejczak, and R. Andersen. 1995. "Creating Capital Markets in Central and Eastern Europe." World Bank and Central and Eastern European Privatization Network, Washington and Ljubljana.

Ribnikar, I. 1997. "The Path from Social Ownership to Ownership of Business Enterprises." *IB Review* 1(1): 37–50.

Securities Market Agency of Slovenia. 2003. *Annual Report 2002*. Ljubljana.

World Bank. 1994. *Averting the Old Age Crisis: Policies to Protect the Old and Promote Growth*. New York: Oxford University Press.

NOTES

1. The SMA could refuse permission to establish a new privatization investment fund or issue new shares in an existing fund if the total market share of such funds under the control of a management company exceeded 10 percent.

2. With constant changes in the Investment Fund Act and other regulations, these activities were only partially restricted with the strengthened supervisory powers of the SMA.

Chapter 18
Labor Market Developments in the 1990s

Milan Vodopivec

Slovenia's transition to a market economy has brought dramatic changes to the workings of the labor market. The government abandoned its traditional paternalistic attitude toward firms and workers.[1] Firms were allowed to lay off redundant workers, thus ending the virtually absolute job security that had prevailed under self-management. Labor mobility has been facilitated by collective bargaining, which has replaced the previous rigid system of wage determination. And the focus of protection has shifted from jobs to workers, with many more unemployed workers relying on unemployment benefits than under self-management.

How has this disruption of a previously stable economic system affected labor market outcomes? In all transition economies, unemployment soared and employment declined during the transition, but what kinds of worker flows have produced these developments, and what has been their magnitude? Also, how large have the job flows been that were associated with these worker flows—in particular, how many jobs have been destroyed and how many created? Moreover, how have the market forces that have been unleashed affected the return to human capital? For example, has the wage advantage of more educated and more experienced workers increased? Last but not least, how have specific groups of workers been affected? In particular, has transition brought more hardship to women than to men?

This chapter addresses these questions using an exceptionally rich data set covering all formal sector workers and firms in Slovenia.[2] It finds that the labor market transition strongly affected not only employment and unemployment, but also worker and job flows as well as wages, and it caused a major dislocation of workers. The bulk of the adjustment occurred in the early 1990s; by 2001, when the labor market transition was mostly complete, a relatively favorable picture had emerged: the unemployment rate was below 6 percent, and employment and average wages exceeded their 1991 levels. The pattern of worker and job flows also suggests completion of the labor market transition: after a period of sharp increases in flows in the early 1990s, flows declined and then stabilized by the end of the 1990s. Other results show that, in the early 1990s, the returns to education dramatically increased; that returns to experience slightly decreased for those with long service and increased for those with short service; and that the male-female gap was kept constant at a level that was low by international standards throughout the 1990s.

The chapter proceeds by outlining the institutional background, describing key labor market reforms, and comparing the main policy parameters with those of other transition economies. Empirical evidence follows, with a presentation of the main trends in the labor market during 1990–2001, an analysis of worker and job flows, and an analysis of wage developments. The last section concludes.

INSTITUTIONAL BACKGROUND

Profound changes in the political and economic system, some of which started while Slovenia was still part of SFR Yugoslavia, heavily influenced outcomes in the Slovenian labor market in the 1990s. Above all, the 1988 Yugoslav Law on Enterprises transferred decisionmaking rights from workers to equity owners, thus formally ending the era of self-management. Important changes occurred in both employment and wage policies. The major novelty in the area of employment was the right of employers to lay off workers, although exercising this option remained extremely costly for the employer. On the wage setting front, self-management was replaced by a system with three components: a new Labor Code, collective bargaining, and incomes policy.

The following subsections summarize the main labor market policies of Slovenia in the 1990s and compare them with those of other transition economies. In keeping with its general approach to transition reforms, Slovenia undertook labor market reform rather cautiously.[3] It retained rather strict employment protection legislation, particularly for regular employment; it maintained a costly unemployment benefit system, which, even after a strong reduction in entitlements in 1998, remained the most generous among transition economies; it imposed a heavy tax burden on labor; and it kept minimum wages relatively high. To stimulate reemployment, Slovenia also spent considerable resources on active labor market policies.

Employment Protection Legislation

In SFR Yugoslavia, layoffs were not permitted except on disciplinary grounds. Reforms undertaken during the transition crossed the Rubicon of permanent job security and allowed employers to lay off workers, but imposed large costs for doing so (see Riboud, Sanchez-Paramo, and Silva-Jáuregui 2001). In case of a layoff "for economic reasons," the 1991 Labor Code (which with minor modifications remained in power until 2003) called for six months advance notification and severance pay of half the worker's monthly earnings for each year of service; it also imposed large procedural costs (Vodopivec 1996). Regulations governing the use of fixed-term employment were more liberal, with no limit on the number of successive contracts or on the maximum cumulated duration of fixed-term contracts.

Compared with other transition economies, Slovenia had much stricter regular employment protection throughout the 1990s (Riboud, Sanchez-Paramo, and Silva-Jáuregui 2001). In the early 1990s its rules on fixed-term employment were also more restrictive than in other countries, but that changed with the introduction of temporary work agencies in 1998. Still, as judged by a combined score of regular and temporary employment throughout the 1990s, Slovenia had the strictest employment protection among a group of transition economies, with a score of 3.8, compared with a group average of 3 (Haltiwanger, Scarpetta, and Vodopivec 2003).[4]

Taxation of Labor

Throughout the 1990s Slovenia imposed high taxes on labor. Its tax wedge (defined as the sum of social security contributions and personal income taxes, as a proportion of total labor costs) was equaled only by Poland among all transition economies, at 48 percent. This is well above the level in many OECD countries but less than in the high-tax countries of Continental Europe and Scandinavia (Haltiwanger, Scarpetta, and Vodopivec 2003). At 37.4 percent, the average tax wedge in transition economies was much smaller.

Minimum Wages

Slovenia introduced mandatory minimum wages in 1995; earlier in the 1990s, minimum wages were determined through collective agreements. After 1995 their relative level—the ratio of the minimum to the average wage—stayed remarkably constant at 40 percent. This ratio is toward the high end among transition economies: over the 1990s as a whole, the Slovenian average ratio was 36.3 percent, significantly above the average of 28.7 percent for other transition economies (Haltiwanger, Scarpetta, and Vodopivec 2003). In general, Slovenia retained substantial control over wage setting, with minimum basic wages for different categories of workers determined through collective agreements, and mandated, automatic wage increases for older workers (Haltiwanger and Vodopivec 2003).

Unemployment Benefits

Unemployed workers in Slovenia may apply for unemployment benefits, first under the unemployment insurance program and then—if they qualify—under a means-tested unemployment assistance program. Workers who have paid contributions and lose their job are eligible if they neither quit their job nor were dismissed for cause. Duration of potential eligibility for receipt of benefits ranges from 3 months for workers with few years of service to 24 months for workers with many, and for older workers. After amendments in October 1998 the benefit duration was substantially reduced (even by more than 50 percent for some categories of workers), although the dependence of benefits on years of service was preserved. The level of the benefit depends on past earnings. The replacement rate is 70 percent in the first three months and drops to 60 percent thereafter.

Even after the 1998 changes, Slovenian unemployment benefits remain among the most generous in transition economies. In most other transition economies, the potential duration of eligibility is between 6 and 12 months. Benefits are also among the highest in transition economies. In the 1990s the average unemployment benefit in Slovenia amounted to 33.6 percent of the average wage, compared with an average of 27.6 percent for a group of comparator countries (Vodopivec, Wörgötter, and Raju 2003). Vodopivec, Wörgötter, and Raju also show that, in the 1990s, an index of generosity of unemployment benefits (defined as the product of the replacement rate and the share of compensated unemployed among all unemployed) in Slovenia was, at 21.8, the highest among all transition economies and well above the average of 12.7.

Active Labor Market Programs

Slovenia spent considerable resources on active labor market programs in the 1990s. As a percentage of GDP, expenditure on these programs was highest in 1991 and 1992, at 0.83 percent and 1.17 percent, respectively; it then declined to about 0.4 to 0.5 percent of GDP in the late 1990s and 2000. Slovenia's average expenditure on active labor market programs in the 1990s (0.5 percent of GDP) was considerably above the average for comparator transition economies, at 0.35 percent of GDP. Expressed as a share of expenditure on passive labor market measures, expenditure on active labor market programs in the late 1990s and 2000 ranged from 38 percent to 70 percent, quite in line with the experience of OECD countries.

KEY LABOR MARKET TRENDS

Transition reforms heavily affected the working of the labor market. The bulk of the adjustment occurred in the early 1990s, and by 2001, when the labor market transition was mostly complete, the picture that emerges is a relatively favorable one. After a short transition "dip" in the early 1990s, both employment and wages started to increase and unemployment to decline, with the turnaround occurring in 1993–95. In 2001 total employment and the labor force exceeded their 1991 levels, and unemployment stabilized at a low level by international standards. The transition changed the structure of employment, reducing the shares of young and older workers, as well as those of unskilled workers, but it did not worsen the relative position of women.

The transition initially reduced real wages sharply. During 1990–92 real monthly wages fell by 24 percent, but they steadily increased after 1993 (Figure 18.1; Table 18.1, top panel). By 2001 they exceeded their 1990 level by 9 percent. Women's wages on average amounted to 85 to 89 percent of men's wages—rather high values by international standards. (In contrast, Orazem and Vodopivec 1995 report an increasing trend of women's relative wages during 1987–91.)

FIGURE 18.1 WAGES AND EMPLOYMENT, 1990–2001

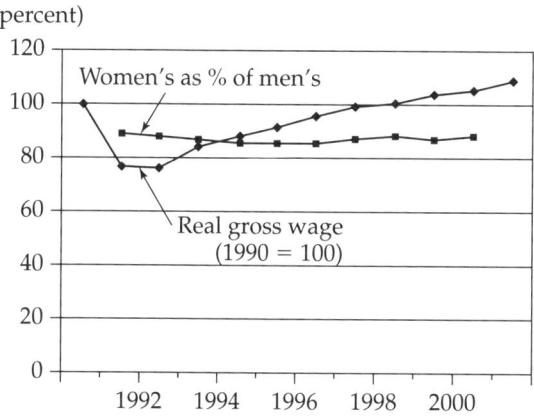

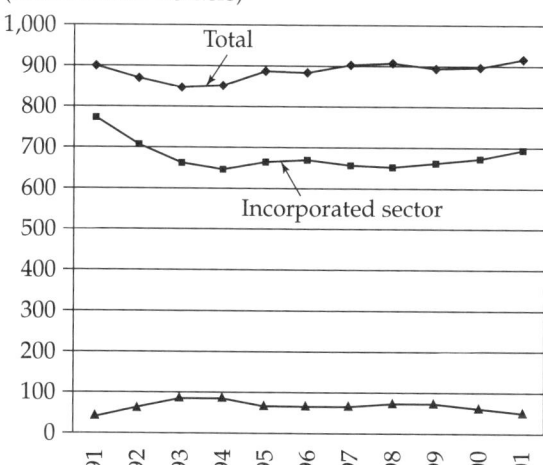

Sources: Statistical Yearbook of Slovenia, various issues; work history database.

TABLE 18.1 SELECTED LABOR MARKET INDICATORS, 1990–2001

Indicator	1990	1991	1992	1993	1994	1995	1996	1997	1998	1999	2000	2001
Wages in the incorporated sector												
Real gross wage (yearly average, 1990 = 100)	100.0	77.0	76.0	84.5	87.6	91.5	95.9	98.9	100.4	103.7	105.4	108.9
Ratio of women's to men's average wage (percent)	..	88.6	88.1	86.4	85.0	85.0	85.4	86.9	88.9	86.5	87.8	..
Employment[a]												
Total employment (000s)	..	896	871	845	851	882	878	898	907	892	894	914
Women (percent of total)	..	46.9	46.7	46.7	46.7	46.4	46.7	46.3	46.3	46.0	46.2	45.6
Employment in incorporated sector (000s)	823	768	702	660	645	666	670	658	656	662	676	692
Women (percent of total)	46.0	46.1	46.1	46.8	47.2	47.1	46.9	46.6	46.1	45.8	45.3	45.3
Age structure of employment (percent of total)[b]												
Age under 20	3.0	2.2	2.3	1.8	2.0	2.2	1.8	1.5	1.5	1.4	1.4	1.2
Age 20 to 30	29.1	28.5	27.1	26.1	25.2	25.3	24.8	24.8	24.8	24.6	24.1	23.7
Age 30 to 40	32.5	33.7	35.1	35.7	34.9	34.1	33.8	33.7	33.7	33.5	33.1	32.6
Age 40 to 50	23.2	25.1	26.1	27.4	28.2	28.5	29.7	30.1	30.2	30.3	30.5	30.5
Age over 50	12.2	10.5	7.6	7.2	7.8	8.1	8.4	7.9	7.8	8.3	8.8	9.7
Education structure (percent of total)[b]												
Did not finish elementary	16.3	15.2	13.3	12.0	10.8	9.5	8.6	7.6	6.8	6.0	5.5	5.0
Elementary school	19.8	19.6	18.5	18.1	17.6	17.7	17.6	17.2	17.1	16.8	16.6	16.5
Vocational school	29.9	29.9	29.5	29.8	29.9	30.2	30.1	30.0	30.0	30.1	29.9	29.6

High school	21.8	22.4	23.6	24.5	25.5	26.3	27.2	28.0	28.6	29.2	29.7	30.2
Higher education	12.1	12.8	13.7	14.3	14.8	15.0	15.3	16.1	16.4	16.8	17.1	17.4
Unemployment[a]												
Total unemployment (000s)	..	49.4[c]	67.2[c]	85	85	70	69	69	75	71	69	57
Women (percent of total)	..	..	..	42.4	43.5	44.3	44.9	46.4	46.7	47.9	47.8	49.1
Unemployment rates (percent)	..	5.2[c]	7.2[c]	9.1	9.0	7.4	7.3	7.1	7.7	7.4	7.2	5.9
Men	..	..	..	9.9	9.5	7.7	7.5	7.0	7.6	7.2	7.0	5.6
Women	..	..	..	8.3	8.4	7.0	7.0	7.3	7.7	7.6	7.4	6.3
Registered unemployed[d] (000s)	35	55	86	112	138	122	126	125	129	122	114	103
Labor force[a]												
Total (000s)	945.5	938	931	934	951	946	967	984	964	963	972	
Men	504.3	502	500	503	514	506	517	528	518	517	524	
Women	441.3	436	430	433	440	441	446	456	444	446	445	
Participation rate (percent)	60.6	59.2	57.8	57.4	58.7	57.5	58.7	60.0	58.3	57.7	57.9	
Men	67.7	66.2	64.8	64.2	66.2	64.5	65.1	66.7	64.9	64.1	64.5	
Women	54.0	52.6	51.1	51.3	52.1	51.3	52.3	53.8	51.8	51.7	51.4	

a. Persons aged 15 years and over, second quarter of each year (data for 1993–96 refer to May).
b. Percentages may not add up to 100 because of missing values of attributes in the data set.
c. Estimates based on 1993 data of unemployment and trends in registered unemployment.
d. As of the end of the year.

Sources: Statistical Yearbook of Slovenia, various issues; work history database.

At the onset of the transition, employment also declined sharply. The decline was particularly intense in the incorporated sector, where employment in 1994 was 80 percent below its 1990 level (Figure 18.1; Table 18.1, second panel). Total employment started to grow after 1995, and by 2001 it had already surpassed its 1990s level; employment in the incorporated sector, in contrast, started to grow only in 1999, and in 2001 it still lagged 15 percent behind its 1990 level. The transition thus pushed a significant number of workers to the nonincorporated sector, that is, to a less formalized working environment, including self-employment.

The structure of employment also changed in various ways. First, as already mentioned, both young and older workers have seen their employment shares decline (Table 18.1, third panel). The share of employed workers who are under 30 decreased from more than 32 percent in 1990 to 25 percent in 2001, and the share of employed workers who are over 50 decreased from more than 12 percent to below 10 percent in those same years. For the young, both push and pull factors were at work. On the one hand, young workers faced more difficult access to jobs because of the tightened labor market; on the other hand, the returns to education increased dramatically (see below), making schooling at the college level more attractive: indeed, the number of college students nearly tripled in the 1990s. Many older workers retired in the early 1990s, some under pressure and with the encouragement of government-sponsored early retirement programs. The trend toward a falling share of older workers was reversed in 1998 by the pension reform, which introduced a gradual increase in the retirement age.[5] Second, the educational structure of employed workers improved markedly: the share of workers who had not completed elementary school fell sharply, and the share of workers with a high school education or higher increased. Interestingly, the share of women in employment remained stable at 45 to 47 percent throughout the period.

One of the most notable changes was the dramatic increase in unemployment. The number of unemployed soared in the early 1990s, from an estimated 20,000 before 1990 to 85,000 in 1993, with unemployment reaching 9.1 percent (Table 18.1, fifth panel). After 1995, however, unemployment started to decline (except in 1998), reaching a low of 5.9 percent in 2001. Trends in unemployment rates were similar for men and women. Because the registered unemployed qualified for a host of benefits, throughout the 1990s and into the 2000s the number of registered unemployed surpassed by a large margin the number of unemployed as counted by labor force surveys (which adhere to the International Labour Organisation's definition of unemployment; Table 18.1, fifth panel).[6]

The number of workers in the labor force—which can be viewed as a summary measure of labor market activity—fell in the early 1990s and again in the late 1990s. Because of strong growth outside those intervals, however, in 2001 the labor force exceeded its 1991 level by 2.7 percent (Table 18.1, bottom panel). Despite this growth, the labor force participation rate declined, reflecting strong flows of the working-age population into nonparticipation. In 2001 the labor force participation rate stood at 58 percent, which is relatively low by international standards (2.6 percentage points below that of a group of six industrialized Western European countries).

WORKER AND JOB FLOWS

The above analysis looked at changes in labor market stocks; this section investigates the flows responsible for those changes. The transition shock of the early 1990s temporarily but dramatically increased worker and job flows, with a rise in separations and job destruction preceding an increase in hiring and job creation (Figure 18.2). The scale of job flows was comparable to that typically found in Western industrialized countries, but, interestingly, the scale of worker flows lagged behind values typical in other countries. The patterns of both worker and job flows suggest that, by 2001, the labor market transition was complete: after a period of intense increase in flows in the early 1990s, flows declined in 1994–96 and had mostly stabilized by the end of the 1990s. In 2000–01 some flows (for example, flows in and out of unemployment) were clearly above pretransition values (for job flows, comparative pretransition values are lacking).

Worker separations and hirings increased in the early 1990s, with separations preceding hirings by several years, and then slowly declined after 1996. In 2001 separation and hiring rates were 14 percent and 15 percent, respectively (Table 18.2, top panel), well below the OECD average of 26 percent for both rates (OECD 1994). It is notable that, except in the early 1990s, separation and hiring rates were well synchronized.

Probabilities of various types of exit from employment also show an interesting pattern, all of them suggesting that the labor market transition had ended by the late 1990s. The probability of job-to-unemployment transitions increased in the early 1990s and only mildly decreased after 1994; job-to-job transitions were kept low in the early 1990s and increased after 1994; and job-to-other transitions increased strongly during 1990–92 but had declined and stabilized at about 4 percent by the end of the observation period (Table 18.2, second panel; Figure 18.2).

Inflows into unemployment also show that the nature of unemployment changed in the late 1990s. Only in the early 1990s did layoffs and bankruptcies contribute a large share of inflows into registered

FIGURE 18.2 WORKER FLOWS, 1990–2001

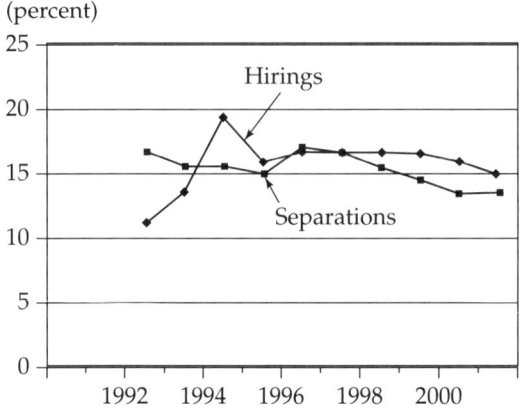

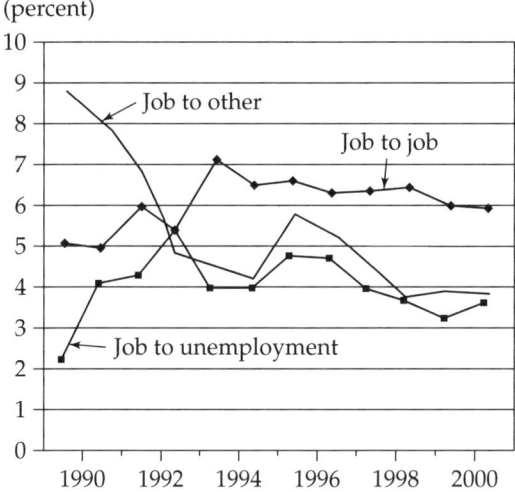

Source: Author's computations based on work history database.

unemployment, peaking at about 30 percent during 1991–93. In the late 1990s the main sources of inflows were terminations of fixed-term appointments and labor force entry (Table 18.2, third panel). Consistent with the decline in the unemployment rate, the probability that an unemployed person would find a job also increased in the late 1990s, stabilizing at just above 50 percent (Table 18.2, fourth panel).

The transition also strongly influenced job flows (Table 18.2, bottom panel). Job destruction and, with a lag of several years, job

TABLE 18.2 WORKER AND JOB FLOWS, 1990–2001

Indicator	1990	1991	1992	1993	1994	1995	1996	1997	1998	1999	2000	2001
Worker flows[a]												
Hirings (000s)	..	..	75.4	86.0	119.8	102.5	108.5	107.2	107.6	108.9	107.4	100.9
Separations (000s)	..	..	113.1	98.3	96.9	94.7	111.6	107.8	99.1	94.1	89.9	93.7
Hiring rate (percent)	..	..	11.4	13.7	19.5	16.1	16.9	16.7	16.8	16.8	16.2	14.8
Separation rate (percent)	..	..	17.0	15.7	15.8	14.9	17.3	16.8	15.5	14.5	13.5	13.8
Probability of exit from employment[b] (percent of total)												
To another job	5	4.9	5.9	5.4	7.1	6.5	6.7	6.4	6.5	6.6	6.2	6.1
To unemployment	2.3	4.1	4.2	5.5	4.0	4.1	4.9	4.8	4.1	3.8	3.2	3.6
To other	8.7	8	6.9	4.9	4.7	4.3	5.8	5.6	4.9	4.1	4.2	4.0
Inflows into registered unemployment[c] (000s)												
Total	46.5	73.6	74.6	90.6	76.1	78.2	82.2	77.7	74.5	77.7	75.9	82.1
New entrant or reentrant	14.5	20.1	15.8	21.2	21.6	21.4	18.8	17.4	18.1	18.7	18.5	20.1
Voluntary separation	5.3	5.2	9.5	9.8	9.0	9.7	8.4	7.4	7.3	8.0	9.3	9.6
Separated for disciplinary reasons	1.8	1.3	0.8	0.7	0.5	0.4	0.3	0.2	0.3	0.2	0.2	0.2
Laid off	0.8	4.1	17.8	16.7	10.4	9.0	11.4	13.0	8.7	6.0	4.3	4.9
End of fixed-term appointment	12.8	18.4	17.8	21.2	20.9	24.7	26.9	27.3	28.3	29.3	27.3	30.8
Employer went bankrupt	8.7	18.9	7.6	11.0	9.2	8.9	9.5	7.7	6.2	5.7	4.8	4.3
Other	2.6	5.7	5.2	10.0	4.5	4.2	6.9	4.8	5.7	9.7	11.5	12.2
Probability of exit from unemployment to employment[d]	40.8	41.4	29.0	42.0	50.5	45.2	44.6	45.9	48.0	52.4	52.6	..

TABLE 18.2—*continued*

Job flows[e]

Job creation (000s)	..	..	53.8	59.9	87.8	70.2	75.9	70.9	70.6	71.5	68.0	62.7
Job destruction (000s)	..	..	91.6	72.2	65.0	62.4	79.0	71.5	62.1	56.7	50.6	55.5
Job creation rate (percent)	..	..	8.1	9.6	14.3	11.0	11.8	11.1	11.0	11.0	10.3	9.2
Job destruction rate (percent)	..	..	13.8	11.5	10.6	9.8	12.3	11.2	9.7	8.7	7.6	8.2
Memorandum: employment (000s)[f]	..	..	664	626	614	637	644	641	641	649	664	681

a. Flow rates are obtained by dividing flows by total employment at the beginning of the year. Hirings are the number of workers of a particular firm on January 1 of the next year that were not employed by the same firm on January 1 of the current (next) year. Separations are the number of workers of a particular firm on January 1 of the current year that are not employed by the same firm on January 1 of the next year.

b. During calendar year, among persons employed as of the start of the calendar year.

c. During calendar year.

d. Within 12 months, among persons entering unemployment during the calendar year.

e. Flows are calculated as described in note a. Job creation is employment gains, summed over all firms that increased employment between January 1 of the current year and January 1 of the next year. Job destruction is employment losses, summed over all firms that decreased employment between January 1 of the current year and January 1 of the next year.

f. Numbers differ from those in Table 18.1 because of imperfect matching of workers to firms (not all workers had valid firm identifiers).

Source: Author's computations based on work history database.

creation sharply increased in the early 1990s. (It is safe to assume that pretransition job destruction rates were much lower.) Starting in 1996 both job destruction and job creation rates slowly declined, dropping below 10 percent in 2001 (Figure 18.3). After reaching rates that were high by international standards in the early 1990s, the intensity of job flows in 2001 was comparable to that in Western industrial countries (for job flows in other countries, see, for example, Davis and Haltiwanger 1999). Interestingly, the share of job creation in hirings

FIGURE 18.3 JOB CREATION AND DESTRUCTION, 1990–2001

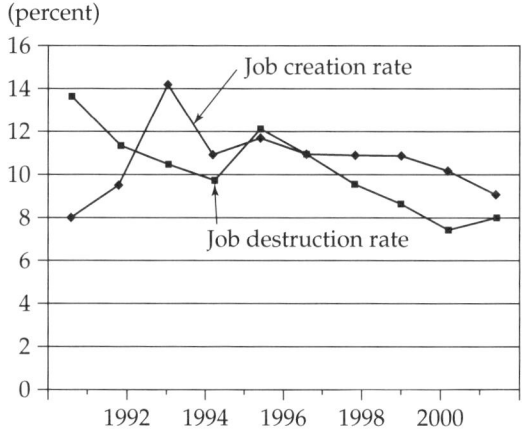

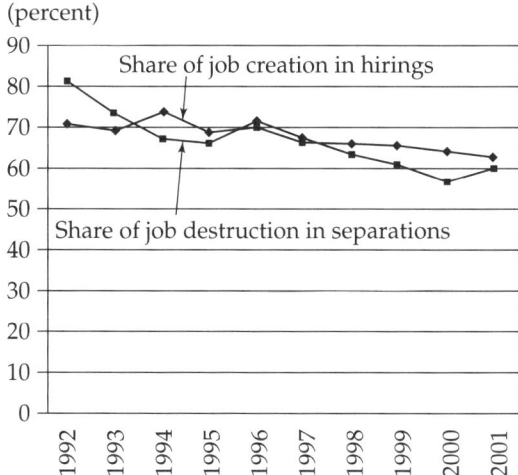

Source: Author's computations based on work history database.

and, similarly, the share of job destruction in separations declined steadily throughout the 1990s, reaching 62.1 percent and 59.3 percent, respectively, in 2001 (Figure 18.3). Even after 10 years of decline, however, these values exceed those typical in Western industrial countries. (Based on eight studies of industrial countries, Davis and Haltiwanger reported average values of 45.2 percent and 47.9 percent, respectively, for the share of job creation in hirings and the share of job destruction in separations.) Although at the end of transition job flows were thus comparable to flows in industrial countries, worker flows seem to have lagged behind.

DETERMINANTS OF WAGES

Results of estimates of earnings function show that the transition unleashed strong and diverse changes in the determinants of pay.[7] In particular, returns to education increased dramatically, primarily at the very beginning of the transition, and have stabilized since the mid-1990s. Returns to experience fell slightly for those with long service and increased for those with short service, but even in 2001 returns were increasing for those with service of more than 25 years—clear evidence of rigidity in the wage-setting mechanism. The male-female gap was kept constant at internationally low levels throughout the 1990s.

Male-Female Wage Gap

When skill and job characteristics are controlled for, Slovenian women were found to earn 9 to 10 percent less than otherwise identical men in the period under observation (Table 18.3, top panel). Orazem and Vodopivec (1995) report a narrowing of the gap during the 1987–91 transition, which came about because predominantly female industries were hit less hard than predominantly male industries.

Education

The most dramatic changes associated with the transition occurred in the returns to education; most of the change in these returns was over by 1993. The returns to more educated workers increased monotonically for all groups, with the highest increases belonging to graduates of two-year colleges (*višja šola*) and, especially, four-year colleges (*visoka šola*; Figure 18.4 and Table 18.3, second panel).[8] For the latter group the wage premium over unskilled workers (those who had not finished elementary school) doubled over the six-year period from

FIGURE 18.4 RETURNS TO EDUCATION AND WORK EXPERIENCE, 1987–2001

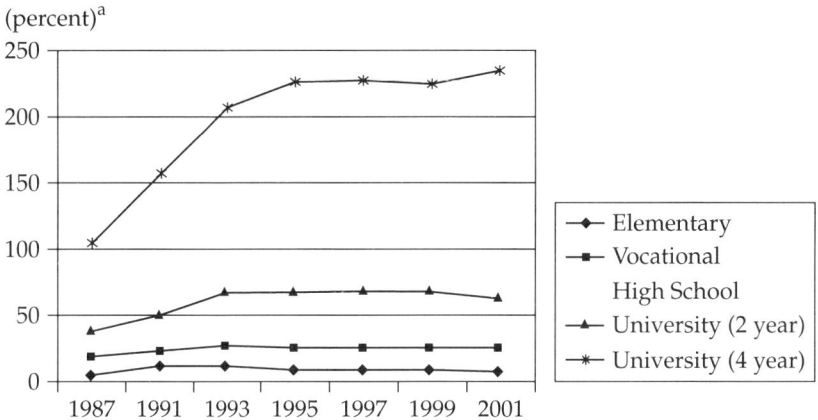

(percent)[a]

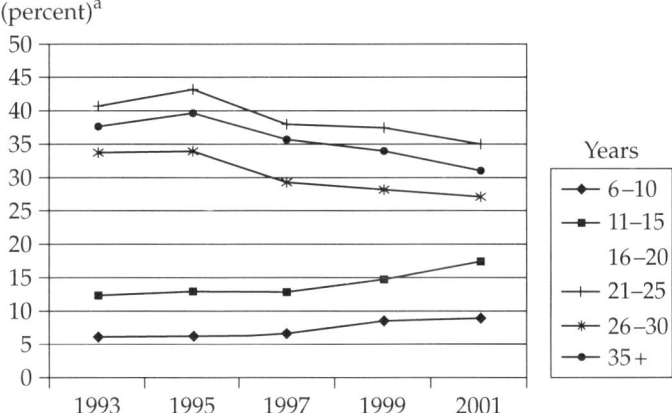

(percent)[a]

a. Coefficients α_i, reported in Table 18.3, are converted to returns as $100 * [\exp(\alpha_i) - 1]$.
Sources: Own computations based on workers' earnings database; Orazem and Vodopivec (1995) for 1987 and 1991 (data refer to males).

1987 to 1993: from 104 percent to 208 percent. After 1995 the value of education for all educational groups remained remarkably constant, with only a modest additional increase for the most educated in 2001. Converted to yearly rates, returns to education in 2001 amounted to 2 percent for those with elementary education, 3 percent for those with vocational education, 8 percent for those with high school, 15 percent for those with a two-year college degree, and an astounding 20 percent for those with a four-year college degree. (These results

TABLE 18.3 RESULTS OF REGRESSIONS EXPLAINING EARNINGS BY SEX, EDUCATION, EXPERIENCE, AND OWNERSHIP OF EMPLOYER, 1987–2001[a]

Independent variable	1987 Coef.	1987 t-statistic	1991 Coef.	1991 t-statistic	1993 Coef.	1993 t-statistic	1995 Coef.	1995 t-statistic	1997 Coef.	1997 t-statistic	1999 Coef.	1999 t-statistic	2001 Coef.	2001 t-statistic
Sex														
Female	..		..		−0.09	−81.0	−0.09	−76.2	−0.09	−85.2	−0.10	−89.1	−0.10	−82.1
Education[b]														
Elementary	0.04	5.3	0.11	6.2	0.09	45.7	0.08	36.5	0.08	34.9	0.07	28.0	0.07	24.9
Vocational	0.16	23.5	0.20	13.8	0.24	123.7	0.22	104.2	0.23	110.4	0.21	98.1	0.21	84.1
High school	0.32	40.0	0.41	24.6	0.52	253.7	0.52	231.4	0.52	241.6	0.52	221.2	0.51	194.9
University (two-year)	0.52	43.3	0.68	27.7	0.85	311.0	0.89	304.9	0.89	327.7	0.89	308.7	0.91	277.8
University (four-year)	0.72	61.8	0.94	41.5	1.12	410.6	1.19	407.8	1.19	440.7	1.18	419.4	1.21	385.4
Work experience[c]														
6–10 years			..		0.06	25.6	0.07	26.1	0.07	30.8	0.08	38.7	0.09	35.5
11–15 years			..		0.12	49.5	0.12	51.3	0.12	56.5	0.14	62.8	0.16	64.4
16–20 years			..		0.19	77.1	0.18	74.1	0.16	74.3	0.17	77.8	0.19	73.9
21–25 years			..		0.24	101.3	0.24	98.4	0.21	96.1	0.22	95.1	0.21	82.7
26–30 years			..		0.29	116.1	0.29	115.4	0.26	113.7	0.25	108.9	0.24	92.5
31–35 years			..		0.32	115.5	0.34	119.0	0.31	120.4	0.30	116.9	0.27	98.1
More than 35 years			..		0.34	100.1	0.36	105.4	0.33	99.3	0.32	99.1	0.31	90.6

Type of ownership[d]												
Social	..	..	0.14	11.7	0.07	5.4	0.08	7.1	0.08	6.2	−0.03	−2.3
Private	..	..	0.10	9.3	−0.01	−0.6	0.00	−0.4	0.08	9.6	−0.02	−2.8
Cooperative	..	..	0.09	4.0	0.09	4.0	0.06	3.0	0.14	6.6	−0.07	−3.2
Mixed	..	..	0.15	10.6	0.04	2.7	0.03	2.2	0.08	6.5	0.01	1.1
No. of observations	15,888	10,822	551,506		529,294		503,059		500,418		401,168	
R^2	0.43	0.34	0.38		0.40		0.47		0.47		0.50	

a. Included but not reported are sectoral dummies and dummies for the type of shift work.
b. Omitted variable is unfinished elementary education.
c. Omitted variable is less than 6 years experience.
d. Omitted variable is state ownership.

Sources: Author's computations based on workers' earnings database; Orazem and Vodopivec (1995) for 1987 and 1991 (data refer to males).

assume that the groups spent 11, 12, 14, and 16 years, respectively, to obtain their education, and that the base category—those who had not finished elementary school—spent 5 years in school).

Work Experience

Throughout the 1990s, experienced workers continued to command a premium, which increased nearly linearly with years of service. Interestingly, however, premiums showed a clear tendency to shrink throughout the 1990s, with the premium for workers with little work experience increasing, and that for workers with long experience decreasing (Figure 18.4 and Table 18.3, third panel). Still, in 2001 each year of work experience brought roughly a 1-percentage-point increase in wages. This pattern differs from the international experience (see below) and is consistent with the regulations of collective agreements, which mandate an increase in the basic wage with work experience (see above). The identified pattern of wages thus suggests a heavy influence of the institutional setup on wages.

Type of Ownership

Interestingly, returns do not reveal any strong differences by type of firm ownership. In particular, workers in private firms were paid an 8 to 10 percent premium over workers in state ownership in some years, but in other years they were paid less than state workers (Table 18.3, fourth panel). This suggests that wages do not differ strongly across firms of different ownership types.

International Comparisons

How do these results on the determinants of the wage structure compare with those in other economies? First, as alluded to above, the female wage gap in Slovenia in the 1990s was very low by international standards. For example, in the late 1990s the gap was 29 percent in Bulgaria, 24 percent in Hungary, 25 percent in FYR Macedonia, and 31 percent in Poland (Rutkowski 2001). Second, virtually all studies on transition economies find that the returns to education have increased and that more-educated groups have received larger increases (Rutkowski 2001, Orazem and Vodopivec 1997). Third, our results on the returns to experience differ from those of most other studies. Both in terms of the pattern (the fact that the premium continues to *increase* for workers with over 30 years of experience) and in terms of size, the experience premium in Slovenia deviates from that in most other transition economies (see Rutkowski 2001) as well from that in Western industrialized countries.

Wage Inequality

Orazem and Vodopivec (1995) report that during 1987–91 the dismantling of government controls produced a strong increase in wage inequality: wage variation increased between and within skill groups, within groups with identical industry and human capital characteristics, and across firms within an industry. Their results show that, later in the 1990s, wage inequality increased only modestly: the Gini coefficient increased from 28.9 in 1992 to 30.0 at the end of 1994, fell to 29.1 following the introduction of the minimum wage in 1995, and increased again to 30.6 in 2001.

CONCLUDING REMARKS

During the transition, Slovenia undertook labor market reforms rather cautiously. It retained strict employment protection legislation, imposed a heavy tax burden on labor, and kept minimum wages relatively high. To help workers dislocated by the transition, it offered rather generous unemployment benefits and spent considerable resources on active labor market policies.

Regardless of whether such policies helped or hindered labor market adjustment—a still open question not tackled in this chapter—the evidence presented in this chapter suggests that by 2000–01 the Slovenian labor market had completed its transition.[9] The systemic shock of the early 1990s dramatically increased worker and job flows, with worker separations and job destruction leading the way, and hirings and job creation lagging by several years. Both worker and job flows declined and had mostly stabilized by the end of the 1990s. Unemployment sharply increased in the early 1990s and then slowly declined. Similarly, after an intense but short-lived reduction in the early 1990s, both employment and wages started to increase, with the turnaround occurring in 1993–95. In 2001 employment and the labor force both exceeded their 1991 levels, and unemployment stabilized at a low level by international standards. The transition also brought important changes to the determination of wages: the returns to more educated workers increased dramatically, and the returns to workers with long service declined, whereas those for workers starting their career increased. Women did not fare worse than men: they only slightly reduced their share in employment while retaining a relatively small wage gap.

These developments clearly show a strengthened role for market forces in the Slovenian labor market. Increased worker flows and, particularly, increased job flows in the early transition suggest that one of the key tasks of transition—the reallocation of labor—proceeded in vigorous fashion. The process was fostered by increased flexibility in the determination of wages, and changes in returns to education show that market forces were strongly at work in this area, too. Among other positive developments, the gender wage gap not only has not worsened but has indeed stabilized at an internationally low level, and the increase in wage inequality was brought to a halt during 1992–2001. Among the worrying signs is the distortion of the structure of wages produced by the automatic increase of the basic wage with seniority, as called for under collective agreements. Because this requirement contradicts the trend in an individual's productivity over his or her career, it hinders the employment or reemployment of older workers. Moreover, it seems that worker flows in the Slovenian labor market have stabilized at internationally low levels, possibly hindering gains from improved matches between workers and employers. This is an area worthy of further investigation.

REFERENCES

Abraham, K., and M. Vodopivec. 1993. "Slovenia: A Study of Labor Market Transitions." World Bank, Washington, D.C. Processed.

Bevc, M. 1993. "Rates of Return of Investment in Education in Former Yugoslavia in the 1970s and 1980s by Region." *Economics of Education* 12(4): 325–43.

Davis, S., and J. Haltiwanger. 1999. "Gross Job Flows." In O. Ashenfelter and D. Card, eds., *Handbook of Labor Economics*, Vol. 3, pp. 2711–2805. Amsterdam: Elsevier Science.

Employment Office of Slovenia. 1996. *Yearly Report 1996*. Ljubljana.

Haltiwanger, J., and M. Vodopivec. 2003. "Worker Flows, Job Flows and Firm Wage Policies: An Analysis of Slovenia." *Economics of Transition* 11(2): 253–90.

Haltiwanger, J., S. Scarpetta, and M. Vodopivec. 2003. "How Institutions Affect Labor Market Outcomes: Evidence from Transition Countries." Paper presented at the World Bank Economist Forum, Washington, April.

OECD. 1994. *The OECD Jobs Study*, Paris.

———. 1999. *Employment Outlook*. Paris.

Orazem, P., and M. Vodopivec. 1995: "Winners and Losers in Transition: Returns to Education, Experience, and Gender." *World Bank Economic Review* (May): 210–30.

———. 1997. "Value of Human Capital in Transition to Market: Evidence from Slovenia." *European Economic Review* 41: 893–903.

Riboud, M., C. Sanchez-Paramo, and C. Silva-Jáuregui 2001. "Does Eurosclerosis Matter? Institutional Reform and Labor Market Performance in Central and Eastern European Countries in the 1990s." In B. Funck and L. Pizzati, eds., *Labor, Employment, and Social Policies in the EU Enlargement*

Process: Changing Perspectives and Policy Options. Washington, D.C.: World Bank.

Rutkowski, J. 2001. "Wage Inequality in Transition Economies of Central Europe. Trends and Patterns in the Late 1990s." Social Protection Discussion Paper Series 0117. World Bank, Washington, D.C.

Svejnar, J. 2002. "Transition Economies: Performance and Challenges." *Journal of Economic Perspectives* 16: 3–28.

Vodopivec, M. 1993. "Determination of Earnings in Yugoslav Firms: Can It Be Squared with Labor Management?" *Economic Development and Cultural Change* 41(3): 623–32.

————. 1996. "The Slovenian Labor Market in Transition: Evidence from Microdata." In *Lessons from Labour Market Policies in the Transition Countries.* Paris: OECD.

Vodopivec, M., A. Wörgötter, and D. Raju. 2003. "Unemployment Benefit Systems in Central and Eastern Europe: A Review of the 1990s." Social Protection Discussion Paper 0310. World Bank, Washington, D.C.

NOTES

The author is grateful to the Statistical Office, the National Employment Office, and the Pension and Disability Fund of the Republic of Slovenia for providing data.

1. For evidence on government involvement in wage setting under self-management, which resulted in massive income redistribution, see Vodopivec (1993).

2. The empirical analysis rests on three unusually rich administrative databases covering all Slovenian work force participants and all incorporated business subjects: a work history database, a workers' earnings database, and a business registry of firms (for details, see Haltiwanger and Vodopivec 2003).

3. See, for example, Svejnar (2002) for an evaluation of the general pace of reform in transition economies.

4. The maximum value is 6. Scores are based on the OECD (1999) methodology, which evaluates regular and fixed-term legislation based on 18 dimensions. Comparator countries include Bulgaria, Czech Republic, Estonia, Hungary, Poland, Romania, Russia, Slovakia, and Ukraine.

5. Older workers also faced increasing difficulties in exiting unemployment (Abraham and Vodopivec 1993).

6. The difference arises primarily from a sizable population of registered unemployed workers whom the survey did not find to be unemployed. Out of 110,000 registered unemployed in 1996, the survey found that 19,000 (17.3 percent) were in fact employed, and 32,000 (29.1 percent) were out of the labor force (Employment Office of Slovenia 1996). On the other hand, the survey also found 10,000 workers counted as unemployed by the survey who were not registered as unemployed with employment offices.

7. The results reflect returns to specific components of human capital and type of ownership of the firm, under the ceteris paribus assumption. They were obtained by estimating standard earnings functions on data for all workers in the Slovenian incorporated sector.

8. This contrasts sharply with the pretransition results. Bevc (1993) reports that, from 1976 to 1986, private returns to education in Slovenia increased dramatically for workers with primary education (from 13.6 percent to 18.5 percent) and only slightly for those with tertiary education (from 4.3 percent to 5 percent), and that they decreased for those with secondary education (from 6.9 percent to 5.2 percent).

9. In an analysis of both OECD and transition economies, Haltiwanger, Scarpetta, and Vodopivec (2003) found that institutions that lead to less labor market flexibility and higher labor costs are associated with adverse labor market outcomes, more generous unemployment benefits, and stricter employment protection legislation.

Chapter 19
Social Sector Developments

Tine Stanovnik

OVERALL ASSESSMENT OF THE
SOCIAL PROTECTION SYSTEM

The social protection system of Slovenia has played an extremely important role in the transition process: it could aptly be described as a rock of stability in a tumultuous and tempestuous period of rapid economic, political, and social change. This does not mean that the system was rigid and inflexible: it did evolve, but in a gradual and orderly fashion. Also, the system has to a large degree remained generous, particularly in comparison with those in other Central and Eastern European (CEE) countries.

The strong performance of the social protection system was made possible by the well-developed administrative capacity of Slovenia's autonomous social security institutions, such as the Institute for Pension and Disability Insurance and the Institute for Health Insurance. Apart from this institutional and administrative capacity, Slovenia is fortunate in having preserved a centralized system of collection of taxes and social contributions. This was the responsibility of the Payment Agency (Služba Družbenega Knjigovodstva, or SDK). The agency maintained a very tight grip on all payments by firms and thus also tight control over social security contributions; this in turn prevented an erosion of compliance. This factor is extremely important, because widespread evasion did wreak havoc in a number of CEE countries, resulting in severe reductions in social benefits. Typically, the deterioration of social protection systems in the CEE economies in transition is ascribed to their very adverse macroeconomic developments (the fall in output, increase in unemployment, and mass retirement); but Slovenia also experienced very adverse macroeconomic developments in the first years of transition, yet the social protection system continued to function with scarcely any disruption. On the other hand, although the social protection system generally deserves good marks for its coverage and adequacy of benefits, it does not necessarily cater equally well to the needs of all relevant population subgroups, as some groups fare better than others. Figure 19.1 illustrates the trends in the numbers of employed, unemployed, pensioners, and old-age pensioners from 1990 to 2001.

Table 19.1 presents data on social protection expenditure in Slovenia and compares them with average values for the 15 EU countries (EU-15). In terms of the costs of social protection expenditure relative to GDP, Slovenia is very close to the EU average. Comparison of the relative importance of various individual social protection programs shows that the composition of social protection expenditure in Slovenia is also more or less similar to that in the EU-15. Expenditure on old-age pensioners is by far the most important category, accounting for 44 percent of all social protection expenditure in 2000; the corresponding

FIGURE 19.1 EMPLOYMENT, UNEMPLOYMENT, AND
PENSION RECIPIENTS, 1990–2001

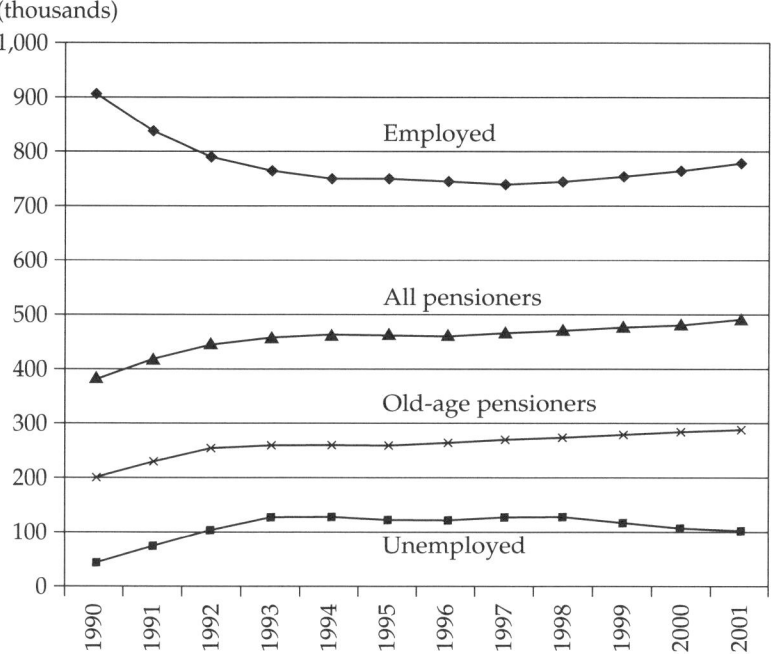

Sources: Institute for Pension and Disability Insurance and
National Employment Office of Slovenia.

figure for the EU-15 is 42 percent. Table 19.1 also shows that housing
allowances are virtually nonexistent in Slovenia: housing subsidiza-
tion mostly takes the form of controlled (below-market) rents for non-
profit and social rentals.

Reform of the various parts of the social protection system in
Slovenia pursued multiple goals, although financial sustainability was
certainly in the forefront. Of course, there are exceptions to this general pattern. For example, the almost continuous changes in child
allowances were mostly driven by family policy considerations. The
1992 and 1999 reforms of the pension system and the 1992 reform of
the health care system were more "mainstream" and were triggered
by the need for cost containment and the desire to ensure the system's
financial viability at least in the medium term. In other words, these
reforms were designed in such a way as to reduce benefits within the
public system. Concomitantly, a greater role was envisaged for private provision, which was to compensate for the reduction in benefits

TABLE 19.1 EXPENDITURE ON SOCIAL BENEFITS BY FUNCTION IN
SLOVENIA, 1996–2000, AND THE EUROPEAN
UNION, 2000
(percent of GDP)

Function	1996	1997	1998	1999	2000	EU-15, 2000
Sickness, health care	7.9	8.0	8.0	8.0	7.9	7.5
Disability	2.2	2.2	2.2	2.3	2.3	2.2
Old age	11.3	11.4	11.4	11.2	11.2	12.7[a]
Survivors	0.5	0.5	0.5	0.5	0.5	n.a.
Family and children	2.2	2.2	2.1	2.3	2.4	2.2
Unemployment	1.1	1.3	1.4	1.2	1.1	1.7
Social exclusion not elsewhere classified	0.5	0.5	0.4	0.4	0.4	1.0[b]
Total	25.5	26.0	26.0	25.9	25.9	27.3

a. Includes survivors' benefits.
b. Includes benefits for housing.
Sources: Statistical Office of the Republic of Slovenia (2002); Eurostat (2003).

from the public system. This strategy proved quite successful in the
health care reform of 1992, and much less so in the 1992 pension
reform; the failure of the latter was due to the complete absence of
tax incentives. The 1999 pension reform corrected this omission and
introduced substantial tax incentives for private collective pension
schemes.

SOCIAL BENEFITS, POVERTY, AND INEQUALITY

An important aim of cash social benefits is to provide income to persons who have temporarily or permanently withdrawn from the labor
force. This income replacement function is in fact the dominant function of all social protection systems. In continental Europe, where social
insurance principles are important for determining the level of benefits,
benefits disbursed by the social protection system are related to previous income, that is, income earned during one's economically active
period. In these systems only a smaller part of total benefits—social
assistance—is devoted exclusively to the needy. This means that one
cannot expect a priori that social protection systems will be efficient
in the alleviation of poverty.

Nevertheless, various studies performed for Slovenia, such as
Stanovnik and Stropnik (1998) and Stropnik and Stanovnik (2002),
have shown that social benefits do contribute significantly toward
poverty alleviation. This can be seen from Table 19.2, which shows the

TABLE 19.2 CONCENTRATION COEFFICIENTS AND FACTOR
INCOME SHARES IN TOTAL INCOME, 1993 AND
1997–99

	Concentration coefficient[a]		Factor income share	
Type of income	1993	1997–99	1993	1997–1999
Income from employment	0.30501	0.30960	0.58615	0.60286
Income from occasional work	0.40096	0.13287	0.02714	0.01519
Self-employment income	0.43987	0.16883	0.09397	0.06302
Pensions	0.09985	0.15602	0.21085	0.25042
Health insurance-related cash benefits	0.19555	0.05623	0.00552	0.01224
Unemployment benefits	−0.20568	−0.18613	0.01431	0.01436
War-related disability benefits	0.07359	−0.05449	0.00325	0.00193
Social assistance	−0.44134	−0.70331	0.00437	0.00257
Child benefits	−0.37404	−0.20977	0.00738	0.01615
Educational grants	−0.00272	−0.08290	0.00688	0.00915
Income from capital and property rights	0.76940	0.67017	0.00617	0.00795
Intrafamily financial gifts and transfers	0.56250	−0.01952	0.03400	0.00416
Total current monetary disposable income	0.26960	0.23557	1.00000	1.00000

a. A coefficient below that for total current monetary disposable income (the Gini coefficient) indicates that the given income source tends to equalize incomes in relative terms across rich and poor; a negative coefficient indicates that the poor receive more of that source of income in absolute terms than the rich.

Source: Author's calculations using data from 1993 and 1997–99 Household Expenditure Surveys. (The 1997–99 survey actually consists of three annual surveys, suitably merged.)

Gini coefficients of income inequality and concentration coefficients for various income sources.

Where the concentration coefficient for a given income source is positive but lower than the Gini coefficient for total current disposable monetary income, the implication is that the given income source is a relative income equalizer, relatively more important for the poor than for the rich. Negative values of the concentration coefficient indicate that the poor receive (in absolute terms) more of the given income source that the rich.

Thus, quite according to expectations, unemployment benefits, social assistance, and child benefits were absolute income equalizers in 1997–99. Nevertheless, their overall effect on income inequality was small, as the share of these income sources in total disposable household monetary income was small (last two columns of Table 19.2).

Poorer households also receive larger educational grants than richer households, because more and more of these grants are being disbursed by the Ministry of Education, for which social criteria are decisive. Pensions are a relative income equalizer, meaning that they are more equally distributed than total household income. This is of course quite according to expectations, as pensions are a social insurance payment, with strong solidarity elements. Also quite according to expectations is the very high value of the concentration coefficient for income from capital and property rights, showing that this income source is strongly concentrated among the rich.

Table 19.2 also shows a large decrease in the Gini coefficient for total current disposable monetary household income: its value dropped from 0.2696 in 1993 to 0.2356 in 1997–99. Although it is true that income inequality peaked in 1993, the subsequent decrease is overstated. It seems that, in the 1997–99 household expenditure surveys, income from self-employment was somewhat underreported, particularly in the higher income groups.

Social transfers have a quite varied effect on the income of recipient groups. In other words, in spite of social transfers, the risk of poverty can be quite high for certain groups. This can be seen from Table 19.3, which shows the incidence of poverty for various vulnerable groups. The table shows that during the transition period, that is, from 1993 to 1997–99, the risk of poverty increased slightly for all persons, although not for all subgroups. Poverty risk decreased for pensioners and for persons aged 60 and over. These two groups, of course, strongly overlap. The relative income position of pensioners and persons aged 60 and over has seen continuous improvement since the mid-1980s; it is caused by a favorable indexation rule for pensions, whereby growth of pensions is closely tied to growth in nominal (net) wages. On the other hand, the large increase in poverty risk for the unemployed was caused by a decrease in the share of unemployed who receive unemployment benefits and a decrease in the average real value of those benefits. Poverty risk also increased for children; weaker targeting of child benefits undoubtedly contributed to this increase.

PENSION REFORM

Slovenia undertook two pension reforms in the 1990s, under two pieces of comprehensive pension legislation: the Pension and Disability Insurance Act (PDIA) of 1992 and the PDIA of 1999. These two acts, together with the PDIA of 1983, can be regarded as good examples of the gradualist approach toward reform of the social protection system. This applies only to the final result, however, as the initial

TABLE 19.3 INCIDENCE OF POVERTY, 1993 AND 1997–99[a]
(percent living below poverty line)

Poverty line as percent of median equivalent household income	All persons		Pensioners		Unemployed		Children aged 18 and under		Persons aged 60 and over	
	1993	1997–99	1993	1997–99	1993	1997–99	1993	1997–99	1993	1997–99
40	3.7	4.2	3.8	3.3	13.6	23.6	4.2	4.8	7.3	5.3
50	7.1	8.0	8.7	5.7	22.5	35.5	7.4	9.4	14.1	10.0
60	12.9	13.9	16.3	11.5	33.5	48.3	13.2	16.7	25.0	17.6
70	20.6	21.1	23.2	19.4	45.5	63.1	21.5	24.6	33.6	28.4

a. For a discussion of methodological issues, see Stropnik and Stanovnik (2002).
Source: Author's calculations using data from 1993 and 1997–99 Household Expenditure Surveys.

proposals for the most recent reform were anything but gradual. Even the "White Paper on the Reform of Pension and Disability Insurance," prepared by the Ministry of Labour, Family, and Social Affairs, which appeared in November 1997, contained quite radical proposals for a fundamental restructuring of the pension system: a large downsizing of the first (public) pillar and the introduction of a mandatory, privately fully funded, second pillar. The reform proposals were obviously strongly influenced by the solutions favored by the World Bank. However, because of strong opposition from various quarters—trade unions, some political parties, and influential economists—the original proposals were watered down considerably.[1] Changes in the first pillar, although substantial, were introduced gradually, with numerous exceptions. Instead of a mandatory second pillar, a voluntary second pillar was introduced, mainly in the form of collective pension schemes.[2] An important concession wrested from the Ministry of Finance was a very favorable tax treatment of premiums for these pension schemes, which are tax exempt up to a certain contribution ceiling. This means that they are not subject to corporate income tax, social security contributions, or personal income tax.

Table 19.4 presents the basic characteristics and defining parameters of the pension reforms of 1983, 1992, and 1999. As the table shows, the 1999 PDIA considerably narrowed the gender gap with regard to pension eligibility criteria. For both men and women, the earliest possible retirement age is 58, and the insured person must have worked a sufficient number of years to qualify.[3] The 1999 PDIA introduced the term *full pensionable age*, set at 63 for men and 61 for women. It serves as a benchmark: strong incentives (in the form of higher accrual rates) are provided to prolong the period of working activity, that is, to retire after the full pensionable age, as well as strong disincentives for retirement before the full pensionable age. Thus, although men are able to retire at age 58 (with a pension qualifying period of 40 years), their pension is subject to "maluses," that is, negative accrual rates, so that they receive a permanently reduced pension. Typically there are exceptions to this rule, and certain categories of workers can retire at 58 without maluses, again provided they have worked for 40 years.

In the 1999 PDIA, new pensions are calculated on the basis of the individual's best 18-year average of net wages,[4] and accrual rates are much lower than the previous accrual rates. The relevant gender parameters are almost the same, but slightly more favorable for women.

The 1999 PDIA retained the principle of pension indexation according to the growth of net wages. It also introduced an important new feature, namely, a downward adjustment of pensions for existing pensioners. This takes account of the fact that new entrants will retire under less favorable conditions and that existing pensions

Table 19.4 Basic Characteristics of the 1983, 1992, and 1999 Pension and Disability Insurance Acts

1983 PDIA	1992 PDIA	1999 PDIA
Eligibility criteria[a]		
Men: p.q.p. = 40 years Women: p.q.p. = 35 years Men: age = 60, p.q.p. = 20 years Women: age = 55, p.q.p. = 20 years Men: age = 65, ins.p. = 15 years Women: age = 55, ins.p. = 15 years	Men: age = 58, p.q.p. = 40 years Women: age = 53, p.q.p. = 35 years Men: age = 63, p.q.p. = 20 years Women: age = 58, p.q.p. = 20 years Men: age = 65, ins.p. = 15 years Women: age = 55, ins.p. = 15 years	Men: age = 58, p.q.p. = 40 years Women: age = 58, p.q.p. = 38 years Men: age = 63, p.q.p. = 20 years Women: age = 61, p.q.p. = 20 years Men: age = 65, ins.p. = 15 years Women: age = 63, ins.p. = 15 years
Minimum insurance period		
15 years	15 years	15 years
Pension base		
Best 10-year average of wages, indexed for inflation	Best 10-year average of net wages, indexed for inflation	Best 18-year average of net wages, indexed for inflation
Accrual rates		
Men: 35 percent of pension base for first 15 years, then 2 percent for each additional year, up to 40 years of p.q.p.	Men: 35 percent of pension base for first 15 years, then 2 percent for each additional year, up to 40 years of p.q.p.	Men: 35 percent of pension base for first 15 years, then 1.5 percent for each additional year of p.q.p.
Women: 40 percent of pension base for first 15 years, 3 percent for each additional year up to 20 years, then 2 percent for each additional year up to 35 years of p.q.p.	Women: 40 percent of pension base for first 15 years, 3 percent for each additional year up to 20 years, then 2 percent for each additional year up to 35 years of p.q.p.	Women: 38 percent of pension base for first 15 years, then 1.5 percent for each additional year of p.q.p.

TABLE 19.4 — *continued*

	Column 1	Column 2	Column 3
Pension indexation	90 percent of growth of net wages	Growth of net wages	Growth of net wages
Minimum pension base	65 percent of national net wage	64 percent of national net wage	Set nominally, but effectively 64 percent of national net wage
Maximum pension base	350 percent of national net wage	310 percent of national net wage	4 times minimum pension base
Early retirement	Men: age = 55, p.q.p. = 35 years Women: age = 50, p.q.p. = 30 years	Men: age = 55, p.q.p. = 35 years Women: age = 50, p.q.p. = 30 years and other required conditions[b]	No special provisions, but certain categories of workers can obtain a pension without deductions for retirement before full pensionable age.[c]
Deductions for early retirement	1.5 percent for each "missing" year until age 60 (men) or age 55 (women); 0.5 percent for each "missing" year of insurance. Deductions are temporary and lifted when age criteria are fulfilled.	1 percent for each "missing" year of insurance. Deductions are temporary and lifted when age criteria are fulfilled.	Not applicable.

Purchase of insurance period

Generous conditions for farmers and the self-employed. In August 1990; possibility to purchase years is extended to certain categories of employees (firm bankruptcy, "technological" redundancy, etc.).	Employer may purchase (for employee) up to 5 years, under certain conditions.[d] Employee may purchase years for time spent in university education and military service.	Employer may purchase (for employee) up to 5 years, under certain conditions.[e] Employee may purchase years for time spent in university education and military service.

p.q.p. = pension qualifying period; ins.p. = insurance period.

a. The increase in pensionable age under the 1992 PDIA was gradual and was completed in 1998. All figures refer to final values. The increase in the pensionable age and pension qualifying period under the 1999 PDIA for women was very gradual. Figures refer to the final values, which will in some cases be achieved in 20 years.

b. "Other required conditions" include bankruptcy of the employing firm, disability, or long-term unemployment.

c. Article 55, 1999 PDIA.

d. Article 214, 1992 PDIA.

e. Articles 195–99, 1999 PDIA.

Source: Štrovs (1984), Kuhelj (2000), and the 1983, 1992, and 1999 PDIAs.

must be adequately aligned with these lower entry pensions. The 1999 PDIA has also narrowed the gap between comparable maximum and minimum pensions: the ratio is now 4:1 instead of the previous 4.8:1. Early retirement is no longer possible, although the period during which persons may purchase insurance (mostly for military service and university schooling) has been retained. The purchase price takes account of actuarial fairness and is thus much higher than in the early 1990s.

The 1999 PDIA also introduced a state pension for persons aged 65 and over who are not entitled to a pension from a public scheme and who have no income but have at least 30 years of residence (between the ages of 15 and 65) in Slovenia. This is in effect a social assistance benefit: it found its way into the PDIA as the result of considerable negotiation among parties in the government coalition.

Pension reform has succeeded in stabilizing public pension expenditure as a percentage of GDP. Following the passage of the 1999 PDIA, the actual retirement age started to increase, and the ratio of the average old-age pension to the average wage started to decrease (Table 19.5). There is no doubt that the single most important measure for cost containment was the downward adjustment of existing pensions, that is, the adjustment undertaken for alignment with the values of pensions of new entrants.

TABLE 19.5 PENSION EXPENDITURE, REPLACEMENT RATES, AND ACTUAL RETIREMENT AGES, 1992–2002

Year	Pension expenditure (percent of GDP)	Average replacement rate[a] (percent)	Actual retirement age (years, months)	
			Men	Women
1992	11.41	77.8	56, 2	52, 6
1993	11.76	73.9	56, 2	53, 3
1994	11.84	75.4	57, 7	53, 2
1995	12.23	76.2	57, 6	53, 1
1996	12.14	74.6	57, 6	54, 0
1997	12.13	74.3	58, 3	54, 11
1998	12.05	74.5	58, 5	55, 3
1999	12.09	75.8	58, 2	54, 10
2000	12.16	75.3	59, 2	55, 5
2001	11.92	73.2	59, 3	55, 5
2002	11.85	72.8	59, 11	55, 6

a. Ratio of the average old-age pension to the average net wage.

Source: Institute for Pension and Disability Insurance (2003).

The development of pension funds has also gained momentum. As of April 2003 there were five mutual pension funds, three pension funds organized by insurance companies, and four pension funds organized by pension companies. Membership in these funds has amounted to 201,100 persons, or about 24.8 percent of all insured persons within the first (public) pillar. Because of tax incentives (premiums are exempt from corporate income tax, social security contributions, and personal income tax), employers are strongly motivated to enroll their employees in collective pension schemes. Individual pension schemes are rare, since premiums paid by individuals are exempt only from personal income tax. Preparations are well under way for employees of the public sector to join these pension schemes; this will result in a further large increase in membership and will approach 50 percent of insured persons in the first public pillar.

HEALTH CARE REFORM

Unlike the pension system, which remained centralized at the republic level during the 1980s, the health care system was highly decentralized and was in effect managed by self-managed communities of interest. Such decentralization resulted in low efficiency, poor control of resources, massive bureaucracy, and large deficits. When the self-managed system was dismantled in 1990, a new state institution, the National Bureau for Health Care, was established, and almost all health care contributions were channeled into the state budget. Only a small contribution rate was retained at the local level (for sickness benefits). Thus, whereas there were virtually no institutional changes in pension insurance (except a change in name), health insurance experienced a sea change. Predictably, the organizational change ("budgetization") could not resolve the problem of chronic lack of resources for health care, which remained in spite of increased out-of-pocket co-payments. In 1992 health reform legislation introduced far-reaching changes in the system.

The state delegated responsibility for health care to the newly founded Institute for Health Insurance (IHI), which was given responsibility for mandatory health insurance. Concomitantly, voluntary health insurance was introduced under the auspices of the IHI. This later evolved into an independent mutual insurance association, Vzajemna; soon thereafter, a private insurance company (Adriatic) also entered the field. The need for voluntary health insurance arose because the reform opted for mandatory health insurance with incomplete coverage of costs for a number of treatments and medications. The previous practice of out-of-pocket co-payment was deemed unacceptable, as the co-payment was to increase considerably. Full cost coverage by the mandatory insurance was to be confined only to a set of very specific needs, such as treatment of certain chronic diseases (cerebral palsy, epilepsy, developed forms of diabetes, multiple sclerosis, and others), regular preventive medical checkups for children in regular schooling, and medical care in prenatal clinics. Not surprisingly, the success of the voluntary health insurance program was swift and massive: it has quickly become quasi-mandatory, and only 5 percent of insured persons within the mandatory program are not also members of voluntary health insurance. The two insurance providers, Vzajemna and Adriatic, collect SIT 65.6 billion in premiums annually, which represented 19 percent of total health insurance payments (mandatory health contributions and premiums for voluntary insurance) in 2002. Meanwhile the retrenchment of public health insurance was quite impressive, as the joint (employee and employer) health insurance contribution rate dropped from 18.15 percent in 1992 to 13.8 percent in 1993.

It was hoped that the success of the health care reform, as manifested by a decrease in the mandatory contribution rate and the introduction of private health insurance, could be replicated in the pension reform of 1992. The latter introduced voluntary individual supplementary pension insurance under an institutional arrangement similar to that for health care. Thus, whereas voluntary health insurance was founded under the auspices of the IHI, voluntary pension insurance was founded under the auspices of the Institute for Pension and Disability Insurance. The introduction of supplementary pension insurance was quite unsuccessful, however, as the number of members never surpassed several hundred. The causes for this failure are twofold: pensions offered by the public pension system were still quite high even after the 1992 reform, and there were no tax incentives to join such a scheme. The 1999 pension reform did not repeat these mistakes: a significant (albeit gradual) decrease in pension rights within the first (public) pillar was combined with very strong tax incentives for membership in the second pillar (private pension funds).

The 1992 health care reform has perhaps become, in a sense, too successful for its own good. There is very little differentiation of premium payments, which means that every member pays nearly the same amount. The scheme is regressive, and this has become a highly contentious issue, as discussed in the *2003 White Paper on Health Care Reform*. It has been suggested that premiums for complementary health insurance be abolished and that a new tax be introduced in their place. Needless to say, should this proposal be accepted, private voluntary health insurance would almost certainly be marginalized and confined to supplementary insurance.

FAMILY AND CHILD BENEFITS

A number of benefits under the social protection system go to parents and their children; among these, parental compensation and child allowances are the most important. Parental compensation is granted in the form of wage compensation during parental leave; there has been virtually no change in this benefit during the transition period. In stark contrast, child allowances have experienced numerous changes during the 1990s. These could hardly be described as reforms, however, since they involve only changes in eligibility criteria and amounts—in effect, only tinkering with the system. From the early 1990s to 1999, coverage has been gradually increasing. Thus, in 1993, families were eligible for child allowance if their income per family member did not exceed 43 percent of the average net wage. This ceiling was increased to 50 percent of the average gross wage in 1994 and further increased to 110 percent of the average gross wage in 1996. Still further changes in 1999 introduced a new schedule, with the ceiling set at 99 percent of the average gross wage. Although the previous schemes were also more inclined toward lower income groups, the latest scheme was even more so, as the child in the lowest income group receives 5.8 times as much as a recipient in the highest income group. The 1999 changes also introduced differentiated benefit levels, with benefits dependent on the number of children in the family (the more children, the higher the average amount per child).

UNEMPLOYMENT BENEFITS

The unemployment insurance system is probably the weakest within the overall social protection system of Slovenia. In accordance with the "workfare" doctrine, greater emphasis in recent years has been placed on various active labor policy measures. Even before the 1998 reform, entitlements for unemployment benefits could hardly be described as generous, as the Organisation for Economic Co-operation and Development (1997) has noted. Changes introduced in 1998 further tightened eligibility conditions for the receipt of unemployment compensation, which is an income-related unemployment benefit. Admittedly, the duration of entitlement has remained unchanged. It still ranges from 3 to 24 months, but the required insurance record is more demanding. These harsher conditions predictably caused a large drop in the number of beneficiaries (Table 19.6).[5] The floor and ceiling of this benefit have also changed: the floor was raised from 80 to percent to 100 percent, and the ceiling lowered from 320 percent to 300 percent, of the guaranteed

TABLE 19.6 RECIPIENTS OF UNEMPLOYMENT BENEFITS,
          1992–2002

Year	Recipients of unemployment compensation (thousands)	Recipients of unemployment assistance (thousands)	Share of all recipients in total registered unemployment (percent)
1992	32.5	18.2	45.0
1993	42.5	20.0	43.1
1994	31.4	11.0	42.1
1995	28.3	5.9	30.3
1996	33.7	4.1	30.3
1997	37.1	3.7	32.6
1998	36.0	2.8	32.6
1999	31.2	3.2	31.0
2000	23.0	3.7	29.1
2001	19.4	4.5	25.3
2002	17.6	5.6	23.6

Source: National Employment Office of Slovenia (2002).

wage.[6] After his or her unemployment compensation has expired, the unemployed person is entitled to a means-tested flat-rate unemployment assistance benefit. The 1998 changes extended the period of entitlement to unemployment assistance benefit from 6 to 15 months, which caused an increase in the number of beneficiaries (Table 19.6).

The 1998 changes also severely reduced entitlements for the elderly unemployed. Before 1998 the duration of entitlement to unemployment compensation could be extended for a further three years, provided the unemployed person was sufficiently close to the normal retirement age. In effect, the elderly unemployed could thus receive unemployment compensation for up to five years. This provision has been abolished,[7] and the only concession granted to the elderly unemployed for whom unemployment compensation has expired and who are sufficiently close to retirement is that the National Employment Office pays their pension and disability insurance contribution.

Although all these new measures did result in reduced expenditure on unemployment benefits, they have doubtlessly further aggravated the income and social position of the unemployed. As Table 19.3 shows, the incidence of poverty among the unemployed is quite high, and the unemployed are the vulnerable group with by far the largest incidence of poverty.

CONCLUDING REMARKS

Broadly speaking, Slovenia has succeeded in maintaining a fairly well developed and generous social protection system. Not all of the functions of this system are equally well developed, however, and not all subgroups of the population are equally well provided for. Housing provision for the needy can be singled out as an example of an underdeveloped function of the system. The young unemployed, the elderly unemployed, and single parents with children are three groups for whom the social protection system does not provide sufficient protection from poverty and social exclusion.

Privatization of the social protection system has been successful in the sense that it stabilized public social protection expenditure and prevented an erosion of the whole social protection system. Private health insurance, introduced in 1992, quickly became quasi-mandatory, as its coverage is nearly universal. Similarly, private pension schemes (collective and individual) introduced in 2000 are rapidly increasing their membership and might well become quasi-mandatory in the coming years. In contrast to these trends toward retrenchment of the public system, the *2003 White Paper on Health Care Reform* proposed that private insurance for co-payments be discontinued, to be replaced by a "new" social security contribution rate. Of course, it remains to be seen whether this reversal will gain public acceptance.

Although Slovenia's spending on social protection is comparable to that in the EU countries as a percentage of GDP, it remains, nevertheless, a cause of constant concern, because the resulting higher labor costs have an impact on the competitiveness of the Slovenian economy. The joint (employee and employer) contribution rate has remained virtually unchanged since mid-1996 and amounts to 38 percent, although this is down from a peak of 50.35 percent in 1992. This decrease did come at a price, as revenue transfers from the state budget to the Institute for Pension and Disability Insurance increased considerably following the cut in the contribution rate in 1996.

Slovenia has so far acted pragmatically in introducing changes in its social protection system and has managed the "balancing act" of providing acceptable benefits from the combined (public and private) social protection system while keeping the costs acceptable to the general population. Of course, these changes must be continuous and must reflect not only public finance realities but also the preferences of the body politic.

REFERENCES

Eurostat. 2003. *Statistics in Focus, Population and Social Conditions*, no. 3. Luxembourg.

Organisation for Economic Co-operation and Development. 1997. "Labour Market Policies in Slovenia." Paris.

Stanovnik, T. 2002. "The Political Economy of Pension Reform in Slovenia." In E. Fultz, ed., *Pension Reform in Central and Eastern Europe*. Budapest: ILO-CEET (International Labor Organization, Central and Eastern European Team).

Stanovnik, T., and N. Stropnik. 1998. "Impact of Social Transfers on Poverty and Income Inequality in Slovenia: A Comparison between the Pre-Transition and the Post-Transition Period." Institute for Economic Research, Ljubljana.

Statistical Office of the Republic of Slovenia. 2002. "Statistical Information No. 143." Ljubljana.

Stropnik, N., and T. Stanovnik. 2002. "Combating Poverty and Social Exclusion: A Case Study of Slovenia." ILO-CEET, Budapest.

Štrovs, M. 1984. *Novi sistem pokojninskega in invalidskega zavarovanja*. Ljubljana: Gospodarski vestnik.

Uršič, C., and T. Stanovnik. 2003. "Invalidity Pensions in Slovenia." In C. Prinz, ed., *European Disability Pension Policies*. Aldershot, U.K.: Ashgate.

NOTES

1. A detailed account of the reform process is presented in Stanovnik (2002).

2. This is somewhat at variance with World Bank terminology, which reserves the term "second pillar" for mandatory privately funded pension schemes.

3. The "pension qualifying period" includes the insurance period and years that are credited by the state. "Insurance period" includes not only years of actual work ("years of service"), but also years that an insured person can purchase.

4. This is being gradually extended from the best 10-year period, which was in force in 1999. One year is being added each year, so that the 18-year period will be reached in 2008.

5. A number of unemployed workers receive disability benefits, which are disbursed by the Institute for Pension and Disability Insurance. Thus the drop in the share of unemployed who receive unemployment benefits overstates the actual drop in the number of unemployed who do not receive any social protection benefits (Uršič and Stanovnik 2003).

6. The guaranteed wage has no relation to wage remuneration and is used mostly as a criterion for social assistance benefits. These benefits are net payments and are not subject to tax. Somewhat exceptionally, it is being used to set a floor and ceiling for unemployment benefits, which are in principle a social insurance compensation. The guaranteed wage amounted to some 20 percent of the average gross wage in 2002.

7. Those receiving unemployment compensation in 1998 and sufficiently close to normal retirement age could still apply the old rule.

Chapter 20
Reentering the Markets of the Former Yugoslavia

Jože P. Damijan

Recent Slovenian trade flows as well as outward flows of foreign direct investment reflect a trend toward increased trade and investment activities in the markets of the other former republics of SFR Yugoslavia (former Yugoslav markets, or FYM). The increased intensity of these flows might point toward a reintegration of trade in the region and the creation of new (or the restoration of former) patterns of trade and production specialization characterized by a supply-chain organization. Before 1990 the FYM provided the Slovenian economy with a base for necessary inputs, such as raw materials that are scarce in Slovenia, semi-manufactured products, and agricultural products. After processing either within Slovenia or in the local affiliates of Slovenian firms, final products were then sold on both Western markets and the single Yugoslav market. (On the other side, many exports of final products from other parts of the region were directed through Slovenian firms licensed for foreign trade operations.) The crucial aspect of these patterns of Slovenian purchases in the region was the vertical supply-chain organization of production as well as the prevalence of the intrafirm trade that is typical of multinational companies (MNCs). In fact, this MNC pattern of trade was based on an appropriate ownership framework, with Slovenian firms the main "foreign" acquirers and greenfield investors in the region. Leaving aside the negative political connotations that this pattern of production and trade has provoked in the past,[1] it is ultimately true that, in the period before 1990, it helped to stimulate economic growth and sustain a kind of economic and social stability in the country. Fidrmuc (2000) shows that, with this pattern of intrafirm and interrepublic trade, the volume of bilateral trade flows between republics of the former Yugoslavia was about 24 times greater than that predicted by a gravity model based on normal trade flows among EU countries.

This chapter analyzes the current trade and investment activity of Slovenian firms in the region of the former Yugoslavia in order to reveal the trends in that trade and the motivation for Slovenian direct investment in the FYM. This is done using official trade and investment data provided by the Statistical Office of the Republic of Slovenia and the Bank of Slovenia, as well as data from a specially conducted survey among the 115 largest Slovenian companies aimed at studying the evolution of their investment motives in the FYM over the 1990–2004 period. One suspects that, at present, motives of trade promotion rather than increased efficiency are the driving force behind the recent increase in foreign investment activity of Slovenian firms. These firms predominantly aim at increasing sales to the region from their Slovenian headquarters, rather than setting up local production facilities for the purpose of jumping trade barriers or exploiting comparative advantage (for example, using cheaper local labor in the other former Yugoslav republics). The reasons for this lie in the past unstable political and economic environment of the FYM, in the poor financial discipline of some local customers, and in the still-underutilized resources of Slovenian firms. But even if trade promotion is the short-run strategy of Slovenian firms, efficiency-seeking and comparative advantage reasons could prevail in the longer run.

This chapter is organized as follows. The first section briefly overviews the consequences for Slovenian firms of the loss of the FYM in the early 1990s. The second section describes the overall patterns of trade and investment between Slovenia and the successor countries of the former Yugoslavia. The third section analyzes the present and planned trade and investment behavior of Slovenian firms with respect to the FYM. The fourth section discusses changes in the different investment motives of Slovenian firms in the FYM over the 1990–2004 period. The final section concludes.

CONSEQUENCES OF THE LOSS OF THE FORMER YUGOSLAV MARKETS

The Slovenian economy has historically been heavily dependent on the markets of the former Yugoslavia. According to input–output calculations, which in the absence of official statistics are the only source for estimating interrepublic trade flows in the former Yugoslavia before 1991, about one-third of total Slovenian manufacturing sales in 1988 was consumed in Slovenia, one-third was exported, and one-third was sold in the other former Yugoslav republics (data from the Statistical Office of the Republic of Slovenia). Hence, after the disintegration of SFR Yugoslavia in 1991, Slovenian firms faced a tremendous shock, as half of the large domestic market almost disappeared. Sales to the other republics of the former Yugoslavia fell from $6.7 billion in 1990 to only $1.5 billion in 1992. One has to bear in mind that Slovenian firms could compensate for only a small part of these losses by increasing exports to other countries. Between 1990 and 1992, exports to other countries increased only modestly, from $4.1 billion to $5.2 billion, and then to $7.0 billion in 1996. In other words, between 1990 and 1992, although Slovenian firms were able to create about $1 billion in new exports, they lost markets in the former Yugoslavia worth about $5 billion.[2] In gross terms, the loss of these markets amounted to about 40 percent of Slovenia's GDP in 1992, and about 20 percent of GDP in net terms. The loss of sales to the FYM in this period can therefore be counted as one of the major sources of the deep depression into which the Slovenian economy fell in the early 1990s (Damijan and Majcen 2000).

The actual decline of Slovenia's GDP between 1988 and 1993 amounted to 20 percent. Several studies have estimated the negative impact of the loss of trade with the FYM on the Slovenian economy. Bole (1992), using a small, aggregated macroeconomic model, predicted that the loss of the FYM would lead to a 6 percent decline in GDP. Potočnik (1992), using a two-region computed general-equilibrium (CGE) model of Slovenia and the rest of Yugoslavia, predicted that the loss of the FYM would cause a 20 percent reduction of output. Buehrer (1994), using a CGE model for Slovenia, estimated that Slovenia's total trade losses in markets in the former Yugoslavia and the countries of the Council for Mutual Economic Assistance could explain two-thirds or more of the decline in GDP. As a consequence, a number of enterprises ran into severe trouble, as many smaller enterprises oriented to import substitution in the domestic market were unable to export at prices that covered their costs. A major restructuring of the manufacturing sector became an absolute necessity, along with the need for rapid reorientation of nondomestic sales and the adoption of an export-oriented development strategy.

RECENT TRENDS IN TRADE AND INVESTMENT FLOWS

Trends in Trade Flows

For purposes of analyzing trends in trade flows between Slovenia and the successor countries of the former Yugoslavia, the period after 1991 can be divided into two subperiods. The first period, between 1992 and 1999, saw a further decline in Slovenian exports to the FYM until 1993 and a modest upward trend afterward (Table 20.1). Between 1993 and 1999, Slovenian exports to the FYM increased by 47 percent when measured in euros, or by 34 percent when measured in dollars.[3] The lion's share of this expansion was in exports to Bosnia and Herzegovina and FR Yugoslavia, which grew rapidly after 1995. Exports to Croatia, which account for half of total exports to the FYM, stagnated over the period.

The story for imports is less favorable. Whereas by 1999 Slovenian exports to the FYM had regained their 1992 level (measured in euros), imports from the FYM had not yet recovered. Between 1992 and 1993 these imports dropped by 37 percent; they fell a further 10 percent from then until 1999. The explanation for this unfavorable trend is straightforward. Before 1990 the FYM provided the Slovenian economy with a base for necessary inputs, such as scarce raw materials, semi-manufactured products, and agricultural products. After the breakup of SFR Yugoslavia and the outbreak of war, these supply chains were interrupted, and Slovenian firms were forced to obtain the necessary inputs from the countries of the Central European Free Trade Area (CEFTA; see Damijan and Masten 2002). Between 1992 and 1999 Slovenia's trade structure indicates a rapid reorientation toward

TABLE 20.1 BILATERAL TRADE BETWEEN SLOVENIA AND OTHER SUCCESSOR COUNTRIES OF SFR YUGOSLAVIA, 1992–2002

(Millions of EUR)

Exports	1992	1993	1994	1995	1996	1997	1998	1999	2000	2001	2002	% 2002
Croatia	736	633	624	690	683	741	727	630	747	893	958	4.5
Macedonia	103	170	184	146	136	133	144	166	172	148	160	1.5
BiH	18	17	58	92	211	255	285	341	406	444	495	4.5
FRY	309	7	14	7	77	99	92	80	155	264	350	3.2
Total FYM	1167	826	880	935	1106	1228	1247	1217	1480	1748	1964	17.9
TOTAL	5168	5208	5772	6437	6636	7411	8073	8023	9483	10341	10999	100

Imports	1992	1993	1994	1995	1996	1997	1998	1999	2000	2001	2002	% 2002
Croatia	659	509	421	446	471	412	385	417	487	452	422	3.6
Macedonia	60	76	68	67	57	50	42	35	52	30	25	0.2
BiH	15	9	4	6	12	27	42	53	63	69	69	0.6
FRY	207	0	0	2	42	37	61	34	45	53	62	0.5
Total FYM	942	595	493	520	582	525	530	538	646	604	578	5.0
TOTAL	4751	5565	6175	7347	7523	8284	9018	9466	10986	11339	11606	100

Balance	1992	1993	1994	1995	1996	1997	1998	1999	2000	2001	2002	% 2002
Croatia	77	123	203	244	212	329	342	213	261	441	536	38.7
Macedonia	43	93	117	80	78	83	102	131	119	117	135	9.7
BiH	2	8	54	86	199	228	243	288	343	374	426	30.7
FRY	102	7	14	5	35	62	31	46	111	211	289	20.8
Total FYM	224	231	387	415	524	703	717	679	834	1145	1386	100
TOTAL	418	−358	−402	−910	−887	−873	−945	−1443	−1503	−998	−607	

Source: Statistical Office of the RS (SURS); author's own calculations.

the European Union. Exports to and imports from EU members in this period grew on average by 8 percent and 12 percent a year, respectively, and increased from 60 percent to more than 66 percent of total trade.

In the second period, after 1999, the picture reverses, with a reorientation of Slovenian exports back toward the FYM and other transition economies (such as Russia and the CEFTA countries). Between 1999 and 2002 Slovenian exports to the FYM grew on average by 17 percent a year, while exports to the European Union grew only by 7 percent a year. There are several reasons for this trend. First, now that the major political constraints in the individual successor countries of the former Yugoslavia have been resolved, there are signs of economic recovery, which will stimulate demand. Second, Slovenia has signed free trade agreements (FTAs) with most of the countries of the former Yugoslavia.[4] Since 1999 these FTAs seem to be further stimulating both Slovenian exports as well as imports from the FYM.

Importance of Former Yugoslav Markets for the Slovenian Economy

The share of exports to the FYM in total Slovenian exports remained relatively stable at about 16 percent from 1993 until 2000 and then increased to 18 percent by 2002. By contrast, imports from the FYM stagnated in the 1990s, resulting in a monotonically decreasing share of these imports in total Slovenian imports. The consequence has been a huge and increasing trade surplus in trade with the FYM. In 2002 that surplus amounted to about €1.3 billion, enough to completely offset Slovenia's deficit in trade with the European Union. In absolute terms, most of that surplus stems from trade with Croatia.

Trade with the FYM seems to have gained attractiveness in recent years, for several reasons. The main one is that Slovenian firms handle the FYM with special care, since they feel they possess a special advantage over competitors from other countries because of their better understanding of local markets. After the recent political stabilization, and with economic recovery under way in the region, Slovenian firms tend to be winning back the market shares they held before 1990. However, during the transition period, part of the Slovenian manufacturing sector was less successful in restructuring and reorienting its sales toward EU markets. Firms in these less competitive industries place special emphasis on gaining market share in the FYM. A study by Damijan (2001) reveals that the export attractiveness of the European Union for Slovenian products is completely the reverse of that of the FYM. Slovenian firms in the agriculture, food, paper, chemicals, and wood industries can on average double their export prices when exporting to the FYM compared with exporting to

EU markets. Consequently, a clear pattern of export specialization by industry is emerging, with industries that are less competitive in EU markets tending to specialize in exports to the FYM. Hence it is not surprising that more than 50 percent of exports of agricultural and food products are sold to the FYM.

These "indecently high" export prices in the FYM, however attractive they may appear to the current operations of firms, may in the longer run lead to unfavorable macroeconomic developments, for several reasons. First, all of the countries of the former Yugoslavia have large balance of payments deficits, which so far have been financed with foreign assistance or, in the case of Croatia, with the inflow of foreign direct investment (FDI). As foreign assistance is diminishing and FDI inflows in most of these countries remain very modest, these countries may run into severe balance of payments difficulties, forcing them—at least in the short run—to cut imports. As pointed out by Mrak, Jaklič, and Veselinovič (2001), in 2000 Slovenia accounted for 7 percent of the overall trade imbalance of FR Yugoslavia, 22 percent of Croatia's trade imbalance, 33 percent of Bosnia and Herzegovina's, and 37 percent of FYR Macedonia's. Second, after joining the European Union in 2004, Slovenia will have to abandon its FTAs with the other countries of former Yugoslavia. This will certainly worsen the present market access advantage of Slovenian firms over their competitors from the current EU members and will probably lower their market share. Third, since exporting to the FYM is less demanding in terms of product quality, any increased export orientation to these markets could potentially hinder the further restructuring of the firms involved and increase the technology gap between these firms and those exporting to EU markets. A kind of dual economy could be the long-run outcome.

Therefore, to forestall possible unfavorable macroeconomic developments in the future, a new strategy is needed to penetrate the FYM. Although a number of Slovenian firms have already adopted a new strategy, a majority of firms in less competitive industries will still have to consider possible relocation of their manufacturing activity, through FDI, to the FYM instead of relying on export specialization.

Patterns of Outward FDI

In the second part of the 1990s, a number of Slovenian firms realized that their competitive advantage in the FYM could be maintained only through establishing affiliates in the local markets. Hence the stock of Slovenian outward FDI going to the countries of the former Yugoslavia has been on an upward trend since 1994. Between 1994 and 2002 the total stock of Slovenian outward FDI has increased from €289 million to €1.4 billion. In 2002 the stock of Slovenian FDI in the

FYM amounted to €823 million, or about 59 percent of the total stock of Slovenian outward FDI.[5] A majority of the Slovenian FDI stock in the FYM (36.5 percent of total Slovenian outward FDI) is located in Croatia; 11.2 percent of Slovenia's total FDI stock is in Bosnia and Herzegovina, 6.9 percent is in FR Yugoslavia, and 4.3 percent is in FYR Macedonia. By the end of 2000, 804 investment projects were being conducted by Slovenian firms in the FYM. Only half of these, however, involved the establishment of a new firm or the acquisition of an existing viable firm. The other half are in real estate, bankrupt local firms, and other investments. In contrast, a majority of Slovenian outward FDI in other countries involves the establishment of new or the acquisition of existing firms. This fact reflects the cautiousness of Slovenian firms regarding the types of investment they make in the FYM. This fact will become even more apparent in the next section, where survey data on the largest Slovenian companies are analyzed.

TRADE VERSUS INVESTMENT IN PENETRATING THE MARKETS OF THE FORMER YUGOSLAVIA

The previous section revealed an increased importance of the FYM for Slovenian firms in recent years and a need to change their market access strategy. This section reports survey evidence on the current exporting and investment activities of 115 of the largest Slovenian companies (see Damijan 2001 for details). Firms' responses give a picture of the prevailing modes of entry into the FYM, entry costs, the main reasons for their choice of entry mode, and the characteristics of individual FYM, as well as firms' present and planned future investment activities in the FYM.

Entry Costs and Modes of Entry

A firm can penetrate its target sales market using either of two alternative market access strategies: conventional exporting (the export approach) or setting up local production in the target market (the FDI approach). The decision between the two strategies depends on many factors, such as entry costs (tariffs, transportation costs, and the like), technology, comparative advantage (differences in labor costs and resource abundance between the home and the foreign country), country risk, and so on. The main advantage of exporting over direct investment lies in the smaller amount of funding needed. The chief disadvantages include lower efficiency where there are high entry costs, and poor financial discipline in export markets. The advantages of investment are seen in the possibility of avoiding high entry costs, the chance to make use of cheaper local labor and materials, and the

FIGURE 20.1 TRENDS IN SLOVENIAN OUTWARD FDI, 1994–2001

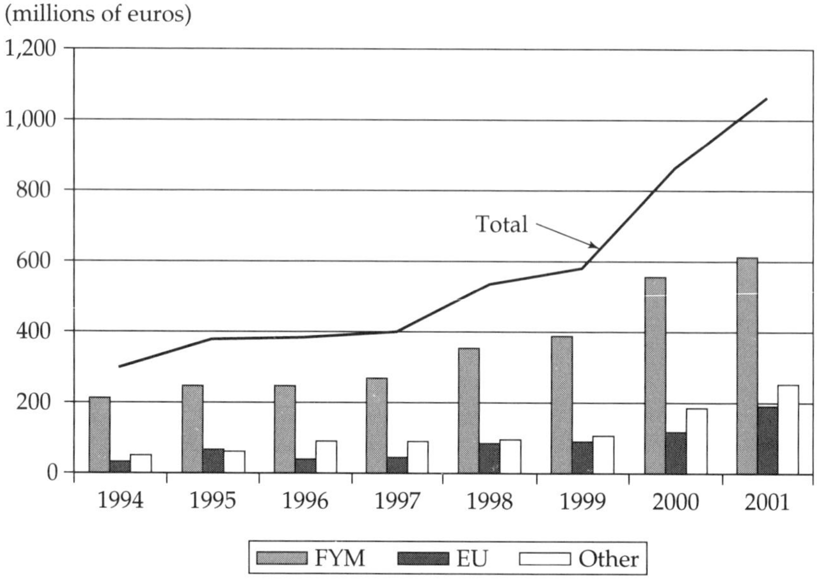

(millions of euros)

Source: Bank of Slovenia (2002).

possibility of influencing local authorities and receiving subsidies or tax exemptions for starting up operations. The major drawbacks of the investment mode lie in the greater amount of funding required to set up local production, distribution networks, and other related activities, and in the potentially higher risk attached to operations in foreign markets.

The survey reveals that the largest Slovenian firms still prefer conventional exports over FDI as the mode of entry for all the countries of the former Yugoslavia. As expected, some FDI-promoted sales take place in Croatia. On average, local affiliates of Slovenian firms account for about one-third of total firm sales to this market. In Bosnia and Herzegovina and in FYR Macedonia, 85 percent of total firm sales have been achieved through exports; in FR Yugoslavia the comparable figure reaches 95 percent. A breakdown of firms' responses by industry reveals an almost unaltered picture. Only in Croatia, in some industries (for example, food, chemicals, metal, and nonferrous products), does firms' market penetration through local affiliates exceed 50 percent of total sales.

The reasons for this dominance of exports in market access to the FYM lie in firms' perception that local markets there remain too unstable to justify a market access strategy based on investment for the purpose of jumping trade barriers. In the case of the FYM, the perception of various entry costs may also play a crucial role in determining a firm's market access strategy. Where entry costs are high relative to other factors (such as the stability of the local business environment and the scale of operations), firms are more likely to penetrate these markets through FDI. Where relative entry costs are low, firms will continue to penetrate the markets through exports. The survey gives a rough estimate of entry costs for individual FYM as well as the stability of the local economic and political environment in each market (Table 20.2).

The main entry barriers that Slovenian firms face in Croatia and in Bosnia and Herzegovina, according to the survey, are high tariffs and hindered entry into local store chains, followed by transport costs. Reflecting the greater distance involved in trade with FR Yugoslavia and FYR Macedonia, firms claim that transport costs are the key trade barrier, followed by high tariffs and hindered entry into local store chains. However, what is important is the magnitude of the estimated entry barriers. In Croatia and in Bosnia and Herzegovina, entry barriers are modest (not exceeding a score of 2.8, where 5 is the maximum value), whereas in FR Yugoslavia and FYR Macedonia, barriers are almost uniformly higher. For comparison, in EU markets, technical and health standards and hindered entry into local store chains are estimated to be higher barriers than in the FYM. Tariff barriers in the European Union are estimated to be much lower than those in the FYM, whereas transport costs are judged to be higher than in Croatia and in Bosnia and Herzegovina, but lower than in FR Yugoslavia and FYR Macedonia.

One can hardly make suggestions on the basis of these estimates alone about the modes of entry into the FYM. For that one should also refer to the estimates of the stability of local business environments. Firms viewed the business environment in Croatia as modestly unstable,

TABLE 20.2 ESTIMATE OF ENTRY COSTS AND OF THE STABILITY
OF THE LOCAL BUSINESS ENVIRONMENT

Entry costs	EU	CRO	BiH	FRY	MK
Transport costs	3.0	2.3	2.8	3.5	3.8
Tariffs	1.8	2.7	2.7	3.4	2.9
Entry into local store chains	3.4	2.7	2.6	2.8	2.6
Technical and health standards	3.4	2.1	1.9	2.0	1.9
Nontariff trade barriers	1.9	2.0	1.8	2.3	2.0
Informal administrative barriers	1.4	1.9	1.8	2.5	2.0
Stability of the business environment	4.4	3.1	2.4	1.5	1.7

Notes: 1 = low; 5 = very high. CRO = Croatia; BiH = Bosnia and Herzegovina; MK = Macedonia.

Source: Damijan (2001).

that in Bosnia and Herzegovina as unstable, and that in FR Yugoslavia and FYR Macedonia as extremely unstable. In sum, firms' estimates of trade barriers relative to the stability of local business environments would not recommend FDI as a way of penetrating the FYM. In Croatia (and partly in Bosnia and Herzegovina), where stability is judged to be modest, trade barriers are also moderate, which may or may not encourage much FDI. Here industry-by-industry and case-by-case considerations become important. In contrast, in FR Yugoslavia and FYR Macedonia, the higher probability of FDI encouraged by the higher trade barriers is offset by the unstable economic and political climate. Hence the finding that exports are the prevalent mode of market access for Slovenian firms to most of the FYM does not come as a surprise. So far, only in Croatia do Slovenian firms feel comfortable enough to set up local production establishments to serve the local market.

Reasons for Choosing the Export Entry Mode

What are the reasons underpinning the preference for exports as the mode of entry into the FYM? Firms exporting to Croatia cite good business cooperation and lower investment requirements compared with FDI as the main reasons for preferring the export mode. In Bosnia and Herzegovina, FR Yugoslavia, and FYR Macedonia, firms stress the low level of investment needed and the small scale of their current operations. In FR Yugoslavia, poor local legislation is also an important reason. Trade and transactions costs seem to play a very small role (Table 20.3).

Reasons for Choosing the Investment Entry Mode

As argued above, despite the presence of trade barriers, Slovenian FDI in the successor countries of the former Yugoslavia may well be driven by lower labor costs and possible relative resource abundance. So far,

TABLE 20.3 MAIN REASONS FOR EXPORT ENTRY MODE IN 2000

Reasons	EU	CRO	BiH	FRY	MK
Good business cooperation	3.9	4.1	3.4	3.2	3.0
Less investment required than in case of FDI	3.8	3.8	3.7	3.6	3.6
Low scale of sales	3.3	3.3	3.4	3.4	3.4
Specific products	3.4	3.2	3.3	3.3	2.8
Good financial discipline	4.1	2.9	2.7	2.7	2.7
Low trade and transaction costs	2.9	2.9	2.6	2.6	2.4
Poor local legislation	1.8	2.7	3.1	3.4	2.9

Notes: 1 = unimportant; 5 = very important. CRO = Croatia; BiH = Bosnia and Herzegovina; MK = Macedonia.
Source: Damijan (2001).

however, none of the key theoretical reasons for FDI enumerated above seem to be very important for the Slovenian firms conducting business in the FYM. On the contrary, Slovenian firms stress the importance of the investment mode of penetrating these markets simply as a means of securing payment. The poor financial discipline of local customers is cited as a major reason for choosing the investment mode. The large volume of sales and access to adjacent local markets also stimulate Slovenian investment in the region. High entry costs and low labor and material costs in the successor countries of the former Yugoslavia are important investment motives relative to the EU figures; however, they are much less important as a motivation compared with security of payment (Table 20.4).

A breakdown by industry reveals some slight differences from the above general picture. Firms in the textiles, chemicals, and rubber and tires industries claim high entry costs as the main reason for choosing the investment mode of entry. Firms in the textiles, wood, rubber and tires, and electrical appliances industries stress the importance of low-cost local labor and materials. These reasons may become more important after the successor countries of the former Yugoslavia have stabilized their political systems and basic macroeconomic situation.

Because some business practices in the FYM are unique to the region, Slovenian firms try to make use of their past experience with the region to achieve some first-mover advantages over Western firms, which are still very cautious in this respect. Doing business with most of the firms in the region is very risky, as there are no solid guarantees that export shipments will be paid for. Firms in our survey claim that the key mode of payment in this region is cash, followed by completely insecure payments to open accounts, and barter. Svetličič and Jaklič (2001), using an independent survey among Slovenian firms, report similar findings on the terms of payment in the FYM. Documentary credits or letters of credit, which are among

TABLE 20.4 MAIN REASONS FOR INVESTMENT ENTRY MODE
           IN 2000

Reasons	EU	CRO	BiH	FRY	MK
Poor financial discipline	1.3	3.8	3.7	3.7	3.4
Large scale of sales	3.8	3.8	3.5	3.2	3.2
Access to adjacent local markets	3.7	3.6	3.5	3.7	3.3
Low labor and material costs	2.3	3.2	3.6	3.5	3.3
Specific products	2.9	2.8	2.7	2.6	2.6
High entry costs	1.8	2.7	3.1	3.1	2.7

Notes: 1 = unimportant; 5 = very important. CRO = Croatia; BiH = Bosnia and Herzegovina; MK = Macedonia.
Source: Damijan (2001).

the most secure modes of payment in international trade, are almost unsuitable in this region, as local banks either are untrustworthy or have no relations with Slovenian or Western banks. Hence, in the short run, Slovenian firms make use of investment in the FYM predominantly to secure payments for their shipments. So far, Slovenian firms have mainly invested in representative offices and their own stores, with their chief task being to promote trade, that is, imports of goods produced by Slovenian parent firms. Only 20 percent of Slovenian firms investing in the region have established local production facilities.

ARE FOREIGN INVESTMENTS TRADE-PROMOTING OR EFFICIENCY-SEEKING?

The main conclusion that can be drawn from this analysis is that, so far, trade promotion clearly dominates efficiency seeking as a motivation for Slovenian FDI in the FYM. This section further explores this finding by analyzing the current and planned investment behavior of Slovenian firms in the region.

In our questionnaires, firms were asked about their past and planned investment activities in the FYM. Their responses suggest that the largest Slovenian firms captured in our survey performed very few FDI projects in the FYM before 2001. Before 1990, out of 115 surveyed firms, there were only 27 FDI projects in the FYM, 80 percent of them in the manufacturing sector. Between 1990 and 2000, 42 FDI projects in the FYM are recorded among our sample of firms, 70 percent of them in the manufacturing sector. Between the survey date and 2004, 42 percent of firms indicated a serious intention to perform FDI in the FYM. The greatest propensity to invest in the FYM was recorded among manufacturing firms: 50 percent of manufacturing firms in our sample confirmed that they have engaged in FDI in the FYM.

To gain further insight into the evolution of investment motives of Slovenian firms in the FYM over the 1990–2004 period, Damijan (2001) used a probit model where the dependent variable (the existence of FDI by a firm) is regressed on a set of firm characteristics such as size, factor intensity, labor and capital productivity, export propensity, research and development (R&D) intensity, and industry (using dummy variables representing industries). The results indicate that common characteristics of firms investing in the FYM before 2001 are large size, high export propensity, and operation in the food industry. These findings confirm that past investments of Slovenian firms were mainly for trade-promoting motives; that is, large firms attempted to increase their capacity utilization by exporting to the FYM. This is especially true of firms in the food industry, which have found themselves to be competitive only in the FYM.

Probit results for the investment plans of Slovenian firms up to 2004, however, reveal some change in firms' investment preferences. It seems that the trade promotion motive for FDI in the FYM has been replaced by a more distinctive efficiency-seeking motive. In the future, firms with higher labor intensity, labor productivity, and R&D intensity tend to wish to relocate part of their production to the FYM in order to combine their firm-specific intangible assets with the lower local labor costs. The results also indicate that past experience with investments in the FYM may significantly affect future investment plans. The results point to positive past experiences, since firms that already have invested directly in one of the successor countries of SFR Yugoslavia tend to extend their investments in the future to other countries in the region.

CONCLUSIONS

This chapter has documented a high attractiveness and an increased importance of the other countries of the former Yugoslavia as export markets for Slovenian firms in recent years. Between 2000 and 2002 the share of exports to the FYM in total Slovenian exports increased from 16 percent to 18 percent. Slovenian firms in the agriculture, food, paper, chemicals, and wood industries can on average double their prices when exporting to the FYM relative to what they would receive in EU markets. Consequently, a clear pattern of export specialization by industry appears, in which industries that are less competitive in EU markets tend to specialize in exports to the FYM. Yet however attractive the FYM may appear to the current operations of Slovenian firms, without a change in their market access strategy, their market shares may be endangered in the near future. The reason is that the large balance of payments deficits recorded in all the countries of the former Yugoslavia may force them, at least in the short run, to cut imports. Another reason for changing the market access strategy is that, after joining the European Union in 2004, Slovenia will have to abandon its FTAs with the countries of the former Yugoslavia, which in turn will reduce the market access advantage that Slovenian firms currently enjoy over their EU competitors.

Therefore, to avoid possible unfavorable trends in the future, Slovenian firms, especially those in less competitive industries, should place more emphasis on possible relocation of their manufacturing activity through FDI to the FYM instead of specializing in exports as at present. The present pattern of market penetration of the FYM indicates that Slovenian firms predominantly aim at increasing sales to the region from their Slovenian headquarters rather than setting up local production facilities in order to jump trade barriers or to exploit the comparative advantage (cheaper local labor) of the FYM. In the past, Slovenian firms used investments in the FYM predominantly to secure payment for their shipments from Slovenian headquarters. So far these firms have mainly invested in representative offices and their own stores, whose major task is to promote trade. Only 20 percent of Slovenian firms that have invested in the region have established local production facilities. The key reasons for this lie in the unstable political and economic environment of the FYM, in the poor financial discipline of local customers, and in the still-underutilized resources of Slovenian parent firms.

The investment plans of the largest Slovenian firms through 2004, however, already point toward a change in firms' long-run investment motivation. The efficiency-seeking motive has become more pronounced. In the future, firms with higher labor intensity, labor productivity, and R&D intensity are likely to relocate part of their production to the FYM in order to combine their firm-specific intangible assets with the lower local labor costs.

REFERENCES

Bole, V. 1992. "The Slovenian Economy in General Disequilibrium." *Gospodarska gibanja* 230. Economics Institute of the Faculty of Law, Ljubljana.

Buehrer, T. S. 1994. "Can Trade Losses Explain the Current Recession in Slovenia?" Ph.D. dissertation, Harvard University, Cambridge, Mass.

Damijan, P. J. 2001. "Slovenian Investment Activity in Former Yugoslav Markets: Trade-Promoting or Efficiency-Seeking Motivation?" *Economic and Business Review* 3(3/4): 229–47.

Damijan, P. J., and B. Majcen. 2000. "Trade Reorientation, Firm Performance and Restructuring of Slovenian Manufacturing Sector." *Journal of Transforming Economies and Societies* 7(1): 24–35.

Damijan, P. J., and I. Masten. 2002. "Time Dependent Efficiency of Free Trade Agreements: The Case of Slovenia and the CEFTA Agreement." *Economic and Social Review* 33(1): 147–60.

Fidrmuc, J. 2000. "Optimum Currency Area Theory, Trade Integration, and EMU Enlargement." RCEF Working Papers Series 115. Faculty of Economics, Ljubljana.

Mrak, M., A. Jaklič, and D. Veselinovič. 2001. "Finančni aspekti gospodarskega sodelovanja Slovenije z državami nekdanje Jugoslavije." In J. Prašnikar, ed., *Izzivi in priložnosti na trgih nekdanje Jugoslavije. Proceedings of the 3rd Slovenian Business Conference.* Ljubljana: Časnik Finance.

Potočnik, J. 1992. "Two-Region CGE Model of Slovenian-Yugoslav Economy." Master's thesis, University of Ljubljana, Ljubljana.

Svetličič, M., and A. Jaklič. 2001. "Neposredne investicije v državah nekdanje Jugoslavije." In J. Prašnikar, ed., *Izzivi in priložnosti na trgih nekdanje Jugoslavije. Proceedings of the 3rd Slovenian Business Conference.* Ljubljana: Časnik Finance.

NOTES

1. At the end of the 1980s political accusations were heard in other republics of the former Yugoslavia that Slovenian firms had "exploited" the other republics by taking their economic resources.

2. The source for the 1990 figures is the Institute of Macroeconomic Analysis and Development; figures for the period after 1992 are normally available from the Statistical Office of the Republic of Slovenia.

3. In the present case, the euro-based figures reflect current trends more accurately given the high volatility of the dollar exchange rate in the 1990s, and because of the de facto export pricing of shipments to the FYM in euro-based currencies.

4. Slovenia signed a free trade agreement with FYR Macedonia in 1996, with Croatia in 1997, and with Bosnia and Herzegovina in 2001.

5. EU countries accounted for 20.6 percent of the outward FDI stock at the end of 2002, and other EU accession countries for 7.6 percent.

Part III: The Quest for EU Membership

Chapter 21
EU Membership: Rationale, Costs, and Benefits

András Inotai and Peter Stanovnik

For at least two specific reasons, Slovenia can be considered a unique case in the transformation process in Central and Eastern Europe (CEE). One is that Slovenia was and remains the most developed country in the region, as measured by its GDP per capita, which is about 70 percent of the EU average. The other is that, by some other indicators, Slovenia enjoyed the most promising initial conditions for managing the transition and quickly catching up to the EU countries, both quantitatively and qualitatively. On the other hand, Slovenia became an independent nation-state as a result of the dissolution of SFR Yugoslavia. In contrast, all the other transition economies either were nation-states even during the Soviet-dominated period (with varying restrictions on their room to maneuver) or could look back to a period of national independence in their history (mainly the Baltics and the Czech Republic but, for a short period, Slovakia as well).

These two factors have largely influenced Slovenia's behavior in seeking accession to the European Union. The result was a less unlimited enthusiasm for accession and greater concerns, but at the same time greater self-confidence as well. The establishment of the Slovenian nation-state could hardly fit into a plan that called for giving up substantial parts of national sovereignty at the moment of joining the European Union. Furthermore, Slovenia's pioneering economic (and social) position and its perception and implementation of its "first-mover advantage" did not make early accession a high priority for economic policy, at least not at the price of giving up part of these real or perceived, long-term or short-lived, advantages.

For both of the reasons mentioned above, and partly because of the reluctance of Italy, Slovenia was the last of the first-wave candidate countries to ratify a Europe Agreement. Even more important, Slovenia applied for membership before ratification occurred.

However, looking back on the developments of the last five years, one can say that Slovenia has made a rather successful adjustment and implementation of the EU *acquis communautaire*. It carried out negotiations without encountering any major obstacle, and it held a highly successful referendum (with 86 percent voting in favor) on accession to the European Union in early 2003. This change of attitude can be explained by the changing attitude of Slovenian society in favor of EU membership. That change in turn can be attributed to two major factors. On the one hand, it became clear to the greater part of Slovenian society that membership in the European Union could offer greater security than staying out. The war elsewhere in SFR Yugoslavia certainly fostered recognition of the need for security through participation in larger organizations (including, of course, NATO). On the other hand, some of Slovenia's first-mover advantages started to turn into disadvantages with the comparative process of transformation in Central Europe and the Baltics.

The repeated delays in privatization, the slow and selective inflow of foreign capital, the weaknesses in the banking sector, and the country's high production costs compared with the Czech Republic, Hungary, Poland, and Slovakia noticeably narrowed Slovenia's competitive advantages in the second half of the 1990s. Even as foreign capital established new and modern factories in Hungary, later in the Czech Republic, and to some extent in Slovakia, multinational companies with regional competence tended to avoid Slovenia, despite its higher level of development and favorable geographic location. Slovenia's originally substantial comparative advantages based on the country's structural development, high-quality export products, previously established trade and service networks, and geographic location started to diminish as foreign companies working out of Hungary and other countries began to offer commodities and services of the same quality at lower prices. More important, many high-technology firms chose to launch their regional and Europe-wide operations from other Central European countries. Although Slovenia managed to keep its share of the German market, it could not keep pace with Czech, Slovak, or Hungarian exports, which spectacularly increased their market shares. No less important, the average price of Slovenian exports of manufactured goods could not be raised in the German market. Hungarian average export prices, in contrast, doubled in a few years. Whereas in the mid-1990s Slovenian prices were still 20 to 30 percent higher than Hungarian prices for similar goods, by 2001 the average export price of Hungarian manufactured products was about 70 percent higher than that of Slovenian goods. It is obvious that the rapid deterioration of the first-mover's beneficial position has led to a reorientation of Slovenian attitudes toward accession to the European Union.

This chapter is organized as follows. The first section briefly overviews the reasons underlying EU accession. In the second section the costs and benefits of the accession process and of membership are analyzed. The third section describes Slovenia's position as a border region of the European Union. The fourth section discusses Slovenia's economic relations with the successor countries of SFR Yugoslavia. The final section concludes.

REASONS UNDERLYING EU ACCESSION

In general, Slovenia and the other CEE countries want to join the European Union for a number of reasons. First, they expect to achieve greater economic, social, and military security, greater legal stability, and stronger democratic institutions from membership. This factor played an important role in the case of Slovenia, not so much for internal as for external security reasons.

Second, several economic arguments speak in favor of membership. Free trade in manufactured goods will be reinforced, and any kind of safeguard clauses contained in the Europe Agreement will be abolished. Trade in agricultural products will be fully liberalized at the moment of accession. More important, the new members will become part of the EU internal market, with additional growth and structural impacts. Finally, trade *among* the new countries themselves, which had faced high levels of sectoral and bilateral protection (despite the original aim of CEFTA), will become completely free at the moment of accession. Slovenia's export pattern suggests that some of these elements—economic and legal security, and the internal market, not least concerning trade in services, as well as trade among the new member countries—argue convincingly in favor of membership.

Third, EU membership will abolish barriers to the free flow of labor in the enlarged union. This is of less importance to Slovenia's economic interests than to those of Poland, for instance. Nevertheless, Slovenia will be interested in an immediate and reciprocal liberalization of the labor market (Bobek and others 1996).

Fourth, access to EU financial resources has always been a major force driving accession in most of the candidate countries. Again because of Slovenia's higher level of development, however, this issue did not play as important a role as it has in other countries, although Slovenia, too, expects a net gain in its EU-related financial balance, and some areas in the country will easily qualify for EU transfers.

Fifth, and of great relevance, was the argument that only membership can solve the problem that Slovenia would in any case be greatly affected by the decisions to be made in Brussels but, absent EU membership, would have no say in those decisions. Accession will settle this issue, and Slovenia, although a small country with modest representation on European public institutions, will be able to adequately influence both the everyday operation of integration and the process whereby the future of Europe is shaped. The country's high-quality public administration, wide political consensus on EU-related issues, and strong social support seem to guarantee the successful incorporation of Slovenian interests and ideas into the decisionmaking process of the enlarged European Union. The fact that the accession negotiations were managed successfully and smoothly is another argument justifying this expectation.

COSTS AND BENEFITS OF THE ACCESSION PROCESS AND OF MEMBERSHIP

There is a general view, both among Slovenia's political elite and among by far the greater part of society at large, that accession to the European Union is a positive-sum game. Without denying the truth of this general statement, however, several qualifications have to be made.

First, Western European public opinion tends to hold that the benefits of EU enlargement lie mainly on the side of the acceding countries, whereas the additional costs will have to be absorbed by the current member states. There is little evidence that most of those who hold this opinion are aware of the substantial benefits that rapid liberalization of CEE markets has meant for Western European business, both in trade and in investment. Moreover, most Western Europeans are fundamentally underinformed about the costs of preparing for membership that the candidate countries face.

Second, a complete accounting of benefits and costs must include a number of qualitative features, such as security, stability, predictability, and reliability, which are important factors in political and economic decisionmaking processes but can hardly be quantified. The real costs of the lack of security, stability, and the rest could, of course, become all too apparent in the case of a devastatingly negative outcome, as, unfortunately, has happened elsewhere in the former SFR Yugoslavia.

Third, the benefits and costs will be unevenly distributed across sectors. Some business activities will, from the very beginning, be among the beneficiaries; others will have to carry heavy investment and restructuring costs. According to Majcen (1999), the first group includes the export-oriented sectors (for example, metal products, machinery, and transport equipment), where positive effects should be expected irrespective of the exchange rate, public finance, or other economic policies adopted. The second group includes sectors where negative effects are expected irrespective of government policies (for example, agricultural and forestry products). A third group includes sectors where the effects depend largely on the exchange rate and public finance policies adopted (for example, electricity and gas, and nonmarket services). In general terms the sectors that were competitive in the preaccession period are likely to improve their market position in the enlarged European market and in the framework of the internal market. Also, those sectors that can count on further investment, both domestic and foreign, as well as rely on potential EU resources (regional support, employment, human resources, and so on) will be among the winners. On the other hand, the less competitive sectors, and especially the highly protected ones, including some "national champions," may face difficult times. Agricultural producers form a special stratum in this regard.

Fourth, the benefits and costs will be unevenly distributed across regions. Paradoxically, at least in the period immediately after accession, the more developed regions have seemed able to absorb EU (and other development) resources more quickly and more efficiently than the backward areas. This discrepancy, which initially may further exacerbate regional income and development gaps, is expected to be narrowed in the medium term, as the absorption capacity of the less developed parts of the country increases and spillover effects from the more to the less developed areas are strengthened. However, even in this case, a clear government policy is badly needed to avoid deepening economic and social divisions and the economic peripheralization of some regions of the country.

Fifth, the benefits and costs may also be unevenly distributed over time. Short-term beneficiaries are not guaranteed to be among the long-term winners, and by the same token, short-term losers should not be written off as long-term losers. In this context much depends on the level of preparation of the participants, their openness to and readiness for reform, their capacity to absorb EU resources as well as domestic inputs (human resources, administrative capacity, management skills), and the supportiveness of government policies. The general experience among countries that have acceded to the European Union in the past is that the benefits from integration start to manifest themselves only after a period of several years. Considering that the next wave of accession will take place at a time when Western Europe finds itself in difficult economic straits, with stagnation in some countries and the need for serious reform in others, the adverse external economic environment may even prolong this initial period. Therefore it is extremely important to find some areas of early success for the society of the acceding country, so as to avoid any kind of backlash or disappointment or even the demoralization of the society, which would surely undermine the success of membership.

Serious and well-founded economic analysis and efficient communication are indispensable elements of successful membership. As in previous accessions and enlargements, there are a number of largely unjustified fears on both sides. This chapter will not attempt to identify, much less refute, all the fears and concerns of the current member states (mainly related to migration, border controls, and budgetary issues). However, some of the domestic concerns of the acceding countries will have to be addressed promptly. These include rising prices, rising unemployment, the bankruptcy of many small and medium-size companies, a growing regional development gap, and the loss of sovereignty. Interestingly, one very real problem is not among the concerns most commonly voiced, namely, a budgetary crunch in the initial years of membership.

Prices will be, in most cases, international prices, the result of free trade and of trade and capital liberalization in the acceding countries, although some commodities—and certainly services in the medium term (through the Balassa-Samuelson effect)—will experience mainly modest price increases. However, with the exception of some agricultural goods, these increases stem from the adoption of EU-conforming value added taxes (the abolition of the zero tax bracket of the VAT) or, in exceptional cases, from higher common external tariffs against third countries. Still, by far the most important price increases can be expected in those areas in which the government, for whatever reasons, has not already liberalized prices but instead maintained a managed or administered price system, either in order to "control" inflation or to support the less well off in society (Inotai 1999).

Similarly, the labor market situation will not be fundamentally affected by accession, or at least not adversely. Free trade with the European Union has already generated a large-scale restructuring of labor demand and supply. On the one hand, as the new members become part of an internal market of about 450 million consumers, new opportunities will be opened up for many companies. Also, domestic and, particularly, foreign investors may be encouraged to start new businesses by the greatly increased legal certainty, by domestic investment and consumption rates that are growing at above-average rates, and by the revealed comparative advantages of the new members in the large European market. On the other hand, companies or industries still struggling with structural problems and facing the consequences of delayed liberalization may, at least temporarily, see unemployment increase. In addition, an ambiguous impact can be expected from the full liberalization of trade among new member countries. Although they have been members of CEFTA for several years, CEFTA fell short of a genuine free trade area in many respects. However, as of May 1, 2004, all domestic protectionist instruments must be abolished immediately, and national authority over trade policy will be transferred to Brussels. Some sectors that used to face protectionist barriers in CEFTA trade will be among the winners, while those that were protected against CEFTA competition may find themselves on the losing side, with clear consequences for the labor market. It is much more difficult to evaluate the impact of membership in the longer term. In this context, significant improvement can mainly be expected from reasonable government policies. The European Union may support higher employment through various financial and other instruments, but these certainly cannot become the driving force of such development.

The conclusions to be drawn about the future of small and medium-size enterprises (SMEs) follow in part the same arguments. It is obvious that the next stage of economic modernization will require a concentration of capital (both domestic and foreign), which will affect the number of SMEs. Mergers, acquisitions, start-ups, and failures will dominate the general picture. However, this would be necessary even without membership in the European Union. In this respect accession to the European Union should be considered as a catalytic factor, cleaning up the market and fostering international competition. It is hard to understand why local companies that have long focused on an extremely limited domestic market would not benefit from access to a market of 450 million consumers. Except for some protected sectors (particularly nontradables) and some service-related companies, all economic actors in CEE have already been exposed to free competition for several years. They will certainly survive, even if they have to adapt to new requirements. It is not only simplistic but indeed dangerous to put all SMEs in the same basket. Some will not feel keener competition (or any competition at all) in the coming years, since they are local suppliers. There is hardly any reason why hairdressers from Stuttgart or Amsterdam should come to set up shop in Slovenia or any of the other acceding countries. Others will prove to be successful exporters to international markets and will discover a larger and more stable market to supply. Still others will become reliable subcontractors to multinational corporations, with good prospects for the period after accession. Those companies, however, that used to enjoy the benefits of a protected domestic market or other preferential treatment may face more difficult—but not hopeless— times. In sum, it has to be emphasized—and widely communicated— that changes in the structure of SMEs are mainly due to a higher level of economic development and to gaining international competitiveness. In this context membership in the European Union is more a supportive element than a barrier.

Finally, the loss of national sovereignty has to be mentioned as a more general concern. Obviously, the European Union is a supranational body, and some traditional areas of national sovereignty have been transferred by the member states to Brussels in the last decades. The accession treaties cover all areas of Community-level policymaking, and more are likely to be added in the near future, partly as a result of the recent Convention on the Future of Europe and the designing of a constitution of the European Union, and partly as a consequence of global developments. However, the national sovereignty of small countries in a globalizing age has become more and more a fiction in any case. Indeed, small countries are expected to exercise more influence if the rules of the game favor shared sovereignty. Thus they should advocate a more federalist approach to European integration rather than an intergovernmental one, which would generally give priority to a decisionmaking process managed by large countries, often going over the heads of the smaller ones. In addition, small countries may find that accession gives them enhanced room to maneuver in negotiating with large third countries such as the United States or Japan, or with other regional groupings, or in the international arena (in the World Trade Organization, for example). Finally, membership in the European Union should be considered a two-way street, expanding possibilities to participate in global developments and processes, while providing an umbrella of protection against the adverse impacts of external developments.

It is quite interesting that the most important adverse impact of accession, namely, the possibility of a budget crunch, has scarcely been mentioned by the critics of accession. The reasons for this negligence are not easy to identify. Most probably, the critics believed that most of the population would fail to understand the argument. Yet it is precisely here that the most important explosive factors lie. A steady and sustainable process of catching up to the EU average will require relatively ample room for budgetary maneuvering, provided that expenditures predominantly (if not totally) finance investment, and not private consumption, as has been the case in various CEE countries in recent years.

The reality for the next few years, however, is quite different. First, the new member countries will have to pay their full contribution to the EU budget from the beginning, whereas their access to EU funds will be based on the phasing-in principle. Second, part of the money necessary to successfully prepare for membership will be needed in the next few years, partly because preparation has been delayed, and partly because of the new tasks emerging from membership. Third, the national contribution to the direct payments to be made to farmers, which can reach 30 percent of the EU average, has to be provided from the central budget. Fourth, national cofinancing ranging between 20 and 50 percent of the total value of an EU-approved project has to be guaranteed as well. Fifth, and in addition, a liquidity problem arises in two areas. On the one hand, direct payments to farmers have to start in 2004; however, EU transfers will occur one year later, based on such statistics as the area cultivated and the yield of the crops that fall under the Common Agricultural Policy. On the other hand, projects cofinanced by EU funds also need anticipated payments from the national budget, since part of the EU transfers are expected to arrive years after the project is finalized. Bills, accounts, and invoices presented by business actors participating in the project's implementation have to be settled immediately, long before EU support is expected to arrive.

As a consequence, serious budgetary pressures may appear between 2004 and 2006, implying that a restructuring of budgetary expenditure can hardly be avoided. The real question is, which items in the budget will get reduced financial support? Cuts in politically and socially sensitive areas are one scenario, with clear consequences for domestic (and maybe also regional) stability. The neglect of sensitive areas would result in reducing expenditure on (and investments in) education, culture, science, and health care—exactly those areas that are crucial for sustainable development, successful catch-up, and enhanced ability to meet global competition. This conflict, which will demand further transformation of the public sector, is expected to dominate political and economic discussions in the new member countries in 2005 and 2006 and could become a key issue for the enlarged union as well. At the moment there is no clear indication that the European Union is aware of this potential conflict, and some political, economic, and research measures would prove that it has started to take action to avoid such a situation, which would not only threaten national and regional stability and longer-term and sustainable growth in CEE, but also the global competitiveness of the European Union itself.

SLOVENIA AS A BORDER REGION OF THE EUROPEAN UNION

As a result of enlargement, the European Union will have two distinctly different kinds of borders: hard and soft. The hard borders will be those with Russia, Belarus, and Ukraine, and the soft borders those with other current or would-be candidate countries. The June 2003 Saloniki declaration on the Western Balkans, by offering future membership to the countries of this region as well, has made this differentiation even more evident. Concerning soft and hard borders, the acceding countries constitute four clear groups. Some (the Baltics, Poland, and Slovakia) will have only hard borders. The Czech Republic will not have any external (Schengen) border. Slovenia will have one soft border (with Croatia), while Hungary will have three soft borders (with Romania, Croatia, and Serbia) and one hard border (with Ukraine). This geopolitical reality has to be taken into account when talking about the border regions, the best forms of cross-border cooperation, the Schengen regime, ethnic minorities, and so on.

EU accession in May 2004 and the establishment of a Schengen border line in late 2006 will bring important economic and social changes to Slovenia and to the populations of neighboring regions and countries. For the period 2004–06, it was agreed with the European Commission that Slovenia as a whole will act as a single NUTS 2 (Nomenclature des Unités Territoriales Statistiques) region, despite several arguments (differing levels of economic development in Slovenia's subregions; its location at a crossroads of the Alps, the Pannonian Plain, the Dinaric Alps, and the Adriatic Sea; its many different types of terrain; its great biodiversity; its border regions with Austria, Italy, Hungary, and Croatia; its national minorities; and so on), which argue in favor of the administrative division of the country into two or three NUTS 2 regions.

Its favorable position in Central Europe will allow Slovenia to build upon the advantages of its geographical situation and achieve solid integration into the wider European area. Integration here means not only closer economic relations (in trade, investment, the euro zone, fiscal, capital movement, regional, technological and research cooperation, and so on), but also an intensification of political and cultural linkages and legal harmonization with neighboring countries and regions.

Given the opportunities and risks of enlargement and regionalization outlined above, it seems essential for Slovenia to follow a development strategy that will

- allow a stable growth path on both sides of the border, with clear emphasis on catching up with the present EU members
- be focused on the joint vision of an integrated regional economy, social cohesion, and good neighborly relations
- provide an infrastructure that will make border crossing easier and be oriented toward the spatial integration of the border regions
- take into account the protection of the environment, natural resources, and the needs of the local resident population, and
- help to build cross-border institutions for regional development and cultural exchange.

Accession will bring to Slovenia (and its neighboring regions) the potential for growth through economic development at a rate clearly above the EU average; the potential to expand its markets into neighboring countries; the realization of benefits through integrated production (cooperation and chains of production across borders), which at the regional level are now also accessible for very small enterprises; the potential for networking, cooperation, and integration to allow growth in markets and quality for SMEs in border regions as well. This strategy is valuable for businesses on both sides of the border, but with a different emphasis on market access and cost reduction (Funck and Pizzatti 2003).

Accession in 2004 will pose some risks for Slovenia and its neighboring regions (Agency for Regional Development 2000). The following effects can be envisaged on both sides of the present borders: a loss of retail markets in a number of product groups and services to competitors from across the border, price changes, and split service performance due to the predominance of customers from the neighboring country.[1] The majority of SMEs, construction, and service industries so far performing on local markets will face competition from neighboring countries. Substitution of local workers with workers from neighboring countries, particularly in jobs with lower skill and language requirements, will put downward pressure on wages. There will be a risk of brain drain through the loss of dynamic and skilled workers to higher-paying areas or regions. Cross-border commuting will increase the volume of passenger transport. Tourist flows will intensify the use of formerly protected (in some cases untouched) landscapes and natural resources. Prices of property and real estate will not develop symmetrically, but according to purchasing power. There will be a risk of loss of control over high-quality property and businesses.

Consequently, the new generation of EU interregional programs and PHARE cross-border cooperation programs

- should follow a proactive approach toward regional economic and social integration
- should be project-driven, with projects ranging from development of strategy to physical investment, and
- should focus on networking and institution building across borders.

After Slovenia's accession in 2004, the free movement of goods, capital, and services will be established within the enlarged European Union. This will have a particularly strong influence on Slovenia's economic relations with neighboring regions in Italy, Austria, and Hungary (although there is a seven-year derogation period for the free movement of labor). Slovenia's special free trade arrangements with the other countries of former SFR Yugoslavia will be abolished.

IMPACT OF SLOVENIA'S EU MEMBERSHIP ON THE OTHER SUCCESSOR COUNTRIES OF SFR YUGOSLAVIA

Apart from its neighbors within the European Union, Slovenia's most important economic partners are the other successor countries of SFR Yugoslavia. The final goal of all the countries on the territory of the former SFR Yugoslavia is to transform their economies into viable market economies and to achieve integration into the European Union. EU accession is considered key to a successful domestic transformation. Because Slovenia is at a more advanced stage of its transition, it should assist those countries in the region that are lagging behind, by relying on well-established connections and on a good understanding of the actual situation in the broader southeastern European region.

Although the individual countries of the region are at different stages of integration into the European Union, all see full membership as their main political and developmental objective. The speed and sequencing of EU integration should be adjusted to the specific characteristics and needs of each individual country in the region within the common procedure called the Stabilization and Association Process. The decision of the EU member states to put the countries in southeastern Europe on the so-called EU accession track is expected to strengthen substantially the efforts of the countries in the region toward accession, especially if accompanied by an appropriate volume and structure of preaccession funds (Peace and Crises Management Foundation 2003).

Proximity, knowledge of the market, and an appropriate institutional framework are the keys to economic cooperation, especially since Slovenia has a large number of SMEs and nongovernmental organizations that have not lost their economic and cultural ties with the former internal market of SFR Yugoslavia. Indeed, in recent years Slovenian companies have greatly intensified their activities in the other successor countries of SFR Yugoslavia, through exports as well as foreign direct investment (see Chapter 20). By signing Stabilisation and Association Agreements with the European Union, the countries of the former SFR Yugoslavia have intensified their political, economic, and social cooperation with the present member states and the new accession countries. Taking a medium- to long-term view, the dynamic effects of market liberalization and economic integration will have a positive impact on the industries subject to scale economies and on the establishment of higher forms of economic cooperation (networking, joint ventures, clustering, and the like). Slovenia, as a new EU member, will be keenly interested in the next round of the EU enlargement process from both a political and an economic point of view. That is why Slovenia supports the invigoration of the integration process provided for by the Stabilisation and Association Agreements with the other countries of the former SFR Yugoslavia.

CONCLUSIONS

Slovenia, as the economically most advanced EU accession country, has undergone three parallel social processes in the relatively short time since independence, all of them complementing and reinforcing each other:

- the transition from a socialist system to a viable market economy
- the transition from a region within SFR Yugoslavia to a sovereign national state, and
- accession to the European Union as a powerful political and economic force for regional integration.

For Slovenia, EU accession has proved to be the most suitable strategic option for achieving external security, legal harmonization, economic stability, involvement in European decisionmaking processes, and access to a large single market of 450 million consumers with free movement of goods, services, capital, and labor. It is expected that the benefits of accession will exceed the costs, taking into consideration both the quantitative and the qualitative effects. The benefits will include the net inflow of financial support through the cohesion and structural funds; active participation in the various political, economic, social, and cultural institutions of the European Union; greater competitiveness of the economy; a more flexible labor market; and inclusion in the euro zone, among others. The costs will include loss of sovereignty in monetary and fiscal policy affairs, the bankruptcy of uncompetitive enterprises; and thus higher unemployment and rising prices in certain sectors, among others. Slovenians should see EU membership as a two-way street: providing the opportunity to become an active partner in European and global development processes, on the one hand, while taking advantage of the EU umbrella of protection against the negative impacts of the global environment on a small country, on the other.

During the transition and preaccession period, Slovenia has gained valuable experience in a number of areas: in developing its institutional and legal framework, in skill formation, in cultural patterns, and in its capacity for participation in European programs. All of these should prove instrumental in the transfer of knowledge to the new candidate countries of southeastern Europe.

REFERENCES

Agency for Regional Development of the Republic of Slovenia. 2000. "Joint Interreg IIIA—Phare CBC Programming Document—Slovenia." Ljubljana.

Bobek, V., J. Potočnik, V. Ravbar, M. Rojec, P. Stanovnik, and F. Štiblar. 1996. "Slovenia: Strategy of International Economic Relations." Ministry of Economic Relations and Development, Ljubljana.

Funck, B., and L. Pizzatti. 2003. "European Integration, Regional Policy and Growth." World Bank, Washington, D.C. Processed.

Inotai, A. 1999. "The Costs and Benefits of Eastern Enlargement of the EU." Institute for World Economics, Budapest. Processed.

Majcen, B. 1999. "Measurement of Costs and Benefits of Accession to the EU for Selected CEECs: Country Report Slovenia." Research Report 256. Wiener Institut für Internationale Wirtschaftsvergleiche, Vienna.

Peace and Crises Management Foundation. 2003. "Cavtat Declaration on Economic Development and Policies in the Region of Former Yugoslavia." Belgrade.

NOTES

1. By split services performance is meant a new division of labor among service providers on both sides of the border.

Chapter 22
Slovenia's Road to Membership in the European Union

Janez Potočnik and Jaime Garcia Lombardero

This chapter describes the basis for and the process of Slovenia's integration into the European Union. The first section deals with the main decisions that Slovenia has made with regard to EU integration, and the second with the EU criteria for membership and the accession process in general. The third and fourth sections explain Slovenia's accession process and its negotiations with the European Union, and the final section concludes.

MAIN STRATEGIC DECISIONS AND DOCUMENTS RELATED TO EU ACCESSION

The main strategic decisions that set Slovenia on the road toward membership in the European Union were first outlined in 1994–95 in the Strategy for Economic Development of Slovenia (Potočnik, Senjur, and Štiblar 1995). The crucial goals of this strategy were to speed Slovenia's economic growth and allow Slovenia to catch up with the more developed European countries; to improve the competitiveness of the Slovenian economy; to allow Slovenia to take part in Europe's integration; and to achieve sustainable economic growth while taking into account environmental, social, and ethical concerns.

The ultimate objective was to develop Slovenia into a modern, democratic country based on the rule of law, a market economy, and private ownership, while attending to important social and environmental concerns. Because the European Union is based on exactly these values and standards, EU membership was seen as an ultimate proof that the transition has been accomplished.

Just as, on the one hand, a successful transition was thus seen as a precondition for accession, so too, on the other, the accession process itself speeded Slovenia's transition. The process helped Slovenia overcome certain obstacles—such as monopolistic firms and entrenched political interests—to necessary change. It established greater order and stability in the economy and society as a whole and contributed to the improved competitiveness of all economic agents—individuals, companies, and the state itself.

To achieve these goals, Slovenia had to undertake several tasks. The first task—separation from the former Yugoslavia—had already been accomplished: the Slovenian economy had been transformed into an independent national economy and had become a participant in its own right in a number of major international associations and organizations. Next, in order to transform its self-managed socialist economy into a functioning market economy, Slovenia had to introduce and develop democratic political institutions, transform the ownership of its enterprises, and develop its financial, labor, and goods and services markets and liberalize its foreign economic relations. In the search for equilibrium between rapid growth and external and internal balance, further stabilization of the economy was needed; the government had to take measures to stimulate domestic saving and to raise the share of investment in GDP, and thus create the conditions for sustainable and stable growth. It was recognized that growth should be driven by exports and that the current account should be kept in balance. Also, the share of general government expenditure in GDP needed to be lowered, and the general government deficit had to be prevented from increasing. In addition, there was a need to accelerate the process of system transformation, that is, to reform the social security system, continue the reform of the tax system, accelerate the privatization process, develop the capital market, reorganize public administration, and introduce long-term budget programming.

In 1996 and 1997 Slovenia adopted two new strategic documents: the Strategy of International Economic Relations (SIERS; Bobek and others 1996), and the Strategy for Increasing Competitiveness Capabilities of Slovenian Industry (Ministry of Economic Affairs 1996). Based on a thorough analysis of the country's situation, the SIERS suggested EU membership as the best option for the country's European integration.

On the basis of these documents, in 1998 Slovenia adopted the Strategy of Slovenia for Accession to the European Union (Mrak, Rojec, and Potočnik 1998). Its main objective was to define and outline a set of consistent medium-term economic and social policies required to complete the economic transformation of Slovenia and prepare its economy for EU accession. The strategy had several operative objectives, the most important being to analyze the level of economic and social transformation already achieved in Slovenia, to identify sector- and area-specific objectives and targets, to design a consistent system of reforms and economic policy measures required to reach this objective, and to establish a proper mechanism for monitoring the realization of reforms and other measures.

Slovenia signed the Europe Agreement on association between itself and the European Union on June 10, 1996, and it applied for EU membership on the same day. The Europe Agreement entered into force in February 1999. The agreement covers free trade and economic cooperation as well as technical assistance, training, and political dialogue.

EU CRITERIA FOR MEMBERSHIP AND THE ACCESSION PROCESS

In 1993, at the Copenhagen European Council, the EU member states took a decisive step toward the current enlargement of the Union, agreeing that the countries of Central and Eastern Europe that so desired could become members. The member states also decided that these countries would be admitted to the European Union once they had met certain economic and political conditions. These criteria for membership (also called the Copenhagen criteria) were the following: stability of the institutions guaranteeing democracy, the rule of law, human rights, and protection of minorities; the existence of a functioning market economy as well as the capacity to cope with competitive pressure and market forces within the European Union; and the ability to take on the obligations of membership, including adherence to the aims of political, economic, and monetary union. The last criterion entails the adoption and implementation of the *acquis communautaire*[1] into national legislation and its enforcement through adequately prepared administrative and judicial bodies.

The submission of an application for EU membership marks the start of an accession process that takes several years. In brief, the process is as follows:

- *Assessment:* The European Commission delivers an opinion on each applicant country, based on the conditions for membership established by the European Union. If the applicant country is judged capable of meeting the accession criteria, the Commission may recommend that negotiations be launched. If not, the application is put on hold or rejected.
- *Screening:* The candidate country must adapt its national legislation to community law. During the screening process, the commission and the applicant country's negotiating teams jointly examine the country's legislation in each area of cooperation, to determine where, why, and how it needs to be adapted and what the possible obstacles are.
- *Negotiations:* The candidate country presents its negotiating positions for each area. Within the European Union, the European Commission is responsible for drafting the EU negotiating positions, which must be approved by the Council of Ministers. The country holding the presidency of the Council chairs the negotiations. During the negotiations the member states are represented by ministers or their permanent representatives to the European Union in Brussels, and the candidate country is represented by its chief negotiators. The aim of the negotiations is to reach agreement on the exact terms of membership.
- *Approval:* Once negotiations have been concluded and the accession country is considered to meet all the formal requirements for EU membership, an accession agreement is drawn up, which must then be approved by the Council of Ministers and the European Parliament. After the agreement has been signed, it requires the approval of the member countries and of the

candidate country (in both cases, through a decision in the national legislature). Most often, the candidate country will also hold a referendum on membership.

SLOVENIA'S ACCESSION PROCESS

In 1997 the European Commission prepared an opinion on the state of fulfillment of the Copenhagen criteria by the six countries that at that time had applied for membership: Cyprus, the Czech Republic, Estonia, Hungary, Poland, and Slovenia. In light of its findings, the Commission recommended to the member states that accession negotiations be opened with all six countries.

In Slovenia's case the Commission concluded that the country could be regarded as a stable democracy fulfilling the relevant level of compliance with the first two Copenhagen criteria. However, the commission stated that Slovenia would have to make considerable effort to be able to adopt and implement the *acquis,* particularly in the area of the internal market, the environment, employment, social affairs, and energy, before it could be granted full EU membership. Further administrative reform would be indispensable if Slovenia was to have the necessary structures in place to apply and enforce the *acquis* effectively.

The Preaccession Strategy: Various Forms of Support

To facilitate preparations for membership, the European Union and Slovenia agreed on a preaccession strategy whereby the European Union would provide financial assistance to help Slovenia adopt and implement the *acquis* before accession. Three main instruments were adopted for the implementation of this strategy: the Europe Agreement between Slovenia and the European Union, the Accession Partnership and National Programme for the Adoption of the *Acquis* (NPAA), and the PHARE financial instrument.

The *Europe Agreement,* or Association Agreement, is based on a shared understanding and shared values and is designed to prepare the way for the political, economic, and social convergence of Slovenia with the European Union. The Europe Agreement became the framework within which Slovenia prepared its legislation and administrative structures for membership.

The *Accession Partnership* and the *NPAA* were the instruments that facilitated the process of programming the European Union's financial assistance to Slovenia. That assistance in turn was linked to Slovenia's progress. The Accession Partnership contains the Slovenia's precise commitments as regards democratic stability, macroeconomic performance, industrial restructuring, and adoption of the *acquis*, focusing on the priority areas identified in the European Commission's opinion on Slovenia's application for membership. The NPAA was a national document giving precise information and details on how Slovenia intended to fulfill the priorities of the Accession Partnership. Beginning in 1998, the commission recorded each year the progress made by Slovenia in the different areas of the *acquis*. This served as a basis for the European Union to make decisions on the conduct and progress of accession negotiations and to monitor and assess the progress made in meeting the Copenhagen criteria.

Slovenia has been receiving assistance from the European Union since 1992. The most important instrument through which this assistance has been channeled is the *PHARE program*.[2] Between 1992 and 1997 the main emphasis in Slovenia's preaccession financial assistance was on promoting economic development through support of privatization and enterprise restructuring, banking sector reform, and increased research and development capacity. With the launch of accession negotiations, the emphasis shifted to preparation for membership; that is, assistance was focused on the priority areas defined in the Accession Partnership and the NPAA.[3] It can thus be said that the PHARE financial instrument evolved from what was originally a demand-driven external aid into a tool that has supported many different aspects of the transition process. It has been an indispensable instrument in the preparation for accession.

Challenges in Adopting and Implementing the *Acquis*

Slovenia could not effectively apply the rules of the internal market without first undertaking the reform of its judiciary and introducing the necessary structural reforms for its transformation into a functioning market economy. Progress in these two areas was absolutely necessary for Slovenia to survive in the new economic environment, even if it were not negotiating accession to the European Union. However, the determination to become an EU member was an overriding argument that helped Slovenian citizens support and accept the difficult and sometimes unpopular decisions made by the authorities.

Reform of the judiciary has continued over the entire period of transition. Legislative changes, continuous training of judges, and the adoption of measures aimed at abolishing the backlog of pending court cases were the main actions implemented to foster the modernization and adaptation of the judicial system to the new political, economic, and social environment. This task is still ongoing, and sustained efforts should be maintained to train judges in dealing with cases arising in particular from the implementation of the single market rules.

Since 1997 Slovenia's economic performance has improved considerably. Macroeconomic stability has been achieved, and *economic reforms* have steadily deepened. Slovenia is today a functioning market economy, and completion of the current reform path should enable it to cope with competitive pressure and market forces in the European Union. However, efforts should still be made to reduce the inflation rate through the further elimination of indexation schemes and through appropriate macroeconomic policy. Slovenia has adopted a gradual but judicious approach to economic reform, which in some sectors could be perceived as lacking determination. It is true that although the role of the state is steadily decreasing, the state is still prominent in the economy. The slow pace of privatization reflects the gradualist approach to structural reform in Slovenia.

The most demanding challenge for Slovenia was, however, *the transposition and implementation of the acquis* and *the development of institutions*. The areas of EU law affecting the liberalization of the economy and the transformation of the labor market, the implementation of the Common Agricultural Policy, and those areas where substantial financial effort was needed (in particular, the environment) proved, unsurprisingly, to be the most difficult to implement. Overall, Slovenia has now achieved a high degree of legislative alignment with the *acquis* in most areas, and the setting up of administrative capacity is well advanced.

The *liberalization of economic activity* is an essential element in the proper functioning of the four freedoms (free movement of goods, persons, services, and capital) that govern the EU internal market. However, liberalization also means equal opportunities for companies and persons, so as to guarantee a fair and competitive environment for companies, the protection of consumers, and preservation of intellectual and industrial property. In this respect Slovenia has not only established the necessary institutions for certification and standardization of products, market surveillance, supervision of financial services, and enforcement of market rules, but is also acquiring the necessary experience through the practical implementation of the relevant rules and provisions. Some progress still has to be made in these areas before Slovenia's accession, in particular on establishing a good track record on enforcement with a view to ensuring efficient competition and transparency for market players.

Agricultural policy, including veterinary and phytosanitary legislation, is another difficult and time-consuming area where steady progress has been made and preparation is proceeding satisfactorily. Slovenia is now focusing attention on an important number of pieces of legislation and provisions that have to be fully implemented by the date of accession, in particular the upgrading or establishment of border inspection posts along Slovenia's frontier with Croatia (which will become the external border of the enlarged European Union). Costly but necessary investments in this area are being undertaken by the administration, with financial support from the European Union, to ensure that Slovenia will effectively manage its share of responsibility in securing the health of all European citizens.

The environment is another area where, in spite of the difficulties, Slovenia has demonstrated its commitment to abide by EU rules. The level of alignment is already very high, although it is still necessary to ensure the effective implementation of industrial pollution control provisions and to secure sufficient investment to ensure implementation of the environmental *acquis*.

Slovenia has also continued to make good progress in the area of *justice and home affairs*. The Schengen border between Slovenia and the European Union will be maintained for some time after accession. Slovenia has set a target date of 2006 for the lifting of the internal border and for the full implementation of the external Schengen border. In the meantime Slovenia is bringing its institutions, management systems, and administrative arrangements up to EU standards, in particular with a view to adopting and implementing measures with respect to external border controls, asylum, and immigration, according to the Slovenia Schengen Action Plan. Some further efforts are also needed to prepare the administration for its responsibilities in preventing and combating crime, terrorism, and illicit drug trafficking.

Preparations are also in progress toward the implementation of the EU *cohesion policy*. The European Union created this policy in 1988, to compensate its less developed regions for the negative effects that the establishment of the internal market might bring to their economies. It is thus very important for Slovenia to make timely preparations for the implementation of a policy that will certainly help its economic agents face the adjustments necessary to fully benefit from the internal market after accession. Training and investments constitute the main actions cofinanced by EU structural instruments with a view to supporting structural change. However, to mobilize funds and to fully benefit from EU assistance, Slovenia must adapt its administrative structures in timely fashion to the management rules of the structural funds.

Given the level of administrative capacity and alignment with EU rules and standards that Slovenia has already achieved , and given its track record in implementing the commitments it has made in the accession negotiations, one can fairly conclude that Slovenia will be able to assume the obligations of membership by the date of accession.

NEGOTIATIONS

Negotiations between the European Union and Cyprus, the Czech Republic, Estonia, Hungary, Poland, and Slovenia started in March

1998. In 2000 negotiations with another five transition economy applicants (Bulgaria, Latvia, Lithuania, Romania, and Slovakia) and with Malta began. The basic principle of the negotiations was that nothing is agreed until everything is agreed. Each candidate country's accession prospects would depend on its progress in the negotiations.

The focus of negotiations was on the *acquis communautaire,* which was structured into 31 chapters covering policies in specific sectors: economic and monetary union; agriculture; fisheries; environment; free movement of capital, goods, services, and persons; external relations; and so on. For each chapter the candidate countries negotiated with the European Union the legislative and policy changes that would be required.

It was clear from the very beginning that the impetus to join the European Union came from the candidates, not from the European Union itself. The *acquis* was not subject to being changed or adjusted to meet the needs of individual candidates, as it was the result of decades of compromises among the existing member states. But in special cases either or both sides might seek exemptions from the *acquis.*[4]

In its earlier stages the negotiating process could thus more appropriately be called a process of adjustment. In that period, at least in Slovenia's case, the real negotiations took place within the country, with respect to its preparation to undertake the necessary changes not only in principle, but also despite interferences with the existing division of economic and political power. Slovenia succeeded in reaching an adequate level of political consensus and support to allow the process to proceed efficiently and in a quite undisturbed manner. Slovenia's favorable starting position, reflected largely in its relatively high level of development compared with the other candidate countries, as well as its small size, which allowed it adequate flexibility, helped Slovenia become one of the most successful candidates in the process of adjustment. One of the reasons for that success may be that Slovenians were aware throughout the accession process that their country's future image as a member state was being created. Slovenia wanted to be seen as a country with great expertise—flexible, constructive, and well-organized—and as a country that strives to achieve its interests but is at the same time aware that, within the Community, those interests can be realized only through agreement on and understanding of the interests of others as well as the common interest. Aware of its small size and relative lack of political significance, Slovenia always sought to do its work correctly. The efficiency of internal preparations was largely in Slovenia's own interest, since it was judged better to enter the European Union well prepared for the challenges of increased competition.

Negotiations on the Financial Arrangements of Accession: Goals and Assessment

The real negotiations—concerning the distribution of a limited amount of funds among the candidates—took place in 2002. These financial negotiations involved candidates' contributions to the EU budget in the period 2004–06 and candidates' drawing of funds under the two most important financial assistance policies: agricultural policies and structural and cohesion policies. Slovenia opted for the most favorable combination, whereby it would be able to meet two of its main goals. The first was that the final agreement with the European Union should allow Slovenia to continue the process of real convergence, that is, of further reducing Slovenia's developmental lag behind the EU average. The second was that the agreement should not worsen the position of Slovenia's public finances or cause difficulties in achieving the necessary fiscal objectives for joining the euro zone.

The results of the financial negotiations can be presented and assessed from these two perspectives. The agreements set clearly defined development and public finance goals for the short term, that is, from the date of membership (May 2004) to the end of the present financial perspective (the end of 2006). But their long-term importance is even greater, since, by these agreements, Slovenia established the basis for its participation in negotiations on the new financial perspective (2007–13) as a full member. In these negotiations a unique amount will be earmarked for all member states of the enlarged European Union.

Results of the Financial Negotiations

The negotiations on the financial package began in January 2002, when the European Commission published a document titled "Common Financial Framework 2004–2006." That document defined the basic framework for discussion of the financial aspects of accession, that is, EU assistance to the accession countries in the areas of agriculture and structural and cohesion policy, and contributions by the accession countries to the EU budget.

In the area of *agriculture,* Slovenia set four strategic goals: that Slovenia should participate fully and equally in EU policies; that the economic position of Slovenian farmers should not be made worse by EU accession; that the negotiated quotas and reference quantities must not be lower than present output in Slovenia; and that any solutions negotiated should be adapted to the specific structural and development problems of Slovenian agriculture and should take into account the changes foreseen in the Common Agricultural Policy. These goals were fully met, and the package of solutions was altogether favorable for Slovenia.[5]

In the area of *structural and cohesion policy,* Slovenia endeavored to meet two major goals: to ensure an amount of funds in the 2004–06 period suitable to the country's level of development; and to reach an agreement according to which the less developed parts of the Slovenian territory would preserve, in the next financial perspective, the status of an Objective 1 region. (Objective 1 regions are granted the widest possible access to EU structural funds.) From a long-term perspective, the agreements reached in this area may be assessed as positive.[6] They provide opportunities for Slovenia to draw funds for structural activities even in the period after 2007. From a short-term perspective, it would have been better if more funds had been approved for structural and development purposes for the period 2004–07. However, the amount of funds approved is understandable in view of the European Union's criteria by which a relatively small share of funds was earmarked for the most developed candidate countries. In previous EU enlargements, new member states were able to draw only a relatively small amount of approved funds in the first year of membership. This means that accepting more structural funds in the first years of membership, when the country is not yet fully qualified to draw them, means also taking on greater public finance risks.

In the area of *contributions to the EU budget* and *Slovenia's net budgetary position in relation to the EU budget,* Slovenia set the following goals: in the period 2004–06, to achieve a better positive net budgetary position than recorded in the year before accession; and, in the period 2007–13, to increase the likelihood that Slovenia would remain a net recipient from the EU budget. The agreed solutions are in line with both goals.[7] Such an outcome of the negotiations gives Slovenia some room to maneuver in managing the risks to which it might be exposed in the event of potentially inefficient drawing of EU funds from the rural development and structural funds.

Slovenia introduced a special issue in the EU budget, namely, the *financing of controls at the EU external border* (the Schengen border). The European Union accepted Slovenia's proposal and undertook to assume part of the cost of establishing and maintaining the Schengen border in the new member states.[8] It is quite realistic that the item for Schengen border expenses will remain in the EU budget in the period of the next financial perspective as well.

CONCLUSIONS

The principle of EU enlargement toward Central and Eastern Europe was decided at the European Council meeting in Copenhagen in 1993.

At the same meeting the main economic and political criteria that the candidate countries should meet were also announced.

At the Council's Luxembourg meeting in 1997, Slovenia was invited to start negotiations toward accession to the European Union. The negotiations started in April 1998 and were completed in December 2002. The basic objective of the negotiations was to reach an agreement on how and when the candidate countries could align their legislation with the European legal framework (the *acquis communautaire*), and whether they had set up the necessary administrative structures and bodies for the effective implementation of the common rules. To facilitate preparations for membership, the European Union and Slovenia agreed on a preaccession strategy whereby the European Union would provide financial assistance.

The hardest part of the negotiations was left for the final phase. This was the agreement on the financial package, that is, the amounts that Slovenia would receive for agriculture, structural funds, and other common policies of the European Union from the EU budget in the years 2004–06, and the amounts that Slovenia would contribute to the EU budget in the same period.

The proposals of the European Union were usually horizontal (that is, the same for all candidate countries) and were in many cases not suitable for Slovenia. Therefore Slovenia actively and successfully endeavored to obtain more favorable solutions. The agreed financial solutions are well balanced for Slovenia in the short run and include elements that should have important positive effects in the long run, thus contributing to the stability of Slovenia's public finances.

Slovenia's accession process and negotiations undoubtedly created a favorable basis for its successful integration into the European Union and enhanced the process of real convergence. Now it is up to Slovenia itself to make the best possible use of the opportunities presented by EU membership.

REFERENCES

Bobek, V., J. Potočnik, V. Ravbar, M. Rojec, P. Stanovnik, and F. Štiblar, eds. 1996. *Slovenia: The Strategy of International Economic Relations—From Associated to Full-fledged Membership in the EU.* Ljubljana: Ministry of Economic Relations and Development.

Ministry of Economic Affairs. 1996. "Strategy for Increasing Competitiveness Capabilities of Slovenian Industry." Ljubljana.

Mrak, M., M. Rojec, and J. Potočnik. 1998. "Slovenia—Strategy of the Republic of Slovenia for Accession to the European Union—Economic and Social Part." Institute of Macroeconomic Analysis and Development, Ljubljana.

Potočnik, J., M. Senjur, and F. Štiblar. 1995. "The Strategy for the Economic Development of Slovenia: Approaching Europe—Growth, Competitiveness and Integration." Institute of Macroeconomic Analysis and Development, Ljubljana.

NOTES

1. The *acquis communautaire* is the European Union's common regulatory framework, a body of EU legislation, practices, principles, and objectives accepted by the member states. It has accumulated over 50 years and amounts to more than 12,000 legislative acts. It includes intra-EU treaties (most importantly the Treaties of Rome, the Single European Act, and the Maastricht, Amsterdam, and Nice Treaties); legislation enacted at the EU level and judgments of the European Court of Justice; principles in the areas of justice and home affairs, and foreign and security policy; and the treaties with third countries.

2. The PHARE (Poland and Hungary: Aid for Economic Restructuring) program started in 1989 as a help to the Polish and Hungarian economies; it developed into a main program for accession candidates.

3. During the period 1998–2003, the Commission allocated €227 million to the PHARE program and three Cross Border Co-Operation programs. In all these years, major work was done with the introduction of targeted institution building, which gave a boost to ongoing reforms of public administration. Particular emphasis was placed on preparing Slovenia for entry into the internal market and the implementation of phytosanitary and veterinary control. An important area was the preparation of what would become the new EU external frontier along the land border between Croatia and Slovenia for all the controls linked to the regulation of the common market and the Schengen border. More recently, investments were also started in the area of economic and social cohesion. The aim was to give Slovenia initial experience in running projects and grant schemes of a regional nature that, after accession, would be financed from structural funds.

4. Possible exemptions are of three types: a *transition period* could be established as a temporary exemption that allows the full implementation of the *acquis* in a certain field, within negotiated time limits, after accession; a *derogation* is a permanent exemption, granted very rarely, usually connected with certain specific features of the acceding country; a *safeguard clause* grants the right to suspend certain provisions of the *acquis* if the country does not fulfill its obligations.

5. Of all the candidate countries, Slovenia achieved by far the highest level of topping up of direct payments to farmers from the national budget. In addition, only Slovenian farmers will have access to direct payments at exactly the same level as their colleagues from EU member states starting in 2007, and in this element of the Common Agricultural Policy they will be on entirely equal footing with the other members.

The outcome of negotiations on quotas and reference quantities is favorable. The agreed quotas and reference quantities even allow further restructuring of the Slovenian agriculture and at the same time improve Slovenia's possibilities in further changes of the CAP.

Slovenia managed to assure itself an exhaustive and developmentally interesting package of solutions for rural development in the period 2004–2006, worth altogether about EUR 250 million. The program allows the formation of a more quality government policy as regards agriculture and rural areas and at the same time improves Slovenia's position in the future debates about the CAP reform.

6. For the period 2004–06, it was agreed that Slovenia would receive altogether €404 million from EU structural instruments, of which €236 million will come from structural funds and €168 million from the cohesion fund. The final decision concerning the regionalization of Slovenia for purposes of the cohesion policy will be made by the end of 2006, allowing a realistic chance that a large part of Slovenia's territory will be eligible to draw on EU structural funds in the period 2007–13.

7. In October 2002 the European Council eliminated the dilemma of whether Slovenia would be a net payer to the EU budget in 2004–06. The European Union decided that no new member should find itself in a worse net budgetary position after accession than in the year before accession. Under the final agreement reached in Copenhagen in December 2002, lump-sum payments to Slovenia amounting to €224 million were approved for the period 2004–06. As a result, Slovenia's net budgetary position improves from a projected €45 million for 2003 to about €82 million projected for each of the three years in the period 2004–06.

8. Slovenia will receive a total of €107 million for this purpose in the period 2004–06.

Chapter 23
Size Matters in the European Union: Searching for Balance between Formal and Actual Equality

Zlatko Šabič, Marjan Svetličič, Dorota Pyszna-Nigge, and Wolfgang Wessels

This chapter discusses the evolution in the institutional position of smaller states within the European Union. Particular attention is devoted to arrangements reached between larger and smaller European countries within the framework of the 1996 Amsterdam Treaty, the Nice arrangement of 2000, and the Convention on the Future of Europe established in 2001. The subject is of key importance for Slovenia, now that it is on the verge of full EU membership.

It has been said that we shall "all be the gainers if we can create a world fit for small states to live in. But the small can preserve their independence in the international as in the national sphere only within a true system of law which guarantees both that certain rules are invariably enforced and that the authority which has the power to enforce these cannot use it for any other purposes" (Hayek 1997). This argument, made back in 1944, conveys an important message. Whatever the preponderance of major powers, and however impressive the outbursts of the so-called arrogance of power might be, the world never is and most likely never will be entirely of their own making. Not a single country in the world as we know it can achieve its national interests on a zero-sum basis without encountering resistance and, ultimately, a costly conflict.[1]

The European Union may be taken as a case in point. Having arisen out of the aftermath of two devastating wars, it has become home to the largest European countries and to smaller states alike. Political events in Central and Eastern Europe at the end of the 1980s and the beginning of the 1990s did catch the European Union slightly off balance. Although the end to the East-West divide certainly came as a relief, it also created immediate problems for the EU member states. They were confronted with such issues as whether, how, when, and under what conditions the former socialist countries—including many small ones, such as Slovenia—would be granted access to the markets of the European Union or even become full members (Dinan 1999). Fifteen years later, the answer is in front of us: the European Union is on the verge of an unprecedented enlargement to Central and Eastern Europe and the Mediterranean.

Slovenia is a part of this process. EU membership can be fairly considered as a reward for all the effort this country has invested in establishing itself as an actor in the international community. However, EU membership is also a challenge to Slovenia in carrying out its own strategies and fulfilling its goals. What, then, should Slovenia, as a future EU member, be prepared to expect?

The history of the European Union is, among other things, a history of relations between smaller members and their larger counterparts. Yet that history notwithstanding (or, indeed, precisely because of it), smallness appears to have limited explanatory power in accounting for the dynamics of decisionmaking in the European

Union. There is no such thing in the European Union as a caucus of smaller states, simply because the Union has not been set up to pursue smaller states' interests alone. Even in those areas where conflict between the smaller and larger states could emerge, for example in institutional affairs, the perception of fair dealing on these matters tends to prevail. Put differently, that which must be sustained with respect to the role of individual member states in an international decisionmaking system such as the European Union is a point of balance between two equalities: formal equality, which is thought to have existed since the Treaty of Westphalia in 1648, and to which all recognized states have since been entitled; and actual equality, which has never existed and therefore must always be actively pursued through international agreement (Šabič 1999).

SMALLER STATES AND DECISIONMAKING IN THE EUROPEAN COMMUNITIES: A HISTORICAL PERSPECTIVE

The European Coal and Steel Community

When the Schuman plan of 1950 was first brought to life, the smaller members made sure that the three largest member states—France, Germany, and Italy—were not the only ones whose interests were reflected in collective decisionmaking. At the beginning of the negotiations, an agreement was reached in principle that decisions in the ministerial council of the European Coal and Steel Community (ECSC) should be reached by majority vote, unless otherwise provided. This raised the issue of how the voting power that the prospective members were to possess in the ECSC Council would be distributed. The smaller states did not want to enter an arrangement in which they would be overpowered by Germany and France. After much negotiation (Küsters 1988), it was eventually agreed that each of the member states would be allocated one vote; yet the treaty also stipulated that whenever the treaty required the concurrence of the ECSC Council to a proposal submitted by the High Authority, an "absolute majority" of the member states, that is, four out of the six members, was necessary. Moreover, the decision was deemed adopted only if at least one of the states voting in favor produced 20 percent of the total value of coal and steel in the ECSC (that is, either Germany or France had to vote in favor).

In the case of an equal division of votes, however, and if the High Authority decided to maintain its proposal after a second reading, the agreement of France and Germany, the two largest producers of coal and steel, would suffice. Thus a kind of weighted voting was introduced in the arrangement: in particular circumstances a special weight was given to the votes cast by France and Germany, which made it impossible for the smaller members to overrule these two acting together. By the same token, however, the French and Germans could not (except in the event of an equal division of votes) impose their policies on the other four member states. This arrangement largely met the demands of both the smaller and the larger prospective members of the ECSC.

The European Economic Community

Decisionmaking in the European Economic Community (EEC) was based on at least two considerations (Westlake 1995). First, the dominance of the larger member states again needed to be checked if smaller states were to be willing to enter. Thus the states agreed that Luxembourg could be used as a starting point for the distribution of votes to other member states. It was awarded one vote. The other two small states, Belgium and the Netherlands, were each accorded twice as many votes as Luxembourg, and France, Germany, and Italy, as the largest members, each received twice as many votes as Belgium or the Netherlands (Article 148/2 of the EEC Treaty). The qualified majority vote (QMV) needed to pass a decision was set at 12 votes. Unless a proposal was submitted by the Commission, in which case 12 votes from any three member states were enough for adoption, the required 12 votes had to be cast by four different member states. The Benelux countries accepted this arrangement because they trusted that the Commission would take account of their vital interests (Schermers 1972, vol. II). Confidence in and support for the Commission has since then become and remained part of the smaller states' decisionmaking doctrine.

The second underlying issue was connected with the increasing importance of the QMV in the ministerial council's decisionmaking. In contrast to the ECSC Treaty, the EEC Treaty was not static. It specifically provided for continued progress toward a common market, which was gradually to increase the number of decisions made by the QMV rather than by unanimity. But this development soon proved to be a major source of dispute between member states.

The First Waves of Enlargement

With three successive enlargements in 1973, 1981, and 1985, and with no significant change in decisionmaking procedures, including the method of distributing the votes, the overrepresentation of smaller states in the Council's decisionmaking became problematic. The UK government argued, for instance, that "a relatively small group of relatively small states, acting in concert, may block progress (on the common market or other areas of Community activity) with relative ease."[2] The British had a point. It was—and still is—true that a great many decisions in the Council are reached by consensus, but, ultimately, heads are always counted. From the perspective of the larger members, the situation further deteriorated after the end of the Cold War. The anticipated enlargement of 1995 was to bring the relative voting power even more into the smaller members' favor. At an informal meeting in Ioannina, Greece, on March 27, 1994, the EU foreign ministers partly agreed that the question of institutional reform, including the weighting of votes and the threshold for the QMV in the Council, would be examined at the next intergovernmental conference (IGC). This decision in a sense announced a new era for the European Union, in which the relative weights of the smaller and larger member states were to be redefined. The process began at Amsterdam in 1996.

FROM AMSTERDAM TO ROME

The Amsterdam Intergovernmental Conference

The European Union added three new members in 1995, and the enlargement to the east was nearing fast, but the Amsterdam IGC failed to meet the expectations of those wishing to reform the existing EU decisionmaking system. Member states were clearly aware of the imminence of reforms in the Council's decisionmaking. Eight of the 10 Central and Eastern European applicants closest to membership in the European Union were smaller countries, comparable in size to Belgium, Austria, or the Netherlands. Only Poland and Romania would qualify even as medium-size countries. Baldwin (1994) calculated that if the mode of vote distribution then in place were left unchanged, the likely new Central and Eastern European members could form a blocking minority among themselves alone. However, the member states could not reach a comprehensive agreement on crucial institutional issues (the so-called Amsterdam leftovers), namely, the size of the Commission and the voting reform of the Council. They could only agree to a protocol on the institutions. Article 2 of the protocol, appended to the Amsterdam Treaty, stipulates that at least one year "before the membership of the EU exceeds twenty, a conference of representatives of the governments of the Member States shall be convened in order to carry out a comprehensive review of the provisions of the Treaties on the composition and functioning of the institutions." It was agreed that such a conference would be convened in Nice.

The Arrangement of Nice

The institutional reforms initiated in 1999 to prepare the EU enlargement to the east showed a tendency toward a redefinition of institutional balance that was partly to the detriment of the smaller countries. In early 2000 the applicant countries expressed their concern about maintaining the equilibrium among the existing EU member states.[3] Already at that stage, it was obvious that the prospective members were especially preoccupied with the question of the future role of smaller states in EU decisionmaking. The IGC 2000 and the bargaining at Nice over the weighting of votes in the Council brought about an intense debate, full of contending arguments.

The agreement reached at Nice and written into the protocol on the enlargement of the European Union (Wessels 2001) envisages a substantial reweighting of the existing voting system, but it rejected the Commission's proposal, supported by the smaller countries, of a double majority of states and populations. The consensus neither guarantees a balance between smaller and larger member states nor simplifies the decisionmaking nor makes it more transparent. The threshold for a QMV was increased and the procedures were made more complicated (three thresholds must be met for a QMV in the Council: a threshold size of population, a majority of countries, and a general threshold of votes), leading to a hybrid constellation, which reduces the role of smaller countries in EU decisionmaking. At that time the applicant countries were expecting a reassessment of the relative weight of member states' votes, but one that would maintain a balance between larger and smaller member states. Therefore Poland was probably the only applicant country whose expectations in this respect were entirely fulfilled: it would probably gain greater political weight in the enlarged European Union and enjoy good assets for the coalition building. Besides, Poland, as a future EU member, was unlikely to make concessions in favor of the smaller member states.

That said, a slight digression is in order. Based on what has just been noted with respect to Poland, one could get the impression that the smaller states might have perceived Poland as a burden to their own aspirations regarding EU membership. But the reality seemed to be quite the contrary. It appears that the smaller states were quite willing to accept certain realities with regard to the accession process, one of which was that Poland would be a future EU member. Poland was simply too big to be left behind. Thus, to maintain the momentum of enlargement, it was in the smaller states' interest to support Poland's case to be admitted in the first wave, since that would avoid a threat to the continent's stability. This "solidarity," as put by Janez Potočnik, head of the Slovenian negotiating team and the current minister without portfolio for European affairs,[4] seems to be yet further proof that relations between smaller and larger European countries are rather complex, and that the mechanism of interdependence between countries of different size actually works.

The Convention on the Future of Europe

With a sense of unfinished business after the Nice IGC,[5] and with preparations for the eastward enlargement proceeding at full speed, the idea of staging a Convention on the Future of Europe was launched at the Laeken Summit in December 2001. The Convention, with a one-year mandate, was meant to bring about solutions to the main challenges facing the European Union at "a defining moment in its existence."[6] Those challenges were defined as greater efficiency, greater representativity, and a stronger role for the European Union in international affairs. Overall, the deliberation within the Convention did not show a clear division of interests between smaller and larger member states, at least as reflected in the coalitions and alliances that emerged in support of specific positions. The institutional questions, predictably, were a remarkable exception. The rotating presidency, the voting system, the composition of the Commission, the relative powers of the Commission and the Council, and the question of representation in the European Parliament, as well as control of subsidiarity by the national parliaments, were all identified as issues for discussion (Magnette and Nicolaïdis 2003).

Coalition building among the smaller states began to take shape. A group of smaller members—the so-called seven dwarfs (Austria, Belgium, Finland, Ireland, Luxembourg, the Netherlands, and Portugal)—organized a meeting in Luxembourg on April 1, 2002, with a view to preparing a joint position on institutional reform (Miller 2003). Slovenia, together with governmental representatives from 15 other smaller states (Austria, Bulgaria, Cyprus, the Czech Republic, Denmark, Estonia, Finland, Hungary, Ireland, Latvia, Lithuania, Malta, Portugal, Slovakia, and Sweden) formed a coalition which was organized around their commonly prepared paper titled "Reforming the Institutions: Principles and Premises."[7] The coalition members argued on several occasions for the equality of member states and for the necessity of safeguarding the institutional balance. They favored the "double-hatting" of the High Representative, no support for any further reliance on demographic factors in reforming the institutions, and a strong Commission (with members from every member state), whose president would be elected either by the European Parliament or by a separate body of electors, and who would be responsible to both the European Parliament and the European Council (either of which could remove the college members from office. Yet the debate on institutions at the Convention failed to bring about a united coalition of all the smaller states, simply because of the traditional posture of individual smaller members. As was noted in the case of Denmark, the smaller states indeed tended to champion the Commission as the guardian of the "common interest" and thus of the weaker and minority players in the game; however, "there is not a direct mapping. Germany for instance has long been a champion of the Commission; and Denmark is no supranationalist" (Magnette and Nicolaïdis 2003). Yet Denmark was but one of several such cases. As the institutional debate unfolded, the Benelux countries also leaned toward forming positions separate from the larger group of smaller states.

Debates became heated on several occasions; one of these occurred early in 2003, when the French and Germans issued a joint proposal on institutions, apparently without even consulting the smaller states, that attacked the rotating presidency by introducing the idea of a president of the European Council (Hughes 2003).[8] The initiative gained momentum and was presented in the form of draft articles for institutions of the European Union on April 23, 2003. Those draft articles were seen as unfavorable not only for many of the existing smaller members, but also for the smaller accession countries, including Slovenia.[9] For instance, the suggested term of office of the Council president (who would be elected by the member states for two-and-a-half years, with an option to renew the term, and would be assisted by his or her own bureau) was seen by many—but not all—the smaller member states as a power grab by their larger cousins at the expense of the Commission.[10] However, as one commentator observed, if "a sizeable number of countries are calling for a full time, long-term President of the European Council and an even larger number of countries are opposed to the idea, whatever the proposal, there will be those left dissatisfied."[11] In the end it was the smaller states that found themselves on the losing side, temporarily at least, on several counts. For example, it was decided that member states would not each have their own commissioner; that the rotating presidency would not be kept; that the president of the Council would be installed (admittedly with lesser prerogatives than originally proposed, but it was left to the future to see how this president would establish himself or herself vis-à-vis the president of the Commission); and that the voting system agreed to at Nice would be modified.

Clearly, things might have turned out differently if the smaller states had organized themselves as a solid bloc. However, that did not take place for several reasons. Among these is the traditional orientation of some of the smaller member states. The Benelux countries, for example, have always been considered as mediators between the interests of bigger and smaller members. They maintained, for example, that the status quo of the Council Presidency within the system was no longer viable,[12] but at the same time they argued that "we must safeguard the principle of equal treatment of all member states, just as the balance between the institutions of the Union."[13] They reacted strongly to the Franco-German proposal, arguing, among other things, that jeopardizing the institutional balance at the expense of the Commission was not acceptable.[14] Meanwhile they were starting to appreciate the arguments for some of the reforms propounded by larger states, such as the reduction in the number of commissioners. It seemed increasingly difficult to see what the gain for smaller states would actually be if "their" commissioner served on an executive body with several dozen invented and mostly obscure portfolios.[15] After May 2003 the Benelux countries shifted toward supporting a smaller Commission and apparently did not oppose the idea of a permanent president (Miller 2003).

The other, perhaps even more compelling reason for the smaller states' failure to coalesce is the sheer experience (or lack thereof) in negotiations within the European Union. A case in point was the debate about the Nice institutional arrangement. The group of governmental representatives, which was headed by Spain, and which, besides the United Kingdom (another major player), enjoyed support from the smaller accession countries, including Slovenia, argued for the Nice system. It turned out, however, that their true reason for defending Nice was not the one that the smaller countries had in mind. The whole battle for Nice, as it were, was largely due to Spain's worries, which were to keep "as much weight as possible in future negotiations on Union financial perspectives, in order to defend European budgetary support when most structural funds are directed to Eastern and Central European countries."[16] After these worries had been dealt with in informal negotiations, Spain changed its course. The British followed the Spaniards, and the stage for an entirely new scenario was set. As Agence Europe put it, "All of a sudden, in the press conference that brought together the 'paladins of Nice' the Spanish and British governments were no longer there!"

It would be beyond the scope of this chapter to evaluate how the countries that were thus left in the dark on such a grand scale accepted this course of events. However, one comment on the outcome of this particular institutional debate did not mince words: "Five Member States and ten accession countries were on their own, paying for their ingenuousness and lack of knowledge of the underside of the affair by having the displeasure of having fingers pointed at them accusing them of 'being saboteurs of the Convention' or at the very least, 'conservatives' opposed to a new Europe!"[17] In Slovenia this verdict tends to be accepted as part of the learning process; it is now considered almost as an informal *acquis* of the negotiations, which a future member needs to absorb sooner rather than later if it wants to establish itself in the Union.[18]

THE ROAD TO ROME: HEAVEN OR HELL
FOR SMALLER STATES?

As already indicated, the final product of the Convention, the Draft of the Constitutional Treaty,[19] redefines the institutional equilibrium in the European Union. The compromise leans toward certain limitations on the role of smaller countries, mainly by abolishing the principle of a rotating presidency, reducing the number of commissioners, and reweighting the voting power in the Council. The outcome of the negotiations goes in the direction of stronger intergovernmental procedure, partly to the potential detriment of smaller countries.

Assembled at the Summit of the European Council in Copenhagen in 2002,[20] the heads of state and government of the EU members emphasized that new members should fully participate in the IGC scheduled for October 2003. Given that the present draft of the constitutional treaty still needs to be negotiated by the heads of state and of government, new coalitions might yet emerge, in particular among smaller countries willing to reestablish the institutional equilibrium from Nice (see Table 23.1). At the time of this writing, it was close to impossible to speculate on the outcome of these negotiations. It seems safe to stress, however, that smaller countries, including Slovenia, might be particularly sensible to the evolving role of their larger counterparts, especially because the former will be anxious about the creation of a Directorium—a constellation that points to intergovernmental cooperation of the larger member states as a starting point for the further development of the European Union.

This is not to say, however, that the European Union that Slovenia will soon be joining will be very different from what it was. The core political and economic advantages of joining remain, and they remain considerable for smaller countries. EU membership means an opportunity to actively participate in EU policymaking, and to form, participate in, and set agendas for coalitions that serve Slovenia's priorities. The history of the European Union has shown how much a smaller member country with limited international influence can contribute to shaping EU policies. (Luxembourg, as a founding member, and Ireland are perhaps the best cases in point.) Smaller countries may even act as a blocking power on some initiatives. The *mise en question* of the Treaty of Nice and its rejection at the first referendum in Ireland illustrate perfectly this interdependence among EU member states.[21]

The challenge for smaller states is how to utilize these new opportunities most effectively, given their limited human and material potential. Used wisely, even the limited resources of a smaller state may make a difference. As Baillie (1996) has argued, once an actor has obtained certain rights in one area of decisionmaking, these rights become entrenched and provide that actor with a certain status and

TABLE 23.1 WEIGHTS OF EU MEMBER COUNTRIES AND ACCESSION COUNTRIES IN EUROPEAN INSTITUTIONS

| Country | Population | | Seats in the European Parliament | | | | Votes in the European Council | | | |
| | | | Currently (until 2004) | | Under Treaty of Nice protocol on EU enlargement | | Currently (until 2004) | | Under Treaty of Nice protocol on EU enlargement | |
	Thousands	Percent of total	Number	Percent of total	Number	Percent of total	Number	Percent of total	Number	Percent of total
Germany	82,264	17.01	99	15.81	99	13.52	10	11.50	29	8.40
United Kingdom	59,817	12.37	87	13.89	72	9.83	10	11.50	29	8.40
France	59,620	12.33	87	13.89	72	9.83	10	11.50	29	8.40
Italy	57,876	11.97	87	13.89	72	9.83	10	11.50	29	8.40
Spain	39,509	8.17	64	10.22	50	6.83	8	9.19	27	7.82
Poland	38,666	7.90			50	6.83			27	7.82
Romania	22,488	4.65			33	4.50			14	4.05
Netherlands	15,760	3.26	31	4.95	25	3.41	5	5.75	12	3.77
Greece	10,570	2.18	25	3.99	22	3.00	5	5.75	12	3.48
Czech Republic	10,267	2.13			20	2.73			12	3.48
Belgium	10,267	2.12	25	3.99	22	3.00	5	5.75	12	3.48
Hungary	10,091	2.08			20	2.73			12	3.48
Portugal	10,016	2.07	25	3.99	22	3.00	5	5.75	12	3.48
Sweden	8,880	1.83	22	3.51	18	2.46	4	4.60	10	2.90
Bulgaria	8,230	1.70			17	2.32			10	2.90
Austria	8,116	1.68	21	3.35	17	2.32	4	4.60	10	2.90
Slovakia	5,393	1.11			13	1.77			7	2.30

TABLE 23.1 — continued

Country	Population		Seats in the European Parliament				Votes in the European Council			
			Currently (until 2004)		Under Treaty of Nice protocol on EU enlargement		Currently (until 2004)		Under Treaty of Nice protocol on EU enlargement	
	Thousands	Percent of total	Number	Percent of total	Number	Percent of total	Number	Percent of total	Number	Percent of total
Denmark	5,349	1.10	16	2.55	13	1.77	3	3.45	7	2.30
Finland	5,181	1.07	16	2.55	13	1.77	3	3.45	7	2.30
Ireland	3,827	0.79	15	2.40	12	1.64	3	3.45	7	2.30
Lithuania	3,700	0.76			12	1.64	—	—	7	2.30
Latvia	2,439	0.50			8	1.09	—	—	7	1.16
Slovenia	1,978	0.41			7	0.95	—	—	4	1.16
Estonia	1,445	0.30			6	0.82	—	—	4	1.16
Cyprus	751	0.15			6	0.82	—	—	4	1.16
Luxembourg	443	0.09	6	0.96	6	0.82	2	2.30	4	1.16
Malta	378	0.08			5	0.68	—	—	3	0.87
Total[a]	483,343	100.0	626	100.0	732	100.0	87	100.0	345	100.0

a. Numbers may not sum to totals because of rounding.

Source: Rousselot-Pailley (2002).

position. This enhances the actor's resources, which can then be instrumental in the defense of interests in other areas.

In terms of external impact, groupings of countries have a greater chance of strongly influencing discussion and decisionmaking at an international level, whereas the influence of an individual smaller country may be close to nonexistent. In this respect one can hardly avoid mentioning the member states' cooperation in what will soon be the former second pillar of the European Union. With regard to the Common Foreign and Security Policy (CFSP), EU membership for smaller countries means a low-cost strategy for upgrading their international position. In particular, the costs of their participation in the CFSP are small, because of the constraints set by the present procedures of "rationalised intergovernmentalism" (Wessels 2001). As stipulated in the draft of the constitutional treaty, a qualified majority shall apply in a very limited number of occasions after a unanimous decision has been made,[22] and there has not been any substantial move in this respect since Nice. It should also be noted that, because the CFSP will remain intergovernmental, moral group pressure on smaller member states to stay within a broad mainstream will be restricted. Thus the new members might continue to follow their policy orientations independently, as the case of the crisis in Iraq has indicated. Finally, participation in the CFSP does not impose on smaller countries the risk of being marginalized among other countries. Intergovernmental procedures, implying a right of veto or a constructive abstention, emphasize the importance of each country in decisionmaking on CFSP issues.[23]

CHALLENGES FOR SLOVENIA AS A NEW, SMALL EU MEMBER

Slovenia is one of the smaller applicant states that have learned some lessons on the way to EU membership. One of those lessons is that although institutional issues matter, they are probably the only area in EU policymaking that could bring smaller states together as a group, especially when they perceive the threat of being marginalized by the larger states. This chapter has demonstrated that the institutional history of the European Union is also a history of an ongoing struggle to strike a balance between formal and actual equality among EU members. This struggle is set to continue at the next IGC and is unlikely ever to be put to rest. The European Union is, after all, a union of states, which will maintain their participation only as long as they feel they are being treated appropriately. A perception of balance between formal and actual equality is the cornerstone of such treatment. If the latter should disappear, the European Union may find itself on the road to collapse.

However, this chapter has also argued that, even when institutional issues are on the agenda, a unified bloc of smaller states is something close to a political fiction—something that rarely, if ever, comes to life. Smaller states that behave rationally will follow their own interests and will choose their allies accordingly. Flexibility in looking for cooperation and support, determined by what a country really wants in a particular area of cooperation, should be the main guideline for Slovenia in pursuing its own goals as an EU member. The Irish Minister for Foreign Affairs, Brian Cowen, has described this approach aptly: "We have affinities with countries like Sweden and Finland on security and defense. Our views on the Commission coincide with that of Benelux. We cooperate with the UK on taxation and with France on agriculture."[24]

What are, or may be, the immediate priorities for Slovenia as a future EU member? Primarily, Slovenia must learn how to grasp the opportunities of an enlarged, open market and to adjust to that market by appropriate restructuring to the new configuration of factors of production within it. However, just as important is to look beyond the present challenges. In this respect, Slovenia should never lose sight of those countries still awaiting full membership. Setting clear roadmaps for future enlargements, in order to create political and economic support for needed reforms in prospective members, must be a priority not only for Slovenia but also for the European Union as a whole. Postponing further enlargements, and eventually the completion of the process of European integration, surely would also mean postponing the transformation and progress not only of future member states but also of existing ones.

The second priority for smaller states is to select the right strategies for specialization, to find niches in which their expertise is comparatively more competitive (Šabič 2002). The future of countries such as Slovenia in the European Union is not determined by their size. On the contrary, size is not a handicap, as many authors never tire of emphasizing.[25] Specialization in economics and in politics is one of the few advantages that smaller states have in an ever more globalized economy with increasing importance of size and scope. On entering the European Union, smaller countries gain some structural and even relational power. If they succeed in specializing, they may become influential in their own right, as the cases of Luxembourg and Ireland demonstrate. Areas of specialization may be many: in Slovenia's case, relations with the western Balkans come immediately to mind. This is an area that is bound to remain one of the European Union's top political and economic priorities for the future (Calic 2003). Slovenia, as a former republic of SFR Yugoslavia, retains profound knowledge about this area. It could make a significant contribution to the greater success of the European Union, notably in changing its rather reactive policies to a more proactive, future-oriented approach. Another possible field of specialization is in dealing with minority issues—an area where Slovenia has expertise and could help to enhance EU standards (Roter 2003).

Last but certainly not least, in estimating Slovenia's chances and discussing its priorities in the European Union, one should never look only from without, but also from within. Katzenstein (1985) and Kindleberger (1984) have pointed out that the goals that a (smaller) country sets for itself can only be achieved if the foundation—the ability to achieve better social cohesion, a better structured labor-capital relationship, and better implementation of policies—is there to provide support. As of 2004, the fortunes of Slovenia will be determined not only by the new environment—an enlarged European Union—but equally by the actions of policymakers back home.

REFERENCES

Baillie, S. 1996. "The Seat of the European Institutions: An Example of Small State Influence in European Decision-making." EUI Working Paper 96/28. European University Institute, Florence.

Baldwin, R. 1994. "Towards an Integrated Europe." Centre for Economic Policy Research, London. Processed.

Becker, G. S. 1991. "As Nations Splinter, Global Markets are Merging." *Business Week,* April 22.

Calic, M. J. 2003. "EU Policies towards the Balkans." Paper presented at the Conference on Italian Presidency of the EU, Rome, June 27–28.

Dinan, D. 1999. *Ever Closer Union.* Houndmills, U.K.: Macmillan Press.

Hayek, F. A. 1997. *The Road to Serfdom.* London: Routledge.

Hughes, K. 2003. "The Battle for Power in Europe—Will the Convention Get It Right?" CEPS/EPIN Working Paper, Centre for European Policy Studies and European Policy Institutes Network, Brussels, February.

Katzenstein, P. J. 1985. *Small States in World Markets: Industrial Policy in Europe.* Ithaca, N.Y.: Cornell University Press.

Kindleberger, C. 1984. *Multinational Excursions.* Cambridge, Mass.: MIT Press.

Küsters, H. J. 1988. "Die Verhandlungen über des institutionelle System zur Gründung der Europäischen Gemeinschaft für Kohle und Stahl." In K. Schwabe, ed., *Die Anfänge des Schuman-Plans 1950–51.* Baden-Baden: Nomos Verlag.

Magnette, P., and K. Nicolaïdis. 2003. "Large and Small Member States in the European Union: Reinventing the Balance." Research and European Issues 25, May. Groupement d'Etudes et de Recherche Notre Europe, Paris.

Milanović, B. 2001. "Nations, Conglomerates and Empires: Trade Off between Income and Sovereignty." In S. Dominick, M. Svetličič, and J. P. Damijan, eds., *Small Countries in a Global Economy.* Houndmills, U.K.: Palgrave.

Miller, V. 2003. "The Convention on the Future of Europe: Institutional Reform." Research Paper 03/56. House of Commons Library, London.

Missiroli, A. 2002. "Conclusions." In "Bigger EU, Wider CFSP, Stronger ESDP? The View from Central Europe." Occasional Paper 34. Institute for Security Studies, Paris.

Norman, P. 2003. "Actors, Institutions and Process: Observations as the Convention Moves into Its Final Months." In *The European Convention—A Midterm Review, January.* Cambridge, Mass.: Minda de Gunzburg Center for European Studies, Harvard University.

Roter, P. 2003. "Language Issues in the Context of Slovenian Smallness." In F. Daftary and F. Grin, eds., *Nation-Building, Ethnicity and Language Politics in Transition Countries,* 1st ed. Budapest: Local Government and Public Service Reform Initiative, Open Society Institute.

Rousselot-Pailley, G. 2002. *Guide to the European Union 2001–2002: An Overview of Current Issues.* Brussels: Roupater.

Šabič, Z. 1999. "Voting in International Organisations: Mere Formality or a Matter of Substance?" Scientific Library, Faculty of Social Sciences, Ljubljana.

———. 2002. "Small States Aspiring for NATO Membership: Some Factors Influencing the Accession Process." In Z. Šabič and C. Bukowski, eds., *Small States in the Post-Cold War World: Slovenia and NATO Enlargement.* Westport, Conn.: Praeger.

Schermers, H. G. 1972. *International Institutional Law.* Leiden: A. W. Sijthoff.

Svetličič, M., and H. Singer. 1996. "World Economy: Challenges of Globalization and Regionalization." In M. Svetličič and H. Singer, eds., *World Economy: Challenges of Globalization and Regionalization.* London: Macmillan Press, and New York: St. Martin's Press.

Wessels, W. 2001. "Nice Results. The Millennium IGC in the EU's Evolution." *Journal of Common Market Studies* 39(2): 197–219.

Westlake, M. 1995. *The Council of the European Union.* London: Cartermill.

NOTES

1. This argument is close to one author's conclusion, if in a different context, that smaller countries are the main gainers from conglomerates and factors of stability within them (Milanović 2001).

2. House of Commons, Foreign Affairs Committee, "Third Report: The Single European Act," para. 37, 1986: 2617.

3. See the positions of the applicant countries on the IGC 2000 in the transmission note to the Conference of the Representatives of the Governments of the Member States. Slovenia: CONFER/VAR 3956/00; Romania: CONFER/VAR 3955/00; Hungary: CONFER/VAR 3952/00; Cyprus: CONFER/VAR 3951/00; the Czech Republic: CONFER/VAR 3958/00; and Poland: CONFER/VAR 3960/00, 24/2/2000.

4. Personal interview with the authors, July 25, 2003.

5. See "Treaty of Nice—White Paper," chapter on "Key elements," p. 9. (*The Irish Times,* special edition; www.ireland.com/newspaper/special/2001/nice/, July 12, 2003).

6. Laeken declaration, Part I (europa.eu.int/futurum/documents/offtext/doc151201_en.htm, July 22, 2003).

7. The contribution was submitted to the Secretary-General of the Convention on March 28, 2003 (CONV 646/03).

8. Contribution submitted by Convention members Dominique de Villepin (France) and Joschka Fischer (Germany) on January 16, 2003 (CONV 489/03): "Franco-German contribution to the European Convention concerning the Union's institutional architecture," p. 3.

9. "Giscard d'Estaing Presents Articles on Institutions, Insisting on Respect of Community Method," Agence Europe, April 25; "Reforming the Institutions: Principles and Premises"; "EU Minnows Raise Their Voice," BBC News, May 16, 2003 (news.bbc.co.uk/1hi/world/europe/3035231.stm, July 15, 2003).

10. See "Institutions—draft articles for Title IV of Part I of the Constitution" (CONV 691/03), Article 16a. Among the smaller states, Sweden and Denmark were reported as being in favor of installing a long-term president (Norman 2003).

11. "Valéry Giscard d'Estaing tries to reconcile partly contradictory demands linked to reform of European Union institutions," Agence Europe, April 24, 2003.

12. In this respect it is indicative that the Benelux countries did not join the Group of 16.

13. "Memorandum of the Benelux: A Balanced Institutional Framework for an Enlarged, More Effective and More Transparent Union," CONV 457/02, December 11, 2002.

14. "Benelux: prise de position des Premiers et des Ministres des Affaires étrangères suite à la Contribution franco-allemande à la Convention." The contribution was retrieved from europa.eu.int/futurum/documents/contrib/cont210103_fr.pdf (July 21, 2003).

15. This was the same reason that eventually led some within the Slovenian political elite to believe that, at the end of the day, the one-state-one-commissioner idea would not be in Slovenia's interest (personal interview with Janez Potočnik, minister without portfolio responsible for European affairs, July 25, 2003).

16. This and the next quotation are from "Somersaults of pride at European convention bode well for final stage of work—spirit of compromise, serenity of president," Agence Europe, June 11, 2003.

17. "Somersaults of pride at European convention bode well for final stage of work—spirit of compromise, serenity of president," Agence Europe, June 11, 2003. However, such incidents could also be interpreted differently. Take the initiative of the Vilnius group, supporting the U.S. intervention in Iraq.

On the one hand, the initiative may have demonstrated a certain lack of political experience; on the other hand, it also indicated how far the acceding countries rely on their autonomy to take strategic decisions touching—directly or indirectly—upon their security interests. In other words, one should not expect smaller states that are about to become EU members to be willing to accept some kind of junior partnership in the European Union.

18. This view was shared by Janez Potočnik (personal interview with the authors, July 25, 2003).

19. CONV 850/03, "Draft Treaty establishing a Constitution for Europe, adopted by consensus by the European Convention on June 13 and July 10, 2003," submitted to the President of the European Council in Rome, July 18, 2003.

20. European Council in Copenhagen, December 12–13, 2002, Presidency Conclusions, 1591/02.

21. It is always useful to stress the specific character of the European Union, especially in times of political crisis: political disintegration is only the other side of the coin of economic integration (Svetličič and Singer 1996).

22. The use of the QMV, as defined in Article III-201(2), applies when adopting decisions that implement a European Council decision relating to the Union's strategic interests and objectives; decisions that implement the Foreign Minister's proposal following a specific request to him or her from the European Council; decisions implementing an action or position of the Union; and decisions concerning the appointment of a special representative.

23. It is worth noting that the acceding countries seem open regarding the use of constructive abstention (Article 23 of the Treaty on European Union), which "would preserve their formal status, but without confronting them with responsibilities that may challenge their resources or internal cohesion" (Missiroli 2002).

24. *Le Monde*, April 4, 2003, as quoted in Magnette and Nicolaïdis (2003).

25. "The advantages of a large internal market have been offset by trade pacts among independent states and growing trade between all states" (Becker 1991; see also Milanović 2001).

Chapter 24
Political Economy of Slovenia's Transition

Janez Šušteršič

Slovenia is a prime example of the gradualist approach to transition. One of the main arguments in favor of this approach was that big-bang reforms entail unnecessary shocks, leading to excessive losses of output and jobs, and consequently to social unrest and ultimately reversal of the reforms. In contrast, a more gradual approach should give economic agents more opportunities to adapt, and at least some economic activity and jobs may be transformed rather than lost altogether.[1] Numerous examples of such reasoning, used in Slovenia as justification for being cautious with reforms, are presented throughout this book. If the argument is correct, a country that adopts a gradualist approach should suffer relatively small output losses and enjoy a comparatively stable economic growth rate.

Table 24.1 confirms these expectations. Slovenia has achieved one of the highest average economic growth rates among the transition economies that are current EU accession candidates (second only to Poland), and it has had by far the least volatile growth during the transition process. Moreover, this stable and reasonably high growth rate was achieved without any major macroeconomic imbalances over the 1990s.[2] Much the same can be said regarding social and political developments. Slovenia's unemployment and poverty rates are both below the EU average. Spending on social benefits, as a percentage of GDP, is also comparable to the EU average, which indicates a rather generous welfare and social security system. Slovenia developed a working system of social partnership and experienced relatively little social unrest or political turmoil during its transition.[3]

Slovenia's overall economic, social, and political stability is a clear benefit of gradualism. However, if one looks beyond the headline figures, structural and institutional weaknesses become evident, which

TABLE 24.1 REAL ECONOMIC GROWTH IN CURRENT
EU ACCESSION COUNTRIES, 1993–2001

(percent a year)

Country	Average real growth rate	Standard deviation
Poland	4.8	1.8
Slovenia	4.3	0.9
Slovakia	4.2	3.2
Estonia	3.9	5.4
Latvia	3.8	7.1
Hungary	3.5	2.0
Czech Rep.	2.2	2.4
Lithuania	1.9	8.2

Source: International Monetary Fund (2003).

may, if not appropriately remedied, prevent Slovenia's future development from being as successful as the past. Caution in reform is not without its costs: a slow pace of economic restructuring may weaken the competitiveness of the economy and lead to macroeconomic imbalances, such as excessive growth of public spending and persistent inflation.

The second section of this chapter addresses the pitfalls of gradualism. First, however, the political economy reasons why the gradualist approach was a natural choice for Slovenia are discussed, and the argument is made that the advantages of gradualism are at the same time also the underlying reasons for its weaknesses. The final section concludes with some perspectives on appropriate economic and structural policies for the future.

GRADUALISM AS A NATURAL POLITICAL
AND ECONOMIC CHOICE FOR SLOVENIA

Unlike in some other Central and Eastern European countries where the main impulse for the breakdown of the socialist regime came from the outside, the transition in Slovenia was endogenous.[4] The gradual transformation of the political and economic system was triggered by forces within the old system. The key difference was in the behavior of the established political elites. In some countries these elites stuck to the unreformed centrally planned system until the very end, and the breakdown thus came unexpectedly for them as a result of international developments and domestic pressures. In other countries, including Hungary and Russia as well as Slovenia, the established elites anticipated the possible breakdown and tried to prepare themselves for the coming changes. From their point of view, the main change that transition would bring was that their own political and economic fortunes would no longer depend on their loyalty to the autocratic leaders or on their own ability to distribute favors and economic rents. To secure their future in the new system, they had to obtain private economic and political capital.

They have done so in two important ways. First, they acquired economic assets through what has been called "spontaneous privatization," using the laws adopted in the last years of the socialist system to appropriate the resources of viable enterprises to themselves. In Slovenia the legal ground for such privatization was the laws on employee share ownership and social capital passed by the last federal government of SFR Yugoslavia as part of the economic reform package introduced at the end of 1998.[5] Second, they acquired political capital by presenting themselves as "reform communists," initiating some cautious changes toward market socialism and pluralistic democracy. The Slovenian reform communists advocated economic reforms in the direction of market socialism at the federal (SFR Yugoslavia) level and a greater decentralization of decisionmaking. They also tolerated a more open political debate and the emergence of civil society groups.[6] By doing so, they clearly increased their popularity among the Slovenian population and were able to enter the first democratically elected legislature as one of the strongest parties.[7]

Using opinion poll data, Schnytzer and Šušteršič (1998) showed that the single most important political issue in the last years of the socialist federal system was whether Slovenia should become more independent, and if so, how much more independent, from SFR Yugoslavia. Politicians' attitudes on this issue were crucial to their popularity, even more than their views on democracy or economic liberalism. Secession, of course, was a risky undertaking, and it could not be accomplished successfully if not backed by an almost unanimous consent among the population and political groups. Because of this, political decisionmaking was based on a search for a wide consensus on all the important decisions.[8]

These political factors made gradualism a natural choice for Slovenia. The threat of repressive intervention by the federal institutions prevented the emerging opposition from being very radical in its statements and claims, forcing it to seek consensus with the existing political elite. The elite, in turn, was able to gain some popularity by carefully supporting some of the opposition's ideas and by resisting pressure from Belgrade to stop the liberalization process. As a result of this imposed consensus, the political transition was smoother and less radical in Slovenia than in other postcommunist countries. The successor party to the League of Communists mustered considerable public support, and the formal interest groups of employers and employees were able to largely retain their organizational structure and resources throughout the regime change. Their political influence was used to ensure that the economic and political transformation proceeded in a less radical fashion, thereby preserving the value of their specific networks and skills, for example, in conducting politics and business in a semirestricted environment. The natural consequence of the search for consensus was that radical reforms with uncertain outcomes were avoided.

Another factor contributing to Slovenia's "natural" inclination toward gradualism was the country's relatively favorable initial economic conditions. Slovenia was not only the most developed part of the former SFR Yugoslavia and indeed of the whole socialist bloc, but also the one where economic reform in the pretransition period had gone the furthest. Producing the lion's share of Yugoslavia's exports to the Western markets, Slovenia's economy had been rather open for a long time before transition, and Slovenians traveled freely to the

West. During the pretransition reforms, the Slovenian people and enterprises learned at least some of the behavior patterns consistent with a market economy, and their perceptions of the world and their values evolved in a direction that conformed with a market economy and capitalism. Gradualism meant that transition reforms could build on these acquired knowledge, skills, and value orientations, allowing for smooth adaptation to the changing environment.

A paramount case where the importance of political and economic legacies for the design of transition reforms could be clearly observed was the debate on privatization.[9] The first proposal was based on the idea of decentralized and gradual insider buyouts, subsidized by the state. Its economic justification was that it would employ the valuable experience and skills of existing management toward the successful restructuring of firms. Political support for this proposal, which clearly favored enterprise insiders, came from the left-wing parties, mainly because of the personal networks that remained among enterprise managers and the former communists, and because workers are a natural constituency for leftist parties. Right-wing parties within the government coalition soon came out with an alternative proposal, based on centralized privatization through a voucher scheme and investment funds. The economic advantages of this proposal would be the short time needed to accomplish it, and the possibility for quick establishment of strategic owners through the secondary market for shares. Politically, the proposal was expected to muster general public support for the new government, because it would give each citizen an equal initial share in the distribution of the firms' social capital. The power of the old elites to control firms would be significantly diluted, and, at least in the initial period, the new government would be able to exercise some control over the economy through the investment funds.

None of the initial proposals gained sufficient political support to pass the legislature. The centralized voucher scheme proposal was blocked by the third chamber of the legislature, which consists mainly of delegates elected by employees in the firms, thereby effectively representing the interests of the old elite networks.[10] The disagreement on privatization led to dissolution of the ruling coalition and to the government losing a vote of confidence. A new, center-left government was elected, and a compromise privatization proposal was prepared by the major parties, combining the equal distribution of vouchers to all citizens with sizable discounts for decentralized insider buyouts and with a fifth of assets allocated directly to two quasi-governmental funds. The privatization law finally passed just a few days before general elections, after a two-year political debate and a standstill in actual ownership restructuring.

The case of privatization shows clearly not only how gradualism and compromise in reforms were the result of balancing conflicting and equally strong political and economic interests, but also that there are costs to such an approach in terms of economic development. The obvious direct cost is the postponement of key reforms that would, if enacted earlier, contribute to the faster restructuring of the economy. Another cost is that compromise solutions are not always economically optimal. Many firms that decided for insider buyouts faced the problem of employeeism and the preference of many workers to use the income for consumption rather than to reinvest it in the firm. Others faced a stalemate between inside and outside owners, which prevented serious restructuring from taking place. This mode of privatization also discouraged foreign investment; given evidence that enterprises with foreign capital were generally restructured faster and more efficiently, this meant that important opportunities were missed. The reluctance of the government to sell shares acquired by the quasi-governmental investment funds, and the problems with providing enough assets for privatization to match the value of outstanding vouchers (the so-called privatization gap), also slowed restructuring. Only in the last few years have strategic and active owners been able to gain stronger control of firms at the expense of the state, the investment funds, and employee ownership.[11]

COSTS OF GRADUALISM: SLOW STRUCTURAL REFORMS

Assuming that the extent to which transition reforms have been accomplished in any given country can be objectively measured, it is interesting to look at one of the most commonly used indicators of reform progress, namely, the transition index of the European Bank for Reconstruction and Development. Table 24.2 shows that the relative lag of Slovenia has been constant over the last decade; the country neither gained nor lost ground relative to the country with the highest transition index. Slovenia did not accomplish less reform than other countries in any given year; it simply carried them out a year or two later than the leading country. Hence it might be more appropriate to call the Slovenian transition a cautious rather than a gradual one.

Strict proponents of gradualism might even say that lagging behind with reforms is a virtue; after all, almost by definition, gradualism does not call for quick structural reforms or across-the-board privatization and liberalization. Bearing in mind that it is sometimes indeed wise to be cautious, however, it is important to point out some of the costs of gradualism.

The effects of slow and gradual privatization on the economic restructuring of the business sector have already been described. Privatization of the financial sector was delayed even further and indeed

TABLE 24.2 RELATIVE EBRD TRANSITION INDEX FOR SLOVENIA

Year	Country with highest index (leading country)	Transition index[a] For leading country	For Slovenia	Ratio of Slovenia's TI to leading country's TI (percent)
1991	Poland	2.4	1.9	79.2
1992	Czechoslovakia	2.6	2.0	76.2
1993	Czech Republic	3.0	2.6	86.7
1994	Czech Republic	3.2	2.9	91.4
1995	Hungary	3.3	3.0	91.3
1996	Hungary	3.4	3.1	90.5
1997	Hungary	3.7	3.3	90.4
1998	Hungary	3.7	3.3	89.5
1999	Hungary	3.7	3.3	89.5
2000	Hungary	3.8	3.4	89.5
2001	Hungary	3.7	3.4	91.0

a. Index is calculated as the average of country's scores in nine (eleven since 1997) key areas of transition reforms. Countries included in this comparison are the eight that will join the European Union in 2004.

Source: European Bank for Reconstruction and Development (2002).

has still not been accomplished. Moreover, the peculiar institutional arrangements that were in place throughout almost the whole transition period, such as the general use of indexation clauses and the cartelization of interest rate setting, effectively protected the banking sector from competition. Development of the capital market was hampered by a protectionist stance against foreign investment and by the chosen mode of privatization, since most insider-owned firms did not opt for public listing of their shares. As a result, financial intermediation remained relatively small in scale and nondiversified.[12]

Economic policy could also have done more to initiate faster economic restructuring. Industrial policy was used predominantly to help unviable enterprises rather than to support innovative and technologically advanced companies. The institutional framework retained many inefficiencies that increased the uncertainty of property rights and hampered the development of entrepreneurship. Tariff policy, after initial liberalization, retained some protection and even increased it for agricultural products. Monetary policy used managed exchange rate floating and capital controls to prevent excessive capital inflows that could trigger macroeconomic instability, but by doing so it also effectively prevented some foreign direct investment and created an exchange rate buffer for marginal exporters that would otherwise have been forced into more comprehensive restructuring.[13]

Empirical evidence collected in Murn and Kmet (2003) and Bednaš and others (2002) shows clearly the detrimental effects of slow reform on private sector competitiveness. The market share of Slovenian exports in EU markets remained largely constant in the 1995–2000 period, while, for example, Hungary increased its share by around 130 percent, Slovakia by 90 percent, Czech Republic by a third, and Poland by a fifth. The underlying reason for Slovenia's failure to match their performance is the slow restructuring of Slovenia's manufacturing industry, which made possible only very modest increases in export shares of technologically advanced and knowledge-based products.[14]

Despite an unfavorable export structure, Slovenia has so far been able to avoid excessive current account deficits. The largest deficits, recorded between 1999 and 2001 and amounting to around 3 percent of GDP, were mainly a result of excessive domestic spending and rising oil prices. In the years thereafter, deficits were avoided thanks to low domestic spending and rapid growth of exports, especially to Central and Eastern European markets. However, recent developments indicate that these alleviating factors may disappear, posing the risk of a deteriorating trade balance if export competitiveness is not significantly improved.

Reforms of infrastructure and the public sector were even more cautious than those in the private sector. Electricity markets were gradually opened for industrial consumers first, but plans to privatize production and distribution facilities have been postponed, mainly on the grounds that restructuring has to be accomplished first, to improve the economic viability of enterprises and ensure security of supply. With respect to the rail system, a law was passed in 2002 that will enable the separation of service operations from infrastructure. In telecommunications, the existing legal monopoly was abolished only in 2001, and an efficient market structure has still not been established. Plans to privatize the main operator have been postponed because of low demand in takeover markets. Local utilities are regulated by the municipalities, which in practice creates very different local situations, mostly characterized by underinvestment, local monopolies, and inefficiency. Independent regulators of electricity supply, rail service, and telecommunications markets have been established, but some time is still needed for them to gain the necessary experience in establishing an efficient market structure. The competition authority also has very limited resources and is mainly concerned with deciding on applications for mergers and acquisitions; it seldom endeavors on its own initiative to tackle cases of market power abuse and cartelization.

Serious reforms to improve the efficiency of public administration, reduce the overregulation of private economic activity, and improve the legal system have been initiated only very recently (see Chapter 13).

Pension reform was implemented in 1999 and was able to reduce the fiscal burden somewhat. However, it took several years to reach agreement among the social partners on the reform, and some important elements of the initial proposal were significantly diluted (see Chapter 19). A similar difficulty in reaching consensus has hampered the introduction of comprehensive labor market reform, and it remains to be seen whether the enacted legislative changes were sufficiently extensive to create a significantly more flexible labor market. Health sector reform is still in the pipeline.

Public sector inefficiency and the inability to resist interest group pressure were reflected in rising public expenditure as a share of GDP during the second half of the 1990s. Expenditure on public sector wages and social transfers contributed the largest share of this increase (see Chapter 12). The relative inefficiency of the nontradables sector was also the main structural reason for persistent inflation after 2000. Nontradables industries compensated for their lower productivity growth by raising their relative prices and channeled the earnings into higher wages.[15] Administered prices have been consistently increasing faster than overall inflation. Fiscal policy, which responded to increasing fiscal expenditure by raising sales taxes, thereby created significant additional inflationary pressure in 2000 and 2001. Monetary policy reacted accommodatively, through depreciation of the tolar, motivated by the ambition to offset part of the excessive costs of an inefficient public sector on exporters, but depreciation in turn exerted yet more cost pressure on inflation.

A LOOK AHEAD

The same underlying reasons that led naturally to the choice of gradualism in Slovenia's transition are also responsible for the costs of that choice, which must be tackled if Slovenia wants to accelerate its development in the future. This chapter has shown that a strong political consensus and an established tradition of economic and political reform were the main reasons why it was natural for Slovenia to choose a gradual approach. But it has also been shown that the same reasons—a stalemate between interest groups, leading to postponed decisions and suboptimal compromises—were responsible for the country's lagging behind in some crucial reforms. Developments in recent years have warned that continuation of such an approach might seriously hamper economic competitiveness and backfire on an otherwise stable macroeconomic performance.

The process of accession to the European Union created a welcome outside pressure for faster reform. Important steps forward have been made in the last few years in many areas. The partial privatization of one of the two state-owned banks was accomplished, and formal indexation of interest rates was abolished. Capital controls were lifted, and inflows of foreign direct investment were significantly increased. The quasi-governmental investment funds were willing to sell off some of their holdings in important private enterprises. Ownership restructuring in the private sector gained some momentum. State aid and industrial policy are being redirected toward supporting technological improvements, cost efficiency, and innovation, and more support is available for producer networks and small and medium-size enterprises. A streamlining of overregulation has been initiated, and legislation needed to increase efficiency of public service has been passed. The new wage agreement almost completely abolished indexation and alleviated the cost pressure from wages on both the budget and private enterprises.

Slovenia is still the most developed among all the transition countries. However, in order to avoid potential threats to its continued prosperity and to fully reap the benefits of membership in the European Union, more effort is needed in many of the areas discussed in this chapter, to bring greater dynamism and growth potential to the economy. Structural reforms, particularly in infrastructure and the public sector, have to be pursued with greater determination, and industrial policy must concentrate on fostering restructuring and competitiveness in the private business sector. A more restrictive fiscal and wage policy, as well as a less accommodative monetary policy, are needed to bring inflation down to sustainable levels. Social policy has to be streamlined wherever it does not directly target the most vulnerable in the population, the cost efficiency of the public sector has to be improved, and the institutional framework of economic activity has to be made simpler and more transparent. There is no lack of awareness that all this needs to be done, and official government documents are full of declarations on this score. What is most needed now is the determination to act on those good intentions, in spite of pressure from special interests and in spite of the political risks associated with a less cautious approach to reform.

ACKNOWLEDGMENTS

The author thanks Maja Bednaš, Matija Rojec, Boštjan Vasle, and other colleagues at the Institute of Macroeconomic Analysis and Development and the Slovene Macroeconomic Forum for stimulating discussions on Slovenian gradualism, and Andreja Poje and Špela Lesar for sharing data compiled in the framework of their own research.

REFERENCES

Bednaš, M., S. Jurančič, M. Rojec, J. Šušteršič, and B. Vasle. 2002. "Vstop v EU: konec gradualizma v Sloveniji?" 7. letna konferenca Sekcije za ekonomsko politiko Zveze ekonomistov Slovenije, Ljubljana.

Dewatripont, M., and G. Roland. 1992a. "The Virtues of Gradualism and Legitimacy in the Transition to a Market Economy." *Economic Journal* 102: 291–300.

————. 1992b. "Economic Reform and Dynamic Political Constraints." *Review of Economic Studies* 59: 703–31.

————. 1996. "Transition as a Process of Large-Scale Institutional Change." *Economics of Transition* 4: 1–30.

European Bank for Reconstruction and Development. 2002. *Transition Report.* London.

International Monetary Fund. 2003. *World Economic Outlook.* Washington, D.C.

Lydall, H. 1989. *Yugoslavia in Crisis.* Oxford, U.K.: Clarendon Press.

Murn, A. 2002. "Industrijska politika in državne pomoči v Evropski uniji in v Sloveniji." Delovni zvezki Umar 11(2). Institute of Macroeconomic Analysis and Development, Ljubljana.

Murn, A., and R. Kmet, eds. 2003. "Poročilo o razvoju." Institute of Macroeconomic Analysis and Development, Ljubljana.

Murrell, Peter. 1995. "Reform's Rhetoric-Realization Relationship: The Experience of Mongolia." In Kazimierz Z. Poznanski, ed., *The Evolutionary Transition to Capitalism.* Boulder, Colo.: Westview Press.

Pejovich, S.. 1994. "The Market for Institutions vs. Capitalism by Fiat." *Kyklos* 47: 519–29.

————. 1996. "The Market for Institutions versus the Strong Hand of the State: The Case of Eastern Europe." In B. Dallago and L. Mittone, eds., *Economic Institutions, Markets and Competition: Centralization and Decentralization in the Transformation of Economic Systems.* Aldershot, U.K.: Edward Elgar.

Poznanski, K. Z. 1992. "Market Alternative to State Activism in Restoring the Capitalist Economy." *Economics of Planning* 25: 55–77.

————. 1995. "Institutional Perspectives on Postcommunist Recession in Eastern Europe." In K. Z. Poznanski, ed., *The Evolutionary Transition to Capitalism.* Boulder, Colo.: Westview Press.

Roland, G. 1993. "The Political Economy of Restructuring and Privatization in Eastern Europe." *European Economic Review* 37: 533–540.

————. 1994a. "On the Speed and Sequencing of Privatisation and Restructuring." *Economic Journal* 104: 1158–68.

————. 1994b. "The Role of Political Constraints in Transition Economies." *Economics of Transition* 2: 27–42.

Schnytzer, Adi. 1995. "Why Do Rational Communists Not Obstruct the Transformation Process?" *Public Choice* 85: 143–56.

Schnytzer, Adi, and Janez Šušteršič. 1996. "Transition by Secession: The Case of Slovenia." *Acta Oeconomica* 48: 375–92.

Šušteršič, Janez. 2000. "From the Socialist Cycle to the Endogenous Transition." *Economic and Business Review for Central and Eastern Europe* 2: 29–59.

NOTES

1. For theoretical arguments see, for example, Murrell (1995), Pejovich (1994, 1996), and Poznanski (1992, 1995), or, within a more neoclassical methodology, Roland (1993, 1994a, 1994b) and Dewatripont and Roland (1992a, 1992b, 1996).

2. See Chapter 8. The extent to which the increase in fiscal and current account deficits in 1999 and 2000, and the persistence of inflation after 1999, can be explained as a result of gradualism is discussed later in this chapter.

3. Both Prime Minister Janez Drnovšek and President Milan Kučan were elected to their offices for three consecutive terms, and the Liberal Democratic Party was the leading party in the government coalition during most of the transition period.

4. The distinction between endogenous and exogenous transition and its path dependency on pretransition reform are explained in Šušteršič (2000).

5. It is no surprise that one of the first measures taken by Slovenia's independent democratic government was to declare these laws invalid in Slovenia. For a model explaining spontaneous privatization as a phenomenon induced by uncertainty regarding the stability of the socialist system, see Schnytzer (1995); on its extension to political popularity and the acquiring of political capital, see Schnytzer and Šušteršič (1996).

6. See Lydall (1989) for a well-informed review of developments in the last decade of SFR Yugoslavia.

7. The first government in independent Slovenia was formed by a coalition of newly formed center and right-wing parties, but the strongest individual party in the proportionally elected chamber was the Liberal Democrats, a group that emerged from the Socialist Youth Organization; the ex-Communist Party obtained 17.3 percent of the votes.

8. This imperative for consensus also influenced the structure of the emerging democratic political institutions. The most important chamber of the legislature was elected on the principle of proportional representation, producing a balanced distribution of seats among a number of parties and forcing them to form broad and heterogeneous coalition governments. Collective bargaining, largely organized with the help of inherited trade union and chamber of commerce structures, soon became important not only in wage policy but also in deliberations over other major reforms.

9. For a detailed exposition of the debate and the actual privatization proposals, see Schnytzer and Šušteršič (1996) and Chapters 5 and 14 in this volume.

10. The first democratically elected legislature retained the three-chamber structure from socialist times. The main legislative chamber was elected on a

proportional system in free competition among the political parties. The second chamber was elected at the community level based on a majority system and was intended to represent local interests. The third chamber was elected at the enterprise level on a majority principle and was intended to represent the interests of economic entities.

11. The pitfalls of privatization and their economic consequences are described in more detail in Chapters 14, 15, and 17. Employeeism is defined and investigated in more detail in Chapters 14 and 15.

12. For accounts of developments in the banking sector and the capital market, see Chapters 10, 16, and 17, and Murn and Kmet (2003).

13. For detailed explanations see Murn (2002) and Murn and Kmet (2003) for an analysis of industrial policy and state aid expenditure, and Chapters 13 (on institutional rigidities), 9 (on trade protection), and 11 (on exchange rate policy) in this volume.

14. Slovenia managed to increase the share of knowledge-based products in its exports from 22 percent to 26 percent between 1993 and 2000, while Hungary increased it from 24 percent to 42 percent, and the Czech Republic from 20 percent to 33 percent. In 1999, 26 percent of Slovenian exports consisted of technologically advanced products, compared with 32 percent in the Czech Republic and 46 percent in Hungary. Slovenia and Poland scored lowest among the more advanced transition economies on an indicator of the intensity of structural change in manufacturing.

15. Unit labor costs declined by 17.5 percent in manufacturing in the 1995–2000 period, but by only by 11.9 percent in other sectors, mostly in nontradables. In this period the cumulative rise in prices of nontradables was consequently 35.5 percent higher than that in prices of tradables (Bednaš and others 2002).

About the Editors

Mojmir Mrak, of Slovenian nationality, obtained his bachelor's degree and M.Sc. in economics from the Faculty of Economics in Ljubljana and his Ph.D. in economics from the Faculty of Economics in Belgrade. Upon completion of his studies, he first joined the Center for International Cooperation and Development and later became a visiting fellow at the Inter-American Development Bank in Washington, D.C., and at the OECD Development Center in Paris. Between 1990 and 1992 he served as an economist in the Research Branch of the United Nations Industrial Development Organization (UNIDO) in Vienna, where he was responsible for preparing a part of the organization's *Global Report* dealing with international finance issues of importance for industrial sector development. From July 1992 to July 1996 he served as a chief external debt negotiator for Slovenia with the multilateral financial institutions, the Paris Club, and the London Club.

Mr. Mrak is currently a professor of international finance at the University of Ljubljana and a regular visiting professor in the postgraduate program of the University of Siena and at the doctoral program organized jointly by three universities in Vienna: the Wirtschaftsuniversität, the Technische Universität Wien, and the Universität Wien. Since 1997 he has also been an adviser to the Slovenian government on financial aspects of the country's accession to the European Union. Over the last decade Mr. Mrak has served as a member of the supervisory boards of the Slovenian Export Corporation (1993–2001), the Agency for Securities Markets (1997–98), and Nova Ljubljanska Banka (1998–2001).

Mr. Mrak is author, coauthor, or editor of numerous books, including *Multinationals of the South* (London, 1986) and *Succession of States* (The Hague, 1999), and of articles published in such international journals as *Eastern European Economics, Revue d'etudes comparatives Est-Ouest,* and *Savings and Development.* In addition, he has conducted various consultancy assignments for several international organizations (the Organisation for Economic Co-operation and

413

Development, the European Union's PHARE program, the World Bank, the European Bank for Reconstruction and Development, the International Finance Corporation, and the Inter-American Development Bank), a number of UN agencies (including UNCTAD and UNIDO), and numerous private sector consultancy firms from various EU member states.

Matija Rojec, of Slovenian nationality, received his Ph.D. in economics at the University of Ljubljana. He is Associate Professor in the Faculty of Social Sciences at the University of Ljubljana and a Senior Research Fellow at the university's Center for International Relations. He is also Adviser to the Government at the Institute of Macroeconomic Analysis and Development of the Republic of Slovenia.

Mr. Rojec's research interests include foreign direct investment (FDI), the transformation process in Central and Eastern Europe, enterprise restructuring, and the process of EU enlargement. He has published books and numerous articles in journals such as *Transnational Corporations, Management International Review, Eastern European Economics, Communist Economies, Economic Systems, Industry and Innovation, International Relations and Development, Journal of East-West Business,* and *Prague Economic Papers.* He has coordinated or participated in numerous international research and consulting projects in the fields of FDI, internationalization, enterprise restructuring, transfer of technology, EU integration, and others, in the framework of PHARE-ACE, the OECD, UNCTAD, UNDP, UNIDO, United Nations University/WIDER, The Economist Intelligence Unit, and the International Center for Economic Growth.

M. Rojec has served as a consultant to various ministries and agencies of the Slovenian government on matters related to FDI, the transition process, and the EU accession process. He has been heavily engaged in Slovenia's activities related to the EU accession process, including as one of the coordinators of the preparation of major strategic government documents related to EU accession, such as "Slovenia in the European Union: Strategy of Economic Development of Slovenia" and "EU Accession Strategy of the Republic of Slovenia: Economic and Social Part." Recently he has been involved in the Stability Pact and the activities of other organizations in southeastern Europe in the field of FDI and EU integration.

Carlos Silva-Jáuregui, of Mexican nationality, studied applied mathematics and economics at the Instituto Tecnológico Autónomo de México (ITAM) and did his graduate studies in economics at the University of Chicago. Mr. Silva-Jáuregui began his professional career by working in the research department of the Banco Nacional de México (BANAMEX), the largest commercial bank in México. He spent a number of years in academia, doing research and lecturing in areas such as macroeconomics, microeconomics, and statistics and econometrics at ITAM, the Universidad Autónoma de Barcelona, the University of Chicago, and Pennsylvania State University.

In 1991 Mr. Silva-Jáuregui joined the World Bank, where he worked as an economist in the Latin America region on Brazil, Perú, and Venezuela. Three years later he took the position of country economist for the Czech and Slovak Republics in the Europe and Central Asia region of the World Bank. In 1996 he was named country economist for Slovenia as well. He worked until 2000 as Senior Economist on Central European countries, particularly the Czech Republic, Slovakia, Slovenia, Hungary, and Poland, and on labor and regional EU accession initiatives. Mr. Silva-Jáuregui joined the Middle East and North Africa region of the World Bank in late 2000, working initially on Lebanon, Syria, and Jordan, and more recently on Iran and Iraq as Lead Economist. He has done research on regional issues in the Middle East and North Africa region such as economic volatility and migration. Mr. Silva-Jáuregui is also a member of the regional Gender Advisory Group.

Mr. Silva-Jáuregui is author, coauthor, or team leader of numerous studies at the World Bank, including *Poland—Reform and Growth on the Road to EU Accession* (1997), *Slovenia—Labor Market Issues* (1998), *Slovenia—Trade Sector Issues* (1998), *Slovenia—Economic Transformation and EU Accession* (1999), *Czech Republic—Toward EU Accession* (1999), *Czech Republic—Enhancing the Prospects for Growth with Fiscal Stability* (2001), *Slovakia—Living Standards, Employment and Labor Market Study* (2001), *Lebanon—Sources of Growth* (2001), "Does Eurosclerosis Matter? Institutional Reform and Labor Market Performance in Central and Eastern Europe" (2002), *Jordan—Development Policy Review* (2002), "Is Economic Volatility in the Middle East Really High?" (2003), and "Migration and Trade: Problems or Solutions?" (2003).

Contributors

France Arhar is Chairman of the Management Board, Bank Austria, Ljubljana, and former Governor of the Bank of Slovenia.

Velimir Bole is Senior Researcher, Economics Institute at the Law School, Ljubljana, and a former member of the Governing Board, Bank of Slovenia.

Bistra Borak is an undergraduate student in political science, Faculty of Social Sciences, University of Ljubljana.

Neven Borak is Director of the Securities Market Agency, Ljubljana, and a former adviser to the President of the Slovenian Parliament and to the Prime Minister and the Presidency of the Republic of Slovenia.

Bojko Bučar is Professor in the Faculty of Social Sciences, University of Ljubljana.

Milan M. Cvikl is Chief Financial Officer, Nova Ljubljanska Banka; a former State Secretary for Public Finance in the Ministry of Finance, Republic of Slovenia; and a former economist in the Central and Eastern Europe Area, World Bank.

Jože P. Damijan is Assistant Professor, Faculty of Economics, University of Ljubljana, and Research Fellow, Institute for Economic Research, Ljubljana.

Polona Domadenik is Assistant Professor, Faculty of Economics, University of Ljubljana.

Janez Drnovšek is President and former Prime Minister of the Republic of Slovenia and a former member of the Presidency of the Socialist Federal Republic of Yugoslavia.

Mitja Gaspari is Governor of the Bank of Slovenia and a former Minister of Finance of the Republic of Slovenia.

Vladimir Gligorov is Senior Researcher, Wiener Institut für Internationale Wirtschaftsvergleiche, Vienna.

Aleksandra Gregorič is Assistant Professor, Faculty of Economics, University of Ljubljana.

András Inotai is Director, Institute for World Economics, Hungarian Academy of Sciences, Budapest, and Visiting Professor, College of Europe, Bruges and Natolin, Belgium. He is the former head of the Task Force for Hungary's Integration Strategy, Budapest, and a former Visiting Professor at Columbia University, New York.

Božo Jašovič is a member of the Governing Board of the Bank of Slovenia; a former State Secretary for Treasury at the Ministry of Finance of the Republic of Slovenia; a former member of the Expert Council of the Securities Market Agency, Ljubljana; and former President of the Board of the Bank Rehabilitation Agency, Ljubljana.

Bartlomiej Kaminski is Associate Professor, Department of Government, University of Maryland at College Park, and Senior Fellow, Center for the Study of Post-Communist Societies.

Tomaž Košak is Assistant Director, Analysis and Research Department, Bank of Slovenia.

Boštjan Kramberger is a candidate for the M.Sc. degree in the Faculty of Economics and Business, University of Maribor.

Jaime Garcia Lombardero is Head of the Slovenia Team, DG Enlargement, European Commission, Brussels.

Boris Majcen is Director, Institute for Economic Research, Ljubljana.

Jože Mencinger is Rector of the University of Ljubljana, Professor in the Law Faculty, University of Ljubljana, and Senior Researcher, Economics Institute at the Law School, Ljubljana. He is a former member of the Governing Board of the Bank of Slovenia, and a former Vice Prime Minister of the Republic of Slovenia.

Dušan Mramor is Minister of Finance of the Republic of Slovenia and Professor in the Faculty of Economics, University of Ljubljana. He is the former Chairman of the Expert Council of the Securities Market Agency, Ljubljana.

Rasto Ovin is Dean, Faculty of Economics and Business, University of Maribor.

Janez Potočnik is Minister for European Affairs of the Republic of Slovenia. He is the former head of the negotiating team for accession of the Republic of Slovenia to the European Union, and former Director, Institute of Macroeconomic Analysis and Development, Ljubljana.

Janez Prašnikar is Professor, Faculty of Economics, University of Ljubljana and Head of the Institute for South-East Europe, Ljubljana. He is Research Fellow at the Centre for Economic Policy Research, London, and at the William Davidson Institute at the University of Michigan Business School.

Dorota Pyszna-Nigge is Research Associate, Jean Monnet Chair for Political Sciences and European Affairs, University of Cologne.

Andrej Rant is Vice Governor of the Bank of Slovenia.

Ivan Ribnikar is Professor, Faculty of Economics, University of Ljubljana, and member of the Governing Board of the Bank of Slovenia.

Marko Simoneti is Professor, Faculty of Law, University of Ljubljana, and member of the board of the Ljubljana Stock Exchange; he is a former member of the Expert Council of the Securities Market Agency, Ljubljana and former Director, Agency for Privatization, Ljubljana.

Peter Stanovnik is Senior Research Fellow and former Director, Institute for Economic Research, Ljubljana.

Tine Stanovnik is Professor, Faculty of Economics, University of Ljubljana, and Senior Research Fellow, Institute for Economic Research, Ljubljana.

Marjan Svetličič is Professor, Faculty of Social Sciences, University of Ljubljana.

Zlatko Šabič is Associate Professor, Faculty of Social Sciences, University of Ljubljana.

Franjo Štiblar is Professor, Faculty of Law, University of Ljubljana; Senior Researcher, Economics Institute of the Faculty of Law, Ljubljana; and Chief Economist, Nova Ljubljanska Banka.

Janez Šušteršič is Director, Institute of Macroeconomic Analysis and Development, Ljubljana.

Milan Vodopivec is Senior Economist, Human Development Network, Social Protection Unit, World Bank. He is Professor and the former Dean of GEA College of Entrepreneurship, Piran, Slovenia.

Marko Voljč is Director General, Central Europe, KBC Bank and Insurance Holding. He is former Chief Executive Officer, Nova Ljubljanska Banka, and former Division Chief, Central America and Panama Division, World Bank.

Wolfgang Wessels is Professor, Jean Monnet Chair for Political Sciences and European Affairs, University of Cologne.

Index

Note: f = figure; t = table; and n = note.